ESCAPE TO CONFLICT

*A Biblical and Archaeological Approach to
the Hebrew Exodus and Settlement in Canaan*

by
GEORGE L. KELM

8\11

IAR Publications, Fort Worth, Texas.

ISBN 0-9629145-0-9

To LINDA

whose love and encouragement
have sustained my efforts

Table of Contents

LIST OF MAPS

COMPARATIVE CHRONOLOGY FOR MAJOR PERIODS OF EGYPTIAN HISTORY

The following chronological table is intended to provide a general chronological context for our discussion. The three columns of dates provided here for comparative purposes indicate the general consensus that has been achieved for the history of Egypt.

		Stiebing[1]	Finegan[2]	Aharoni[3]	A. Mazar[4]	Wente/Van Sicle[5]
I.	Archaic Period Dynasties 1-2	3100-2700	3100-2686	3100-2600	3100-2700	
II.	Old Kingdom Period Dynasties 3-6	2700-2200	2686-2181	2600-2175	2700-2160	
III.	First Intermediate Period Dynasties 7-11	2200-2060	2181-2040	2175-1991	2160-1991	
IV.	Middle Kingdom Period Dynasty 12	2060-1800	2040-1786	1991-1786	1991-1786	
V.	Second Intermediate Period Dynasties 13-17	1800-1560	1786-1552	1785-1570	1786-1567	
	(Hyksos Rule)	(1665-1560)	1660-1552	1678-1570		
VI.	New Kingdom Period	1560-1070	1552-1070	1570-1065		
	Dynasty 18	1570-1293	1552-1306	1570-1303		
	Ahmose I	1570-1546	1552-1527	1570-1545	1550-1525	1570-1546
	Amenhotep I	1551-1524	1527-1506	1545-1525	1551-1524	
	Thutmose I	1524-1518	1506-1494	1525-1508	1524-1518	
	Thutmose II	1518-1504	1494-1490	1508-1490	1518-1504	
	Thutmose III	1504-1450	1490-1436	1490-1436	1479-1425	1504-1450
	Hatshepsut	1503-1483	1490-1468	1484-1469		
	Amenhotep II	1453-1419	1438-1412	1436-1410	1453-1419	
	Thutmose IV	1319-1387	1412-1402	1410-1402	1419-1386	
	Amenhotep III		1387-1350	1402-1364	1402-1364	1386-1349
	Akhenaton	1350-1334	1364-1347	1364-1346	1352-1336	1350-1334
	Smenkhkare	1336-1334	1351-1348		1336-1334	
	Tutankhamun	1334-1325	1347-1338	1346-1337	1334-1325	
	Ay		1324-1321	1338-1334	1337-1333	1324-1321
	Horemhab	1321-1293	1334-1306	1333-1303		1321-1293
	Dynasty 19	1293-1185	1306-1186	1303-1175		
	Ramesses I	1293-1291	1306-1304			1293-1291
	Seti I	1291-1279	1304-1290	1303-1290	1294-1279	1291-1279
	Ramesses II	1279-1212	1290-1224	1290-1223	1279-1213	1279-1212
	Merneptah	1212-1202	1224-1204	1223-	1213-1203	1212-1202
	Amenmesse					1202-1199
	Seti II					1199-1193
	Siptah					1193-1187
	Tausert					1193-1185
	Interregnum					1185-1185/4
	Dynasty 20	1184-1070	1186-1070			
	Setnakht					1185/4-1182
	Ramesses III	1182-1151	1184-1153	1175-		1182-1151
	Ramesses IV-IX			1153-1109	1144-1090	1151-1108
	Ramesses IV					1151-1145
	Ramesses V					1145-1141
	Ramesses VI					1141-1133

	Stiebing	Finegan	Aharoni	A. Mazar	Wente/Van Sicle
Ramesses VII					1133-1127
Ramesses VIII					1127-1126
Ramesses IX					1126-1108
Ramesses X					1108-1098
Ramesses XI					1098-1070
VII. Late Period	1070-525	1070-525	1065-525		
Dynasty 21	1070-946	1069-945	1065-935		
Siamun		978-959			
Dynasty 22	946-745	945-715	935-		
Sheshonk I		945-924	945-924		
Osorkon I		924-889			
Osorkon II		874-850			
Dynasty 23	745-718	818-715			
Dynasty 24	718-712	727-715			
Dynasty 25	712-656	716-656	751-656		
Shabako		716-702	710-696		
Taharqa					
(Tirhaka)	689-664	690-664	685-663		
Dynasty 26 (Saite)	664-525	664-525	663-525		
Necho II		610-595	609-594		
Psammetichus II			595-589	593-588	
Psammetichus III		526-525	526-525		
VIII. Persian Conquest		525	525	525	

NOTES

[1] W.H.Stiebing,Jr. *Out of the Desert? Archaeology and the Exodus/Conquest Narratives.* Buffalo, NY: Prometheus Books, 1989: 38.

[2] Jack Finegan, *Archaeological History of the Ancient Middle East.* Boulder, CO: Westview Press, 1979.

[3] Yohanan Aharoni, *The Land of the Bible.* London: Burns and Oates, 1979.

[4] A. Mazar, *Archaeology of the Land of the Bible 10,000 - 586 B.C.E.* New York: Doubleday, 1990.

[5] E.F. Wente and C.C. Van Sicle III, A Chronology of the New Kingdom. Pp.217-261 in *Studies in Honor of George R. Hughes. (Studies in Ancient Oriental Civilization,* 39) Chicago: Oriental Institute, 1976.

LIST OF ABBREVIATIONS

AASOR	*Annual of the American Schools of Oriental Research*
ADAJ	*Annual of the Department of Antiquities of Jordan*
AJA	*American Journal of Archaeology*
AJSL	*American Journal of Semitic Languages and Literatures*
AS	*Anatolian Studies*
ASAE	*Annales du Service des Antiquités de l'Egypte*
ANEP	J.B. PRITCHARD (ed.), *The Ancient Near East in Pictures*
ANET	J.B. PRITCHARD (ed.), *Ancient Texts relating to the Old Testament (3rd ed.)*
ᶜAtiqot	*ᶜAtiqot: Journal of the Israel Department of Antiquities and Museums*
AUSS	*Andrews University Seminary Studies*
BA	*The Biblical Archaeologist*
BAR	*Biblical Archaeology Review*
BASOR	*Bulletin of the American Schools of Oriental Research*
BAT	*Biblical Archaeology Today: Proceedings of the International Congress on Biblical Archaeology, Jerusalem 1985*
BIES	*Bulletin of the Israel Exploration Society*
BSAE	*British School of Archaeology in Egypt*
CAH³	I.E.S. EDWARDS, C.J. GADD, and N.G. HAMMOND (eds.), *The Cambridge Ancient History (3rd ed.)*
COWA 3	R.W. EHRICH (ed.), *Chronologies in Old World Archaeology*
EAEHL	M. AVI-YONAH and E. STERN (eds.), *Encyclopedia of Archaeological Excavations in the Holy Land*
EA	*Die El-Amarna Tafeln*
EI	*Eretz-Israel: Archaeological, Historical and Geographical Studies*
Glueck Festschrift	J.A. SANDERS (ed.), *Near eastern Archaeology in the Twentieth Century: Essays in Honor of Nelson Glueck*
HTR	*Harvard Theological Review*
HUCA	*Hebrew Union College Annual*
IDB	*The Interpreter's Dictionary of the Bible*
IEJ	*Israel Exploration Journal*
JAOS	*Journal of the American Oriental Society*
JBL	*Journal of Biblical Literature*
JCS	*Journal of Cuneiform Studies*
JEA	*Journal of Egyptian Archaeology*
JNES	*Journal of Near Eastern Studies*
JPOS	*Journal of the Palestine Oriental Society*
JQR	*Jewish Quarterly Review*
JSOT	*Journal for the Society of the Old Testament*
JSS	*Journal of Semitic Studies*

Kenyon Festschrift	P.R.S. MOOREY and P. PARR (eds.), *Archaeology in the Levant: essays for Kathleen Kenyon*
Magnalia Dei	F.M. CROSS et al. (eds.), *Magnalia Dei: The Mighty Acts of God. Essays on the Bible and Archaeology in Memory of G.E. Wright*
OIP	*Oriental Institute Publications*, Chicago
PEQ	*Palestine Exploration Quarterly*
Qedem	*Qedem: Monographs of the Institute of Archaeology, The Hebrew University of Jerusalem*
QDAJ	*Quarterly of the Department of Antiquities of Jordan*
QDAP	*Quarterly of the Department of Antiquities in Palestine*
RB	*Revue Biblique*
Rose Festschrift Glen Rose	L.G. PERDUE, L.E. TOOMBS, and G.L. JOHNSON (eds.), *Archaeology and Biblical Interpretation: Essays in Memory of D. Glen Rose*
Symposia	F.M. CROSS (ed.), *Symposia Celebrating the 75th Anniversary of the American Schools of Oriental Research (1900-1975)*
TA	*Tel Aviv: Journal of the Tel Aviv University Institute of Archaeology*
Tufnell Festschrift	J. TUBB (ed.), *Palestine in the Bronze and Iron Ages: Papers in Honour of Olga Tufnell*
VT	*Vetus Testamentum*
WHJP	B. MAZAR (ed.), The World History of the Jewish People
ZAW	*Zeitschrift für de alttestamentliche Wissenschaft*
ZDPV	*Zeitschrift des Deutschen Palästina-Vereins*

PREFACE

The date and the nature of the Israelite exodus from Egypt has not lacked for space in books and periodicals during the last century. The reader is justified in requesting an explanation for yet another volume on a subject that so dramatically has captivated the minds and pens of so many scholars of the past. Past approaches to the subject obviously have not been uniform. Each scholar in his own way has attempted to make a contribution to the subject out of his own area of expertise using a slightly different approach, attempting to reconcile the intricacies and seeming contradictions within the biblical narratives or between the biblical account and the extra-biblical sources available to us.

For various reasons, the end result has been less than gratifying. A lack of appreciation for the relative importance of the physical conditions of the Sinai for an understanding of the historical event often has resulted in a superficial portrayal of the Israelite plight during the forty years of the sojourn. Too often a casual interpretation of the biblical text has resulted in a failure to recognize some of the implications of statements of topographical and geographical importance. Other writers appear intentionally to have avoided the rather obvious correlation of the exodus experience and the Israelite conquest of the Promised Land. Some scholars have forced the details of both events reflected in the historical sources and the archaeological evidence supposedly related to those events into a preconceived concept.

Without significant historical sources or continuous population to preserve oral traditions, the Sinai has been subject to sheer speculation for most of the last two millennia. Since archaeological evidence for an understanding of the nomadic lifestyle required in the Sinai is at best sparse, the additional disregard of topographical and geographical considerations often has permitted imaginative and fanciful reconstructions of the Exodus event and the plight of the Israelites in preaching and print. Only during the brief periods when the Israelis controlled the area in relatively recent times have there been serious efforts at learning the region's past. While the work of the Israeli geologists, prehistorians, and archaeologists has been impressive, the integration of their results into the area of biblical studies has been limited, and the prevailing perception of the Exodus among most biblical scholars generally continues to follow traditional lines: a single body of Hebrews left Egypt under the leadership of Moses to languish in the Sinai for some forty years prior to entering Canaan either by infiltration or frontal attack. The event is either placed in the fifteenth or thirteenth centuries, and the details are integrated into the reconstruction following the biblical account or several other historical formats. The fact that for many scholars the narratives of Exodus and Numbers are less than historical precludes, for them at least, a serious attempt at formulating a holistic portrayal. Inevitably the biblical record does present a major problem. Some of the historical evidence appears clearly contradictory, and reconciliation of biblical details, even apart from extra-biblical data, is not simple.

The so-called "unreliability" of the biblical chronological data can be attributed, in some instances, to the uncritical and haphazard approach of those who claim to be critical scholars. In many cases, no attempt has been made to reconcile chronological details which "uncritically" appear to deal with the same historical event. In the case of the Exodus, the assumption that the Hebrew movement from Egypt to Canaan was a single, unified Moses-led event obviously results in a problematic integration of biblical data that were never intended to be understood in that way. Any critical reading of the biblical description of this event in the books of Exodus, Numbers and Deuteronomy (however fragmentary and disjointed) provides a complexity of details in time, place and personalities far beyond the traditional simplistic reconstruction generally used to show the inadequacies of the biblical text. A fair-minded evaluation of the biblical materials requires a legitimate attempt at creating a scenario that integrates all biblical and extra-biblical data rather than the depreciation of a pseudo-biblical, historical caricature.

Obviously, details of historical interest are less complete prior to the United Monarchy and the development of official archives for a centralized administration. It is precisely for this reason that modern scholarship must commit greater diligence and perseverance to the reconstruction of pre-monarchial history based on the more fragmentary data available. Unreliability of self must be assumed by the interpreter rather than casually attributing such unreliability to the sources available to him. Scarcity of data should never be construed as unreliability. It is clear that on occasion the biblical writer of necessity or intentionally was selective in portraying historical developments. The period of the "judges" is a good example. These local heroes, identified with different parts of Canaan, were not intended to be chronologically sequential, but rather representative to show that for the most part their exploits were confined clearly to their own tribal interests and participation (in some instances, two or three other tribes joining in common cause).

Whether this attempt at a comprehensive reconstruction of this important event in the life of ancient Israel is a successful integration of the available data is for the reader to decide. Whatever the judgment, it is hoped that some enlightenment has been provided, and that the reader will have been stimulated to private study that will enrich his awareness of the biblical message and that others with clearer insights will be motivated further to enhance our understanding of this fascinating period of biblical history.

This study is intended for the layperson who has a genuine interest in understanding biblical history. Its aim has been to provide a basis for untraditional thinking about the nature of the Hebrew exodus from Egypt and the Israelites' formative integration into a confederacy with the land of Canaan. The approach has been not to enter into critical and analytical evaluation of detailed discussions on the various aspects of the subject, but to provide the broad scope of data relevant to any holistic scenario and some of the details that appear especially significant to an understanding of the biblical data. For those who question the validity of a historical framework based on the biblical narratives, this study will have limited value. For others whose omniscient grasp of biblical truth for these events is beyond challenge, these pages clearly will provide little insight. For the majority between these positions, there hopefully will be some kernels of truth to evoke new thoughts and challenge for study.

Credit for the wealth of data available on the subject has been provided in a general way to avoid exhaustive notes. The extensive bibliography reflects the interest and relevance of the topic within biblical scholarship beyond the primary interests of the author reflected in the notes. The scope of the bibliography has been expanded to provide the interested reader with additional opportunities for continued study. Indebtedness extends far beyond the factual data that has been used in the preparation of this work. The inspiration and stimulation of those whose views differ has been especially appreciated.

The academic and intellectual contributions, to whatever the merits of this work might be, extend far beyond those who provided direct assistance in its preparation. To my parents who provided the initial opportunities and motivation for academic pursuits, to my teachers and professors who prodded and challenged to greater excellence and to my students in more recent years who, by their reluctance to believe, sharpened content conception and communication, I am so very deeply indebted. My profoundest gratitude belongs to my dear wife, Linda, who through the long years of patient support and sustaining encouragement has contributed immeasurably to any and all of my accomplishments. In the preparation of this text as with most other aspects of our work, she has been a active participant in its completion. To Lin and to my office assistant, Jean Foley, I am indebted for helpful suggestions in clarifying intended meanings and proofreading the final text. Thanks also to Miss Foley for the preparation of the informative maps that contribute so meaningfully to an understanding of the text.

George L. Kelm
Fort Worth, Texas
December 15, 1990

INTRODUCTION TO THE STUDY

The historian must be concerned with the reliability of his sources. That concern must be foremost and constant in attempting a reconstruction of events as complex and problematic as the Hebrews' exodus from Egypt and their settlement in Canaan. It is logical therefore that sooner or later he will question the nature of the biblical text in reference to the information it provides concerning these formative stages in the history of the Israelites. It is not too much to ask that the biblical accounts be judged by the same criteria that historians use in determining the reliability of other ancient documents. If events such as the exodus and conquest really happened, then the record of those events as they appear in the Bible should withstand the most rigorous internal analysis and comparative evaluation possible. The theory of this principal is accepted by most scholars.

The 'historical-critical' method intent on subjecting the biblical text to rigorous internal analysis to determine the historical reliability of the text on occasion has succumbed to its own inherent shortcoming, the subjective prejudice of the critic. The unfortunate outcome as a result has been a reflection of the analyst rather than the text. When such vested interests are obvious (for example, in reconstructions of the Hebrew exodus from Egypt to prove an 'early' or 'late' date), the 'skewing' of data is entirely possible. In other instances, the historical reliability is discounted on the presupposition of its etiological or mythical nature.

The interpretive process unfortunately also may be undermined by the acceptance of a simplistic understanding of the biblical text that seems to disregard completely the possibility of a far more complex historical record than a casual reading would suggest. The suggestion that an eyewitness to the events of the exodus should have been able to avoid 'obvious' inconsistencies, duplications, contradictions, and differences in style and vocabulary in the biblical account of the exodus may be satisfying to some. It may even be used as a basis for ridiculing of Mosaic authorship of the Pentateuch, for example. Such thinking lacks objectivity and hardly takes into account the complexity of Israel's formation. In fact, the more serious the attempt to reconstruct, not only events of the biblical record but events related to ancient history in general, the more convinced the researcher becomes that even mundane events have a far greater complexity than initially imagined.

It is a relatively simple matter, with our twentieth century conceptions, and in some cases, preconceptions or misconceptions, to create historical or quasi-historical caricatures of past events in the elemental sense, and then to point out the shortcomings, the lack of authenticity and historical reliability on the part of authors, known or unknown. To credit those authors with a legitimate recording of events out of their complex context and to attempt even a limited understanding of that event from the fragmented sources available to us is slightly more difficult.

Obviously, the ability to recall the intention of the authors of by-gone days is beyond us. Suffice it to say that in most instances they had little, if any thought, of writing to a twentieth century audience (This is intended as an understatement!). In fairness, therefore, criticism of ancient documents must recognize that the primary inadequacies in the appreciation and understanding of those works lie primarily with the twentieth century critic rather than with the ancient author. We must assume that for his purposes and audience, the author's statements were appropriate and adequate. He assumed an orientation and awareness on the part of his reader that was sufficient to provide a clear conception of his intent and the validity of his record. On us, then, in the twentieth century lies the burden of understanding the historical context of the ancient author before we may judge, in any valid way, the accuracy and factualism of his statements.

The question concerning the historical documents in our Bible clearly is not whether this material, or an individual book, could have been written by the same person. It obviously was not, since generation after generation individual scribes faithfully copied and updated the text. Such problems assumed to abound in the account of the Exodus thus can hardly be attributed with certainty to Moses (assuming a Mosaic authorship?) or the original source. The scribes, confronted with a complexity of details, clearly were at a loss in their process of integrating data related not just to a single event, but to a series of distinct 'exodus' experiences that ultimately would be told as a common, corporate experience in the past of a unified Israel. How these separate events may be related to four distinct documents or sources generally assumed to be reflected in the Pentateuch remains to be seen. However, it is interesting to note that two books, Leviticus and Deuteronomy, that reflect the legal system attributed to Moses are essentially unitary, though generally attributed to P (Priestly) and D (Deuteronomist) respectively. The books of Exodus and Numbers, containing the diary-like details of the exodus experience interestingly are assumed to have had a much more complex literary history. The simplistic, traditional approach that has viewed the Exodus from Egypt as a single monolithic event under the leadership of Moses, not only has been frustrated into a defensive apologetic by biblical 'critics' but has vitiated the more complex view of the event that the Bible attempts to portray.

The analysis of biblical texts often has found its shortcoming in a failure to recognize the scribal role in transmission -- a role that in itself accounts for much of the complexity of the text in terms of inconsistencies, duplications, contradictions, and especially differences in style and vocabulary. Obviously, whatever the origin of the text, the freedom with which the scribes dealt with their manuscript as they copied the document and commented on its meaning to assure comprehension on the part of their contemporary readers gave the successive generations of manuscripts individualities that have complicated, to say the least, the role of the modern critical reader.

We tend to disregard the intricacies and implications of literary transmission and the intense responsibility assumed by ancient scribes for communicating the meaning of their texts to their contemporary readers. It was the scribal tradition of 'giving the sense' that prompted them to change, revise, restate to achieve the nuance that would assure a retention of the meaning and their perception of the original words.[1] Surely the so-called anachronisms, so often used to malign the texts, may be attributed to the scribes who in their own way were attempting to update the text for the sake of the 'provincial' readers of their day. Their modernization of the text assured the constant transition of meaning that ultimately was short-circuited by canonization. When the sanctity of the text precluded the interpretive process of the scribe, its meaning was fixed within the literary concepts of that time and place, far removed, unfortunately, from the twentieth century mind.

The recognized creativity of the Israelite scribe, however, has confronted us with a textual dilemma. The date of a biblical document need not be determined by the latest historical or textual allusion. The inclusion of 'late' data may be attributed to a perceptive scribe in the transcriptional process. Late dating of the biblical text on that basis now appears unduly exaggerated, and as some 'exodus' data suggests, there may be good reason, on the other hand, to look more closely for earlier parallels for the biblical materials in extra-biblical sources.

Our problem is a twentieth century mind that approaches the biblical text as though no interpretive process were required for its comprehension. A mere restatement of biblical text in simple English may provide very little insight into the true meaning of the text intended by the original writer. And yet, for totally different reasons, the defender and the critic seem at times to disregard totally the complexity of the text and the context out of which it came to make sweeping statements of its values or shortcomings. If in true scribal tradition we were to commit equal time in attempting to recover the historical, cultural and contextual settings of the biblical text as we do in bolstering or undermining its accuracy, possibly more lasting value could be attributed to our efforts.

In any case, difficulties in understanding the nature of the composition of the text does not of necessity undermine the historical nature of that text. Few will deny the existence of the Hebrew exodus as an historical event. The solution obviously lies in the formulation of an event in which the available data, both written and archaeological, may be integrated in a consistent and meaningful manner.

To approach the study of the Exodus with a presupposition that biblical 'history' often is biased and propagandistic seems no less problematic to a legitimate reconstruction of historical reality than to accept a simplistic, literalist interpretation. The emergence of ancient Israel in Canaan following an extended period of oppression in Egypt was a complex, multi-faceted process that a historical record would tend to reflect. Theological idealization of the Exodus event obviously does not contribute to an awareness of the historical reality that underlies it. But when the basic nature of the commentary portrays the participants in a negative light, the basic honesty of the document appears intact and legitimate for historical reconstruction.

Since it seems highly unlikely that the authors of the biblical text in their historical discussions functioned with malice of forethought in reference to the twentieth century, it is logical to assume that the events of the exodus and conquest, though skeletal at times, were intended for our enlightenment, and that the responsibility for accuracy of interpretation has fallen our academic lot. That the different formulations of 'wandering' traditions in Exodus, Numbers, and Deuteronomy are based on historiographical motifs has been rejected in this presentation.[2] It is our contention that these narratives contain dependable historical evidence in regard to the itineraries and provide a logical basis for a realistic reconstruction of the exodus event. The impact of that event on the subsequent religious life of Israel was too powerful to have less than an historical basis. Our search therefore is for the complex historical reality behind the sketchy outlines of our biblical passages.

Literary Approach to the Exodus Traditions

Studies devoted to the exodus itinerary of the Hebrews from Egypt to Canaan naturally fall into three sections: the routes from Egypt to Sinai, from Sinai to Kadesh-barnea, and Kadesh-barnea to the border of Canaan. The first section is problematic in reference to the location of the 'sea' crossing and the identification of Mount Sinai. The intermediate stage provides a series of place names with unidentifiable locations. The third segment provides multiple routes (often disregarded) that have a direct bearing on the understanding of the nature of the event.

Some scholars in studying the different versions of the itineraries in their entirety according to Pentateuchal literary sources have suggested a degree of mutual dependence and originality.[3] Others have suggested that the descriptive narrative of the Hebrew wanderings in

Exodus and Numbers forms the authentic tradition with later compilations and accretions of details from various sources. The result has been an arbitrary core of reality and a body of suspect details that obviously require explanation. Others have suggested that a much later description of a pilgrimage route to Mount Sinai in part has been reformulated and presented as a list of 'exodus' stations in Numbers 33. Various aspects of borrowing and reconstruction of the text are viewed as an editorial process by numbers of compilers at various times. Thus, for some scholars, the final form given some of these accumulated borrowings are completely erroneous and contribute nothing to an understanding of the historical reality they were intended to describe.[4]

In fact, the possibility exists that the complex nature of the historical event dictated the divergent details that are evident in the biblical text. The seeming incompatibility in the biblical narratives of what traditionally has been accepted as a single Hebrew exodus may reflect two or more major traditions that had their origin in the historical nature of a much more complex process. Thus, Numbers 33 may reflect an earlier migration, or series of movements, that met no military resistance along the King's Highway in the Transjordan. A later or final 'exodus' phase under the leadership of Moses and Joshua avoided confrontation with Edom and Moab by using a long, discouraging detour where the Israelites ultimately were forced to fight their way through Amorite territory north of the Arnon.[5]

The 'Exodus Story' has been described as the ...*structural framework that unifies originally distinct traditions into a meaningful whole.*[6] Israel's wilderness experiences have been linked together as though the consecutive events and locales formed a continuous route from beginning to end. It has been suggested that these diaries, or itinerary notes, ultimately belonged to the royal archive. Their similarity to official military records describing royal campaigns need not be explained by the late annalistic texts of Neo-Assyrian kings of the ninth century B.C.[7] The reliance of the writer on Egyptian scribal conventions related to the documentation of the pharaoh's administrative and military exploits resulted in a 'day-by-day' dairy and the topographical place-name list for the exodus record. But beyond this basic record of the Moses-led exodus, the harmonization of the separate traditions of separate family and clan emigration and the wanderings in the wilderness constituted a major challenge.

Is it not possible that Numbers 33 is a stylized product of an extended literary process that appropriately modified the details of the historical process for the purpose of presenting a single direct route to the Land of Canaan, the Promised Land?[8] May it not be possible that Numbers 33 rather resembles Egyptian prototypes in the form of topographical lists used by the pharaohs to catalog the results of their military expeditions abroad. The recognition that the 'stylized' summary of Numbers 33 is *consistent in its literary form* and that the *...sequence of the stations, as far as can be ascertained, is geographically sound*[9] lends credence to a recognition of a document consistent with its literary milieu. The geographical grouping of place names not found in the itinerary narratives was intended to integrate the events of an extended, complex process into a consolidated historical roster, a listing of noteworthy places in Israel's pilgrimage from bondage to the land of promise.

Archaeology and Historical Reconstruction

Our understanding of the complexity of ancient Near Eastern cultures and the historical events of the distance past has come to us from archaeological research. Inscriptions from Mesopotamia, Egypt and other Near Eastern areas have complemented the limited historical glimpses of the biblical text. Unfortunately inscriptions with historical content from Palestine, the focus of most of biblical history, are few, especially for the formative stages of Israel's history prior to the United Monarchy. However, during the past century, extensive scientific archaeological excavation in all those regions related to biblical history has produced a wealth of knowledge and understanding about the human past. Although this information is of an indirect nature, the careful, systematic excavation of the occupational strata in the mounds of ancient town sites has provided us with correlations of time and culture that have broadened our sense of the ancient Near Eastern environment in which the biblical personalities functioned. For those periods in which no written sources were produced or preserved, this archaeological data is our primary source of information and the basis on which reconstruction of early human lifestyles are possible.

For later periods, the correlation of archaeological data and written insights, whether biblical or extra-biblical, is not a simple matter. The archaeological data is fragmentary, partially the result of the limited exposure of any given archaeological site. The arbitrary selectivity of the ancient writer has provided limited historical glimpses into his time and place. Thus, the chance possibility of a positive correlation of these two types of data tends to frustrate the researcher's commitment in providing his reader with a satisfactory, factual portrait of the past. The reader, on his part, must be satisfied with the realization that very few words from the so-called 'biblical archaeologist' now or ever have come from Mt. Sinai. Any historical reconstruction based on the 'present' level of understanding (at any time) is the result of an interpretive correlation of a subjective corpus of available data. The probability of achieving a 'true' picture of the historical event that lies behind the cultural and historical evidence is dependent upon the skill and objectivity of the scholar and the amount of relevant data available to him. It is the current paucity of relevant data that should prompt greater commitment of effort and funds to archaeological research by those interested in the understanding of the biblical text and the ancient Near Eastern civilization out of which it came. Obviously our commitment must be to understanding... an understanding of those cultural details that reasonably can be expected to contribute to our comprehension of individual biblical events.

The validity of recent attempts at an integration of archaeological and historical data regarding the date and nature of the exodus is undermined by presuppositions. On the one hand, the primacy of biblical statements is affirmed as though the Mind of God is revealed apart from the interpretative process of fallible man. On the other, the veracity and validity of the biblical record is depreciated at the slightest seeming inconsistency with archaeological data, however tentative its interpretation may be. The rigidity of these commitments obviously is not uniform, nor consistent. Between the two extremes is a multiplicity of positions purporting uncompromised objectivity in the recognition of irreducible facts. The unfortunate result for biblical studies has been a division of scholarship into basically two defensive camps (with variations and nuances, of course) committed to the preservation and/or primacy of a position that realistically is difficult to maintain in all its tenets.

The need in reference to the date and nature of the exodus and 'conquest' is to begin again with a different, if not novel, premise. Apart from presupposition and prejudice concerning the primacy of one form of data or another, the basic commitment should be understanding of both historical fact and artifact at 'face value' with a recognition that traditional reconstructions have no merit beyond the limited scope of the originator. The *modus operandi* consequently requires a return to 'Square One' where the naiveté of the uninitiated researcher assembles again the raw, relevant data, from all available sources, to form the corpus of disjointed parts and to challenge a fresh integration.

Critical in the process of analysis and correlation of data in pursuit of a meaningful reconstruction is a consistent acceptance of all relevant information. If any biblical numbers or historical inferences have legitimacy and relevance at all, then selectivity for the sake of a particular reconstruction appears suspect. The question of reliability must be directed at the interpreter of historical or archaeological data as well as at the sources. It is, after all, the interpretive process that brings the reconstruction into being and ultimately it will be the interpretive process that will highlight the limits of its validity. The basic nature of the interpreter's 'stuff' will remain the same. But, the scope of the 'stuff' will be determined by the presuppositions the interpreter brings to his task.

The insurmountable handicap in the formulation of a valid reconstruction is the interpreter who assumes himself above prejudice and presupposition. Convincingly acting the part of omniscient objectivity to his own delusion, he, unfortunately, becomes an ally of the obscurity he hopes to dispel among his hearers or readers.

How, then, may the interpreter structure the data into a meaningful whole? Reconstruction must begin with the isolated restatement of the relevant parts apart from long established structure or assumed relatedness. In other words, "What does this statement or artifact mean in its own right?" A general consensus at this point forms the first step toward new meaning, especially as additional relevant data becomes available. The traditional stereotypes of either 'early date' or 'late date' reconstructions with their respective proponents and arguments have too long held sway. Though models of another nature (*i.e.*, sociological) have not been totally convincing as alternatives, what is even clearer is the fact that the wealth of new data relevant for an understanding of the period and nature of the exodus and 'conquest' has not been used to its best advantage. Repeated attempts to use the results of more recent archaeological research to reinforce or challenge the existing 'early/late' reconstructions have largely failed.

In our attempt at a reconstruction of the Hebrew exodus and the emergence of the Israelite nation in Canaan, one essential point must be maintained concerning the correlation of archaeological and historical data, whether from the biblical or extra-biblical sources. Historical and archaeological data must be exposed to critical evaluation in terms of legitimacy and relevance without reference to traditional or acceptable views. The demand, again, is for objectivity. On the one hand, preconceptions in the interpretation of historical sources, including the biblical text, have led the excavator to compromise his archaeological data. On the other, over-emphasis on archaeological data, on occasion, has led to a misunderstanding of the biblical narrative. Obviously a legitimate integration allows both the biblical text and archaeological evidence an opportunity to clarify the other.[10] Where integration and correlation appear to be impossible, the recognition of current inadequacy must be accepted without prejudicing the general public against that area of study in which our commitment or expertise does not lie. Here the call is for humility in the realization that the basic problem lies in the sphere of interpretation where human fallibility resides. It is highly superficial to suggest that just because an adequate correlation of a set of archaeological details and a series of historical statements from the Bible dated to the same period cannot be found that the problem lies either with the archaeological or the biblical data. It is almost inconceivable that a scholar should suggest that ...*if the archaeological evidence does not correlate well with the biblical narratives, it is probable that these narratives are not historically accurate, and believing Jews and Christians should seek some other way to view them in the context of their faith.*[11] The implication that archaeological evidence and historical references in the biblical narratives are in a confrontational mode, or that one or the other must be declared at fault unless total compatibility can be achieved appears to overlook the obvious inadequacy of the so-called scholar who established the parameters of the relationship in the first place. It is a fallacy that frequently appears in discussions about the contributions and\or shortcomings of biblical archaeology. The fact is that apart from the interpretive process the historical fact and the archaeological artifact have absolutely nothing to say to each other. Their objective reality is totally independent. It is the interpreter who suggests a relationship that may be mutually instructive for understanding their independent reality, or for reconstructing and understanding a greater context. If the results do not achieve expectation levels, the fault surely must lie with the human interpretive process. In fact, the interpretive process has a three-fold jeopardy for human error: the interpretation of the historical fact, the interpretation of the archaeological artifact, and the correlation of the two interpretations. Because of the subjectivity that is inherent in this three-fold process, the work of the biblical archaeologist is never complete and his conclusions can never be assumed to be final. At any point in time, his best efforts are an objective attempt at producing a tentative reconstruction on the basis of the data available to him. To expect more is to be sadly disappointed and unrealistic.

One final, and possibly the most critical, issue must be addressed. Any historical and cultural ramifications for understanding and correlating archaeological and biblical data are based on chronology.

How can we know anything with certainty about the past (in this case, ancient Palestine and Israel), if we cannot even date the major phases of historical and cultural development within a margin of a century of (sic!) less?[12]

The dilemma is not limited to the variety of chronological questions regularly being addressed by individual scholars on the basis of their personal research. The independent chronologies recognized by the academic communities for the cultural history within the confines of modern geographical and political borders are in a constant state of flux. The confusion of 'dates' the student and layperson must confront in the process of even casual interest is both bewildering and discouraging. Most withdraw with their confidence in the scholarly world completely shattered and their initial commitment to independent study often frayed beyond repair.

On the other hand, it is important to recognize that the formulation of an 'absolute' chronology is in a constant state of adjustment and dependent on the ongoing academic process. By the very nature of the process, it is not realistic to anticipate a 'final' integration of all the variables and the ultimate presentation of an 'absolute' chronology for the ancient Near Eastern world. While we attribute numerical 'dates' to specific historical events, we must be willing to accept the fact that we continue to deal with a 'relative' structure in which we are endeavoring to provide some sequential order to a specific discussion. For those who seek 'ultimate truth' such a situation is most difficult to accept in spite of its reality. To fail to recognize the situation, or to refuse to accept its existence, is unfortunately self-deluding.

In this discussion, therefore, the attempt has been made to emphasize the sequential order of things rather than to deal with critical minutiae based on the preference of one chronological structure rather than another. It is hoped that lapses that reflect conflicting 'dates' are limited to those unavoidable integrations of divergent academic discussions. Clearly, the problems of chronological integration demand first priority within the scholarly community. Unfortunately, in the first place, few scholars view themselves, in interest or commitment, as adequate for the task. Secondly, because of vested interest, fewer appear willing to recognize and accept the competence of others to formulate an 'absolute' chronology for them. This impasse, however unfortunate, is the real context in which we must function. It is specifically for this reason that ongoing historical research is a necessity. The legitimacy of our study is based on the premise that our lot will ever be in the realm of the 'relative' rather than the 'absolute.'

The History of the 'Exodus' Problem.

The record of God's deliverance of the Israelites from the bondage of Egypt became the subsequent cornerstone of their religious and political life. The nature of that deliverance, therefore, took on an unusual significance in thought and ritual. Corporate identification as a covenanted people linked the nation to the historical event at Mount Sinai. The impact of this dramatic event in the formation of Israel's national life gave an abiding significance to the wilderness locales identified with the recorded episodes along the way. The detailed description of the events and the consistent agreement in content and structure of the 'exodus' itinerary ultimately may have been the result of reliance on official governmental archives.

Following the Babylonian exile, much of subsequent Jewish, and ultimately Christian interpretation sought the 'spiritual' meaning of the biblical account of the 'exodus from bondage.' However, at least from the fourth century onward, pilgrimage to 'holy places' in Bible lands became appealing and tended to preserve those geographical and topographical traditions that had persisted in oral and written word.

The consistent problem of ancient as well as modern commentators has been the irrepressible desire to harmonize the biblical data into a single corporate event in which all the data of the biblical narratives is carefully integrated. The translators of the Septuagint limited their use of contemporary geographical terms to the confines of Egypt. Most Hebrew names in the LXX simply were transliterated or occasionally translated with some indication of the direction in which the departing Hebrews were thought to have gone. Only the single equation of *Yam Suf* with the Red Sea is clear. Philo, using the LXX text, primarily was interested in the didactic and symbolic value of the Old Testament.[13] Josephus, as a historian rather than a biblical scholar, using both the LXX and the Hebrew texts, took special interest in the route of the Israelite exodus. His descriptions and identifications in recounting the exodus event imply Jewish pilgrimage to some sites, especially in Egypt and the Transjordan. A footnote to his discussion about the lack of water at Rephidim and God's command for Moses *...to smite the rock which they saw lying there...* is informative:

This rock is there at this day, as the travellers agree, and must be the same that was there in the days of Moses, as being too large to be brought thither by our modern carriages.[14]

Talmudic and midrashic traditions generally indicate considerable interest in the location of the wilderness events and suggest that the site of the Israelites' encampment in the Plains of Moab was being pointed out to travelers in the region. Geographical interpretation primarily arose out of a theological or practical interest and for the most part such literature provides few significant insights. A number of Talmudic statements about Mount Sinai, however, provide an interesting perspective. In the Midrash on Genesis in the Babylonian Talmud (*Megila* 29,1; *Mechilta Jethro* 4):

For the Holy One, Blessed be He, left all the other mountains and revealed His Presence on Mount Sinai, although Mount Sinai was not very high; Rav Joseph said: A man should always learn from his Creator (Rashi: to love humility), for the Holy One, Blessed be He, left all the other mountains and revealed His Presence on Mount Sinai.

The perception of the highest, most impressive mountain in the region as the most likely candidate for Mount Sinai appears to be lacking in early Jewish thought.

The New Testament exhibits limited interest and acquaintance with the details of the Exodus. The 'sea' of the Israelites' escape is identified with the Red Sea (Acts 7:36; Hebrews 11:29), probably a general awareness based on the Septuagint. The only other reference is Paul's rather questionable identification of Mount Sinai with 'Arabia' (Galatians 4:25). The Roman inclusion of the Sinai peninsula within the region of Arabia Petraea, however, makes such an identification quite reasonable and accurate.

Christian interest in biblical geography appears to begin with Eusebius of Caesarea who identified Mount Sinai with the southern part of the peninsula. His *Onomasticon* compiled about A.D. 330 reveals a lack of interest or awareness of the nature of the early exodus route from Rameses to Rephidim. Comment on about half of the place names mentioned in the exodus itineraries are grouped in three locales: the area of Feiran in the southern peninsula, the vicinity of Petra east of the Arabah, and the Transjordanian plateau east and northeast of the Dead Sea. This emphasis undoubtedly was based on Jewish tradition and the accounts of Christian travelers intent on identifying places of biblical interest. The *Onomasticon* and Jerome's translation with some revisions, dated ca. 390, suggest that some time before the fourth century A.D. the Wilderness of Sinai and the Wilderness of Paran were understood to be in close proximity in the southern part of the Sinai Peninsula. A town Φαϱαν, located near the mouth of a large valley draining the southern mountain massif into the Gulf of Suez, has been preserved in the Arabic name of the ravine, Wadi Feiran. Since the names of the town and the biblical Wilderness of Paran take the same form in the Greek text, readers of the Septuagint would have had no reason to suspect that the two did not refer to the same region.

Significant development of Christian settlement of the southern Sinai is dated to the mid-third century A.D. Egyptian Christians, subject to Roman persecution and Saracen and Arab slavery, sought refuge in the mountains of southern Sinai. Three primary settlements developed at Raithu (E-Tur), Feiran and Jebel Musa. Already an important commercial port during Phoenician times, Raithu became the primary coastal center from which pilgrims traveled along Wadi Hibran to the monasteries of Feiran and later, St. Catherina. It arbitrarily was identified with biblical Elim. A 10-acre tell that prominently rises in the center of the Feiran oasis has remains dated from the ninth-eighth centuries B.C. of the Judean Kingdom period to the beginning of the early Arab period in the seventh century A.D.[15] It is the only tell discovered thus far in the Sinai with such a prolonged continuous history. Thus, it is not unusual that the town would assume the name Paran which has been suggested as the original name of the entire Sinai peninsula in biblical times. The identification of Paran at this location by Ptolemaeus, a Roman geographer in the first half of the second century A.D. clearly indicates that the name predated the advent of Christianity in the region and therefore was not introduced by Christian monks. (The biblical wilderness of Paran therefore was not confined to the desert of et-Tih or its northern part but was a general name for the whole of the peninsula. The wilderness of Sinai, like other regional names, appears rather to have been limited to the immediate vicinity of the holy mount.)

During the Byzantine period, Feiran was an important city with a cathedral and bishop. Its prosperity was linked to the important caravan route that linked the Gulf of Suez through the Jebel Musa region with the Gulf of Elath (Aqaba) at Dhahab. Hundreds of Nabataean, Greek and Arabic inscriptions by merchants in Wadi Feiran and adjoining wadis suggest the vitality of commercial activity that supported this primary oasis along the route. The Christian community established by a Palestinian monk, Sylvanus, at the end of the fourth century, appears to have vied with another monastic community established by a Syrian monk, Julian Saba, who had built a church on the peak of Jebel Musa earlier in the century. The monks of Feiran identified biblical Rephidim and the wilderness of Paran with the Feiran oasis and the biblical Sinai with Mount Serbal at the eastern end of their oasis, about 72 km. inland from E-Tur. All three centers, Raithu, Feiran and Sinai, sent delegates to a council at Constantinople in A.D. 536.

The earliest Christian monks who had dotted the southern mountains with their prayer chapels ultimately were drawn into Christian community in a church at the base of Jebel Musa. In the sixth century, to protect the lives and property of the numerous monks from roving desert bands in the region, the Emperor Justinian built a fortified monastery. It was dedicated to the sainted memory of a young Alexandrian Christian girl who, in A.D. 307, had been tortured and put to death for publicly accusing the Emperor Maximinus of idolatry. According to the tradition, her bones were recovered from a nearby mountain (where angels had buried her body) to the monastery church. Justinian's recognition and the annihilation of the Christian community and destruction of the Byzantine city of Feiran established the primacy of Jebel Musa as the 'mount of God.'[16] The isolation and fortifications of St. Catherina provided a refuge following the Islamic invasion in the seventh century.

Subsequent history of the Sinai peninsula, obviously, has little bearing on our attempts to reconstruct the Hebrews' wilderness experiences. The identification of Wadi Feiran and biblical Paran provides little, if any enlightenment for the itinerary or location of

Mount Sinai. The biblical descriptive use of 'Paran' suggests a general designation of most, if not all, of the peninsula which consists of smaller regions (Shur, Sin, Sinai, Zin, etc.). Historical discontinuity in the Sinai has precluded significant insights into its distant past. However, there is the hope that in a restatement of the isolated details from a different perspective some enlightenment for the nature of the Hebrews' exodus through this barrenness may be derived. The reader alone must judge.

NOTES

[1] In the tradition of the great scribe Ezra (Nehemiah 8). The biblical manuscripts from Qumran reflect the development of scribal traditions in the three primary Jewish communities (Mesopotamia, Egypt and Palestine) following the destruction of the Second Temple in 586 B.C. A study of variant readings indicate both a rigid commitment to maintaining the 'sense' of the original text and a personal freedom in the selection and integration of variant readings and commentary in the copying of a new manuscript.

[2] Z. Kallai, The Wandering-Traditions from Kadesh-Barnea to Canaan: A Study in Biblical Historiography. Pp. 175-184 in *Essays in Honour of Yigael Yadin,* eds. G. Vermes and J. Neusner. Totowa, NJ: Allanheld, Osmun and Co., 1983.

[3] M. Haran, Pp. 308-310 in *Interpreter's Dictionary of the Bible, Supplementary Volume.* Nashville, 1976.

[4] M. Noth, *Aufsätze zur biblischen Landes- und Altertumskunde,* I, Neukirchen-Vluyn 1971: 55-74, 84-91.

[5] B. Mazar, The Exodus and the Conquest. Pp. 69-79 in *The World History of the Jewish People, First Series: Ancient Times,* III: Judges.

[6] G.W. Coates, *CBQ* 34 (1972): 147-48.

[7] G.I Davies, The Wilderness Itineraries and the Composition of the Pentateuch. *Vetus Testamentum* 33 (1983): 8,9.

[8] Z. Kallai, The Wandering-Traditions from Kadesh-Barnea to Canaan: A Study in Biblical Historiography. Pp. 175-184 in *Essays in Honour of Yigael Yadin,* (eds.) G. Vermes and J. Neusner. Published for The Oxford Centre for Postgraduate Studies. Totowa, NJ: Allanheld, Osmun & Co., 1983.

[9] *idem,* 181.

[10] See, for example, I. Finkelstein, On Archaeological Methods and Historical Considerations: Iron Age II Gezer and Samaria. *BASOR* 277/278 (1990): 109-120.

[11] William H. Stiebing, Jr. *Out of the Desert? Archaeology and the Exodus/Conquest Narratives.* Buffalo, New York: Prometheus Books, 1989: 35.

[12] W.G. Dever, Of Myths and Methods. *BASOR* 277/278 (1990) 127.

[13] G.I. Davies, *The Way of the Wilderness. A Geographical Study of the Wilderness Itineraries in the Old Testament.* Cambridge: Cambridge University Press, 1979: 4-13.

[14] *Antiquities of the Jews* III:II, 7.
[15] Y. Aharoni, Kadesh-Barnea and Mount Sinai. Pp. 166-170 in Beno Rothenberg, *God's Wilderness: Discoveries in Sinai*. London: Thames and Hudson, 1961.
[16] G.I Davies, *The Way of the Wilderness*, 56-61.

Chapter I

AN INTRODUCTION TO THE SINAI PENINSULA

*...A visit to the traditional Mount Sinai suffices to dispel
all...doubts. The huge granite formations are an awe-inspiring
spectacle. The atmosphere, the light and the colours, the
incredible stillness, all conspire to make the scene an unforgettable
setting for the meeting of God with man.*[1]

In the awesome terrain of the Sinai, the crass caravaneer as well as
the penitent pilgrim may sense the presence of God, not in one place
alone, but in every place where the unspoiled expanses of undulating
sand dunes, the high jutting granite mountains, and narrow coastal
ravines conspire to reveal God's handiwork in nature. It seems,
therefore, quite inadequate to justify even long-standing tradition on
sense alone. Scholarly identification of at least thirteen different
locations for the *'Mount of God'* suggests a certain uncertainty about
even the most important aspects of the 'exodus' event. Even the
uncertainty, however, may not be adequate justification for an
additional study of the Hebrews' exodus. But whatever the end result
of this study, the significance of the exodus event in the subsequent
life and religion of Israel requires a more serious approach that
inevitably must begin in the event's supposed physical setting -- the
Sinai Peninsula.[2]

Confined within the extended arms of the Red Sea and the gentle
curve of the Mediterranean shoreline, the triangular land mass that
forms the Sinai Peninsula historically provided the cultural and
commercial bridge between Asia and Africa. The great international
trade route, generally referred to as the *Via Maris*, linked Egypt with
a complex network of roads frequented by caravans burdened with
foodstuffs and luxuries from Asia and Europe. Through the Red Sea,
ships laden with exotic goods from India and East Africa plied the
waters of the Gulf of Elath (Aqaba) on its eastern shore and the Gulf
of Suez on its west. The harbor terminals of these gulfs were linked
by a caravan route that could be viewed as the second most important
thoroughfare in the Sinai. This route, known today as the Darb el-Hajj,
or Pilgrim's Way (from its use by western Islamic pilgrims to the
Hejaz), probably also may be identified (at least in part) with the *Way
of Mount Seir* (Deut. 1:2). From Elath a northern branch led directly

to the mountains of Edom or Seir. A third primary route, the *Way to Shur* (Gen. 16:7; Ex. 15:22) linked the eastern border of Egypt with Kadesh-Barnea and continued eastward through the Arabah south of the Dead Sea to the King's Highway, the major north-south route along the Transjordanian plateau. Apart from these routes with their international implications, the Sinai lies in isolation and seeming arid desolation. Its generally dry wadi beds and deep ravines provide reluctant access to its remote interior to the occasional stray traveler and the nomadic bedouin who call the Sinai 'home.'

Covering an area of 61,000 square kilometers (approximately 24,000 square miles), the Sinai peninsula is separated from the African continent on the west by the 300 kilometer Gulf of Suez and the 160 kilometer Suez Canal that links a series of lakes along the traditional eastern border of Egypt. Similar features on the east, the 170 kilometer Gulf of Eilat and the Arabah, an extension of the Great Rift, provide a natural boundary to Saudi Arabia in the south and modern Jordan in the north. Though the Sinai forms a natural link between the great Sahara and Arabian deserts and its arid conditions preclude permanent settlement, its role in history periodically is dramatic and worthy of detailed scrutiny.

Geological and Geographical Characteristics

The geological formations of the Sinai Peninsula may be divided into a series of distinctive regions. While a variety of geological formations is expected to produce distinctive landscapes, it is the combination of dramatic changes in elevation and the extreme climatic conditions of a desert environment that contributes to the distinctive heterogeneity of its terrain.[3]

Coastal Sand Dunes Along the Mediterranean Shoreline in the North.
A band of shifting sand dunes along the Mediterranean coast 70 kilometers wide at the border of Egypt (Suez Canal) narrows to 45 kilometers as it stretches to Raphia on the border of Canaan. Deposited on the shoreline by the counter-clockwise currents created by the Nile in the Mediterranean, the Sahara sands are gradually carried inland by the prevailing sea breezes. While the average depth

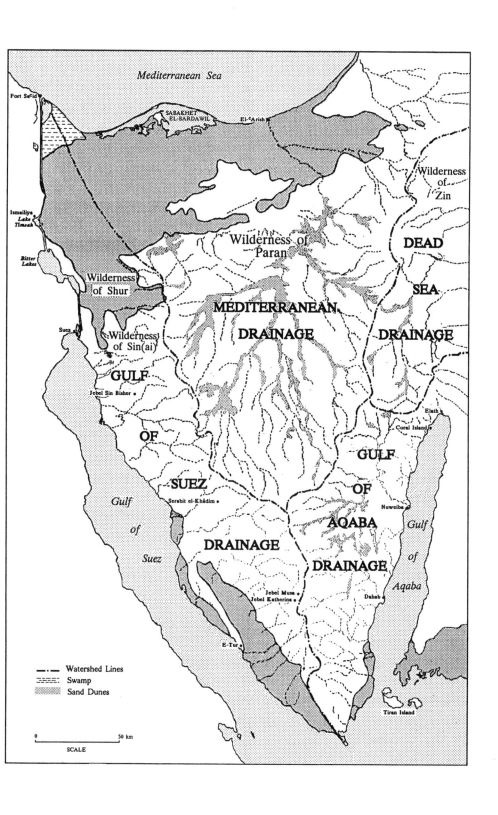

Mediterranean Sea

Port Sa'id

SABAKHET
EL-BARDAWIL

El-ʿArish

Wilderness
of
Zin

Ismailiya
Lake
Timsah

Bitter
Lakes

Wilderness of
Paran

DEAD

Wilderness
of Shur

SEA

MEDITERRANEAN

Suez

Wilderness
of Sin(ai)

DRAINAGE

DRAINAGE

GULF

Jebel Sin Bisher

Elath

Coral Island

OF

GULF

SUEZ

OF

Gulf

Serabit el-Khâdim

Nuweiba

of

AQABA

Gulf

DRAINAGE

of

Suez

DRAINAGE

Aqaba

Jebel Musa
Jebel Katherina

Dahab

E-Tur

Tiran Island

—·— Watershed Lines
▭▭▭ Swamp
▨▨▨ Sand Dunes

0   50 km

SCALE

of the dunes is 30 meters, their height on occasion may reach 80 meters. This band of undulating and constantly changing terrain, though noted for its numerous, relatively shallow fresh water wells, hindered easy passage across the northern Sinai except along the Mediterranean shoreline where the *Via Maris* became Egypt's primary link to Asia.[4]

The sand dunes so dominate the terrain that only one drainage system achieves access to the Mediterranean coast. All other gullies or streams merely disappear beneath the dunes. The Wadi el-Arish channels the run-off of a full two-thirds of the central Sinai northward, finally reaching the sea through a primary riverbed approximately a hundred meters wide.

The Sirbonis Sea (or Sabkhat Bardawil) is a distinctive feature along the Mediterranean coastline. Formed by an arching sandbar 100 kilometers long, it is believed to have been formed by the Pelusiac branch of the Nile much as other lakes and swamps (such as the Menzeleh, El-Burlus, etc.) presently are being formed in the delta region. This saline swamp has a width of 20 kilometers and has a depth of 1.5 to 3 meters. Although bushes and palm trees grow in the southern part of the swamp where ground water is near the surface, the Bardawil sandbank often is submerged in salt water except at its center where a high sand plateau provided an adequate base for Mont Cassius fortress.

The North-Central Foothills and Isolated Geological Formations

Beyond the sand dunes to the south, a series of limestone and sandstone massifs, geological folds sometimes referred to as 'hogbacks' are punctuated by isolated mountains reaching elevations of 2300 to 3500 feet and delineated by faults in which water tables are relatively shallow. These SW-NE depressions with their regularly spaced oases provided convenient lines of communication into the central Negev. The effects of erosion on these relatively soft geological formations with a high concentration of flint have resulted in an irregular terrain with a dark cover of flint gravel and rock. The abrasive actions of wind-blown flint and lack of rainfall contribute to the most barren desert conditions in the Sinai. Only the Wadi el-Arish alleviates the harshness of the region. Limited rainfall on the et-Tih plateau is channelled by the tributaries of the wadi into a single course that escapes into the Mediterranean. The residual water sources in this drainage system and the relatively level terrain gave rise to the major transit routes that traversed the Sinai peninsula.

Three distinctive geological formations punctuate this region. Jebel (Mount) Yelleg is a hard limestone mountain range that rises to an elevation of 1090 m near Bir Hassaneh. Jebel el-Hallal (890 m) near El-Quseima and Ein el-Qudeirat is an extensive crater of sandstone with a hard limestone shell. Jebel Maghara (735 m), farther to the west and north of the Nitzana-Ismailia road, is a similar crater with some cultivable land. Both craters contain ample water sources for pilgrimage and commercial routes and local bedouin settlements.

The et-Tih Plateau

The central band of the Sinai is a massive sedimentary plateau, limestone in the north and sandstone in the south, broken on east and west by the Gulfs of Eilat (Aqabah) and Suez. Formed between the Jurassic and Eocene periods, the central limestone and chalk plateau is lined by occasional magmatic '*dike*' formations. The geological strata are inclined to the south to expose sandstone formations from the lower Cretaceous period,[5] reaching elevations of 1600 meters above sea level. While the ascent from the north is gradual, the southern border of the et-Tih region is marked by an abrupt decline that breaks off in steep sandstone crags. The plateau is practically devoid of water sources and vegetation. In spite of the harsh, inhospitable conditions, numerous flint implements among the black-and-white gravel (*hammada*) on the et-Tih plateau tend to confirm Bedouin folklore that the Tih (meaning '*wanderings*') was associated with the wanderings of foreign tribes in the remote past.[6] The Pilgrims' Route (the famous Darb el-Hajj) linking the northern tips of the Gulfs of Suez and Eilat and the major route followed by North African Moslems on their way to Mecca crossed this region of the Sinai. In the west the Mitla and Giddi Passes provide access to the eastern border of Egypt. Slightly to the south, a secondary fault between et-Tih and the Gulf of Suez created a fold in the plateau where the major oil resources of Ras Matarma, Ras e-Suder and Ras Abu-Rudeis are being exploited. Wadi Suder is a relatively easy passage between the shores of the Gulf of Suez and the plateau. Rich in water sources for this region, its eastern end is dominated by Jebel Sin Bisher, an isolated mountain rising 618 m above sea level. Farther to the east along this route, Saladin, in the 12th century A.D. built an impressive fortress, Ras el-Jundi, on a high limestone promontory to control access into the pass. Limited rainfall is absorbed by the pervious limestone and conducted northward to escape in a line of springs along et-Tih's northern edge.

Bordering the northeastern coastal plain of the Gulf of Suez are limestone hills with deposits of gypsum and marl. Because of these formations, most of the wells and springs of this region are saline.

The Suez Coastal Plain

The region of westerly drainage may be divided into three distinct areas. The dunes of the western slope north of Suez continue to the south of Suez where marl and upcroppings of limestone, gypsum and gravel become more prevalent. On the east the plain is bordered by 300- to 500-meter hills, cut by broad, shallow wadis where only hardy vegetation survives in the saline soils. The limited water sources at the mouths of these valleys similarly are saline.

The Eilat Coastal Plain

An extremely narrow coast line in the north, crowded by a chain of crystalline mountains that fall almost directly into the gulf near Eilat, gradually widens toward the south where decomposing sandstone and limestone formations have contributed to an expanded shoreline. At the mouths of the drainage systems from the higher elevations of the southern plateau, the alluvial fans have extended the coastal plain. On these fans a series of pleasant oases, Nabq (or Nabek) in the south, and Dahab and Nuweib'a on the central gulf shore, with their wells and palm groves provide seasonal camp sites for modern Bedouin. The underground water table is high enough to be reached by wells dug from the surface, with ample water to sustain a relatively large population for the Sinai, especially during the winter season when the southern population gravitates toward the pleasant shorelines from the harsh cold conditions in the higher elevations. Indentations along the southern shoreline provide harbor facilities for fishing, especially at

Sharm el-Sheikh. The strategic location of this site, together with two islands, Tiran and Sanafir, at the southern tip of the Gulf of Eilat, facilitated trade with the Arabian coast at Maqna and provided defensive positions from which to control access into the gulf from the Red Sea proper.

The Region of Nubian Sandstone

Impressive geological formations of brilliant purple, red, dark-brown and black sandstones provide this region of the Sinai's richest mineral deposits with an unusual scenic beauty. Like the area of King Solomon's mines in the Arabah, the hills of Serabit el-Khadim in the western Sinai bear evidence of copper exploitation from earliest times. Remains of an ancient settlement and copper slag piles scattered over a wide region in the Nasb Valley are evidence of smelting operations by the Egyptians that may date back to Old Kingdom times. Some of the copper ore appears to have been transported from the eastern peninsula for smelting. The wood of acacia trees, that still dot the Nasb Valley, probably fueled the smelting operations. A series of Egyptian dynasties sponsored major mining expeditions into the Maghara and Serabit el-Khadim regions for extracting turquoise from the grey sandstone.[7] In modern times, the area's Bedouin population is clustered around a number of oases like Abu Rudeis and Bir Nasb that are lush with date palm groves and small gardens and orchards.

Where the sandstone and limestone of the Carboniferous period meet, near Umm-Bugma, manganese, the Sinai's most important mineral, is found in abundance. Other deposits exist in the Nasb, Malha and Haliq valleys. Sandglass is found near Jebel Dalal. Limited water sources in the region hindered exploitation of these rich mineral deposits.[8]

The Magmatic Region of the South

Once a part of the Arabian-Nubian massif, the southern triangular point of the Sinai was fractured by volcanic eruption, faulted and isolated by the formation of the twin rifts, the Gulf of Suez and the Gulf of Eilat (Aqaba). The higher elevations in the vicinity of Jebel Catherina consist of dark metamorphic schist and contrasting light

granite together with diorite, gneiss, porphyry, dikes and lava. While
the intense faulting has resulted in near total erosion of top soil, the
deep ravines contain natural springs and lush oases.[9]

Snow-covered in the winter, the mountains in the south are grand
geological formations reaching elevations beyond 2600 m. This region
covering over 7500 sq km is fragmented by irregular faults creating
deep ravines and valleys that add to the grandeur of steep, rugged
peaks. Most impressive are Mount Serbal (2070 m) slightly isolated
to the west, Mount Musa (2285 m) and Mount Catherina (2641 m)
centrally located, and Mount Umm-Shomer (2586 m) in the south.
While most of the valleys are devoid of soil and vegetation, the region
is dotted with small oases that are sustained by the greater amounts of
rainfall at the higher elevations.

The Climatic Conditions

Location and elevation are dominant factors determining climatic
conditions in the Sinai peninsula. The extreme fluctuations of
temperature characteristic of the desert belt that stretches from the
North African Sahara to the Saudi-Arabian Desert are tempered by the
Mediterranean and along the eastern and western shorelines by the
Gulfs of Aqaba and Suez. This moderating influence, dispelling desert
cold in the winter and increasing humidity during the unbearable heat
of summer, extends as far as 40-45 km inland, especially in the north.
In the south-central peninsula where elevations reach over 2000 m the
summers are characterized by more pleasant temperatures and winters
may provide infrequent rains and snows at higher elevations.

Annual rainfall in the peninsula varies from 10 mm in the south to
100 mm in the north along the Mediterranean coast. However, because
of the unpredictability of weather conditions in the region, the total
precipitation for a year may occur on a single day without
significantly alleviating the harsh arid conditions for the rest of the
year. Rainfall at the higher elevations anywhere within the extensive
drainage system of Wadi el-Arish may create flood conditions that
pose a serious threat to the temporary settlements of bedouin
downstream or the town of el-Arish at the mouth of the wadi.

While north-south and northwest-southeast wind and weather patterns prevail, local conditions may create temporary east-west air flows of varying intensity. The winds are hot and dry and far less predictable than the daily exchange between the desert and the sea across the narrow arable land mass of Palestine.

The higher elevations of the mountainous southern Sinai may receive as much as 300 mm annually. Intermittent masses of huge rock bear witness to the treacherous force of the sudden torrents in the wadis such winter rains can cause. Aware of the danger bedouin avoid camping in the wadi beds during the winter months.

Oases in the Sinai

Three natural factors contribute to the nature and location of water sources in the Sinai peninsula. Topographical features and the amount of precipitation determine the quantity of water in a region and the geological formations that retain the water determine its quality. Where water during flow or seepage is exposed to marl, gypsum or Eocene limestone, the result is an alkaline, saline or even sulfuric condition unsuitable for human consumption. Impervious rock shelves and clay deposits provide suitable surfaces for the flow of underground water to spring and well locations. Only four major water supply centers exist in the Sinai: along the Mediterranean shoreline, near the isolated mountains of the lowlands, on the northwestern part of the et-Tih plateau, and the higher mountains of the southern peninsula.

Water Sources Along the Mediterranean Coast
Shallow surface wells beyond the beaches along the Mediterranean shoreline provided a constant water source for the commercial and military traffic along the great international trade route, the *Via Maris*, that linked Egypt with the civilizations and cultures to the north. Though wells were rare within the sand dune region, a 15-20 km band along the northern Sinai enjoyed adequate rainfall to sustain isolated wells. Deeper wells could be established along the wadis of Rafah and el-Arish that drained much of the Negev and Sinai.

The Isolated Mountains of the Lowlands

Desert gravel and chalk contribute to the scarcity of water sources in this region. Isolated mountains, because of their higher elevations, such a El-Quseima, Yelleg, Maghara and Hallal receive more precipitation that issues forth at their bases in springs. El-Quseima, especially, with its four major springs of which Ein Qudeirat and Ein Qadis are best known, has the most plentiful supply of sweet water in the entire northern Sinai. Forty to fifty cubic meters of water per hour flow from Ein Qudeirat along the stream where the early Hebrews coming from Egypt temporarily established their religious center and where later the Israelites during the monarchy established a major military fortress. South of this important oasis water sources are very limited.

Water Sources on the et-Tih Plateau

Pervious limestone absorbs the limited moisture that falls in this region. Most of the water that does exist is highly alkaline and unsuitable for human consumption. However, in the northwest corner of the plateau, in the Sumar mountain range and the er-Rahah plateau, a concentration of water sources include ⁶Ayun Musa where 12 springs supply a sizable oasis. Other water sources, such as Bir el-Murah and Bir Abu-Qteifa, are extremely alkaline.

Oases in the Mountainous South

Extensive underground water reserves have been identified at four locations in the south: Wadi Feiran, Wadi es-Sheikh, Wadi Gharbi and at the base of Jebel Hadid. These reserves are annually replenished by the snow and rainfall at the higher elevations of the southern mountains. Reliable springs and wells are more plentiful in the northern sectors along Wadi Hibran and Wadi Feiran, diminishing as one moves farther toward the southern tip of the peninsula. Though surface water in reservoirs and cisterns in the valley beds may vary in quality, well and spring water is pure and plentiful.

While other factors contributed to the formulation of trade routes, the dominant consideration for a traveler in the Sinai, whatever his objective or cause, was the location and reliability of the water sources within the territory to be traversed. In the region of the Sinai where water was so scarce, ignorance or misjudgment on the part of caravaneer and emperor alike could have dire consequences. Dominant trade routes linked the major oases providing an extension of the crucial land bridge between Asia and Africa.

Trade Routes and Travel in the Sinai

For millennia the Levant had served as the buffer zone of the great civilizations along the Euphrates in the north and the Nile in the south, and the southeastern shoreline of the Mediterranean had provided the thoroughfare for the destructive military expeditions that ravaged the hinterland for daily provisions.

The Way of the Sea (Via Maris)

The most important link between Egypt and Canaan since prehistoric times has been the Egyptian *Ways-of-Horus,* the biblical *Way of the Land of the Philistines,* or the Classical *Via Maris,* that commercial caravans and military expeditions frequented. Its role as a land bridge between Asia and Africa gave the northern Sinai an unusual strategic importance. Of utmost military importance to the Egyptians for the control of Canaan, this route followed the Mediterranean shoreline from Sile to Raphia on the southern border of Canaan, a distance of 150 miles. As a result, this northern sand-duned region along the Mediterranean shoreline was more densely populated through most of its history. The northwest corner of Sinai, between the Egyptian border and the Bardawil lagoon (Classical Lake Sirbonis) was an extension of the densely populated eastern Nile Delta. In antiquity, this plain was criss-crossed by irrigation, drainage and navigational water systems. Ancient remains of forts and large settlements including Pelusium (Tell Tarama), Magdolo (Tell el-Her) and Sile (Tell Abu-Seifeh) are scattered throughout the area that served as a commercial, industrial and military region, especially from the New Kingdom onward.[10]

This important international thoroughfare, mentioned in Exod. 13:17, and its regular use by military expeditions to the north appears to have been eliminated as a likely itinerary for the passive Hebrews.

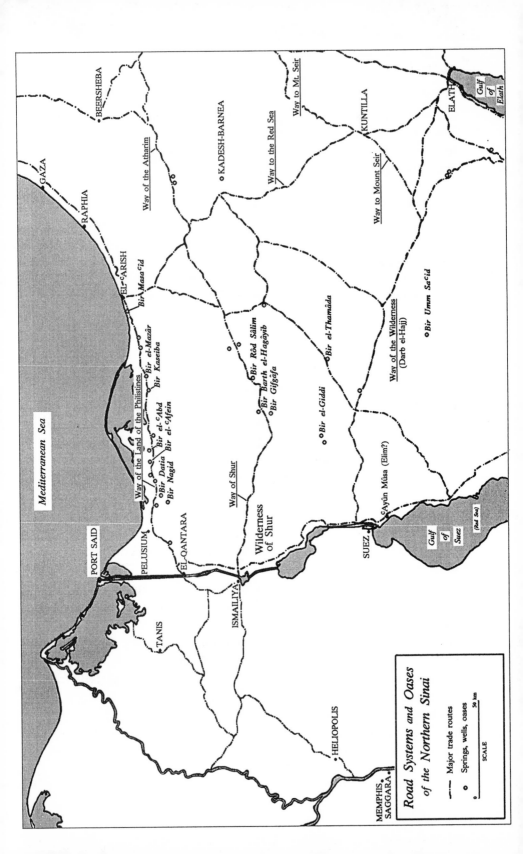

Road Systems and Oases of the Northern Sinai

The annals of the Eighteenth and Nineteenth Dynasty pharaohs refer to the regular campaigns of Thutmose III, Amenhotep II, Seti I, and Ramesses II along this route.

The harsh, desert-like conditions of the Sinai and the limited water sources tended to magnify the importance of secondary routes for movement by subservient peoples for whatever reason. Such a route, suitable for caravans, is the Darb el-Hajj that links Egypt and the upper end of the Gulf of Suez with Midian and the head of the Gulf of Eilat. Its name, *the Pilgrimage Road,* derives at least from the seventh century A.D. when Moslem pilgrims began using it regularly to visit the holy shrine at Mecca. At least six such secondary routes crossing the northern part of the Sinai are mentioned in the Bible.

The Way of Shur

This route crossed the Wilderness of Shur east of the lakes region along the eastern Egyptian frontier and moved in a northeasterly direction toward Ein Qudeirat and Quseima and beyond to Beersheba. This route avoiding the wide band of sand dunes to the north primarily was used by nomadic herdsmen in their seasonal migrations.

The Way of the Wilderness

...But God led the people round by the way of the wilderness toward the Red Sea. (Exod. 13:18)

This route crossed the northern border of the et-Tih plateau from the Gulf of Suez to the Gulf of Eilat, a distance of 150 miles. Also known as the Darb el-Hajj, it linked a network of fortresses from Suez to Aqaba. In the west the route well may have forked with the Giddi Pass providing a northern approach and the Mitla Pass a southern approach to the Egyptian frontier.

The Way to the Red Sea

...Now, since the Amalekites and the Canaanites dwell in the valleys, turn tomorrow and set out for the wilderness by the way to the Red Sea. (Num. 14:25)

The route, commencing at Gaza, linked Ein Qudeirat and Quseima with the Gulf of Eilat. It is clearly identifiable on the ancient Roman road map, the Tabula Peutingeriana.

The Way of Mount Seir and The Way of the Hill Country of the Amorites

...It is eleven days' journey from Horeb by the way of Mount Seir to Kadesh-barnea.

...And we set out from Horeb, and went through all that great and terrible wilderness which you saw, on the way to the hill country of the Amorites, as the Lord our God commanded us;... (Deut. 1:2,19)

These routes, if in fact separate, may be identified with secondary accesses along the tributaries of Wadi el-Arish northward into the mountains of the central Negev. The context of the Exodus itinerary may provide additional clues as to their location.

Routes in the Southern Sinai

Routes in the southern peninsula, not important for international commercial and military enterprises, were developed for the exploitation of natural resources, including copper, turquoise and manganese. A major lateral route along the wadis of Feiran, Zaghra and Nasb provided relative ease of passage across the rugged plateau. However its limited water resources prompted pilgrimages to the south-central plateau to use Wadi Hibran with its more plentiful water supply. The one major longitudinal route into the heart of the mountainous south, used by the mining expeditions into the region of Serabit el-Khadim, Maghara, and Nasb, followed the eastern shoreline of the Gulf of Suez. From the Monastery of Saint Catherine, the major route to the Gulf of Aqaba (or Eilat) followed the longitudinal fault of Wadi Watir with its adequate water resources, including Ein Hudherah and Ein Furtagah, to the shores of the gulf. More difficult, secondary passages approached the northern et-Tih through the Mureiha and E-Rakhinah Passes.

The King's Highway

Though most of the second millennium was characterized by Egyptian domination, the thirteenth century B.C. saw the emergence of a series of ethnic confederacies both in Canaan and in the

Transjordan where Ammonites, Amorites, Moabites and Edomites claimed territorial rights. The nature of this political consolidation is peripheral to our study apart from the fact that a major international trade route along the Transjordanian watershed, the *King's highway*, passed directly through these emerging political entities. This important route linked the head of the Gulf of Eilat with Damascus and provided the most direct channel for the distribution of the luxury items flowing from Saudi Arabia and East Africa to Upper Mesopotamian and Mediterranean markets. At times it rivalled the *Via Maris* in commercial importance, especially during those times when relations between Egypt and the northern powers were strained.

Flora and Fauna

As the natural land bridge between the continents of Africa and Asia, the Sinai exhibits representative flora in spite of the harsh conditions which are overcome only by the more hardy varieties. The palm identifies locations of relatively high ground water, with groves providing unusually pleasant conditions at major oases, where nomads may cultivate ground crops such as gourds and melons and maintain groves of tamarisk, olives, pomegranates and figs. Tributaries of some of the wadis occasionally have been used for growing cereal crops.

In addition to the harsh weather conditions, the soils of the Sinai, often mostly gypsum, marl or sand, are often saline and unproductive. Still the vegetation is varied with over five hundred different varieties of plant life with some unique to the region. Most varieties must not only overcome soil and weather conditions but also the exposure of roots to soil erosion and the abrasive sandstorms that are characteristic of regions with such dramatic changes of atmospheric pressures and temperatures. The agriculture of the Sinai is never adequate to provide for the needs of the generally limited population and historically the inhabitants have looked to Egypt to supplement their meager lifestyle.

Most tolerant to the Sinai's limitations of pasturage and water, the goat and the camel are the most common of the domesticated animals. They provide the basic necessities of food, clothing and shelter for the local nomads, while the camel also became the primary mode of transport. The scarcity of pasturage severely limits the raising of livestock and the uncertainty of water resources requires annual reevaluation of grazing migrations. The migratory quail, using the Sinai for its annual flight from Egypt and North Africa to East Central Europe, contributes to the food supply of the inhabitants along the western and northern shorelines of the Sinai peninsula. The Moroccan and desert locusts from the Sudan, while considered suitable food from ancient times, is a periodic scourge in the Sinai. Borne on southern winds, swarms of locusts of African varieties periodically have extended their destructive path through Palestine and Syria to Anatolia and the Mesopotamian regions.

Population and Settlement

Permanent settlement in the Sinai, as in other desert regions of the world, has been extremely limited and determined by economic factors beyond the borders of the peninsula. The ports at the heads of the Gulfs of Suez and Aqaba, the mines of southern Sinai and the logistical needs of military efforts, especially on the part of Egypt, have dictated the logic of settlement in a basically hostile environment. Nomadic and semi-nomadic populations have dominated the oases unless displaced by foreign intruders and have allowed local conditions to dictate the nature and extent of tribal life.

NOTES

[1] L.H. Grollenberg, *Atlas of the Bible,* trans. & eds. Joyce M.H. Reid and H.H. Rowley. London and Edinburgh: Thomas Nelson & Sons, Ltd., 1957: 48.

[2] Recent studies on the geology and physical geography of the Sinai are relatively few. Our summary of the region's physical conditions is primarily based on Menashe Harel, *The Sinai Journeys: The Route of the Exodus.* San Diego, CA: Ridgefield Publishing Co., 1983. Harel's personal familiarity with the Sinai's terrain and harsh living conditions is based on an extended stay among the Sinai Bedouin tribes. Another volume reflecting personal experience is Beno Rothenberg, *God's Wilderness: Discoveries in Sinai.* London: Thames and Hudson, 1961. Other relatively recent studies include: H.J.L. Beadnell, *The Wilderness of Sinai.* London: Arnold Co., 1927; L. Eckstein, *A History of Sinai.* London and New York: The Macmillan Co., 1921; C.S. Jarvis, *Yesterday and Today in Sinai.* London: W. Blackwood & Sons, 1938; H. Skobucha, *Sinai.* London: Oxford University Press, 1966.

[3] E.Orni and E. Efrat, The Sinai Peninsula. Pp. 123-132 in *Geography of Israel*. Philadelphia: The Jewish Publication Society of America, 1977.

[4] B. Hellstrom, Note on the Ground Water Supply of Northeastern Sinai, *Bulletin de l'Institut du Desert d'Egypte III*, 1 (Janvier 1953).

[5] H. J. L. Beadnell, *The Wilderness of Sinai* (Note Central Sinai cross-section).

[6] I. Beit-Arieh, Fifteen Years in Sinai: Israeli Archaeologists Discover a New World. *BAR* 10/4 (1984): 26-54.

[7] T. Barron, *The Topography and Geology of the Peninsula of Sinai*. Cairo: Egypt survey Department, 1907: 209-10.

[8] R. Said, *The Geology of Egypt*. New York: Elesevier, 1962. (See geological map of central Sinai).

[9] H. Sadek, *The Principal Structural Features of the Peninsula of Sinai*. Madrid: Congress Geologique International, 1928: 900.

[10] E.D. Oren, Migdol: A New Fortress on the Edge of the Eastern Nile Delta. *BASOR* 256 (1984): 7-44.

Chapter II

HISTORICAL BACKGROUND OF THE EXODUS

The background of the Hebrew Exodus from Egypt as a historical event, according to the biblical narratives, must be sought in the early second millennium B.C. The cultural vitality that had marked the Early Bronze urban centers came to an abrupt end toward the end of the third millennium. Throughout the Levant, the destruction levels discovered at every Early Bronze urban site suggest a dramatic, comprehensive upheaval of the local population. Yet, when the cities were resettled a century or two later, distinct cultural advantages of the past were retained in initiating one of the most prosperous periods of ancient times.

Canaan in the Early Second Millennium B.C.

The Middle Bronze Age in Palestine was characterized by a revival of urbanization with a radical shift in the distribution, size and character of the settlements. This reoccupation of long abandoned Early Bronze sites, with new fortifications, saw a dramatic increase of population and a density of settlements especially along the coast and well up into the central hill country. The period between 2000 and 1800 B.C. was marked by a radical change in technology, economic basis, social structure and political organization. Nearly 400 sites are known to have existed in Palestine during the Middle Bronze Age. Their size distribution is especially important in anticipating the dramatic changes in the country before the end of the second millennium B.C.: 5% were large urban sites (20 to 175 acres); 10% were medium-sized towns (7-20 acres); and 85% were villages and hamlets (1-7 acres).[1]

Urban growth, complex social organization, increased prosperity and advanced technology ultimately prompted the proliferation of massive defensive systems as inter-city rivalries and international intervention became more imminent. Many sites, such as Achzib and Accho in the north, Tel Zeror, Tel Poleg, Tel Burga, Yabneh-Yam and Aphek on the

coastal plain, already had been fortified with city walls and gates
before ca. 1800 B.C.[2] Defensive construction continued throughout the
Middle Bronze Age. Even towns and villages as small as 2-4 acres
were surrounded with formidable fortifications.

During this period of prosperity and sophisticated technology,
Canaan's international connections with Egypt became increasingly
important. Following Egypt's 'Dark Age' of the First Intermediate
Period (ca. 2000 B.C.), the Middle Kingdom was founded. (The
accession date of Amenemhet I, founder of the Twelfth Dynasty, has
been fixed astronomically at 1991 B.C.) The Twelfth and Thirteenth
Dynasties that reigned for nearly 500 years reestablished sea trade
with Byblos and the Phoenician coast. Luxury items from Egypt
flowed into Syria, and throughout Palestine archaeological evidence
of Egyptian trade is prevalent. The Execration Texts of the Twelfth
Dynasty suggest intense Egyptian political interest in the region.

The cultural vitality and consolidation that Canaan experienced
ultimately had its effect on Egypt as well. The Second Intermediate
Period (ca. 1720-1570 B.C.) was a time of intense disorder in Egypt.
Increasing numbers of Asiatics (various groups of West Semitic
peoples from Syria and Palestine) succeeded in penetrating the Delta's
eastern frontier and by the Fifteenth Dynasty they had achieved
control. A series of Asiatic kings actually ruled northern and central
Egypt for almost a hundred and fifty years as a 'foreign' Dynasty.
These 'foreign rulers' *(Hyksos)* were from Syria-Palestine. At least
three of the six names of the pharaohs of this dynasty are clearly West
Semitic (Amorite).

Austrian excavations at the site of Avaris,[3] the *Hyksos* capital, at
Tell ed-Dab°a in the Nile Delta, exposed a large urban center founded
ca. 1900-1800 B.C. with domestic and temple architecture, pottery,
metal implements and burial customs very similar to Palestinian MB
IIA. Avaris' population was clearly Canaanite (Amorite). The
settlement of the town was pre-*Hyksos* (dated to the late Twelfth or
early Thirteenth Dynasty) and seemed to represent a gradual, peaceful
process of colonization. There definitely was no evidence of a sudden
military invasion. The Asiatics, over a long period, had been settling
in the Delta. The *Hyksos* (foreign ruler) takeover appears to have
followed ca. 250 years of gradual migration before the central

Egyptian authority finally collapsed. With a large Semitic population providing an expanding power base in the Delta, they took control from an internally weak Egyptian rule. Only the united forces of the late Seventeenth and early Eighteenth Dynasties were able ultimately to dislodge them about a century and a half later.

The continued buildup of fortifications in Palestinian sites (that attained its peak in MB III (or IIB), ca. 1650-1550 B.C.) seemingly anticipated the loss of *Hyksos* control in Egypt. These Palestinian cities originally had provided the power base for Asiatic expansion and ultimate control in the Delta. The end of *Hyksos* rule finally came ca. 1570 B.C. when Kamose (last pharaoh of the Theban Seventeenth Dynasty) reasserted Egyptian power in the Delta. The siege and destruction of Avaris ca. 1570 B.C. (Tell ed-Dabʿa was burned and remained unsettled for centuries) was followed by Ahmose's campaigns and other pharaohs' military efforts in Palestine and Syria into the fifteenth century B.C. Every Middle Bronze III (or IIB) Palestinian site excavated thus far has one or more destruction levels between 1550 and 1480 B.C. (not only major cities, such as Shechem, Gezer, etc., but also smaller sites, such as Tel Mevorakh). The MBIII cities, at the peak of their prosperity after 500 years of peaceful development, in spite of their massive fortifications, succumbed to the relentless Egyptian campaigns. A generation or more lapsed before the cities, depopulated and impoverished, began their recovery in the Late Bronze, stimulation ultimately coming under the Egyptian hegemony in the Late Bronze II (1400-1200 B.C.).

Canaan under Egyptian Control

The end of the Middle Bronze Age in Palestine generally is identified with the expulsion of the *Hyksos* from Egypt, an event supposedly corroborated by destruction levels at a number of Palestinian sites.[4] The military campaign of Ahmose that ushered in the Eighteenth Dynasty and the Late Bronze Age is dated between ca. 1580 and 1545 B.C.[5] Analysis of relevant chronological data seems to date Thutmose III's accession at 1505 B.C., with Ahmose's campaign ca. 1570 B.C. The transition in Palestine from Middle Bronze IIC to Late Bronze IA probably is best understood as a longer time frame (possibly 50 years) in which the expelled *Hyksos*, later Egyptian pharaohs such as Thutmose II or Amenhotep II, or even inter-city rivalries could have been responsible for the destruction layers dated to that period throughout the country. The three-year siege and ultimate destruction of Sharuhen by Ahmose following the expulsion of the *Hyksos* may be reflected in the massive destruction of City III/Palace I at Tell el-ᶜAjjûl. City II/Palace II that follows, characterized by new types of pottery, probably should be assigned to Late Bronze IA.[6]

But, while the date of the event within the chronological sequence of Egyptian history appears secure, the nature of the 'expulsion of the *Hyksos*' may require some serious rethinking at least in two major areas. The suggestion that the expulsion of the *Hyksos* involved a large-scale population shift with dramatic impact ('dislocation of life')[7] on the city-states of Canaan appears questionable. The Theban state obviously had suffered some economic restriction during the Second Intermediate Period, but at the same time, in the fields of art, trade and military prowess, the *Hyksos* must be credited with extending the openness of Egypt to outside influences that had been initiated during the vibrant Middle Kingdom. The defeat of the *Hyksos* at Sharuhen immediately was followed by an Egyptian campaign against Nubia in which ...*His Majesty made a great slaughter...* and Ahmose was rewarded a second time.[8] Extensive trade relations in Nubia, Asia, Cyprus and probably even Crete quickly were revived during the reign of Ahmose I. Internally, rapid recovery of temple building and funerary practices and the dramatic improvement of artistic standards suggest that this period of foreign rule had no major long-term negative effects. Apart from the obvious relief from paying tribute to the *Hyksos*, no dramatic changes in the economy and culture are evident during the early years of the Eighteenth Dynasty.[9] Though Egypt had been divided with the *Hyksos* controlling Lower Egypt from Cusae in Middle Egypt northward, two historical documents, the Carnarvon Tablet[10] and the Kamose Stela,[11] indicate that the final phase of *Hyksos* reign was peaceful with secure borders and the courtiers of Kamose's court in Upper Egypt maintaining grazing rights for their cattle in the Delta. With little or no friction between Upper and Lower Egypt, Kamose's lone motive for launching his attack on the *Hyksos* may have been his personal ambition to be 'King of Upper and Lower Egypt.'[12]

The campaign of Ahmose, responsible for the expulsion of the *Hyksos* element, clearly appears focused on Sharuhen, and the three-year siege of that city appeared intent on the capture and punishment of a relatively few *Hyksos* bureaucrats. Certainly no great population increase was involved that rapidly would have diminished the food supply of this border town under siege. The need of a three-year siege to force the city's surrender seems evidence of such a limited number of high-ranking *Hyksos* who were the focus of Egyptian concern.[13]

The suggestion that the 'expulsion of the *Hyksos*' resulted in a widespread destruction of Canaanite cities and cultural disruption also is open to question. The *Amurru* population of Canaan and the subjugators of Lower Egypt during the *Hyksos* period had a common origin. It appears totally inconceivable that the expulsion of the 'foreign' elements from Egypt would result in widespread devastation throughout Canaan during the mid-sixteenth century B.C. For the 150 years usually attributed to its foreign domination, Egypt and Canaan had coexisted within a single political administrative system. Even if we assume the possibility of a major withdrawal or 'expulsion,' on what basis must we attribute any urban destruction levels to *Amurru* elements returning from Egypt? The only solid historical evidence in this connection at Sharuhen suggests rather that the Canaanite city of Sharuhen sheltered the *Hyksos* against the Egyptians. In fact, the entire Late Bronze period, the historical frame of the Hebrew exodus event, probably is best understood on the basis of Egyptian records. It is for this reason that a brief summary of the lives and exploits of the Eighteenth and Nineteenth Dynasty pharaohs becomes so important. Egyptian political and economic policies concerning neighboring states clearly impacted Canaan's cultural vitality, possibly more than generally imagined. Egyptian military incursions during this period of Egyptian dominance clearly had multi-faceted motivation: punishment, in terms of the stigma of 150 years of foreign domination by Asiatics; paranoia, in attempting to extend Egyptian control ever farther to the north away from its eastern border; and economics, in the integration of prisoner and *corvée* labor forces into various forms

of public and municipal works projects, including basic food supply
in the land of Goshen.

The Nature of the Eighteenth Dynasty

Political conditions in Egypt during the Eighteenth Dynasty have
been used to argue for a fifteenth century date for the Exodus. The
expulsion of the *Hyksos* ushered in the powerful Eighteenth Dynasty
that reestablished Egyptian control over Lower Egypt. The early
pharaohs of the dynasty assumed an energetic resolve to extend and
defend the frontiers of Egypt deep within Asian territory. The
Egyptian army with a revolutionary mobility based on a light, horse-
drawn chariot and greatly perfected weapons including the composite
bow repeatedly swept through Canaan. Town after town fell victim to
Egyptian violence, many left in ruins and abandoned. Already in the
reign of Thutmose I, the Egyptian army reached the Euphrates where
the pharaoh planted a victory stele commemorating his military
successes. Egypt had reestablished nominal control over the entire
southern Levant.[14]

Ultimately, however, succession constituted a serious problem when
Amenhotep I (ca. 1551-1524 B.C.) had no son and chose a military
general, Thutmose I (ca. 1524-1518 B.C.) to succeed him. His rule
was legitimatized by marrying the pharaoh's daughter who,
unfortunately, also failed to have a son. Her only daughter,
Hatshepsut, married her half-brother, Thutmose II (ca. 1518-1504
B.C.) to reinforce his claim to the throne. Again, the Great Wife
(Hatshepsut) failed to produce a son and as a consequence, Thutmose
III, son of a concubine, as a youth became the heir to the throne. As
regent, Hatshepsut named herself pharaoh and co-ruler with the young
Thutmose III. Later expressions of hatred for Hatshepsut (erasure of
her cartouche from statues and inscriptions and attempts at removing
all traces of her reign) have been interpreted as revengeful acts for the
humiliating subordination suffered during the coregency. The possible
scenario suggests that a distraught Hatshepsut claimed a Hebrew child
by adoption who was trained to become the heir to the Egyptian
throne. It was this son, the biblical Moses, who (it has been suggested)
possibly received favored status as foster son over Thutmose in the

rather ambivalent roles of aunt/stepmother/mother-in-law that Hatshepsut played in his life.[15]

During the early part of the Eighteenth Dynasty, the Egyptian campaigns in Canaan faced stiff opposition and represented little more than a show of strength. No effective administrative structure was established to maintain political or economic control. As a result, Egyptian campaigns, conducted with regularity had a devastating effect on the local Canaanite population and economy, but limited success in establishing Canaanite allegiance to the Egyptian overlord. In archaeological terms, this period from the expulsion of the *Hyksos* from Egypt by Ahmose, the first pharaoh of the Eighteenth Dynasty, to the first military campaign by Thutmose III, sixth pharaoh of the dynasty, generally is identified as the Late Bronze IA period. In Canaan this period was characterized by destructions and partial abandonments at many sites. However, the transition from Middle Bronze to Late Bronze appears to suggest continuity in local ceramic wares, a situation that would tend to preclude the suggestion of an incursion by new populations.

The Campaigns and Policies of Thutmose III

Following the Second Intermediate Period and the collapse of *Hyksos* control in Egypt, the military campaigns of the early Eighteenth Dynasty established an Egyptian empire that ultimately reached from the Fourth Cataract of the Nile to the banks of the Euphrates. Primarily the long series of expeditions by Thutmose III (1504-1450 B.C.)[16] forged the dimensions as well as many of the administrative policies of the New Kingdom. Archaeological evidence and many relevant Egyptian documents provide a comprehensive insight into the intimate cultural contacts and commercial interchange between Egypt and its subservient neighbors to the northeast.[17] It was during this period of almost 300 years that the Northern Sinai gained special significance as the land bridge for military domination and commercial exploitation of Upper and Lower Retenu. The primary and shortest route along the Mediterranean shoreline, identified in the Bible as *the way of the land of the Philistines* (Exodus 13:17), was known in Egyptian sources as *The Ways of Horus*. From the eastern Delta to the border of Canaan, this route was maintained by a network of fortified way stations providing supplies for Egyptian military efforts and those non-Egyptian caravans qualified for using its convenience by payment of required customs and road tax. Egyptian garrisons manning the forts effectively secured access to the oases along the 250 km. (150-mile) distance between Sile and Gaza and assured free, uninterrupted flow of military and materiel across the northern Sinai.

An attempt to correlate Megiddo's Stratum IX destruction layer[18] and Thutmose III's first campaign in his 23rd year may be problematic in the possibility that a subsequent Egyptian campaign or local conflict brought about the city's destruction. In spite of the detailed description of other aspects of Thutmose's first expedition, the actual destruction of Megiddo is not mentioned.[19] It seems reasonable however that the scope of the rebellion (350 Asiatic princes) instigated by the kings of Kadesh and Megiddo could culminate in no less than the ultimate of Egyptian punitive actions. The military activities of Thutmose III probably contributed significantly to a general dispersion of the urban population to the countryside to account for some of the decline of urban settlement between the Middle Bronze and Late Bronze periods.[20] The suggestion that Palestine virtually was depopulated for a century by early Eighteenth Dynasty military activities is hardly consistent with Egyptian opportunities for exacting tribute from the region.[21] Nor do the regular military incursions intended to put down rebellious elements suggest a decimated Palestinian population.

At Megiddo a distinct deterioration and paucity of significant architectural and cultural remains following the destruction of the Late Bronze I city (possibly by Thutmose III) provides a clear division between LB IA and IB when the country experienced economic recession. It is important to note, however, that Megiddo was taken by siege.[22] The kings surrendered after seven months as a result of famine and took a pledge of loyalty. There is no reference to burning or otherwise destroying Megiddo in any of the four inscriptions that refer to this episode. If Thutmose actually destroyed Megiddo, it seems inconsistent with his character not to take credit for its destruction. Since the king of Kadesh had been the primary culprit, Thutmose, having received a loyalty pledge from the king of Megiddo, possibly deemed punitive action counter-productive to the role that Megiddo could play in his plans for an Egyptian-controlled Canaan.[23] The LB I pottery shows a gradual but distinct deterioration in quality. The period, however, also provided the occasion for the infiltration of a large, ethnically diverse population that ushered in the vibrant international culture of the LB IIA.[24]

Subsequent campaigns by Thutmose III suggest an Egyptian need for constant surveillance to assure Egyptian interests in Canaan. The temporary nature of the local vassals' commitment to fulfilling their obligations required more than annual punitive raids and a show of Egyptian military strength. Thutmose appears to have instituted at least two effective policies for maintaining more adequate control in Canaan. The first was the imposition of a political structure to facilitate administration.[25] A second policy initiated by Thutmose III was recorded in the annals of his sixth campaign:

> ...Now the children of the princes and their brothers were brought to be captives ('hostages') in Egypt. Now, whoever of these princes died, his majesty was accustomed to make his son go to stand in his place... (ANET, 239)

The taking of the children (sons) and brothers of the vassal kings as hostages and their indoctrination in the obligations of loyalty to the Egyptian pharaoh achieved two primary goals: the present king was held hostage in the knowledge that the well-being of his sons and other male members of his family depended upon his loyalty and faithful fulfillment of treaty obligations. The rebellion or death of the present ruler provided an opportunity for installing an ethnic ruler (acceptable to the local population) who had been 'brain-washed' into an Egyptian mind-set and was fully aware of acceptable behavior as an Egyptian vassal. It is precisely this form of policy that appears operative in Moses' preparation for appointment among his own people in Goshen.

The Campaigns of Amenhotep II

Amenhotep II (ca. 1436-1410 B.C.), an excellent military strategist, successful like his father Thutmose III, was able to consolidate Egyptian control over an expansive empire. Both Thutmose III and Amenhotep II as prodigious builders expended major energies in the delta of the Nile.[26] The inclusion of Semites among the construction workers of this period, as seen in inscriptions and tomb paintings from Thutmose I and III, should be expected since the beginning of the New Kingdom obviously ended the 'favored status' such Asiatic Semites had enjoyed under the *Hyksos* rulers.[27] Furthermore, severity of such 'bondage' under Thutmose III and Amenhotep II surely could provide ample justification for emigration from Egypt.

The pharaoh's annals have preserved information about three military campaigns conducted by Amenhotep II. The documents that remain suggest that the general scribal practice was not to provide a continuous description of the campaign. Rather, a selection of events was intended to show the courage of the pharaoh.[28] This selectivity is evident from the annals of the first campaign in which the account jumps from place to place (with great distances between) without any connecting text (e.g., Hashabu in the Lebanon Valley to the Sharon Plain where the Naharin emissary was captured).[29]

It was during Amenhotep II's first expedition in the land of Takhsi while he was still crown prince or coregent that Thutmose III died. His second campaign followed the *Via Maris* through the Lebanese Beqaᶜ to Ugarit and the Land of Ni. Rebellious elements were dispensed: *...His majesty killed them by shooting,* or forced them to take oaths of fidelity in submission. Although the pharaoh paused in the vicinity of Kadesh to hunt, limited details concerning the specific events of the campaign may suggest that major objectives were not achieved. In fact, Egyptian loyalties were very tenuous, even in southern Canaan.

During the return from this campaign, while crossing the Sharon Plain, an emissary of the Prince of Naharin was captured

> *...carrying a letter of clay at his throat. He (Amenhotep) took him as a living prisoner at the side of his chariot. His majesty went forth in chariot by the track to Egypt, with the marya as a living prisoner in the chariot alone with him.* (ANET, 245-248)

Subsequent events indicate that this courier from the King of Mitanni was attempting to incite rebellion among the cities and towns of Canaan against their Egyptian overlord. The cuneiform tablet carried in a pouch around his neck contained a personal message from Mitanni, possibly offering some inducement for rebellion against

Egypt. The treatment of the prisoner suggests the pharaoh's method of extorting information concerning Mitanni's seditious activities in the Sharon. The prisoner appears to be walking or running ...*at the side of his chariot*... until he was willing to talk, and then the pharaoh took him *in the chariot alone with him.*

Ultimately, the efforts of Mitannian emissaries were successful. Rebellion broke out in the Sharon and Jezreel Plains and the Lower Galilee. An urgent campaign was conducted in November in imminent danger of the rainy season. The timing suggests a desperate attempt by Amenhotep to thwart an imminent open rebellion against Egyptian supremacy. At least six cities and towns in the Sharon alone were forced into submission. Anaharath (identified with Tell el-ᶜAjjûl near Naᶜûra), north of the Hill of Moreh in the Lower Galilee was plundered. It is important to note that this town is located within the region later assigned to the tribe of Issachar (Joshua 19:15).[30] The Prince of Geba-shemen (Tell ᶜAmr, 18 km northwest of Megiddo), at the southern end of the Accho Plain was replaced. All Amenhotep's punitive actions were directed against sites located along the major trade route system through the country, a possible indication of Egypt's concern for maintaining the flow of beneficial commerce.

Amenhotep's ease of movement in the immediate vicinity and the Taanach Letters (dated to the 15th Century B.C.) indicate that an Egyptian garrison was stationed at Megiddo during Amenhotep's reign.[31] During the Amarna period, early in the fourteenth century, Biridiya, King of Megiddo, requested the return of the garrison that previously had been stationed there.[32] It is not certain that Megiddo was the only Egyptian base in the Jezreel during the fifteenth century. The Beth-shean excavations, however, indicate that city became the primary base during the fourteenth century, a situation reflected in the Amarna letters.[33] Thus Megiddo reverted to an ordinary Canaanite royal city, a decision undoubtedly based on Egyptian strategy. The punitive actions against Anaharath and Geba-shemen indicate that Amenhotep's primary concerns were focused on the main northern access routes to the Jezreel Plain. Amenhotep's selection of Beth-shean as Egypt's primary military center anticipated the increasing challenge to Egypt's supremacy in the Upper Jordan Valley and the Lower Galilee.[34]

Amenhotep's prisoner list included 36,300 *Huru* (Horites), 15,200 *Shasu* (Bedouin), 15,070 *Neges* (possibly from Nuḥassi in northern Syria), and 3,600 *ʿApiru* (unlanded, sojourners, having no permanent status). If these categories are representative of the composition of the country's population, as has been suggested, fifteenth century Canaan may have had approximately 66% Horites, 27.5% *Shasu*, and 6.5% *ʿApiru*. The next two centuries saw a marked increase in the *Shasu* and *ʿApiru* populations.

This is the first mention in Egyptian records of *ʿApiru* as a troublesome element in Canaan. The nature of Amenhotep's campaign would suggest that these prisoners were taken either in the Sharon Plain or in the Lower Galilee during the plunder of Anaharath. It may be of significance to note that later campaigns were directed specifically against the *ʿApiru* in this same region.

The Tell el-Amarna Period and the ʿApiru Problem

Amenhotep II's successor, Thutmose IV, was followed by Amenhotep III (ca. 1387-1350 B.C.) and Amenhotep IV, or Akhenaten (ca. 1350-1334 B.C.) whose reigns generally are identified with the troublesome Amarna Age in Canaan. The diplomatic correspondence recovered from Tell el-Amarna, the ruins of Akhenaten's capital on the Middle Nile, depicts the unstable political conditions existing among the vassal kings of Syrian and Palestinian city-states.[35]

These Amarna Letters describe a variety of imperial problems[36] including inter-city rivalries, especially the activities of Labʿayu, Prince of Shechem, who together with his sons, maintained a comprehensive alienation on all fronts. Biridiya, Prince of Megiddo, claimed that Labʿayu had besieged his city (*EA* 244), and his sons had continued later attacks (*EA* 246). The sons threatened war against Giti-padalla (Gath in the Sharon) if that city's prince did not join an alliance against Qena. Labʿayu reportedly destroyed four towns. He, in turn, claimed to have been attacked and one of his towns destroyed (*EA* 252). Abdu-Heba, Prince of Jerusalem, and Milkilu of Gezer were in conflict (*EA* 286). Tagu of Gath and Milkilu were accused of taking Rubutu, a town supposed under Jerusalem's jurisdiction (*EA* 287, 289).[37] Shuwardata from the Hebron region (possibly?) was a co-conspirator in the action (*EA* 290). Abdu-Heba was accused of taking

Keilah (*EA* 279), a town later recaptured by Shuwardata (*EA* 280). Reports of such infractions against tranquil coexistence and common commitment to Egyptian interests were filled with claims of loyalty and accusations and counter-accusations of disloyalty to the pharaoh himself. Always the call was for Egyptian intervention and preservation of Egyptian rights to cities and land in Canaan.

The second major problem was the *Hapiru*/SA.GAZ conflict in various parts of the country.[38] This group, generally conceived of as being outside the bounds of society or political acceptance, possibly caused by economic conditions, with warlike (at least, disruptive) qualities, or alien status, was identified with various economic activities, including donkey drivers, smugglers, transient farmers, slaves and mercenaries.[39] Thus, Biriyawaza of Damascus wrote that a unit of *ʿApiru* was in the army protecting the land (*EA* 195).

...Now, I, with my infantry and my chariotry and with my colleagues and with my ʿApiru and with my Shutu (will be) at the head of the troops to wherever the king, my lord, shall say. (*EA* 205)

In the Amarna tablets, the term *ʿApiru* identified persons of similar character or served as a general pejorative term against one's enemies. For the most part, therefore, the pleas of the local princes were for the Egyptian pharaoh's concern and military involvement in providing assistance against the encroachment of *Habiru* or *ʿApiru*. The plaintive cry for help from Yapaʿu, king of Gezer, echoed throughout the land of Canaan.

...Now, the ʿApiru are prevailing over us, and may the king, my lord, send his hand to me, and may my lord take us (me?) away from the hand of the ʿApiru, so that the ʿApiru will not destroy us. (*EA* 299)[40]

The attempt to identify the ʿApiru with 'feudalistic renegades,' disenfranchised members of the old feudal regime who were attempting to reestablish themselves within the Syro-Palestinian urban structure of the New Kingdom is not totally satisfying. The refinement of the term ʿApiru with such restricted limitations appears necessary to show that an equation *ʿibrî* = *ʿapîrû* cannot stand.[41] That such individual renegades were among the broad scope of disruptive elements referred to in the diplomatic correspondence is highly probable. However, the numerical strength and pervasive nature of the

Apiru seems more consistent with a more general category such as 'unlanded' persons who desperately were seeking opportunities for integrating themselves into the established social and political structures of the region.

A third major problem expressed in these diplomatic messages was the disruption of trade and communications, a basic indication of a general breakdown of the government and local economy. Thus, Abdu-Heba of Jerusalem complained about the lack of security on the caravan routes:

> ...I have sent [gifts(?)] to the king, my lord: [...] captives, five thousand [silver (shekels)] and eight porters for the caravans of the king, my lord; (but) they were captured in the plain of Ajalon. Let the king, my lord, know that I cannot send a caravan to the king, my lord... (EA 287)

Even more disconcerting to some of the avowed loyal vassals was the general disregard of imperial orders, bureaucratic incompetence and corruption. Legitimate institutions clearly continued and only few letters suggest that local princes refused to follow the orders of the pharaoh or his agents. And when it appeared clearly possible that a major infraction had been committed, ignorance seemed an appropriate claim. Even so, criticism was rampant:

> ...Milkilu does not break (his alliance) with the sons of Lab'ayu... Behold Milkilu and Tagu! The deed which they have done is that,... And now as for Jerusalem... shall we do like Lab'ayu, who gave the land of Shechem to the *Apiru*? (EA 289)

Some accusations of bureaucratic incompetence appear to have been well-founded:

> ...Ilimilku is causing the loss of all the king's land...All the governors are lost; the king, my lord, does not have a (single) governor (left)! (EA 286)

Complaints of administrative ineffectiveness and corruption also abounded:

> ...the deed which Yanhamu did...saying to me: "Give me thy wife and thy children, or I will smite!" (EA 270)
>
> ...the men...of Nubia have committed an evil deed against (me); I was almost killed by the men...in my own house. Let the king (call) them to (account). (EA 287)

It must be recognized, however, that lawlessness obviously existed prior to the Amarna period and certainly inter-city conflict continued later. Texts throughout the ancient Near East document the problems and turmoil created by those 'unlanded' *ʿApiru*.

The problem unique to the Amarna Age was the disruption of trade. This problem was related directly to economic structure and administrative directives instituted by the pharaohs of the Eighteenth Dynasty. The acquisition of goods no longer relied on raiding and booty. Caravans moved between primary depots along established routes with local kings responsible for facilitating the transshipment and providing local protection against raiding and looting of caravans. These recently established obligations provided opportunity for three types of punishable misconduct: disloyalty (*EA* 254), failure to facilitate transshipment of goods (*EA* 255) and stopping tribute payments (*EA* 287). In pleading innocence, Lab'ayu the king of Shechem claimed:

> ...*I have not rebelled, and I have not sinned, and I do not withhold my tribute, and I do not refuse the requests of my commissioner.*
> (*EA* 254)

To minimize such misconduct on the part of the Canaanite vassals, the pharaoh established an extensive imperial bureaucratic system. The Egyptian officers were commissioned to assist the local princes in their efforts to protect caravans in their immediate vicinity, to provide and forward tribute and taxes to the pharaoh, to supply the imperial troops during their passage or stay in the area, to provide and supply *corvée* labor for imperial lands and projects, and to safeguard their towns, cities and lands as a sacred trust from the pharaoh.[42]

Examples of disloyalty obviously are reflected in the Amarna documents. But for the most part, the letters display the effectiveness of the administrative policies introduced by the Eighteenth Dynasty pharaohs. They recorded a fairly consistent expression of loyalty, whatever the motivation. The bureaucratic system was functioning, possibly not to the highest level they had known, but the expectation was there. The level of commitment was clear. Armed units sustained defense of the cities. Agents assumed responsibility for the delivery of trade goods and tribute was sent in relative safety. The local princes were more than willing to provide food and lodging for any

military units that would sustain peaceful coexistence with their
neighboring city-states. Complaints were lodged against those who did
not share adequately in the supply of *corvée* labor. The first half of
the fourteenth century B.C. saw Egypt's imperial administrative
institutions in Canaan functioning with effectiveness. It has been
suggested, in fact, that the Amarna interlude was far less revolutionary
in its social and political aspects than at first imagined. The stability
of the political and economic institutions, so strongly ingrained, even
among the distant vassals, may have contributed to the failure of the
religious reform at el-Amarna.[43]

The nature of Egyptian domination in Canaan has far-reaching
implications for the nature of the exodus and Israelite settlement
patterns in Canaan. With the possible exception of Hazor (an explicit
distinction in the biblical narrative), the local Canaanite kings of the
New Kingdom period were mercenary commandants whose natural
resources had been exploited. Palestine and Syria had been reduced by
repeated Egyptian expeditions to the status of provinces under the
jurisdiction of Egyptian bureaucrats and local garrisons.[44]

The appearance of *ᶜApiru* among prisoners taken during Amenhotep
II's second military campaign may not be construed as 'proof-
positive' that the Moses-led exodus accordingly had taken place. Nor
may it be assumed that the absence of letters in the Amarna archive
from Jericho, Gibeon, Bethel and Hebron is possible evidence of
Hebrew control while those cities represented among the diplomatic
correspondents continue in Canaanite control with a measure of
loyalty to the Egyptian overlord.[45] On the other hand, the taking of
such prisoners can hardly be conceived of as descent of the Hebrews
to Egypt at the beginning of their sojourn.[46]

The importance of a number of other significant Egyptian
inscriptions has been overstated in reference to the evidence they
provide for dating the Moses-led exodus in the fifteenth century B.C.
A badly damaged temple wall inscription at Speos Artemidos, dated
to Hatshepsut's reign, reflects her anger against the activities of
Asiatics who had dwelt in the Delta and her intention to rebuild ruined
buildings (possibly temples).[47] That Hatshepsut annulled their 'former
privileges' and forced them to participate in public works projects is
totally consistent with what would be expected following the *Hyksos*

period without having any direct bearing on the biblical exodus.[48] An initial resistance to such tasks and permission to leave Egypt as an alternative similarly is quite consistent with the biblical progression of deteriorating Hebrew-Egyptian relations in the Delta. If this inscription were assumed to be the Egyptian counterpart of the biblical exodus account, then Hatshepsut (ca. 1503-1483 B.C.) could be identified as the pharaoh of the oppression and the exodus. Such an identification is helpful only for those who are hoping to explain various aspects of the 'plagues' and the Red Sea escape by the coincidental eruption of Thera (Santorini) in the Aegean Sea, a catastrophic event usually dated between 1500 and 1470 B.C.[49]

The Horemheb tomb relief at Saqqara, dated about 1334 B.C., portrays Asiatics requesting permission to enter Egypt, famished because their town had been destroyed and they had been forced to live like animals in the desert.[50] Dated to the turbulent days of the Amarna period, there is obviously no need to attribute such conditions to Joshua's so-called military campaigns in Canaan.[51] The fact that these Asiatics sought refuge in Egypt suggests an hospitable environment rather than a period of intense bondage for such foreign elements.

The Exploits of the Nineteenth Dynasty Pharaohs

A break in the royal succession following the death of Tutankhamun brought Ay and Horemheb to the throne. Not only were they not of royal blood, but neither provided an heir. The appointment of Horemheb's elderly vizier, Pramesse, as his successor with the name Ramesses I, and the death of Horemheb (ca. 1320 B.C.) ushered in the 19th Dynasty. Ramesses I's reign was brief. A coregency with his son, Seti I, was initiated already in his second year, and as a result no major building projects or military campaigns have been attributed to him. Some faience cartouches of Ramesses I, recovered under the Egyptian temple at Beth-shean, may be attributed to Seti I's Asiatic campaign during Year 1 when he relieved a siege on that city.[52]

The Campaigns of Seti I

The uncertain policies of Amenhotep IV clearly contributed to the deterioration of Egyptian prestige and influence in Palestine during the Amarna period. The hostility of many of the Palestinian cities included warlike operations against isolated towns that had remained loyal. Beth-shean and Rehob, and probably Megiddo, presumably maintained a semblance of control in vital areas along the *Via Maris* trade route. An alliance of Pehel beyond the Jordan and Hamath had besieged both Beth-shean and Rehob, towns controlling major trade routes from the Jordan Valley into the Jezreel, a situation the Egyptians could not tolerate. With Beth-shean and Rehob in immediate jeopardy, Seti's first campaign so early in his reign reflected the urgency of restoring Egypt to her former role as a great power in Palestine.

Four campaigns (or, possibly better, four primary objectives of a single campaign) by Seti I are portrayed in a series of scenes carved on the north and east walls enclosing the hypostyle hall of the Amun Temple at Karnak.[53] The reliefs depict Seti's military field operations, the subjugation of hostile chieftains and the dedication of prisoners to Amun. The detailed portrayal of these reliefs and the information contained in a stela found at Beth-shean also make possible a reconstruction of Seti's campaign itinerary. His departure from Sile on Egypt's northeastern frontier was along Egypt's primary military road to Palestine (the biblical *'way of the land of the Philistines'*). This road over a distance of 150 miles from Sile to Raphia on the Canaanite frontier was maintained by nine fortified wells.[54] The portrayal in the Karnak reliefs of battles raging among the wells suggests not only the need for fortifications protecting the vital water sources along the way, but also the hostile environment of the northern Sinai.

Military occupation in the northern Sinai was enhanced dramatically during the reign of Seti I. Punitive raids against Sinai *Shasu* obviously were intended to ensure safety along the primary trade routes and the establishment of permanent fortified, administrative centers, a significant innovation of the Nineteenth Dynasty, demanded a greater urgency for constant control on all vital links between Egypt and the strategic centers scattered throughout Canaan and beyond Damascus in southern Syria.

After Raphia (possibly controlled by the *Shasu*) and Gaza 'the town of the Canaan' fell to Seti, his army appears to have encountered no other opposition through the Sharon and Jezreel Plains to the outskirts of Beth-shean. The fact that Megiddo, guarding the Aruna Pass through the Carmel ridge, is not mentioned would seem to suggest that this major stronghold along the *Via Maris* was pro-Egyptian.

In the rescue of Beth-shean, Seti's punitive action was directed against Hamath, the instigator of the siege on Beth-shean, Pehel, also in the Jordan Valley just beyond the river, and the *ʿApiru* in Mount Yarmuta, just to the north of Beth-shean. To maintain stability in the region, Seti stationed three of his armies (garrisons or battalions) at Hamath, Beth-shean and Yenoʿam (probably ʿUbeidiya),[55] on the banks of the Jordan just south of the Sea of Galilee. Following the success of his efforts in Lebanon, Seti returned to the region to punish Pehel for its role in the Beth-shean siege.[56] It is interesting to note, however, that Seti did not station his troops beyond the Jordan even though part of the problem clearly was centered at Pehel. The commemorative stela recovered in the Beth-shean excavations refers to the *ʿApiru* of Mount Yarmuta:

> *Then his majesty said, 'How can these wretched Asiatics think (of taking) their (arms) for further disorder?* (ANET, 255)

The pharaoh seems to suggest that these Asiatics previously have been a problem, possibly a reference to the second campaign of Amenhotep II against Anaharath in the region of Mount Yarmuta in which 3600 *ʿApiru* were returned to Egypt as living captives. In any case, this campaign focused on the upper Jordan Valley and the Lower Galilee as a troublesome area for the pharaohs of the Eighteenth and Nineteenth Dynasties in their attempts to reestablish Egyptian control over Canaan. The trouble-making *ʿApiru* are identified with this region to which later the tribe of Issachar was assigned.

Having achieved its objectives in the Beth-shean area, Seti's army captured the seaports of Accho and Tyre and imposed tribute upon the Lebanese chieftains who are depicted in the reliefs as

> *...cutting down (cedar for) the great barque upon the river,...as well as for the great flagpoles of Amon...* (ANET, 254)

The success of this campaign not only alleviated Egypt's dire need for lumber but it set the stage for the subsequent assault on Kadesh and *Amurru*-land and the reconquest of Syria. It possibly was for this purpose that the first settlement at Tell Abu Huwâm, as a naval base and port for the Jezreel Plain, was established by the Egyptians in the mouth of the Kishon River.[57]

Seti's third campaign (if the Karnak reliefs depict a chronological sequence) was directed against the Libyans on Egypt's western frontier. The record suggests that the Egyptians were victorious. It is clear, however, that this event signalled the beginning of serious pressures from the west, a problem that progressively plagued subsequent pharaohs.[58] Seti's final campaign again was directed against the Hittites somewhere north of Kadesh where he claimed a great victory with many prisoners returned to Egypt as hostages. Obviously, whatever his successes in the far north, they were temporary.Later, Ramesses II's battle at Kadesh indicates that early in his reign, the effective Egyptian frontier clearly was to the south. Seti's peace treaty with Muwatallish, the Hittite king, demonstrated Seti's success in reestablishing Egyptian control over all of Syria-Palestine to the Hittite frontier.

Seti I's Domestic Affairs

The Ramesside dynasty seemingly had family traditions and personal devotion to the god Seth of Avaris (biblical Zoan), the earlier *Hyksos'* capital in the Delta. The unpopularity of Seth beyond Lower Egypt and the need of the newly established Ramesside dynasty for the support of the Theban priesthood required the retention of Thebes as the state and religious capital and Amun as the national deity. Much of the damage and neglect of the iconoclastic furor of the Amarna period was repaired. Seti built a large part of the hypostyle hall in the great Amun temple at Thebes and his tomb in the Valley of the Kings is of the finest quality. His temple at Abydos was his greatest achievement, though it was completed by his son, Ramesses II.[59]

In spite of Seti's building efforts throughout Egypt, the pharaohs of the Nineteenth Dynasty from the beginning associated themselves with the *Hyksos'* religious tradition in the Delta. The strong cultural ties between Egypt and Canaan at the beginning of the Nineteenth Dynasty were not confined to political and economic affairs but included an adoption of cultic and ritual practices.[60] Ramesses I established his residence at Memphis and Seti I built his palace at Qantir. The *'Stele of the Year 400'* set up by Ramesses II in Zoan commemorated the 400th year of the god Seth, an anniversary Seti I had celebrated in ca. 1320 B.C. when the dynasty was founded.[61] This commemoration of the establishment of *Hyksos* rule in ca. 1720 B.C. appears to be a claim to legitimacy and suggests that the Ramesside pharaohs viewed themselves as the heirs of the *Hyksos* tradition.

The Campaign and Times of Ramesses II

Ramesses II (ca. 1290-1223 B.C.) began an amazing 67-year reign following an indefinite period as coregent with his father Seti I.[62] The administrative capital at Memphis in the north was distinct from the state and religious center at Thebes. The location of the Delta residence of the pharaohs (*Per-Ramesse*, 'House of Ramesses') in the eastern delta from the reign of Ramesses II onward was a practical decision for a pharaoh whose concerns in Palestine and Syria were far too remote from Thebes.[63] The armies of the Nineteenth Dynasty pharaohs also were stationed at Memphis and *Per-Ramesse* was on constant alert to challenge incursions on both western (Libyan) and northern (Syrian) fronts. Commercial considerations also contributed to the establishment of the Delta capital. A stela bearing the names of Seti and Ramesses II found at Serabit el-Khadim in the Sinai indicates that the turquoise mines still were being exploited during the period of the coregency.[64]

The Battle of Kadesh

Following a brief three-year period of administrative reform, Ramesses II's reign was committed to a defense of Egypt's northern frontier against the Hittites. His first campaign into Asia, into the vicinity of Beirut and Byblos, seemingly issued the challenge to the Hittites. Following the military successes of Šuppiluliumaš, the Hittites considered the kingdom of Kadesh-on-the-Orontes (Kinza) and *Amurru*, their southern vassals. The Egyptian pharaohs, on the other hand, since the rise of the Nineteenth Dynasty, sought to recover these lands by driving the Hittites as far to the north as possible. A Syrian campaign by Seti I successfully forced the kings of *Amurru* and Kadesh to break their treaty agreements with the Hittites, but Syrian lands to the north remained under Hittite control.[65] Therefore, it fell the lot of Ramesses II, in his fifth year, to mount a major campaign against the newly crowned Hittite king Muwatalliš who assembled his army near Kadesh-on-the-Orontes.

The Egyptian army was organized into four divisions (named after four Egyptian deities: Amun, Re, Ptah and Sutekh). Ramesses himself commanding the lead division (Amun) crossed the Orontes at the Shabtuna ford south of Kadesh and on the basis of false information concerning the location of the Hittite forces (provided by two captured Hittites; Egyptian intelligence sources could provide no information to the contrary!), Ramesses marched his division into an Hittite ambush. Ramesses' second division (Re) was routed by a superior Hittite chariot charge, the Amun division was surrounded, and only a surprise *Amurru* attack on the Hittite rear guard rescued Ramesses from sure defeat. However, with his forces redeployed, Ramesses was able to withstand six successive charges of Hittite chariotry and ultimately, with the arrival of the Ptah division, forced the Hittites beyond the Orontes River. An Egyptian account claims that Muwatalliš, with his chariot forces greatly diminished, requested an armistice. Ramesses, on the other hand, with at least half of his forces badly demoralized, was delighted with the opportunity to withdraw. Realizing the vulnerability of his situation so far from home, Ramesses accepted a 'draw' as preferable to outright defeat. The verdict of history concerning the Kadesh confrontation is clear. The subsequent advance of the Hittites southward to the outskirts of Damascus indicates undeniably that strategically the Egyptians suffered an embarrassing defeat with ongoing consequences.[66]

The satisfying outcome of the Kadesh encounter for the Hittites was unquestioned control over Syria. Kadesh and *Amurru* were integrated into the Hittite administrative structure as vassals. Only the serious challenge of Assyria on the Hittites' eastern frontiers and a general deterioration of relations along its over-extended border in Asia Minor and the northeast kept the Hittites from pressing their advantage against the Egyptians in Canaan. As a result, after 16 years of intermittent skirmishes and military probes along the border, a reciprocal Peace Treaty between Egypt and the Hittites was concluded. A recognized border was established, military hostilities were renounced and a mutual defense pact was signed. Diplomatic correspondence was initiated and 13 years later at least one diplomatic marriage sealed an ongoing, amiable relationship between Ramesses II and Hattušiliš.

Some of the petty vassal city states in Palestine saw the unsuccessful Kadesh campaign as an opportunity to rebel. Egypt was forced to respond with punitive expeditions directed against the Negev, Edom, Moab, Ashkelon and the Galilee. Libya constituted a serious threat requiring the construction of a string of forts to control the western tribes. The Hittite Peace Treaty appears to have been Ramesses' ultimate response to an untenable military and administrative position. His inability to reclaim territories occupied by the Hittites in the north and the appearance of military weakness fostered internal unrest and instability among vassal states and areas subject to foreign infiltration. Internal instability, on the other hand, tended to signal military and administrative weakness to the Hittites who, apart from a treaty agreement, might see such internal trouble as an opportunity for additional encroachment or worse. It is precisely this type of dilemma concerning internal administrative policy that underlies the ambivalence of the pharaoh when confronted with Moses' request, "Let my people go!"

Papyrus Anastasi I[67]

A satirical letter, possibly used in the training of apprentice scribes, describes the shortcomings of a fellow scribe assigned to Asiatic military service. The composition dated to the late Nineteenth Dynasty (late thirteenth century B.C.), possibly toward the end of Ramesses II's reign, begins with a critical evaluation of the scribe's letter-writing ability:

...Thy statements mix up this with that; all thy words are upside-down; they are not connected...Lo, thy speeches are (only) vain talk...Thy letter is (too)inferior to permit that one listen to it...

Following a discussion of logistical problems related to expedition management, seemingly the responsibility of the scribe as quartermaster, the letter summarizes a litany of topographical and geographical details a skilled scribe must understand as chief information officer in the pharaoh's military expeditions to Hatti-land. These details are arranged in geographical sequence from the land of Hatti and Upi (Damascus) in the north to Gaza on the southern border of Canaan. In his comments concerning the area of Megiddo and the hazards of passing through the Aruna pass south of Megiddo, our scribe reminds his colleague of an episode about *"Qazardi, the Chief of As(h)er,"* and then describes the serious danger of 'Bedouin' who ambush travelers in the narrow pass.

The presence of this *Chief of Asher* at the end of the thirteenth century B.C. in the immediate vicinity to which the Israelite tribe of Asher ultimately was assigned by Joshua is an interesting coincidence. If these tribes of Asher are one and the same, then we may assume some early infiltration by the Asherites into this region of low, rolling terrain that links the Carmel range to the central hills of Manasseh and Ephraim.

The Campaigns of Merneptah

Merneptah became the thirteenth Crown Prince in the 55th year of Ramesses II's long reign and succeeded to the throne 12 years later when his father finally died after a reign of 67 years. During the final years of Ramesses II, a weakened army and slackened security along Egypt's western frontier provided easy access to Libyan raiding parties who ravaged the western Delta to alleviate famine at home. The threat of outright invasion steadily grew until, in Merneptah's fifth year, a confederacy of Libyan tribes (*Libu, Meshwesh,* and *Kehek*) and 'Sea Peoples' (*Sherden, Sheklesh, Lukka, Tursha* and *Akawasha*) advanced on the Delta. Merneptah's reorganized army, following approval from the Amun Oracle at Thebes, mobilized within a fortnight, took the offensive and marched to meet the enemy at the western frontier. In a six-hour battle Merneptah's forces killed 6000 of the enemy and took many prisoners and much booty. The primary records of this Libyan victory were found in a long inscription at Karnak and a stela from Athribis.

The 'Israel' Stela

The more familiar record to commemorate Merneptah's military successes against the Libyans and Canaan is found in the famous 'Israel' Stela. For the Egyptians, the pharaoh's victories resulted in jubilation and dramatic relief from the great anxiety that had accompanied the obvious decline of national security toward the end of Ramesses II's reign.

> *...Men come and go with singing, and there is no cry of men in trouble. Towns are populated once again and he who plants his harvest shall eat it. Re has turned himself back to Egypt.* (24-25)

Perceptions of conditions on the northern frontier also had changed dramatically:

> *The princes are prostrate, saying 'Peace';*
> *Not one raises his head among the Nine Bows.*
> *Tehenu is destroyed; Hatti is pacified (at peace).*
> *Canaan has been plundered with every evil.*
> *Ashkelon has been deported.*
> *Gezer has been captured.*
> *Yenoᶜam has been wiped out.*
> *Israel has been made waste, without posterity.*
> *Hurru(land) has become a widow because of Egypt.*
> *All lands have united themselves in peace.*
> *The restless have been subdued by the King of Upper and Lower Egypt, Ba-en-Re-mery-Amun, son of Re, Mer-en-Ptah Hotep-her-Maᶜat, granted life like Re, daily.*
>   (lines 26-30)[68]

This important Egyptian document, discovered in 1896 among the ruins of Merneptah's funerary temple in western Thebes, provides a number of significant details for understanding the context of the Hebrew exodus.[69]

1. The mention of peaceful relations with the Hittites (*Hatti*) clearly suggests that the treaty established by Ramesses II was still in effect. Part of the enduring nature of this agreement may reflect the diminishing power of the Hittite kings and the specific internal, economic problems Arnuwandash III, Merneptah's Hittite contemporary, was having at home. A Karnak inscription refers to a shipment of grain to Hatti during a time of famine.[70]

2. The imminent dangers on the western frontier and incursions from Libya appear to have been complicated by a widespread revolt against Egyptian domination in Canaan. Whether the mention of Ashkelon in the southern coastal plain, Gezer in the northern Shephelah and Yeno°am, south of the Sea of Galilee in the Jordan Valley, was intended to indicate the extensive nature of the rebellion, or whether these major urban centers were the instigators, and/or perpetrators of the hostility, is not clear. The fact that Merneptah assumed the title *Subduer of Gezer* following this successful campaign would seem to suggest that these centers were responsible for the problem and worthy of the pharaoh's wrath.[71]

3. The first and only mention of 'Israel' in any known Egyptian text is important especially in reference to Egyptian understanding of the situation in Canaan. The 'determinative' signs provided by the scribes using the Egyptian hieroglyphic system identify the words '*Hatti*,' 'Canaan,' 'Ashkelon,' 'Gezer,' 'Yano°am,' and '*Hurru*' as names of places, the determinative meaning 'land' or 'country.' Israel is assigned the determinative of 'people' rather than 'place,' suggesting to most scholars that Israelites as "people" were in the land without a specific place with which they could be identified.[72] Such a conclusion, in fact, would militate against an early (15th century B.C.) 'all out' exodus because it is difficult to visualize a 200-year period (from the end of the 15th century to the reign of Merneptah) in which Israel was unable to establish herself in the land to the point of being identified with a locale.

The identification of Israel as 'people' apart from place or locale has been explained in various ways to overcome problematic reconstructions. The simplest explanation is to assume a careless scribe.[73] It has been suggested that despite the use of the determinative for 'people,' Israel was a territorial designation, and that those population groups mentioned in the Bible (Danites, Gibeonites, Asherites, etc.) arriving primarily from the lowland city-state regions became 'Israelites' because they settled in the central highlands.[74] Others have suggested that Israel, like Canaan, is an inclusive term, representing approximately half of Palestine (Canaan in the coastal plains and Israel in the central hill country), a situation in effect at the time of Merneptah's campaign following a fifteenth century exodus.[75]

Wall Reliefs of the Amun-Re Temple at Thebes

Wall reliefs adjoining the great Hypostyle Hall of the Amun-Re temple at Thebes recently have provided some clarification of the nature of the 'Israel' stela, and possibly of the situation in Canaan. The central focus of the reliefs is the Peace Treaty between Ramesses II, Merneptah's father, and Hattusilis III, the Hittite king. Their treaty was signed some 16 years following the Battle of Kadesh between Ramesses and Muwatalliš. It was intended to stabilize Egypt's northern frontier against the Hittites' continuing southward encroachment into what was considered traditional Egyptian territory.

Four battle reliefs, two on either side of the Peace Treaty now have been attributed to Merneptah instead of Ramesses II who actually built the wall.[76] These battle scenes appear to correspond with the four primary trouble spots mentioned in the Merneptah Stela. One relief identifies Ashkelon and portrays the siege of a fortified town. A siege ladder, being scaled by an Egyptian soldier armed with shield and spear (or dagger), leans against the crenelated city wall, a feature common to two of the other three reliefs.[77] The besieged residents crowded upon the walls and towers of the besieged towns appear in an attitude of prayer, burning incense and sacrificing (dangling?) children from the heights of the city wall. (We assume precisely this type of crowding of the defensive walls and towers by the besieged residents of Jericho in response to the strange strategy of the invading Israelites.) The fourth battle scene depicts an enemy in open country with low hills but without a fortified town. The 'hill country' setting is consistent with papyrus evidence dated to Merneptah's third year that claims Egyptian controlled strategic positions in the central hill country of Canaan following the pharaoh's military expedition.[78] The correlation of these four reliefs with the stela statement is quite remarkable. Ashkelon and two other fortified cities (Gezer and Yenoᶜam) were besieged by the pharaoh while the fourth battle appears to have been against a population without urbanized fortifications. An additional interesting coincidence is the discovery near the battle reliefs of a fragmentary duplicate of the stela text containing a Canaanite expedition description. If, in fact, both inscriptions depict Merneptah's Canaanite campaign, then we have not only the first mention of 'Israel' but the earliest portrayal of 'Israelites' (Israelite soldiers, chariot, etc.), approximately 600 years before Sennacherib's dramatic presentation of the siege and conquest of Lachish on the walls of his Nineveh palace. The 'Israelite' dress is comparable to Canaanite garb, depicted elsewhere. However, the dress is quite distinct from the Bedouin-type *Shasu*, wearing short kilts and turban headdress, commonly identified with Canaan and the Sinai and portrayed among the prisoners being returned bound to Egypt. The depiction of these 'Israelites' in Canaanite rather than *Shasu* apparel suggests a clear Egyptian distinction between Israelites and *Shasu* who obviously were also Semitic but maintained a distinct nomadic lifestyle.[79]

The references to the Canaanite campaign as a postscript to the Merneptah Stela and its primary subject, the Libyan campaign and defeat of the Sea Peoples in his fifth year, suggest that the northern expedition came early (possibly during his second or third year) in Merneptah's brief ten year reign. His death was followed by a struggle over succession rights within Ramesses II's large, extended royal family. Merneptah's campaign, however, appears to have stimulated a tightening of Egyptian control over Canaan with the establishment of a series of administrative centers and systematic taxation.[80] Excavations along the coastal plain from Tell el-Farᶜah (south) to Accho, Masos in the Negev, a series of sites throughout the Shephelah and even in the Jordan Valley have recovered artifacts bearing the names of Merneptah and his successors of the Nineteenth Dynasty. A destruction level at Gezer dated to Late Bronze IIB has been attributed to Merneptah's campaign.[81] It seems highly possible that Merneptah's campaign initiated renewed vitality in Egyptian domination in Canaan, especially along the coast, in the Shephelah and strategic locations in northern Canaan. The significant decline of Egyptian administrative control and military surveillance contributed to Israelite encroachment on the agricultural lowlands of Egyptian vassals and possible interference in the free movement of commerce and trade along the main trunk line and branches of the *Via Maris*. Merneptah's campaign appears not to have reached into the Transjordan where vassals brought under Egyptian control by Ramesses II seemingly remained loyal.[82]

The simultaneous decline of Egypt, Assyria and Hatti left Syria and Canaan in a political vacuum without the stabilizing forces that had controlled the quarrels and infrequent inter-city rivalries of the petty local kings. The rise of the Twentieth Dynasty and the invasion of the 'Sea Peoples' soon overshadowed the ambitions of local kings.[83] An emerging Israelite confederation surely was weakened by such renewed Egyptian activity in Canaan, a condition continued into the reign of Ramesses III when the full force of the 'Sea Peoples' invasion challenged Egyptian domination.[84]

Summary

With the expulsion of the foreign rulers (*Hyksos*) of the Second Intermediate Period, Egypt's New Kingdom (18th & 19th Dynasties) pharaohs reestablished control over most of the Levant with military expeditions that reached the Euphrates. Domination of the region as an extensive buffer zone against Egypt's enemies to the north proved problematic with local urban rulers exerting their independence against the Egyptian overlord. Punitive military expeditions failed to maintain regional loyalties to the Egyptian interests and treaties in the area. As a result, the pharaohs of the Nineteenth Dynasty imposed a bureaucratic administrative structure and basically integrated Canaan as a province of Egypt.

The annals of Amenhotep II's campaigns, early in the fourteenth century B.C. for the first time, mention the capture of *ʿApiru* among the offending Canaanite populace and their return to Egypt as prisoners. The annals of subsequent campaigns appear to reflect the growing problem of these *ʿApiru* at the focus of Egyptian punitive action. Ultimately, the Stele of Merneptah identified the people 'Israel' as a distinct population that had been subdued in Canaan toward the end of the thirteenth century B.C. Our review of conditions in Sinai and Canaan and Egyptian involvement in the region during the period of our study provides the setting for the exodus of the Hebrews from Egypt and their subsequent integration into their 'Promised Land.' For the sequential development of this important phase in Israel's quest for nationhood we now must return to Egypt and developments in the Land of Goshen.

NOTES

[1] W.G. Dever, The Middle Bronze Age: The Zenith of the Urban Canaanite Era. *BA* 50 (1987): 148-177.

[2] W.G. Dever, The Beginning of the Middle Bronze Age in Syria-Palestine. Pp. 3-38 in *Magnalia Dei: The Mighty Acts of God*, eds. F.M. Cross, W.E. Lemke and P.D. Miller. New York, 1976; M. Kochavi, P. Beck and R. Gophna, Aphek-Antipatris, Tel Poleg, Tel Zeror and Tel Burga: Four Fortified Sites of the Middle Bronze IIA in the Sharon Plain. *Zeitschrift des Deutschen Palästina-Vereins* 45 (1979): 121-165.

[3] M. Bietak, *Avaris and Piramesse: Archaeological Exploration in the Eastern Nile Delta*. London: Oxford University Press, 1981.

[4] W.F. Albright, *The Archaeology of Palestine*. 4th ed., rev. Harmondsworth, England: Penguin Publication, 1960: 96; K.M. Kenyon, Palestine in the Time of the Eighteenth Dynasty. In *CAH³* II/I, 1970-1975: 528; J.D. Seger, The Middle Bronze IIC Date of the East Gate at Shechem. *Levant* 5 (1974): 117-130; *idem,* The MB II Fortifications at Shechem and Gezer - A Hyksos Perspective. *EI* 12 (1975): 34*-35*; J.M. Weinstein, The Egyptian Empire in Palestine: A Reassessment. *BASOR* 241 (1981): 1-28.

[5] Range from high to low chronology. V. Hankey and P. Warren, The Absolute Chronology of the Aegean Bronze Age. *Bulletin of the Institute of Classical Studies of the University of London* 21 (1974): 142-152; Note, R. Gonen, Megiddo in the Late Bronze Age - Another Assessment. *Levant* 19 (1987): 83-100. (Late Bronze Subdivisions: Late Bronze I (1550-1400 B.C.) - 18th Dynasty; Late Bronze II (1400-1300 B.C.) - 18th Dynasty; Late Bronze III (1300-1150 B.C.) - 19th Dynasty).

[6] City II/Palace II pottery includes a local (ᶜAjjûl) Bichrome, Chocolate-on-white, Black Lustrous, White-Slipped, and modified types of MB II-III. For MB II-III date, see A. Kempinski, Tell el-ᶜAjjûl - Beth Aglayim or Sharuhen? *IEJ* 24 (1974): 145-152; for LB IA date, see O. Negbi, *The Hoards of Goldwork from Tell el-ᶜAjjûl*. SMA 25. Göteborg: P. Åström, 1970.

[7] K. Kenyon, Palestine in the Time of the Eighteenth Dynasty. Pp. 526-556 in *CAH³* II, 1. Cambridge: Cambridge University Press, 1973.

[8] A.H. Gardiner, The Defeat of the Hyksos by Kamōse: The Carnarvon Tablet, No. I. *JEA* 3 (1916): 95-110.

[9] T.G.H. James, Egypt: From the Expulsion of the Hyksos to Amenophis I. *CAH³* II, 1: 302-303.

[10] A.H. Gardiner, The Defeat of the Hyksos by Kamose: The Carnarvon Tablet, No. I. *JEA* 3 (1916): 95-110.

[11] L. Habachi, Preliminary Report on Kamose Stela and Other Inscribed Blocks found ... at Karnak. *Ann. Serv.* 53 (1955): 195-202.

[12] T. Säve-Söderbergh, The Hyksos Rule in Egypt. *JEA* 37 (1951): 53-71.

[13] A. Leonard, Jr. The Late Bronze Age. *BA* 52 (1989): 8; W.G. Dever, The Middle Bronze Age: The Zenith of the Urban Canaanite Era. *BA* 50 (1987): 149-77.

[14] A.F. Rainey, Egyptian Military Inscriptions and Some Historical Implications. *JAOS* 107 (1987): 89-92.

[15] J.W.Jack, *The Date of the Exodus in the Light of External Evidence*. Edinburgh: T. & T. Clark, 1925: 251-255; Siegfried H. Horn, What we Don't Know About Moses and the Exodus. *BAR* 3/2 (1977): 23,24; Leon J. Wood, *A Survey of Israel's History*. Grand Rapids, Mich.: Zondervan, 1986: 93-95.

[16] L.W. Casperson, The Lunar Dates of Thutmose III. *JNES* 45/2 (1986): 139-150.

[17] Weinstein, J.M. The Egyptian Empire in Palestine - A Reassessment. *BASOR* 241 (1981): 18-21.

[18] W.F. Albright, Further Light on the History of Israel from Lachish and Megiddo. *BASOR* 68 (1937): 22-26; G.E. Wright, The Archaeology of Palestine. Pp. 85-139 in *The Bible and the Ancient Near East*, ed. G.E. Wright. Garden City, NY: Doubleday, Anchor, 1961.

[19] R.O. Faulkner, The Battle of Megiddo. *JEA* 28 (1942): 2-15; W.H Shea, The Conquests of Sharuḥen and Megiddo Reconsidered. *IEJ* 29 (1979): 1-5.

[20] R. Gonen, Urban Canaan in the Late Bronze Period. *BASOR* 253 (1984): 61-73.

[21] K.M. Kenyon, The Middle and Late Bronze Age Strata at Megiddo. *Levant* 1 (1969): 25-60.

[22] *ANET*: 234-238.

[23] W.H. Shea, The Conquests of Sharuḥen and Megiddo Reconsidered. *IEJ* 29 (1979): 1-5.

[24] W.F. Albright, The Amarna Letters from Palestine. Pp. 98-116 in *CAH³* II/2, 1970-1975; K.M. Kenyon, *Amorites and Canaanites*. Schweich Lectures. London: Oxford University, 1966: 76; M. Several, Reconsidering the Egyptian Empire in Palestine During the Amarna Period. *PEQ* 104 (1972): 123-133; M. Weippert, *The Settlement of the Israelite Tribes in Palestine; A Critical Survey of Recent Scholarly Debate*. Trans. J.D. Martin. Studies in Biblical Theology (2nd series) 21. Napierville, IL: A.R. Allenson, 1971: 71-74.

[25] S. Yeivin, The Third District of Tuthmosis III's List of Palestino-Syrian Towns. *JEA* 36 (1950): 51-62.

[26] Alan Gardiner, *Egypt of the Pharaohs*. Oxford: Oxford University Press, 1961: 188-9, 199; John J. Bimson, *Redating the Exodus and Conquest*. 2nd. ed. Sheffield, England: The Almond Press, 1981: 230-31.

[27] Siegfried H. Horn, What We Don't Know About Moses and the Exodus. *BAR* 3/2 (1977): 24.

[28] J.A. Wilson, *The Culture of Ancient Egypt*. Chicago, 1957: 195ff.

[29] Y. Aharoni, Some Geographical Remarks Concerning the Campaigns of Amenhotep II. *JNES* 19 (1960): 177-78.

[30] ibid., 177-183.

[31] W.F. Albright, A Prince of Taanach in the 15th Century B.C. *BASOR* 94 (1944): 24-27.

[32] *EA* 244, 10.

[33] *EA* 218, 19.

[34] Y. Aharoni, Some Geographical Remarks Concerning the Campaigns of Amenhotep II. *JNES* 19 (1960): 182-83.

[35] W.F. Albright, A Prince of Taanach in the 15th Century B.C. *BASOR* 94 (1944): 24-27; E.F. Campbell, Jr., The Amarna Letters and The Amarna Period. *BA* 23 (1960): 2-22.

[36] M.W. Several, Reconsidering the Egyptian Empire in Palestine during the Amarna Period. *PEQ* 104 (1972): 123-133.

[37] Y. Aharoni, Rubute and Ginti-Kirmil. *VT* 19 (1969): 137-145. Rubute = Khirbet Bîr el-Ḥilû, a large stronghold, but too small for a Canaanite royal city, on the edge of the Valley of Aijalon; Giti-Kirmil = Tell eṣ-Ṣâfi, between Gezer and Lachish = Gath of Shuwardata and Tagi of the Amarna Period.

[38] W. Helck, Die Bedrohung Palästinas durch einwandernde Gruppen am Ende der 18. und am anfang der 19. Dynastie. *VT* 18 (1968): 472-480.

[39] W.F. Albright, Abram the Hebrew: A New Archaeological Interpretation. *BASOR* 163 (1961): 36-54.

[40] S. Izre'el, Two Notes on the Gezer-Amarna Tablets. *Tel Aviv* 4 (1977): 159-167.

[41] A.F. Rainey, Unruly Elements in Late Bronze Canaanite Society. Paper delivered to the Egyptology and the History and Culture of Israel Consultation Section, AAR-SBL Annual Meeting, New Orleans, La., Nov. 19, 1990.

[42] I. Mendelsohn, On Corvée Labor in Ancient Canaan and Israel. *BASOR* 167 (1962): 31-35.

[43] C. Aldred, The End of the El ʿAmarna Period. *JEA* 43 (1957): 30-41; The Beginning of the El-ʿAmarna Period. *JEA* 45 (1959): 19-33.

[44] J. Gray, Canaanite Kingship in Theory and Practice. *VT* 2 (1952): 193-220.

[45] Moshe Greenberg, *The Ḥab/piru*. New Haven, CT: American Oriental Society, 1955: 7,8; T.J. Meek, *Hebrew Origins*. New York: Harper & Bros., 1960: 21; J.J. Bimson, *Redating the Exodus and Conquest*. Sheffield, England: The Almond Press, 1981: 227; L.J. Wood, *A Survey of Israel's History*. Grand Rapids, MI: Zondervan, 1986: 83.

[46] H.H. Rowley, The Exodus and the Settlement in Canaan. *BASOR* 85 (1942): 27-31.

[47] I. Velikovsky, *Ages in Chaos*. Garden City, N.Y.: Doubleday, 1952: 51,52.

[48] H. Shanks, The Exodus and the Crossing of the Red Sea, According to Hans Goedicke. *BAR* 6/5 (1980): 49,50.

[49] H. Shanks, *op cit.*, 46-48; I. Wilson, *Exodus: The True Story Behind the Biblical Account*. San Francisco: Harper & Row, 1985: 131-2, 136-7.

[50] A. Gardiner, *Egypt of the Pharaohs*. Oxford: Oxford University Press, 1961: 243.

[51] S.H. Horn, *op.cit.*, 24.

[52] *ANET*: 253-255.

[53] All four campaigns are subsumed under Year 1, although obviously four successive wars were not fought in one year. Such single dating to cover several expeditions was general in Egypt. Note, Thutmose I's *Tumbos Stela* and Thutmose III's *Armant Stela*.

[54] A.H. Gardiner, The Ancient Military Road between Egypt and Palestine. *JEA* 6 (1920): 99ff., pls.11,12.

[55] N. Zori, Survey of the Beth Shan Basin. *BIES* 18 (1954): 78-90; 19 (1955): 89-98.

[56] Recorded on a stela recovered at Tell esh-Shihab in the Hauran. See W.M. Müller, The Egyptian Monument of Tell esh-Shihab. *PEF* (1904): 78ff.

[57] B. Mazar (Maisler), The Stratification of Tell Abū Huwâm on the Bay of Acre. *BASOR* 124 (1951): 21-25.

[58] R.O. Faulkner, The Wars of Sethos I. *JEA* 33 (1947): 34ff.

[59] A.M. Calverley and M.F. Broome, *The Temple of King Sethos I at Abydos*. 4 vols. London and Chicago, 1933-58.

[60] S. Yeivin, Canaanite Ritual Vessels in Egyptian Cultic Practices. *JEA* 62 (1976): 110-114.

[61] *ANET*: 252f.

[62] K.C. Seele, *The Coregency of Ramses II with Seti I*. Chicago, 1940. Note rationale for accession dates of 1304 and 1279 in L.W. Casperson, The Lunar Date of Ramesses II. *JNES* 47/3 (1988): 181-184.

[63] A.H. Gardiner, The Delta Residence of the Ramessides, III. *JEA* 5 (1918): 179ff.

[64] A.H. Gardiner and T.E. Peet, *The Inscriptions of Sinai*. ed. 2, rev., J.Černý. 2 vols. London, 1952: nos. 246-50.

[65] R.O Faulkner, The Wars of Sethos I. *JEA* 33 (1947): 34ff.

[66] J.A. Wilson, The Texts of the Battle of Kadesh. *AJSL* 43 (1927): 266ff.; M.B. Rowton, The Background of the Treaty between Ramesses II of Egypt and Hattušiliš III. *JCS* 13 (1959): 1ff.; A. Gardiner, *The Kadesh Inscriptions of Ramesses II*. Oxford, 1960; K.A. Kitchen, Some New Light on the Asiatic Wars of Ramesses II. *JEA* 50 (1964): 47ff.

[67] *ANET*: 475-479.

[68] The Merneptah 'Israel' Stela, containing the complete text of the pharaoh's military exploits against Libya and Canaan, now in the Cairo Museum is a black granite monolith, ca. 7.5 x 3.75 feet high. Originally an Amenhotep III stela of the Amarna Period, Merneptah's text was inscribed on the back (verso) side of the Amenhotep Stela. In the semi-circular (lunette) space above the text, Merneptah is depicted twice (in mirror fashion) accepting the sword of victory from Amun flanked by Mut and Khonsu.

[69] W.F. Albright, The Israelite Conquest of Canaan in the Light of Archaeology. *BASOR* 74 (1939): 11-23.

[70] G.A. Wainwright, Merneptah's Aid to the Hittites. *JEA* 46 (1960): 24ff.

[71] The title is attributed in an inscription at Amada; J.H. Breasted, *A History of Egypt*. New York: Chas. Scribner's, 1912: 465-466; A.H. Gardiner, *Egypt of the Pharaohs*. Oxford: Oxford University Press, 1961: 273.

[72] J. A. Wilson, Egyptian Historical Texts, Egyptian Hymns and Prayers, and Egyptian Oracles and Prophecies. P. 378 in *ANET*.

[73] J.A. Wilson, Egyptian Hymns and Prayers. P. 378 in *ANET*; Roland de Vaux, *The Early History of Israel*. trans. David Smith. Philadelphia: The Westminster Press, 1978: 390.

[74] G.W. Ahlstrom, *Who Were the Israelites?* Winona Lake, IN: Eisenbrauns, 1986.

[75] G.W. Ahlstrom and D. Edelman, Merneptah's Israel. *JNES* 44/1 1985: 60,61; H. J. Katzenstein, Gaza in Egyptian Texts of the New Kingdom. *JAOS* 102 (1982): 111-113.

[76] F.J. Yurco, 3,200-Year-Old Picture of Israelites Found in Egypt. *BAR* 16/5 (1990): 20-38.

[77] A. Badaway, *A History of Egyptian Architecture: The Empire (The New Kingdom)*. Berkeley and Los Angeles: University of California Press, 1968: 448-474.

[78] *Papyrus Anastasi* III

[79] F.J. Yurco, Merneptah's Palestinian Campaign. *JARCE* 23 (1986): 197ff.; L. Stager, Merneptah, Israel and Sea Peoples: New Light on an Old Relief. *EI* 18 (1985): 56-64. For arguments identifying early Israelites with Shasu, see: R. Giveon, *Les Bédouins Shosou des documents égyptiens*. Documenta et Monumenta Orientis Antiqui, 18. Leiden: E.J. Brill, 1971: 267-271; M. Weippert, The Israelite 'Conquest' and the Evidence from Transjordan. Pp. 32-34 in *Symposia Celebrating the Seventy-Fifth Anniversary of the American Schools of Oriental Research (1900-1975)*, ed. F.M. Cross. Cambridge, MA: American Schools of Oriental Research, 1979: 32-34; D. Redford, The Ashkelon Relief at Karnak and the Israel Stele. *IEJ* 36 (1986): 199-200; I. Finkelstein, Searching for Israelite Origins. *BAR* 14/5 (1988): 44ff.

[80] E.D. Oren, Governors' Residences' in Canaan under the New Kingdom: A Case Study of Egyptian Administration. *JSSEA* 14 (1984): 37-56.

[81] W.G. Dever et al., Gezer II: Report of the 1967-70 Seasons in Field I and II. *HUCA*. Jerusalem: Keter, 1974: 52; L. Stager, Merenptah, Israel, and Sea Peoples: New Light on an Old Relief. *EI* 18 (1985): 62.

[82] K.A. Kitchen, *Pharaoh Triumphant: The Life and Times of Ramesses II*. Mississauga, Ont.: Benben Pub., 1982: 67-68.

[83] A. Malamat, Cushan Rishathaim and the Decline of the Near East around 1200 B.C. *JNES* 13 (1954): 231-242.

[84] L. Stager, The Archaeology of the Family in Ancient Israel. *BASOR* 260 (1985): 1-24.

Chapter III

FROM GOSHEN TO MOUNT SINAI

The 'Amorite' World of the Early Second Millennium B.C.

The destruction of the great Early Bronze city states of Canaan was only one aspect of a very turbulent time throughout the Levant toward the end of the third millennium B.C. Great urban centers seemingly were overwhelmed and destroyed by a successful infiltration of pastoralists. The result was a century or more of nomadism, followed by a vibrant renewal of urbanization. The revitalization of the great city-state system, once thought the product of a mass migration of Northwestern Semites from Upper Syria and Mesopotamia, came from an integrated, indigenous population of these biblical *Amorites*.[1]
Apart from a return to vibrant urbanization, there is little in the material culture of Syria-Palestine to support the idea of a recent external origin for the Middle Bronze IIA culture. Undeniable ties with the civilizations of the upper Mesopotamian region already were well established. The linguistic evidence suggests an extensive 'Amorite' (West Semitic) population throughout Syria-Palestine during the late third and second centuries B.C.

Ultimately these Amorites controlled the entire Fertile Crescent, and the southward trends of traceable cultural innovations within the Levant did not reflect incursions of *foreigners* but aspects of the natural movement of peoples toward improved cultural and economic opportunities.[2] The development of this indigenous population under more favorable conditions, both climatic, economic and political, produced the high order of urbanization and culture (reflected in the MB IIA pottery repertoire).[3] In Egypt similar political and economic stability resulted from the reunification and establishment of the Middle Kingdom.

The Nile Delta During the Second Intermediate Period: The 'Hyksos' Period as a Prelude to the Exodus

Developments in the Levant had a dramatic impact upon Lower Egypt, especially the Nile Delta. The last phase of the Middle Bronze

Age in Palestine (MB IIC) chronologically corresponds precisely with the late *Hyksos* period in Egypt (ca. 1650-1550 B.C.) when Lower Egypt experienced Asiatic influence and political domination (15th Dynasty). That the material culture of these *Hyksos* possessed strong affinities with Syria-Palestine has been recognized for some time, especially in reference to so-called *Hyksos* fortifications.[4] The massive MB IIA-C fortifications in both Syria and Palestine varied in complexity and structure with enormous earthen embankments, glacis and fosses, stone and mudbrick revetments and perimeter walls, in various combinations. The rationale for such structures extended well beyond local attempts to defend against a variety of offensive weapons, such as chariotry and battering rams.[5] The Asiatic developments in Canaan appear focused on Egypt. The early MB IIA fortifications, evidence of the Amorite expansion southward anticipated renewed infiltration of Lower Egypt, a process already evident during the Old Kingdom period. In the MB IIB period nearly all sites in Palestine had been fortified and used as base-camps for the advance into the Delta where the Fourteenth (Asiatic) Dynasty rivalled the Theban Thirteenth Dynasty. The union of Palestine and Lower Egypt under the Fifteenth Dynasty, during a period of relative tranquility and the decline of Syria, produced a cultural zenith for Palestine during MB IIC (ca. 1650-1550 B.C.).[6]

The *Hyksos* maintained close contact with Asia from which they drew technical strength in warfare during the final struggles against the Egyptians who, in turn, received their support from Nubia. It was a basic struggle between Asian and African cultures. Ultimately, however, Egypt would claim some benefits. Through the *Hyksos*, the Egyptians adopted many innovations in warfare, in mental character and internal political organization, that would stimulate their ultimate successes during the New Kingdom.[7]

Of special importance in this relationship is the identification of Tell el-Dabᶜa in the Nile Delta with the *Hyksos* capital of Avaris.[8] The material culture of this large, well-established town-site is nearly identical to that of Middle Bronze II sites in Palestine and clearly represents a settled Asiatic or Canaanite population in Egypt.[9] There can no longer be any doubt that the 'Asiatics' or *Hyksos* were from Palestine (and possibly southern Syria) and that ethnically they were

Western (*Amurru*, or Amorite) Semites (the progenitors of the Canaanites of the Late Bronze Age). The cultural assemblage including domestic and religious architecture, burials, metal tools and weapons, cultic objects, and both local and imported pottery, not only at Tell el-Dab^{c}a but also at Tell el-Yehudiyeh and Tell el-Maskhuta in the Wadi Tumilat, is typically Syro-Palestinian MB IIA-C. The Palestinian material became predominant after the initial phase of settlement (within the Palestinian MB IIA, ca. 1850 B.C.) that appears to have developed peacefully and to have been sustained over a long period. The Asiatic settlements in the Delta retained strong links with Syria-Palestine throughout the Thirteenth Dynasty (ca. 1786-1633 B.C.). Assimilation of Egyptian culture appears to have been very limited until relatively late, and it was this general lack of acculturation that preserved the 'foreign' status among Egyptian officialdom.

By 1725 B.C., prior to the establishment of the Fourteenth and Fifteenth *Hyksos* Dynasties, Tell el-Dab^{c}a already was the center of a local Canaanite dynasty. A long process of immigration from Palestine preceded the ultimate *Hyksos* takeover. As the *Hyksos* capital of the Fifteenth Dynasty (ca. 1674-1567 B.C.) at its cultural peak, it became the ideal base for expansion in Lower and Middle Egypt.

The destruction of Tell el-Dab^{c}a (Avaris) and the expulsion of the *Hyksos* during the revival of Egyptian strength under Kamose, the last king of the Seventeenth Dynasty, and Ahmose and his Eighteenth Dynasty successors, was followed by a long series of punitive raids into Palestine and beyond (as far as the Upper Euphrates). Their destructive nature, possibly motivated more by revenge than the reestablishment of an Asiatic empire, is attested in destruction levels at most Syro-Palestinian sites during the MB IIC - LB I transition (ca. 1550-1500 B.C.).[10] Following the fall of Avaris (ca. 1540 B.C.), Ahmose (ca. 1570-1546 B.C.) besieged Sharuhen (probably Tell el-^{c}Ajjul rather than Tell el-Far^{c}ah) in southern Palestine. Additional campaigns under Amenhotep I (ca. 1546-1526 B.C.) and Thutmose I (ca. 1526-1512 B.C.) were followed by the decisive military efforts of Thutmose III whose Asiatic campaigns began in his 23rd year (ca. 1482 B.C.) with his successful assault on Megiddo and the Canaanite confederacy.

The Nile Delta During the New Kingdom Period

The population of New Kingdom Egypt included large numbers of Asiatics, especially in the Nile Delta. The basic population of these foreigners surely was the residual effect of the Amorite incursion that resulted in Egypt's domination by 'foreign rulers' (*Hyksos*) during the Second Intermediate Period. With the advent of the Eighteenth Dynasty, their numbers swelled as a result of successful Egyptian military expeditions into the lands of Lower and Upper Retenu.[11] Mass deportation of captives by ship or by land from the Asiatic lands for consignment as land peasants on the expansive temple estates was common.[12] Branded with the name of the pharaoh or the god to be served and assigned to special administrative departments, these Asiatic 'prisoners of war,' by the mid-Eighteenth Dynasty, dominated the temple work force.[13] The great temples were ...*filled with male and female slaves, children of the chiefs of all the foreign lands in the captivity of his majesty...surrounded by the settlements of H³rw.*[14] In keeping with the basic skills of the agrarian society from which they had come, most of these new arrivals were assigned to garment manufacturing and agriculture: ...*to fill the (god's) ergastulum, to be weavers, to make from his byssus, fine white linen, shrw-linen and thick cloth; to trap and work the fields, to produce corn to fill the granary of the god's-income.*[15]

The '*children of the chiefs*' were a distinct class of prisoners intended to serve a special Egyptian purpose. An official New Kingdom policy, stated for the first time in the annals of Thutmose III's sixth campaign and probably instituted by him, claimed the male offspring and relatives of the Asiatic kings and chieftains as hostages for special training and indoctrination ('education') to develop loyal vassals for subsequent generations. In the meantime, the captive relatives ensured the pharaoh against any actions by the current ruler that were not in the best interest of Egyptian domination in the region.[16] For these better educated members of Asiatic nobility, positions of higher rank or specialized trades were possible by appointment (guardsman, construction engineer, etc.) or marriage.[17] An Asiatic became chief draftsman for the design of the Temple of Amun during the reign of Thutmose III, a position that his descendants still held six generations later.[18] Such examples strongly suggest Egyptian willingness to integrate intelligent, capable captives into the economic fiber of the kingdom in responsible positions beyond the subservient agrarian and textile industries. Native Egyptians, as a result, were relieved from *corvée* conscription in public works projects. Unskilled labor in heavy construction and tomb excavation was performed by foreign Asiatic work gangs. Already during the reign of Thutmose III at least 75% of the unskilled laborers were H^3rw.[19] Ultimately, especially from the Akhenaten reign onward, not only Nubians but Asiatics as well were integrated into all aspects of the active military (shield-bearers, swordsmen, spearmen, charioteers, etc.), government and commercial enterprises.[20] Asiatics even have been identified among the priesthood and palace staff. Canaanite names and their equivalents and Canaanite dialects became increasingly more common throughout Lower Egypt.[21]

The employment and commercial opportunities and the size of the Asiatic population seemingly attracted laborers and entrepreneurs who voluntarily entered Egypt's eastern frontier as well. As in earlier centuries, Canaanite herdsmen with their livestock were allowed entry and limited movement within Asiatic-dominated regions.[22] But by the late Eighteenth and early Nineteenth Dynasties, an Asiatic merchant class became so active that ...*to do business speaking the H^3rw-tongue* became synonymous with ...*to haggle*,[23] a possible indication of the prominent commercial role the Asiatics had assumed.

Obviously, the Egyptian records make no reference to a specific ethnic minority in the Delta that may be linked directly to the descendants of Jacob or the Hebrews of the Exodus account. Such a reference should not be expected, nor is such a reference necessary to corroborate the general impression the biblical text gives concerning the situation Moses encountered in his confrontation with the pharaoh. However, in a slave list in a Thirteenth Dynasty papyrus, thirty-seven of 95 names are identified as *'male Asiatic'* or *'female Asiatic'* and presumably Semitic. The names include Issachar and Asher (two of the northern tribes descended from Leah and her maid, Zilpah) and Shiphrah and Puah (Exodus 1:15 - the names of the midwives in Egypt) which are perfectly good Northwest Semitic names of women from the first half of the Second Millennium B.C. and thus authentic in their appearance in the Exodus narratives.[24]

The integration of Jacob's descendants into the economic fiber of the Delta surely was achieved during the period of *Hyksos* dominance. It seems more than reasonable that following a century and a half of foreign rule, a perennial concern for the Egyptians would be the threat that any incident among the various ethnic groups represented among the ever-expanding Asiatic population might spark a concerted Asiatic revolt. The preponderance of Egyptian evidence for the Eighteenth and Nineteenth Dynasties is that the economy of Lower Egypt and especially the Delta region was permeated with a dominant Asiatic population and labor force. It is important to recall that the pharaoh's reluctance in responding positively to the request for the Hebrews' release was two-fold: He was concerned that the Hebrews might become a 'fifth-column' in aiding and abetting an enemy; and he was concerned about their departure. If in fact their numbers had so completely permeated every aspect of the Egyptian economy, as Egyptian records seem to indicate, a mass exodus seriously could have disrupted the entire economy of the Delta. The pharaoh's concerns for the security and the economy of the region appear legitimate within this context.

During the reign of the Nineteenth Dynasty pharaohs, the northern border of Egyptian control in Upper Retenu was a constant concern. If the Moses-led exodus falls within the reign of Ramesses II, as the prevailing evidence seems to suggest, the pharaoh's concern, following the Egyptian-Hittite confrontation at the Battle of Kadesh in 1286 B.C.E., was with the subsequent gradual but persistent Hittite encroachment southward into traditional Egyptian territories. It was this greater concern of a more powerful Hittite presence on his northern frontier that forced Ramesses in 1270 B.C. to vie for permanent borders on a line just beyond the outskirts of Damascus. To assure the *status quo* on his northern frontier, the pharaoh could not risk a major internal revolt by his sizable Asiatic population. Even their departure would have meant a disruption of the region's economic infrastructure sufficiently serious to undermine his country's security. For this reason, it seems totally unnecessary and illogical to suppose that the details of the biblical context of the exodus account should be sought in the Late Period (that is, after 671 B.C.) when the Twenty-sixth Dynasty was threatened so seriously by a succession of Assyrian, Babylonian and Persian military incursions.[25]

The limited reference in the biblical narratives to Egypt and dramatic efforts of her pharaohs during the New Kingdom period is an important fact that must be considered in any reconstruction of the nature and time of the Hebrews' exodus. There is no account of Egypt's conquering armies ravaging the countryside, pillaging and burning villages and towns, nor of the deportation of thousands of peasants into Egyptian bondage, demand and transport of the region's wealth through tribute, nor of towns or cities established and dedicated to the honor of the pharaoh. If, therefore, the Egyptian evidence concerning the New Kingdom period and the biblical portrayal of the temporal context of the exodus may be correlated at all, the exodus event must be found near the end of the period rather than near its beginning. But when we arrive chronologically to the reign of Ramesses II, so many of the isolated details seem to fall into a single sequential whole that *anachronistic aetiology* fails to be descriptive of the biblical narrative.

The Biblical Background of the Hebrews' Exodus

The sequential summary of events leading to the Hebrews' exodus from Egypt provides details essential to an adequate reconstruction of the Sinai itinerary:[26]

1. The original migration to Egypt included 70 members of Jacob's extended family.

2. Joseph died in Egypt, together with his brothers and their generation.

3. The Israelites prospered and their population increased to the point of dominating their region, generally identified with the land of Goshen ...*so the land was filled with them* (Exod. 1:5-7).

4. A new pharaoh arose in Egypt ...*who did not know Joseph.* In view of the fact that Joseph and his generation had long since died, it seems clear that the new pharaoh would have had no opportunity for a personal acquaintanceship with Joseph. It must be assumed, therefore, that *knowing* in this case must refer to the fact that the new

pharaoh 'was not related' to Joseph in the sense that earlier pharaohs possibly were. This change in the relationship of the Hebrews to the Egyptian administration clearly is evident in the biblical reference to the 'policy' change that the new pharaoh instituted in reference to the Hebrews who now seemed to be identified with a dangerous foreign element within Egyptian borders.

a. The new pharaoh clearly differentiated between his own people and the people of Israel.

...*he said to his people, 'Behold, the people of Israel...'* (Exod. 1:9).

b. Israelite numerical strength was viewed as a definite threat to Egyptian political stability.

c. The pharaoh's proposed *new* policy anticipated the possibility that these Israelites could become a 'Fifth Column' within the borders of Egypt.

...*if war befall us, they join our enemies and fight against us...* (Exod. 1:10). If this new pharaoh represents the introduction of Egypt's New Kingdom following a decade and a half of foreign rule under the *Hyksos*, the implications of this danger were vivid in Egyptian minds.

d. The policy also anticipated the possibility of the Hebrews' sudden departure:...*and escape from the land.* This statement seems to pose an additional threat for the Egyptian pharaoh. The departure of the Hebrews clearly was not considered a total solution for the pharaoh in spite of the primary threat Israel posed as a potential 'Fifth Column.' A possible explanation could be the important and possibly essential role the Hebrews played in the economy of the land of Goshen.

5. The new Egyptian pharaoh's policy integrated the Hebrews into public works projects that included the ...*building of store cities, Pithom and Raamses.* This oppressive policy appears not to have achieved the desired results:

a. The population of the Hebrews increased in spite of the oppression.

b. The increased population resulted in a more comprehensive Hebrew control in the land of Goshen.

c. Egyptian concern was heightened rather than diminished.

6. The modification of the Egyptian policy called for an increase in 'quota' requirements of the *corvée* contingents.[27] The rigors of the oppression appear to have spread from the public works projects to the agricultural scene (*...in all kinds of work in the field;...*).

7. The failure of this policy in achieving the desired results prompted the drastic measures of requiring the Hebrew midwives to participate in infanticide.

The Role of Moses[28]

It was into this situation that Moses was born, hidden by his mother along the banks of the Nile, found by the pharaoh's daughter and taken to the pharaoh's courts where he grew into manhood with all of the advantages of the pharaoh's own offspring. Obviously, he received the finest education the pharaoh's court could provide, a preparation that was intended to assure his leadership in the management of the Hebrew enclave in the land of Goshen. The indoctrination of an 'Asiatic' bureaucracy in serving Egyptian interests was a policy initiated by Thutmose III when military incursions and punitive raids into Canaan failed to assure loyalty on the part of local kings. The taking of male family members of Canaanite city rulers to Egypt as hostages tended to ensure faithful conformity to the demands of the Egyptian overlords, and, at the same time, provided an opportunity for 'educating' the hostages into an Egyptian mind-set.

Moses' first assignment among the Hebrews in the land of Goshen unfortunately ended in the pharaoh's displeasure.

When Pharaoh heard of it, he sought to kill Moses. (Exod. 2:15) Moses' flight to the land of Midian, beyond the Sinai, outside Egyptian jurisdiction, was a form of self-imposed exile that lasted until the pharaoh who had sponsored Moses' rise in the Egyptian bureaucracy and who now sought to kill him, died. Integrated by marriage into the family and economy of Jethro, the Midianite priest, Moses ultimately found himself shepherding his father-in-law's flocks in the Sinai. It was there that Yahweh met him at the 'mount of the burning bush' to instruct him in his role as the deliverer of Hebrews from Egyptian bondage.

Moses' instructions in negotiating the Hebrews' release with the
pharaoh and subsequent conversations with the pharaoh are most
instructive in determining the location of the 'mount of the burning
bush' or Horeb which became Mount Sinai of the law-giving:

1. Moses was shepherding his sheep on the 'backside' (in reference
to Midian) or the west side of the desert (Sinai) when he came to
Horeb, 'mount of the burning bush.'

*...and he led his flock to the west side of the wilderness, and came
to Horeb, the mountain of God* (Exod. 3:1).

Since Moses was told specifically that he would return to this
mountain with the Hebrews during the exodus from Egypt, an
awareness of the specific location of this mountain would suggest an
approximate line of march within the border of Egypt.

*...when you have brought forth the people out of Egypt, you shall
serve God upon this mountain.* (Exod. 3:12).

2. The location of Mount Sinai must be sought within a three-days'
journey from the border of Egypt, a site that the pharaoh understood
was not very far away.

*...and you and the elders of Israel shall go to the king of Egypt and
say to him, 'The Lord, the God of the Hebrews, has met with us; and
now, we pray you, let us go a three days' journey into the
wilderness, that we may sacrifice to the Lord our God.'* (Exod.
3:18)

*...Then they said, The God of the Hebrews has met with us; let us
go, we pray, a three days' journey into the wilderness, and sacrifice
to the Lord our God, lest he fall upon us with pestilence or with the
sword.* (Exod. 5:3)

*...We must go three days' journey into the wilderness and sacrifice
to the Lord our God as he will command us. So Pharaoh said, I will
let you go, to sacrifice to the Lord your God in the wilderness; only
you shall not go very far away. Make entreaty for me.* (Exod.
8:27,28)

These statements are consistent and clear. The location of the 'holy
mount' was only *...a three days' journey* from the Egyptian border and
even the pharaoh understood the location as being *...not very far away.*
These details must be considered in determining the specific location
of Mount Sinai. They also have a immediate bearing on the general

direction of the first phase of the itinerary within the borders of Egypt.

Escape from the Land of Goshen

The biblical account of the Exodus begins in the Nile Delta region to which the Hebrews migrated centuries before during a time of drought and famine in Canaan (Gen. 45:10; 46:28). This 'land of Goshen' appears to be situated in the eastern delta where its location was equated with the 'land of Ramesses' in which Ramesses II (ca. 1279-1212 B.C.) built his capital. It was at Raᶜamses and Pithom that the Hebrews were forced to labor in the construction of store-cities during the latter part of their Egyptian sojourn (Exod. 1:11). Pithom (the Egyptian pr-ᶜitm, Per-Atum or Pi-Atum), the 'House of Atum' (sometimes mistakenly identified with Heliopolis), the major worship center of the creator and solar deity of the Egyptian pantheon,[29] also appears to have been located in the eastern delta, near the eastern end of Wadi Tumilat. It is here that two ancient sites, less than 9 miles apart, have claimed identification with the biblical Pithom, Tell er-Retabeh and Tell el-Maskhuta. The discovery of a Roman mile-marker found at Tell el-Maskhuta giving a distance of 9 miles west to Ero (Roman Pithom) seemed convincing evidence for identifying Tell er-Retabeh with Pithom which is exactly 9 Roman miles to the west.[30] Archaeological finds at Tell er-Retabeh indicate that this Middle Kingdom city was abandoned at the end of the *Hyksos* period and was reestablished during the Nineteenth Dynasty.

Our primary focus for understanding the Hebrew sojourn and exodus from Egypt is on the eastern Nile Delta, the frontier of Egypt most vulnerable to a continuous pressure by Asiatic immigrants from the arid Sinai Desert desirous of establishing themselves in its lush, verdant lands. Periodically, Egyptian precautions and defenses were inadequate to stem the tide of Asiatic infiltration. Following the first such instance (The First Intermediate Period), serious effort was committed to the construction of *The-Wall-of-the-Ruler*, a defensive system, generally assumed to be a line of fortresses along the eastern frontier, intended specifically to *...keep out the Asiatics.*

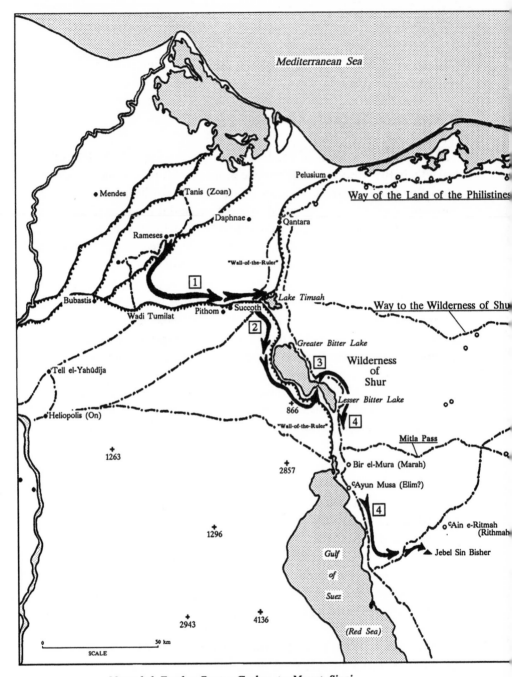

Mediterranean Sea

Pelusium

Way of the Land of the Philistines

Mendes

Tanis (Zoan)

Daphnae

Qantara

Rameses

"Wall-of-the-Ruler"

① →

Lake Timsah

Bubastis

Pithom • Succoth

Wadi Tumilat

②

Way to the Wilderness of Shu

Greater Bitter Lake

③

Wilderness
of
Shur

Tell el-Yahûdîja

Lesser Bitter Lake

866

④

Heliopolis (On)

"Wall-of-the-Ruler"

Mitla Pass

1263

2857

Bir el-Mura (Marah)

ᶜAyun Musa (Elim?)

1296

④

ᶜAin e-Ritmah
(Rithmah

Gulf

Jebel Sin Bisher

of

Suez

2943

4136

(Red Sea)

0   50 km

SCALE

Moses-led Exodus Route: Goshen to Mount Sinai

1. Departure from Rameses along Wadi Tumilat
2. Diverted from Way of Shur at border near Lake Timsah (Etham)
3. Possible crossing of 'Sea' at narrows between Bitter Lakes
4. Followed southerly route to Mount Sinai (Jebel Sin Bisher)

Unfortunately, these defensive structures appear to have been totally inadequate, or the precautions too lax against the so-called 'Amorite Invasion,' that major northwestern Semitic expansion and infiltration that ultimately engulfed the entire Fertile Crescent from the Persian Gulf to Lower Egypt. The impact of this event on the Delta was most significant. The 'foreign rulers' (*Hyksos*) of Lower Egypt established their administrative center in the Delta and for about 150 years Lower Egypt became the western province of Asiatic control.

This focus on the Delta was renewed about two and a half centuries later when the Nineteenth and Twentieth Dynasties established their administrative control over their territories in Syria-Palestine. The archaeological recovery of the nature of these administrative centers and other town sites in the Delta has been problematic due to mudbrick construction rather than the stone and marble construction that characterizes most other Egyptian centers. Recent research at Tell el-Dab'a,[31] a mound ca. 500 m in diameter, has discovered the remains of a vast town site about 7 km north of Faqus on the Tanis road. A natural lake basin, north of the mound, extended 1 km east and west and 500 m to the north. This lake had given Tell el-Dab'a its earlier name, Tell el-Birka (*the mound of the lake*). Ground survey confirmed the existence of an ancient feeder channel (on early survey maps) from the former Pelusiac branch of the Nile to the lake. The overflow of its fresh water supply emptied into the large Bahr el-Baqar drainage system. This means of controlling the lake's level created an ideal inland harbor for the city.

Tell el-Dab'a at one time had extended over 1 km westward to the valley of Khata'na on the east bank of what was the bed of the old Pelusiac branch of the Nile. Within the crescent created by the Pelusiac, Edouard Naville in 1882 excavated graves that yielded Tell el-Yehudiyeh juglets and columns and a sphinx of Queen Sebeknefru (ca. 1789-1785 B.C.) within the enclosure wall of a large temple. More recently, additional statues of the Queen and a Thirteenth Dynasty king named Qemau Sehernedjherjotef were recovered,[32] probably originally kept in the small temple dedicated to their local cult. The immediate vicinity is crowded by a series of mounds. The excavation of Ezbet Rushdi, one of the mounds, has uncovered a large urban center built by Ammenemes I and rebuilt by Sesostris III.

The heterogeneous population at Tell el-Dabᶜa during the Middle Bronze Age had close ties with Phoenicia and secondary links with Cyprus and northern Palestine. Middle Kingdom Egypt maintained intensive relationships with Byblos and Megiddo. Although funerary evidence is limited, the strong Egyptian cultural influence on these Asiatics is reflected in burial customs. While Egyptian luxury items, especially jewelry and alabaster jars, were common in Middle Bronze tombs, the tombs of ethnic Egyptians toward the end of the eighteenth century B.C. appear to reflect the lower economic strata of society.

When, in the late Thirteenth Dynasty, Nehesy or his father established an independent kingdom at Avaris (ca. 1730-1720 B.C.), coincidentally a large royal residence (palace) appeared in the Middle Bronze stratum at Tell el-Dabᶜa. Finds within the palace complex with its Egyptian architectural style suggest an Asiatic presence.

Treasure Cities of Pithom and Rameses

The biblical record identifies three place names associated with the final stages of the Hebrew sojourn in the land of Goshen: Pithom, mentioned only once together with Rameses, as one of the 'cities of store places' (Exodus 1:11);[33] Succoth, the first stop on the exodus itinerary, is mentioned three times in that context (Exodus 12:37; 13:20; and 33:5,6); and Rameses, the store city that was the initial point of departure.

Rameses

The 'land of Ramesses' (Gen. 47:11) generally has been identified with the northeastern Delta or a part of the land of Goshen. According to the Egyptian records, *Per-Ramesses*, the Royal Residence, located between Djahy (Syria) and Egypt, was a substantial place, intended to have the permanence of Memphis. Four separate quarters dedicated to four principal deities surrounded the central core of the city where the royal cult with the worship of Ramesses was maintained. Surrounded by a vast urban population, the city plan was comparable to Thebes. Situated within the productive Delta plain, its granaries were full of barley and emmer wheat -- a massive complex with huge storage buildings and magazines. A lake, possibly artificially constructed, was located near the Residence and a port with seagoing vessels was located either in or near the town.[34] The construction of such supply depots, the public works projects assigned to the Hebrews, obviously facilitated the distribution of supplies to the various institutions operating in or out of the land of Goshen.

Rameses may be identified with two primary centers in the Delta:[35] the Delta capital built by Ramesses II (Pharaoh Ramesses I reigned for only 16 months.) called *Per-Ramesses* (or 'the estate of Ramesses') in the eastern Delta, and a fort guarding an oasis on the route to the Sinai sometimes referred to as 'the dwelling of Ramesses.' (Tanis, with its massive and impressive Ramesside architectural remains, once was considered as the possible site until it became obvious from the French excavations there that the Ramesside materials had been transferred to Tanis and were all in secondary use.) More recently Rameses has been identified with Tell el-Dab°a, dated to both the Middle and New Kingdom periods. Excavations at Qantir (Tell el-Dab°a) have provided ample evidence in foundational materials, bases of statuary, etc. of massive Ramesses II building operations that seemingly at some later time were robbed for construction at Tanis farther north in the Delta where natural building stone for the new capital was unavailable. In spite of such looting, ample evidence of the Twelfth and Nineteenth Dynasty towns have been recovered. It was a large urban center with a vast palace establishment, workshops, magazines, temples, barracks and military quarters. Excavations also produced a rich collection of Middle Bronze pottery of Canaanite/Palestinian origin. To the north the Ramesside palace has been excavated with its monumental architecture and statuary identified with Ramesses' cartouches.

During the Middle Kingdom, Rameses, at an important intersection in the northeastern Delta, became the summer palace of the pharaohs of the Twelfth and Thirteenth Dynasties. When Egypt fell under foreign control, basically the same location, now known as Avaris, became the summer capital of the *Hyksos* kings. With the expulsion of the *Hyksos* in the sixteenth century B.C., a wall was built through the site by one of the early Eighteenth Dynasty pharaohs and then the site was abandoned until the reign of Horemheb, the last pharaoh of the dynasty.

The *Hyksos'* partiality for Tanis and monuments erected there by them (Ramesses II and Merneptah often mentioning Seth and even 'Seth, lord of Avaris') resulted from the fact that Avaris was the *Hyksos* capital and Seth, its god. Thus, the return to *Per-Ramesse*, the northern capital of all the earlier Ramessides, required the dominant recognition of the city's patron deity.[36] A temple dedicated to Seth, the deity of Avaris was constructed, and with the beginning of the Nineteenth Dynasty the city was revived. Seti I's building projects included a summer palace on the northern outskirts, and Ramesses II revived royal interest by building an entirely new city, *Per-Ramesses*, that continued as the second capital during the entire Nineteenth Dynasty. After the reign of Ramesses VI, the city's decline was rapid. Its port succumbed to the silting of the Nile's action and ultimately a new port had to be established farther to the north at the site of Djanᶜnet or Tanis (biblical Zoan). With the building of Tanis came the dismantling of *Per-Ramesses*, the glorious capital of the Ramesside dynasty in the Delta. Its monuments and buildings were dismantled and transported approximately 17 miles northward to construct a new capital for the Twenty-first, Twenty-second, and Twenty-fifth Dynasties. From about 1100 to 600 B.C., throughout what is generally known as the Third Intermediate Period, Zoan (Tanis) served as the administrative center of the Delta.

Pithom

Pithom, a probable transcription of the Egyptian *Pi-Atum* (actually *Per-Atum*, where the *r* has been dropped), may best be sought in the vicinity of Succoth. Succoth (in Hebrew) appears to be a transcription of the Egyptian word *Tjeku* which is associated with the eastern frontier and the urban centers along Wadi Tumilat. In Papyrus Anastasi IV, *Tjeku* is located in close proximity to *Per-Ramesses* and is a region suitable for keeping horses (near the frontier where military expeditions utilizing chariotry were initiated). Ostracon 106 from Deir el-Medina refers to the *three waters of Pharaoh* in this region of *Tjeku*, possibly the same water pools mentioned in Papyrus Anastasi IV, from the reign of Pharaoh Merneptah, the son and successor of Ramesses II. According to this document, the *Shasu* tribes, possibly from Edom, were allowed to cross the eastern border and pass the fort of Merneptah in *Tjeku* to reach the water pools in order to replenish their food and water supply. The pools are referred to as *the water pools of Merneptah in Tjeku.*

Succoth

The name 'Succoth' seemingly is retained in the Arabic Tell el-Maskhuta, which also appears to be the location of the biblical site. Tell el-Maskhuta is located 15 km west of Ismailia in the Wadi Tumilat, one of the major corridors between Egypt and the Levant or Arabia. The canal along Wadi Tumilat, begun by Pharaoh Necho ca. 610 B.C. and completed by Darius the Great during the Persian Period, served east-west shipping as well as irrigation of extensive agriculture in the area. However, an earlier canal along the wadi is possibly dated to the early Middle Kingdom period.[37] The wadi may have played a major role in the immigration of the Asiatic pastoralists who were the forerunners of the *Hyksos*.[38] At both Tell el-Mashkuta and Tell el-Dab^c^a there is ample evidence of large scale incursions of 'pre-*Hyksos*' Asiatics from Syria and Palestine, seemingly drawn to an attractive, underpopulated eastern frontier region during the Middle Kingdom.[39] The identification of Succoth with this site, however, appears to be problematic archaeologically because of the cultural gap which appears to extend from the end of the MB IIa to the Saite/Persian period. The implication of 'Succoth' (*temporary dwellings*) at the point of departure of the itinerary is consistent with a gap in legitimate urbanization. If limited to the exodus experience, the term may refer to the temporary Israelite encampment. If, as generally accepted, Tell el-Maskhuta may be identified as the location of Succoth, Tell el-Retabeh, about eight miles to the west along Wadi Tumilat, seems a logical location for Pithom. A temple from the reign of Ramesses II honoring the gods Atum and Seth suggests that the city at Tell el-Retabeh gave its allegiance to the god Atum of *Tjeku* during the Nineteenth Dynasty. The identification of the Egyptian term *Tjeku* with the urban center, Succoth, and the region of the eastern frontier along the Wadi Tumilat, including Pithom, appears most probable.

Farewell to Goshen

Theories regarding the points of departure from Egypt and the Sinai itineraries may be categorized according to the major routes across the Sinai and the principal bodies of water located along Egypt's eastern frontier (from north to south): Lake Balah, Lake Timsah, The Great and Lesser Bitter Lakes, and the Gulf of Suez. The northern route, identified in the Bible as *'the way of the land of the Philistines'* beyond Qantara was known as the 'Way of Horus.' The Egyptian military presence along this route (*Via Maris*) during the New Kingdom period included supply depots at primary water sources. Any movement along this route inevitably would have resulted in an Hebrew confrontation with Egyptian military for access to the limited capacity of these springs. Whatever the exodus route, concern about the location of water sources, evident in the regular reference to water in the exodus narrative, and the adequacy of such sources for the migratory Israelites, was constant.

The Way of the Land of the Philistines

According to the biblical account, the itinerary of the Hebrews began at Rameses with a southeastern movement toward Succoth. This initial move required the explanation that the *Via Maris*, or *the way of the land of the Philistines* would not be followed because the departing Israelites were not willing (or able) to overcome the military resistance that they would encounter along that route. The obvious detour in the Sinai and later through the Transjordan was prompted by a clear knowledge of the firm control the Egyptians maintained not only on the *Via Maris* but also on the coastal plains of Canaan itself. (The sole exception of Egyptian interest and overt domination appears to have been the central hill country.)[40] Archaeological excavation at a number of oases located on the coastal road along the northern shoreline of the Sinai has confirmed the existence of military forts that guarded the intermittent water sources and served as overnight stops for Egyptian couriers and garrisons moving back and forth between Egypt and the provinces to the northeast. This reluctance to risk the return of the Hebrews to Egypt partially explains the southeastern detour chosen by Moses.[41] As we will see later, the negative attitudes and indecisiveness of the Hebrews and their ingratitude and periodic rejection of Moses' leadership may be explained by the fact that Moses was called upon to lead those Hebrews who had insufficient initiative and motivation to leave Egypt on their own. After 430 years in Egypt, many Hebrews not only had an Egyptian orientation but had succumbed to a 'slave mentality' that appreciated leeks and onions over freedom and the Promised Land. While other evidence obviously is more direct, the Bible seems to infer that others had left Egypt in earlier times when it states:

...at the end of four hundred and thirty years, on that very day, all the hosts of the Lord went out from the land of Egypt. (Exod. 12:40)

A possible implication is that though others had departed in earlier times, this particular exiting group...on that very day completed the process. Following the Second Intermediate Period and the collapse of Hyksos' control in Egypt, the military campaigns of the early Eighteenth Dynasty established an Egyptian empire that ultimately reached from the Fourth Cataract of the Nile to the banks of the Euphrates. Primarily the long series of expeditions by Thutmose III (1504-1450 B.C.) forged the dimensions as well as many of the administrative policies of the New Kingdom. Archaeological evidence and many relevant Egyptian documents provide a comprehensive insight into the intimate cultural contacts and commercial interchange between Egypt and its subservient neighbors to the northeast.[42]

It was during this period of almost 300 years that the Northern Sinai gained special significance as the land bridge for military domination and commercial exploitation of Upper and Lower Retenu (Syria and Palestine). From the eastern Delta to the border of Canaan, the Via Maris was maintained by a network of fortified way stations providing supplies for Egyptian military efforts and those non-Egyptian caravans qualified to use its convenience by payment of required customs and road tax. Garrisons manning the forts effectively secured access to the oases along the 250 km (150 mile) distance between Sile[43] and Gaza and assured free, uninterrupted flow of military and materiel across the northern Sinai. Military occupation in the area was enhanced dramatically during the reign of Seti I who revived Egyptian control in Canaan following the uncertain policies maintained by Amenhotep IV. Punitive raids against Sinai nomads obviously were intended to ensure safety along the primary routes. The establishment of permanent fortified administrative centers, a significant innovation of the Nineteenth Dynasty, demanded a greater urgency for constant control on all vital links between Egypt and the strategic centers scattered throughout Canaan and beyond Damascus in southern Syria.

While Merneptah's military efforts (1223-1213 B.C.) already may have shown some signs of a tenuous Egyptian control, the period of his successors, Seti II and Twosert (1199-1185 B.C.) clearly reflected the rapid decline and end of Egypt's domination in Canaan.[44] The interest of the Egyptian pharaoh in the region, however, did not completely wane. A number of monuments dated to the reign of Seti II indicate continued presence and involvement in the turquoise and copper mines of the Arabah and Sinai and some sites in Canaan.[45] Ramesses III's defeat of the Sea Peoples and the subsequent settlement of the Philistines in the southern coastal region of Canaan as vassals of Egypt reflects in part the pharaoh's attempt at maintaining administrative control. The reigns of subsequent pharaohs (Ramesses V or VI) indicate a total withdrawal within the borders of the Nile Delta.

The importance of this primary military road during the reign of Ramesses II is reflected in a papyrus document (Papyrus Anastasi I) that lists not only the major fortified urban centers in southern Canaan, but also the way stations across the northern Sinai.[46] The stations and fortresses guarding the oases along the 'Ways of Horus,' are depicted in Seti I's reliefs on the north wall of the great Hypostyle Hall in the Amun Temple at Karnak. This document appears to commemorate the successes of the Nineteenth Dynasty in reestablishing Egyptian military and administrative control in southern Canaan at least. Punitive raids against the *Shasu* tribes in the Northern Sinai seemingly were deemed necessary to establish control along the coastal road.[47]

The Karnak reliefs depict additional topographical features for understanding the Egypt/Sinai border. A north-south canal, with crocodiles and reed-lined banks, implying a fresh water environment, identified as *Ta-denit* (dividing waters) runs diagonally into the Mediterranean. Traces of such an ancient waterway recently have been discovered between Pelusium and Qantara.[48] This canal primarily served a dual role along Egypt's eastern frontier. As a major fresh water source for irrigation along the eastern extremity of the Delta region it served as a vital inland waterway for maritime trade. At the same time it became a most effective barrier against nomadic infiltration and a deterrent against possible military invasion. These factors became primary considerations during the reign of the Nineteenth Dynasty when *Pi-Ramesse* in the eastern Delta became the political and administrative center of Lower Egypt.

It is now clear that the biblical Ramesses is identical with *Pi-Ramesse* and that the starting point of the exodus was from Tell el-Dabᶜa-Qantir. At that point the possible options for escape appear to have been limited by the current water courses and irrigation channels. The Pelusiac and the Bahr el-Baqar drainage system created a relatively narrow passage from the Nile Delta to the Darb el-Sultan (Hajj).[49]

The Hebrews' move from *Per-Ramesses* to Succoth clarifies the reason for Pithom's exclusion from the exodus itinerary. Pithom's location west along Wadi Tumilat removed it from the direct line of march toward the frontier. The Hebrews' subsequent move to the Egypt-Sinai border at Etham *on the edge of the desert* seems to imply an easterly direction in the vicinity of modern Ismailia near Lake Timsah.

Etham

When the Israelites moved eastward from Succoth to Etham ...*on the edge of the wilderness* (the eastern frontier of Egypt), they logically assumed that, having avoided the shortest route along the *Via Maris*, they naturally would take the next shortest route, departing Egypt in the vicinity of Lake Timsah and continuing directly to Kadesh-barnea. Along this route they would have followed the line of oases on the southern edge of the sand dunes that extend across the northern Sinai. It was at this point that Moses was instructed to redirect the line of march, by a retreat from the eastern frontier, back to Succoth, and a continuation of the southeastern march within the borders of Egypt (Exod. 13:20; 14:1). Moses' instructions were very specific:

Tell the Israelites to return and encamp near Pi-Hahiroth, between Migdol and the sea. (Exodus 14:1)

The instructions to Moses appear to direct the Hebrews to return to the original line or direction of march originally established from Rameses to Succoth. Following this adjustment, they were facing (or 'directly opposite', according to 14:2) *Baal Zaphon* (in a southerly direction), with *Migdol* and the sea they were about to cross on either side. It is not too difficult to assume that this *Baal Zaphon* was located at the head of the Gulf of Suez, a sanctuary dedicated to the deity by Phoenician sailors plying the Red Sea in Egyptian interests. In fact, if the Gulf of Suez, the Bitter Lakes, Lake Timsah and Wadi Tumilat were all linked by inland waterways permitting shipping into Succoth, Pithom and other urban centers in the Delta, the reference to a prominent sanctuary dedicated to a Semitic deity would be quite natural.

The Environmental 'Trap'

The continuation on this southeastern line brought the Israelites into a region where the physical conditions made escape impossible. Even the pharaoh recognized that with his military he could force their return: *...They are entangled in the land; the wilderness has shut them in* (Exod. 14:3). This locale, as described in the biblical text, is distinguished by four specific features: *Pi-hahiroth*, *Migdol* (fortress), *Baal-zaphon*, and *the sea*. The combination of these features, the wilderness and the pharaoh's army meant the Israelites' position was completely untenable. It was from this impossible situation that the way of escape was provided through the midst of *the sea*.

Pi-hahiroth

The specific details concerning the physical environment in which the Israelites were trapped obviously were intended to clarify and identify the locale of their dilemma. If the term *Pi-hahiroth* may be understood as 'the mouth of the depression, or diggings,' as has been suggested, the reference may be to the eastern end of Wadi Tumilat or other aspects of the man-made water systems that were related to it. The canal initiated by Pharaoh Necho and completed by Darius the Great ran from the eastern branch of the Nile, slightly to the south of Bubastis at the western entrance to Wadi Tumilat, along the entire length of the wadi to Lake Timsah and then turned southward into the Gulf of Suez.

Recently, however, the course of a much earlier canal was discovered that extended northward from Lake Timsah to the vicinity of Qantara and on to the Mediterranean coastline. A cross-section of the canal revealed a 20 m width at the base and a 70 m width at the top. A depiction of this canal has been identified with a relief of Seti I in which the pharaoh, returning from a Palestinian campaign, is shown in his chariot behind three columns of Asiatic captives. Between Seti's entourage and the welcoming Egyptian population is a bridge across a reed-lined canal near the frontier fortress town of Sile. This waterway, extending inland, was identified as *Ta-denit* (with the definite article). The term *Ta-denit* may be translated 'dam,' 'ditch,' 'dike,' 'canal,' or 'revetment.' This canal, its course details clearly identified and defined by modern aerial photos and ground level survey, appears already to have been in use during Seti I's reign in the fourteenth century B.C. Possibly it was constructed as a defensive barrier along the eastern frontier after the expulsion of the *Hyksos* rulers at the end of the Second Intermediate Period.[50]

The canal's construction actually had three possible purposes: navigation, irrigation and defense. The primary purpose undoubtedly was not navigation since Egyptian ships had easier access to the Mediterranean through the branches of the Nile. Irrigation, obviously, could have been a secondary purpose. The area bordering the line of the canal, however, was not ideal for land reclamation. The primary purpose of the canal appears to have been an effective barrier to stop the Asiatics. The 'Wall-of-the-Ruler' already mentioned in *The Story of Sinuhe* probably was constructed at the end of the First Intermediate Period by the early pharaohs of the Middle Kingdom. This line of defense was a canal with high embankments, partially filled with water, that could effectively deter illicit nomadic incursions. In *The Instructions for Merikare*, Merikare was given detailed specifications for the construction of this canal. *The Prophecy of Neferty*[51] which depicts a brief interregnum at the beginning of the twentieth century B.C., between the Eleventh and Twelfth Dynasties, emphasizes the need of dealing with the Asiatic problem. Amenemhet I was to build the 'Wall-of-the-Ruler' so that

*...the Asiatics will not be permitted to come down into Egypt that
they might beg for water in the customary manner, in order to let
their hearts drink.*[52]

The discovery of this canal also appears to clarify the nature of the
'Wall-of-the-Ruler' which probably was not a fortress or a series of
forts along a defensive line, but the actual wall of the earthen ramparts
of the canal. Note the details of Sinuhe's escape at Egypt's eastern
frontier:

*...I came up to the Wall-of-the-Ruler, made to oppose the Asiatics
and crush the Sand-Crossers. I took a crouching position in a bush,
for fear lest watchmen upon the wall where their day's (duty) was
might see me.*[53]

In Merikare's instruction, the 'ramparts' of the canal were to be
...warlike, its warriors many. As a defensive feature, the canal formed
a double wall with a central moat. If one arm of the canal ran from the
northern coast to Lake Timsah, it probably was linked there with the
canal along Wadi Tumilat from the Nile. In the Exodus narrative, the
reference to *Pi-hahiroth* (the mouth of the diggings, or canal?) may
indicate a location near the connection of Wadi Tumilat and the canal
running northward to the Mediterranean. On the other hand, it is
possible that the Necho-Darius canal that ran from Wadi Tumilat to
the Gulf of Suez also had a predecessor in the early second
millennium B.C. It hardly seems logical that the need for stopping the
Asiatics was non-existent south of the Bitter Lakes. A comparable
canal in this area would explain the environmental 'trap' the pharaoh
referred to when he made his decision to force the Hebrews' return:
...They are entangled in the land; the wilderness has shut them in
(Exodus 14:3).

Migdol

The existence of a *Migdol* (stronghold or fortress) along the line of
Egypt's eastern frontier is consistent with any efforts to control access
from the Sinai. If the defensive system associated with the Timsah-to-
Mediterranean canal did not extend to the south, especially between
the Bitter Lakes and the Gulf of Suez, the need for a line of forts
would have been essential to complete control of nomadic incursions.
Though the practice is more in keeping with the period of the

patriarchs (Gen. 12:10; 26:1-6; 42:1ff.) than with a New Kingdom setting, Egyptian hospitality to nomadic groups in allowing them to cross the fortified eastern frontier in time of famine is well documented:

...[We] have finished letting the Bedouin (Shasu) tribes of Edom pass the Fortress of Merneptah... which is (in) Tjeku (Succoth) to the pools of Per-Atum (Pithom) ...to keep them alive and to keep their cattle alive...I have had them brought in a copy of the report to the [place where] my lord is, as well as the other names of days when the Fortress of Merneptah...which is (in) Tjeku, may be passed...[54]

The reference to *the fortress of Merneptah* indicates the existence of free-standing defensive installations at primary points of entry along the Egyptian frontier. Another letter reporting the pursuit of slaves who had escaped to Asia (the Sinai) from Egypt also is informative:

...following these two slaves...when I reached the enclosure-wall of Tjeku...they told [me] they were saying to the south that they (the slaves) had passed by...[Now] when [I] reached the fortress, they told me that the scout (or groom?) had come from the desert [saying that] they (the slaves) had passed the walled place north of the Migdol of Seti-Merneptah...[55]

The most natural reading of these passages suggests that there was a *Migdol of Seti-Merneptah* south of the eastern end of Wadi Tumilat. In fact Cairo papyrus 31169 mentions four places called 'Migdol' that appear to be at least in the vicinity of Wadi Tumilat rather than on the Mediterranean coast. It is entirely possible that one of them was identified with *Baal Zaphon*.[56] Historical and archaeological evidence requires the exodus of at least some groups in the context of the late Nineteenth Dynasty.[57]

The (Red) Sea

The Hebrew term *yam suph* in a number of biblical passages clearly refers to the body of water that we know as the Red Sea (more precisely one or the other of the two arms of the Red Sea known as the 'Gulf of Suez' and the 'Gulf of Aqaba, or Elath'). Attempts at providing a symbolic meaning for the term have been less than satisfying for an understanding of the historical event that delivered the Hebrews from Egyptian bondage.[58] The historical reality of the Hebrews' deliverance and their ultimate formulation of the nation of Israel found its development in specific time-place conditions. Many of those physical locales obviously are beyond our ability to reconstruct, given the sparsity of their documentation.

Baal Zaphon

The term *Baal Zaphon* generally has been associated with the patron deity of Semitic (Tyrian?) mariners and the small temples or sanctuaries established for their use in harbor facilities especially along the Mediterranean coastline. Their activity in the estuaries and canals of the Nile was quite natural in view of the intense Egyptian interest in Lebanese lumber and other products. Access to the Gulf of Suez is totally feasible and the possibility of a shrine dedicated to the 'Baal of the North' would not be unusual in any maritime setting.

In summary, the significant details in the biblical narrative discussion of the Hebrews' progress from Pithom and Ramesses seem to suggest that the *Way of the land of the Philistines* (i.e, *Via Maris*) and the *Way of the Wilderness of Shur*, the two more northerly routes across the Sinai were not taken. They were instructed to "*Turn back!*" when they approached the Shur Road at Etham. Only the great pilgrimage and caravan route linking the northern end of the Gulf of Suez with the northern end of the Gulf of Aqaba remained as a third option across the northern Sinai. But even if this route is rejected as a possible itinerary, their movement within Egypt proper surely brought them southward into the region bordering the Bitter Lakes where the desolation of the region inland to the west and the major bodies of water and the defensive line of the canal and/or line of forts created an untenable situation for escape. The 'low key' description of the miraculous escape of the Hebrews is refreshing in contrast to more recent creative 'flights of fancy' concocted to tickle the imaginations of those who lack an appreciation for the historicity of the biblical text.[59]

Crossing the Red Sea

The location for the crossing of the Red Sea must satisfy a number of basic biblical statements if we consider them to have any historical validity:

1. If the Hebrew word *suf* may be translated 'reed' as well as 'red', it is possible that the body of water the Hebrews crossed was 'fresh,' thus permitting the growth of reeds.

2. The point of crossing must be affected significantly by an East wind to allow for the displacement of the water along the route of crossing (Exod. 14:21,22).

3. The point of crossing must be narrow enough to permit the Hebrew crossing within a single night.

4. The sudden return of the displaced water (resulting from the subsidence of the strong East wind) overwhelmed the pursuing Egyptian army. The biblical account implies that the drowned Egyptian soldiers that the Hebrews saw the next morning should be expected on the eastern shore of the body of water they so recently had crossed (Exod. 14:30).

The possibility that the Bitter Lakes were the 'Sea of Reeds' referred to in the biblical text appears most unlikely under present conditions when these inland lakes are not only salty but alkaline from sulfuric gypsum deposits. However prior to A.D. 767 when Muhammad Abdullah blocked the channel of Wadi Tumilat, the overflow of the Nile from Wadi Tumilat regularly supplied the Bitter Lakes with fresh water.[60] Though these lakes are 22 miles long and 7 miles wide, they are linked by a relatively narrow channel positioned in such a way that the force of an 'east wind' could affect adequate displacement of water to create a passage to the wilderness of Shur on its eastern shore.

The identification of the Bitter Lakes with the Red Sea also provides a possible explanation for the biblical references to *Migdol* and *Baal Zaphon*. The mention of *Baal Zaphon* (*...in front of Baal Zaphon*), possibly a shrine dedicated by Phoenician sailors to their patron saint at the head of the Gulf of Suez, may suggest the Israelite location along the western shore of the Bitter Lakes.[61] Only a single route of escape appeared possible: penetration through the *Wall-of-*

the-Ruler, the defensive system established along Egypt's eastern border following the First Intermediate Period. Thus the reference to a *Migdol* (stronghold) obviously would indicate that one of the fortress along that defensive line stood in the Israelites' escape route. The pharaoh appeared confident that his military unit stationed there would be adequate to thwart the Israelite advance. To the west and south the Egyptian desert provided no hope for the Israelites with not a single oasis within a reasonable distance of their present location.

An additional physical element, emphasized in the biblical account but often overlooked in reconstructions of this aspect of the Israelite escape is the role of the *...strong east wind* (Exod. 14:21). If the biblical account is to be taken seriously, the place of the Red Sea crossing must allow for the displacement of water by a *strong east wind*. The tendency on the part of most conservative students of the Bible is to overlook or willfully disregard the significance of the biblical reference to this physical phenomenon. Of interest is the fact that the 'drift' configuration of the sand dunes east of the Bitter Lakes is irrefutable evidence of prevailing east-west winds in this region. While these elements in themselves do not provide conclusive evidence for the location of *Red Sea* crossing at the 'narrows' between the Lesser and the Greater of the Bitter Lakes, the collective harmony of the itinerary reconstruction and the tentative identification of some locations along the itinerary following the crossing provide a holistic picture with few of the problems that some other reconstructions face.

From the Wilderness of Shur to Mount Sinai[62]

The biblical narrative for the recording of the events between the border of Egypt and Kadesh-barnea takes the form of scribal diary entries, consistent with archival documentation found in official military records. The basic documents quite naturally would derive from the Moses-led contingent at the end of the emigration. The Hebrew leadership, having been educated in the pharaoh's court, were thoroughly familiar with the nature of the official annals of the pharaohs in the periodic military campaigns. It would seem quite natural that the recording of important events of the Sinai wanderings should duplicate the literary forms of the Egyptian scribe. (It seems

almost inconceivable that such parallels should be sought among the
annalistic texts of the Assyrian kings of the 9th century B.C.)[63] The
exodus annals obviously took on a militaristic flavor because their
prototypes probably were the military annals of the Eighteenth and
Nineteenth Dynasties.

The Wilderness of Shur

*...Then Moses led Israel onward from the Red Sea, and they went
into the wilderness of Shur; they went three days in the wilderness
and found no water.* (Exod. 15:22)

The wilderness beyond Etham (Num. 33:6) and the Wilderness of
Shur (wall) beyond the sea may refer to the Sinai frontier approaching
the 'Wall-of-the-Ruler' that had been intended to keep out the
Asiatics. During the next three days in the Wilderness of Shur, moving
generally southward from the eastern shore of the Lesser Bitter Lake,
and finding no water, the Israelites came to *Marah* (bitter).

Marah

*...When they came to Marah, they could not drink the water of
Marah because it was bitter: therefore it was named Marah.* (Exod.
15:23)

An oasis, Bir el-Murah ('bitter well' in Arabic) located less than 10
miles east of modern Suez and 25 miles south of the suggested Bitter
Lakes crossing, may satisfy the location of Marah, a plausible three
day trek through this region of sand dunes. Its *bitter* water, finding its
source in gypsum and sulphur deposits, is highly saline.

Elim

*...Then they came to Elim, where there were twelve springs of water
and seventy palm trees; and they encamped there by the water.*
(Exod. 15:27)

The extended encampment at Elim (Exod. 15:27) may be identified
with ᶜAyun Musa, described as having 12 sources of water and a grove
of date palms and tamarisks extending over half a mile.[64] Located
about 7 miles from Bir el-Mura, ᶜAyun Musa is the largest and richest
oasis along the northern coastal region of the Gulf of Suez. It appears

that the Hebrews' move from Elim into the Wilderness of Sin came only about a month and a half later (Exod. 16:1).

The Wilderness of Sin

...They set out from Elim, and all the congregation of the people of Israel came to the wilderness of Sin, which is between Elim and Sinai,... (Exod. 16:1)

The departure from Elim immediately brought the Hebrews into both the Wilderness of Sin and the vicinity of Rephidim, Horeb, the Wilderness of Sinai and Sinai itself (Compare: Exod. 16:1; 17:1; 17:6; 18:5; 19:1,2). The need for adequate water sources became a logistical problem as they anticipated moving into the Sinai interior. This region may be identified with Wadi Suder, an area of arable land in the valleys and on the slopes of the mountains surrounding it, and a juncture for main routes leading to destinations of primary importance to the Egyptians: a northeastern route led through the oasis of Kadesh-barnea toward Moab and the southern border of Canaan; the route to the east led directly to Edom and Midian (Exod. 18:1-5); and a southern route reached the mining zone being exploited by the Egyptians in the Sinai. All of these roads provided direct access to the eastern border of Egypt. The importance of this juncture well may explain the life-and-death struggle with the Amalekites who seemingly sensed a threat to their domination of these vital trade arteries (Exod. 17:8-16).

Rephidim

...All the congregation of the people of Israel moved on from the wilderness of Sin by stages, according to the commandment of the Lord, and camped at Rephidim; but there was no water for the people to drink. (Exod. 17:1)

It is interesting to note that the visit of Jethro, Moses' father-in-law from the land of Midian, occurred at this juncture of the itinerary (Exod. 18). The impression is that the location of the meeting was prearranged. However that may have been, the meeting appears to take place in the immediate vicinity of Mount Sinai (Exod. 19:1,2).

The encampment before the mount within the Desert of Sinai occurred in the third month following their departure from Egypt, a

destination within an arc of *three-days' journey* from the eastern
border of Egypt (Exod.3:1,18; 5:3; 8:27,28). It seems illogical to think
that Moses' consistent description of the location of the place of
worship during his discussions with the pharaoh were either
misleading or untrue. We must assume that the pharaoh was fully
cognizant not only of the distance but the actual location to which
Moses was referring. The identification of the 'covenant mountain' in
relatively close proximity to the eastern border in keeping with the
biblical description then becomes logical. The 'burning bush'
experience is described as taking place in the western part of the Sinai
peninsula (Exod. 3:1). It is on this basis that the identification of Sinai
with Jebel Sin Bisher (or another mountain in the western peninsula)
becomes reasonable.[65] Jebel Sin Bisher is located approximately
seventy-five kilometers, or forty-five miles from the Bitter Lakes,
within the limits of a *three-days' journey* from the Egyptian border.[66]

The 'Mountain of God'

*...And Jethro, Moses' father-in-law, came with his sons and his wife
to Moses in the wilderness where he was encamped at the mountain
of God.* (Exod.18:5)

The *mountain of God* was the initial destination of the Hebrew
exodus and its identification with Horeb, the place of the burning bush
and Moses' earlier encounter with Yahweh, is clear.

*...Now Moses...led his flock to the west side of the wilderness, and
came to Horeb, the mountain of God...Then the Lord said,
'...when you have brought forth the people out of Egypt, you shall
serve God upon this mountain.'* (Exod. 3:1,12)

Moses' specific request for the release of the Hebrews presumably was
to allow them 'pilgrimage rights' to this mountain which, according
to repeated statements as to its location, was *three days' journey* (Ex.
3:18; 5:3; 8:27) from the border of Egypt. When the pharaoh finally
conceded to Moses' request, his only condition was:

*I will let you go, to sacrifice to the Lord your God in the
wilderness; only <u>you shall not go very far away</u>.* (Exod. 8:28)

From the biblical narrative it would seem clear that the location of
this mountain of the burning bush and the giving of the Law, Horeb

or Sinai, should be sought on the western side of the Sinai peninsula,
not far (within *three days' journey*) from the border of Egypt. The
question then arises, very obviously, why there has been a
proliferation of locations that biblical scholars in the past have tried
to promote as the *real* mountain of Yahweh's visitation with Moses.
At least thirteen locations scattered throughout the Sinai and the
western fringe of the Arabian Desert have been proposed for various
reasons.[67]

Mount Sinai in Arabia

Identifications of Mount Sinai in the Saudi-Arabian peninsula,
primarily based on misinterpretation of geographical data, are largely
discounted today. The Apostle Paul's statement concerning *Mount
Sinai in Arabia* (Gal. 4:25) has misled some biblical scholars to
assume on the basis of more modern boundaries that the sacred
mountain must be sought beyond the Arabah. Greek and Roman
historians including Josephus identified the Sinai peninsula, the Gulf
of Suez and even the area of Goshen within the territory of 'Arabia.'
'Goshen' (Gen. 46:34) was translated *Gesem of Arabia* in the
Septuagint and consequently the New Testament reference to Mount
Sinai in Arabia was consistent with the current geographical context.
This misunderstanding, however, together with Josephus' reference to
Mount Sinai as the highest mountain in the vicinity[68] resulted in the
identification of Mount Baggir, overlooking the northeastern shore of
the Gulf of Aqaba, with Sinai.[69] In this case, as in most others, once
the basic equation with Mount Sinai was made, other physical
conditions in the vicinity generally were found to give credence to the
identification. Thus, a mosque at the base and a saint's grave and a
sacrificial altar on the summit indicate the sacred character of Mount
Baggir. As a consequence, Mount Ertowa nearby has been identified
as Mount Horeb and the location of Rephidim and the plain between
the two mountains became the location of the Israelite encampment
during the giving of the Law. Mount Baggir (elev. 1592 m) is the
highest of the mountains of Seir, followed by Mount Harun (elev.
1336 m), overlooking Petra on the west, which has been identified by
some with Mount Hor.[70]

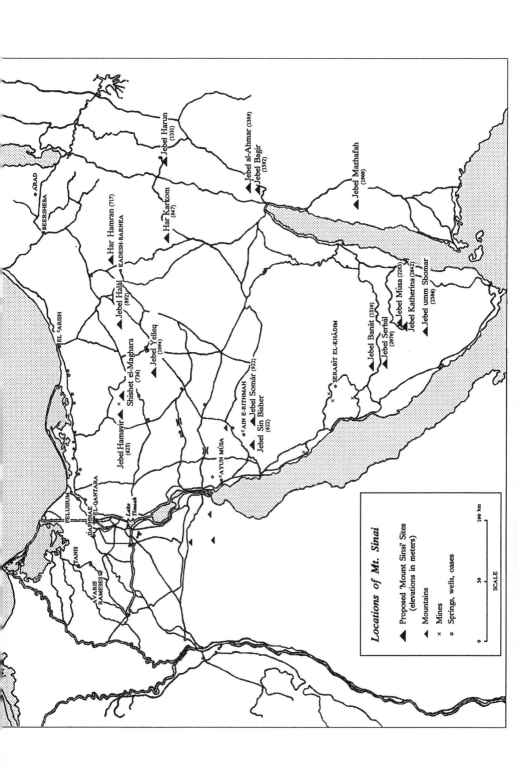

Locations of Mt. Sinai

▲ Proposed 'Mount Sinai' Sites
  (elevations in meters)

▲ Mountains

✕ Mines

o Springs, wells, oases

```
0          50         100 km
SCALE
```

ARAD

BEERSHEBA

Jebel Harun (1331)

Jebel al-Ahmar (1389)
Jebel Bagir (1592)

Jebel Mazhafah (1900)

Har Hamran (717)
KADESH-BARNEA

Har Karkom (847)

EL ʿARISH

Jebel Halal (892)

Jebel Yelleq (1094)

Shishet el-Maghara (736)

Jebel Banât (1350)
Jebel Serbâl (2070)

Jebel Mûsa (2285)
Jebel Katherina (2642)
Jebel umm Shomar (2586)

Jebel Hamayir (625)

SERABÎT EL-KHÂDIM

ʿAIN E-RITHMAH

Jebel Somâr (922)

Jebel Sin Bisher (622)

ʿAYUN MÛSA

PELUSIUM

DAPHNAE
TEL-QANTARA

Lake Timsah

TANIS

AVARIS
RAMESES

The biblical reference to fire and smoke accompanying Yahweh's meeting with Moses on Sinai has required a volcanic setting for some scholars and a location in southern Midian at Se'ib al-Harob, in the volcanic area adjoining Medina and Tebouq. Moses' identification with Jethro, the priest of Midian, and the suggestion that the moon god, the principal deity of primitive Arabs, was identified with Mount Sinai, was used to support the Arabian locale. The theory that *Sin* and *Sinai* originated from the Babylonian moon-god and the references to *Sin* in Arabic and Ethiopian inscriptions also provided a basis for identifying Petra with Sinai.[71]

Mount Sinai in the Southern Peninsula

The most prominent identifications have been clustered in the high, rugged terrain of the granite mountains of the southern part of the Sinai peninsula. However, archaeological research in the southern Sinai has contributed practically nothing to our understanding of the Exodus. No progress has been made in locating the specific Israelite encampments, in identifying their route or in evidence for the location of Mt. Sinai itself. Yet, five primary candidates for Mount Sinai exist in the southern peninsula: the traditional Mount Sinai, Jebel Musa, Jebel Catherina and Jebel Safsafa in the immediate vicinity, and Jebel Serbal and Jebel Banat near the Feiran oasis approaching the Gulf of Suez.

The birth of monasticism in the Byzantine period saw a spread of thousands of monks into the desert regions of the eastern Mediterranean, Asia Minor and Upper Egypt. Before the end of the fourth century, large communities already had established themselves in Sinai, a development that reached its zenith under the Emperor Justinian in the sixth century. Ecological studies within the region have identified the conditions conducive to monastic life. Elevations between 4000-6500 feet where red granite formations enhanced runoff of limited rain and melting snow created conditions that could sustain limited agriculture and orchards in the good alluvial soils of isolated mountain valleys.[72] The identification of various mountains with the *Mount of God* of the Israelite exodus has been related, for the most part, with the five monastic centers that developed in the southern Sinai:

Jebel Musa, the traditional Mount Sinai

Since Byzantine times, Jebel Musa has claimed the biblical name Mount Sinai (or Horeb). Its peak rises to 7370 feet within the southern granite range. The most prominent monastic order developed at the base of Jebel Musa in the monastery of Santa Catherina.

Jebel Catherina

The crest of Jebel Catherina at nearly 9000 feet dwarfs Jebel Musa as one of a number of lesser peaks to its north. Nabataean inscriptions identify the mountain as a pilgrimage center in pre-Byzantine times. Its sanctity also was identified with the worship of Hathor-Baalath as a result of mining operations in the region.

Jebel Safsafa

Jebel Safsafa, near St. Catherina's monastery, reaches an elevation of 6739 feet above sea level. Though its actual height above the El-Raha plain is only 1870 feet, its isolated grandeur and prominence apart from the range often has robbed Jebel Musa of the distinction as the *Mountain of God.*[73] It was identified in Byzantine times with biblical Horeb. Its slopes are steep and barren of vegetation, except for several small mountain valleys with fertile alluvial soil within its heights.

Jebel Serbal

Among the lower mountains of the southern region, Jebel Serbal (elev. 6825 feet) is the most impressive peak because of its isolation from the southern range. The desert oasis of Feiran that stretches for several miles from the base of Mount Serbal is watered by springs fed by the melting snows that enshroud the high summits of these mountains in winter. Dominating the central part of the oasis is a tell and extensive ruins dated to the Judean kingdom (Iron Age II), Hellenistic, Nabatean, Roman-Byzantine and early Arab periods. The tell of this oasis is the only evidence of a fairly prolonged continuity of settlement in the southern Sinai.

The Feiran oasis is located on the primary road from the Gulf of Suez leading into the Jebel Musa region and from there continuing to Dhahab on the Gulf of Aqaba (Elath). In Wadi Feiran and especially in nearby Wadi Mukattab (Valley of the Inscriptions), hundreds of drawings and inscriptions (Nabatean mostly, Greek and Arabic) suggest the vitality of mining (turquoise and copper) in the vicinity and caravan trade along this important thoroughfare. Jebel Maghara, the 'mountain of the caves,' to the northwest with its numerous hieroglyphic rock inscriptions was one of the primary centers of Egyptian mining operations already during the third and second millennia B.C. Just south of Abu Zenima where this trans-Sinai trade route approaches the Gulf of Suez an ancient Egyptian port dated from the fifteenth-thirteenth centuries B.C. provided shipment to and from mining operations as well as a maritime link for caravan trade that passed near the northern base of Jebel Musa. Primarily maritime transport appears to have provided food supplies for the military, mine workers and their support animals. et-Tur (Raithou in monastic records) which served as a port into the southern Sinai also saw the development of monastic settlements at the nearby oasis of Bir Abu-Sueira.

Feiran, or Paran, the name already identified with the oasis by the Roman geographer Ptolemaeus, clearly is not a name introduced by Christian monks or pilgrims but probably is the biblical Hebrew name associated with the settlement during the Judean kingdom period. It is, in fact, very possible that 'Paran' was the original name of the entire Sinai peninsula in biblical times.[74] It is logical that the sole continuous settlement site should assume the name of the peninsula. The designation *Wilderness of Paran* in the biblical narratives, thus appears to have been an inclusive term in which the wildernesses of Shur, Sin, Sinai, Zin, etc. are best understood as regional designations within the peninsula.

Jebel Banat

Jebel Banat (elev. 1510 m) is located directly north of the Oasis of Feiran. Its southwestern base forms the inland slopes of the ravine of Wadi Feiran as it winds is way toward the Gulf of Suez ca. 40 km to the west.

Mount Sinai in the North

Growing numbers of scholars in more recent years have been committed to seeking possible candidates for this important historical site in the northern peninsula. Four isolated massifs (known as 'hogbacks') Jebel el-Maghara, Jebel Libni, Jebel Yelleq and Jebel Hallal tend to parallel the Mediterranean coastline (SW-NE) along the southern edge of the sand dune region.[75] Jebel el-Maghara and Jebel Libni form the more northerly barrier against the prevailing winds and the encroaching sands from the coastal region to the north. The trough that separates the line of Jebel Yelleq and Jebel Hallal on a similar SW-NE orientation, though dotted with isolated sandy regions, provided a direct caravan route from Ismailia into the vicinity of Kadesh-barnea generally identified as the 'Way of the Wilderness of Shur.' Greater periodic precipitation on the higher elevations of these mountains contributes to a relatively high water table and the series of wells and oases near their bases.

Jebel Maghâra and Jebel Libni

Jebel Maghâra (elev. 736 m) and Jebel Libni (elev. 463 m) are both crater-shaped with a hard limestone exterior and a sandstone core. A series of wells provide ample water for seasonal Bedouin migrations through the area and the plain at the base of Jebel Maghâra is cultivable land.

Jebel Yelleq and Jebel Hallal

Jebel Yelleq (elev. 1094 m) and Jebel Hallal (elev. 892 m) form the more impressive southern ridge that forms the northern watershed of the Wadi el-ᶜArish (Mediterranean) drainage system of the North-Central Sinai. Bir Hassana at the northeastern base of Jebel Yelleq is the principal oasis in the region along a N-S route that links el-ᶜArish on the Mediterranean with Ras el-Sudr on the Gulf of Suez.

Jebel Karkom

Mount (or Har) Karkom (Saffron) rises 900 meters from the Negev desert near the present Israel-Egypt border overlooking the Wadi Djirafi. Its limestone mountain plateau, 2.5 miles long (N-S) and 1.2 miles (E-W) so dominates the region that it is visible from the

Mountain of Edom across the Arabah. Its identification as a possible site of Mount Sinai is based on the discovery of some 720 archaeological sites including cultic shrines and villages within a 200 km² area around the mountain. Additionally about 40,000 rock engravings concentrated near the cultic sites along the slope and at the base of the mountain clearly suggest that this was a major prehistoric cultic center. Numerous altars and other assemblages of stones also appear related to the cultic activities. The attempt to relate this region to the exodus traditions has been less than convincing. The disclaimer comes from the fact that most of the datable remains belong to the period 3600-1950 B.C. with materials from the Late Bronze (Exodus) period non-existent or undatable. A small Early Roman sanctuary is located on another mountain facing Mount Karkom about a kilometer away.

The sanctity of the mount appears to have extended from the Neolithic (fifth millennium B.C.) to the Roman period. The archaeological area is covered with shrines, altars, stelae, platforms and funerary tumuli. The scant remains of hundreds of hamlets and campsites appear to have resulted from pilgrimage and temporary assemblies at the base of the sacred mountain. The rejection of Jebel Musa in favor of Jebel Karkom as a candidate for the biblical Mount Sinai is based on a lack of cultic sites in the Jebel Musa vicinity dated earlier than the Byzantine period (4th-7th centuries BC).[76] That Mount Karkom was a holy mountain and a place of pilgrimage at times throughout its existence is clear.[77] Unfortunately, the fact that settlement and activity in the region dwindled after ca. 1550 B.C. and production of rock art ceased for approximately a millennium until the fourth century B.C. tends to discount its importance during the time and following the Israelite exodus event.

Jebel Sin Bisher[78]

Jebel Sin Bisher (elev. 622 m) is located less than 25 km directly east of Ras el-Sudr on the Gulf of Suez. The primary lateral caravan route from el-ᶜArish on the Mediterranean coast to Ras el-Sudr passes at its northern base. From the coastal plain along the eastern shore of the Gulf of Suez, Jebel Sin Bisher forms the first of a series of mountainous ridges, Jebel Somâr (elev. 922 m) and Jebel Budhîya (elev. 1076 m) that ascend toward the watershed of the central Sinai, the et-Tîh. Beyond Wadi el-Sudr on the north, an interior route skirts the western base of Jebel el-Râha (elev. 719 m) and leads directly to the oasis ᶜAyun Mûsa, the possible site of the biblical Elim. Along the southeastern base of Jebel el-Râha, Wadi el-Sudr provides a direct route (ca. 50 km) to the Darb el-Hajj that ultimately led *from Horeb by the way of Mount Seir to Kadesh-barnea* (Deut. 1:2).

The location of Jebel Sin Bisher within a rather barren region of rugged limestone terrain and deep ravines with limited water supply (even though Wadi el-Sudr has the most adequate water resources in the region) is in stark contrast to the lofty mountain grandeur and lush oases that dot the southern peninsula. It is precisely the Hebrews' complaint of lack of water that tends to support a northern location for the *Mount of God.* The additional and more severe complaint following the departure from Mount Sinai also tends to support a location in relatively close proximity to the Gulf of Suez:

...O that we had meat to eat! We remember the fish we ate in Egypt for nothing, the cucumbers, the melons, the leeks, the onions, and the garlic; but now our strength is dried up, and there is nothing at all but this manna to look at. (Num. 11:4-6)

Obviously the reference to Egypt implies a desire to return to Egypt proper. During the first year, two months and twenty days their diet did not evoke rebellion against Moses' leadership. It was only as they moved into the interior of the Sinai Peninsula, away from their camp at the sacred mountain, that the real deprivation of a varied diet became revoltingly obvious. The specific reference to fish may imply a location of their encampment within relatively easy access to the Gulf of Suez and the opportunity to supplementing their staple diet with fish.

In summary, four hundred and thirty years after their seventy ancestors arrived in Egypt during a period of famine, the Hebrews under Moses' leadership escaped the oppressive hardship of Egyptian tyranny. The exodus route avoided the most direct *Via Maris (the way of the land of the Philistines)* to prevent the intimidation of immediate Egyptian military confrontation. From the interior of the Nile Delta *(Goshen)* at Rameses they moved to Succoth and along Wadi Tumilat to Egypt's eastern frontier with the Sinai near Lake Timsah where again they were diverted from *the way of the Wilderness of Shur* that led directly toward the Kadesh-barnea oasis. Their continued southward movement within the Egyptian border brought them into the impossible situation in which the environmental conditions precluded escape from the pursuing Egyptian army. Divine intervention provided an escape route across the narrows between the Greater and Lesser Bitter Lakes into the Wilderness of Shur. Southward movement brought them to Marah and Elim, two oases tentatively identified with Bir el-Murah and ʿAyun Musa, along the primary southern route bordering the Gulf of Suez. Their confrontation with the Amalekites, the principal caravaneers of the northern Sinai, obviously resulted from the perceived threat the Hebrews posed to the commercial monopoly these traders enjoyed. This event in the Wilderness of Sin (Sinai) in the immediate vicinity of *the mountain of God* tends to corroborate Moses' insistence that their destination was only *a three days' journey* from the border of Egypt, on the western side of the Sinai peninsula. The location of Jebel (Mt.) Sin Bisher near the Gulf of Suez allowed for a varied diet that ceased with their move into the Sinai interior.

This northern location for Mount Sinai avoids a serious problem related to the traditional Jebel Musa location in the southern peninsula. The first mention of the Wilderness of Paran in the biblical narrative follows the departure from Mount Sinai (Num. 10:12). The traditional route to Jebel Musa has assumed access to the southern mountains along Wadi Feiran (Paran) with the Hebrews passing through Paran before arriving at the sacred mount. It now appears clear that the ancient (biblical) name of the Sinai peninsula was 'Paran' and that the only biblical town, thus far identified with some semblance of continuous occupation in the entire peninsula, was the 'city of Paran' located near the entrance of the major pass that crosses the southern peninsula. In reference to the period of the exodus, therefore, the Wilderness of Paran should be identified with the entire central watershed of Wadi el-ʿArish, the territory through which the Hebrews passed from Jebel Sin Bisher to Kadesh-barnea.

NOTES

[1] K. Prag, The Intermediate Early Bronze-Middle Bronze Age: An Interpretation of the Evidence from Transjordan, Syria and Lebanon. *Levant* 6 (1974): 69-116; Ancient and Modern Pastoral Migration in the Levant. *Levant* 17 (1985): 81-88.

[2] W.G. Dever, New Vistas on the EB IV (MB I) Horizon in Syria-Palestine. *BASOR* 237 (1980): 35-64.

[3] J.N. Tubb, The MBIIA Period in Palestine: Its Relationship with Syria and Its Origin. *Levant* 15 (1983): 49-62.

[4] P.J. Parr, The Origin of the Rampart Fortifications of Middle Bronze Age Palestine and Syria. *ZDPV* 84 (1968): 18-45; G.R.H. Wright, Tell el-Yehudiyah and the Glacis. *ZDPV* 84 (1968): 1-17; J.D. Seger, The MB II Fortifications at Shechem and Gezer: A Hyksos Retrospective. *Eretz Israel* 12 (Glueck Volume) (1975): 34-45.

[5] W.F. Albright, Presidential Address: Palestine in the Earliest Historical Period. *JPOS* 15 (1935): 193-234; Y. Yadin, Hyksos Fortifications and the Battering Ram. *BASOR* 137 (1955): 23-32; R. Amiran and A. Eitan, Tel Nagila. *IEJ* 13 (1963): 143-144; 333-334.

[6] W.G. Dever, Relations Between Syria-Palestine and Egypt in the "Hyksos" Period. Pp. 69-87 in *Palestine in the Bronze and Iron Ages*. ed. J.N. Tubb. London: Institute of Archaeology, 1985.

[7] T. Säve-Söderbergh, The Hyksos Rule in Egypt. *JEA* 37 (1951): 53-71.

[8] J. Van Seters, *The Hyksos. A New Investigation*. New Haven: Yale University Press, 1966: 127-151; M. Bietak, *Avaris and Piramesse: Archaeological Exploration in the Eastern Nile Delta*. Proceedings of the British Academy, 65. London: Oxford University Press, 1979: 271-283.

[9] R. Giveon, New Egyptian Seals with Titles and Names from Canaan. *Tel Aviv* 3 (1976): 127-133; Some Scarabs from Canaan with Egyptian Titles. *Tel Aviv* 7 (1980): 179-184; A. Kempinski, Jacob in History. *BAR* 14/1 (1988): 42-47.

[10] J.M. Weinstein, The Egyptian Empire in Palestine: A Reassessment. *BASOR* 241 (1981): 1-28.

[11] W. Helck, *Die Beziehungen Agyptans zur Vorderasien im 3 und 2 Jahrtausend*. Wiesbaden, 1971: 107f.

[12] A.H. Gardiner, *Late Egyptian Miscellanies*. Brussels 1933: 108.

[13] K.A. Kitchen, *Ramesside Inscriptions*. Oxford 1968: II, 280: 13-16.

[14] *Urk* IV: 1649.

[15] *Urk* IV: 742:13 - 473:8.

[16] A. Alt, Neue Berichte uber Feldzuge von Pharaonen des Neuen Reiches nach Palästina. *ZDPV* 70 (1954): 31-75; S. Ahituv, Economic Factors in the Egyptian Conquest of Canaan. *IEJ* 28 (1978): 39-108; *EA*, 156:10; 187:22f; 194:30f; *Urk* IV:949).

[17] *Urk* IV:1069; IV:1468f.; IV:1369.

[18] D.A. Lowle, A Remarkable Family of Draughtsmen-Painters from Early Nineteenth Dynasty Thebes. *Oriens Antiquus* S (1976): 91-106.

[19] W.C. Hayes, A Selection of Thutmoside Ostraca from Deir el-Bahri. *JEA* 46 (1960): 29-52; pl. XII:17; P. Berlin, 10621 recto, 9.

[20] L. Habachi, Khanta'na-Qantir: Importance. *ASAE* 52 (1954): 443-562; A.H. Gardiner, *Late Egyptian Miscellanies*. Brussels (1933): 9-10.

[21] W. Helck, *Die Beziehungen Agyptans zur Vorderasien im 3 und 2 Jahrtausend.* Wiesbaden, 1971: 353f.; 505f.

[22] *Papyrus Anastasi* I: 20, 2-4; A.H. Gardiner, The Memphite Tomb of the General Haremhab. *JEA* 39 (1953): 3-12 (fig.2).

[23] J.M.A. Janssen, *Two Ancient Egyptian Shipdogs.* Leiden (1961) 59:14,13.

[24] W.F. Albright, Northwest-Semitic Names in a List of Egyptian Slaves from the Eighteenth Century B.C. *JAOS* 74 (1954): 222-233.

[25] Donald B. Redford, An Egyptological Perspective on the Exodus Narrative. Pp. 137-161 in *Egypt, Israel, Sinai: Archaeological and Historical Relationships in the Bible Period,* ed. Anson F. Rainey. Tel Aviv University. We reject the suggestion that Old Testament sources using the terms 'Amorite' or 'Hittite' for inhabitants of Palestine may not be dated before the 8th Century B.C. in J. Van Seters, The Terms "Amorite" and "Hittite." *VT* 22 (1972): 64-81.

[26] W.F. Albright, From the Patriarchs to Moses: I. From Abraham to Joseph. *BA* 36 (1973): 5-33.

[27] I. Mendelsohn, *Slavery in the Ancient Near East.* New York, 1949; On Corvée Labor in Ancient Canaanite Israel. *BASOR* 167 (1962): 31-53.

[28] W.F. Albright, Moses Out of Egypt. *BA* 36 (1973): 48-76; S.H. Horn, What We Don't Know About Moses and the Exodus. *BAR* 3/2 (1977): 22-31.

[29] E.P. Uphill, Pithom and Raamses: Their Location and Significance, *JNES* 27 (1968): 291-316; 28 (1969): 15-39.

[30] Alan Gardiner, The Delta Residence of the Ramessides, *JEA* 5 (1918): 269; J. Finegan, *Let My People Go: A Journey Through Exodus.* New York: Harper and Row, 1963: 12-13.

[31] Directed by the University of Vienna and the Austrian Archaeological Institute.

[32] L. Habachi, Khanta'na-Qantir: Importance. *ASAE* 52 (1954): 458-70, pls. VI-IX.

[33] D.B. Redford, Exodus 1:11. *VT* 13 (1963): 401-418; W. Helck, Tkw und die Ramses-Stadt. *VT* 15 (1965): 35-48.

[34] E.P. Uphill, Pithom and Raamses: Their Location and Significance. *JNES* 27 (1968): 291-316; 28 (1969): 15-39.

[35] Earlier identifications included the site or vicinity of Pelusium as well. Note, A.H. Gardiner, The Delta Residence of the Ramessides, *JEA* 5 (1918): 127-138, 179-200, 242-271; Tanis and Pi-Ra'messe: A Retractation. *JEA* 19 (1933): 122-128.

[36] A.H. Gardiner, The Defeat of the Hyksos by Kamōse: The Carnarvon Tablet, No. I. *JEA* 3 (1916): 95-110.

[37] A. Sneh, T. Weissbrod and I. Perath, Evidence for an Ancient Egyptian Frontier Canal. *Scientific American* 63 (1975): 542-548; W.H. Shea, A Date for the Recently Discovered Eastern Canal of Egypt. *BASOR* 226 (1977): 31-38.

[38] J. Van Seters, *The Hyksos: A New Investigation.* New Haven, Conn.: Yale University Press, 1966: 92.

[39] B. MacDonald, Excavations at Tell el-Maskhuṭa. *BA* 43 (1980): 49-58.

[40] A.H. Gardiner, The Geography of the Exodus: An Answer to Professor Naville and Others. *JEA* 10 (1924): 87-96.

[41] Exodus 13:17; E.D. Oren, The Overland Route between Egypt and Canaan in the Early Bronze Age (Preliminary Report). *IEJ* 23 (1973): 198-205.

[42] J.M. Weinstein, The Egyptian Empire in Palestine - A Reassessment, *BASOR* 241 (1941): 18-21.

[43] Sile consistently was the point of departure for New Kingdom expeditions to Canaan. A.H. Gardiner, The Ancient Military Road Between Egypt and Palestine. *JEA* 6 (1920): 99-116.

[44] R.O. Faulkner, Egypt: From the Inception of the 19th Dynasty to the Death of Ramesses III. Pp. 217-251 in *CAH³* II, 2. Cambridge, 1975; K.A. Kitchen, *Pharaoh Triumphant: The Life and Times of Ramesses II*. Mississauga 1982: 215-216.

[45] B. Rothenberg, *Timna: Valley of the Biblical Copper Mines*. London 1972: 163, fig. 49:6.

[46] J.A. Wilson, An Egyptian Letter. *Ancient Near Eastern Texts Relating to the Old Testament* (ed. J.B. Pritchard) Princeton 1955: 475-479.

[47] R.O. Faulkner, The Wars of Sethos I. *JEA* 33 (1947): 34-40.

[48] A. Sneh and T. Wiessbrod, Nile Delta: The Defunct Pelusiac Branch Identified, *Science* 180 (1973): 59-61; A. Sneh, *et al.*, Evidence for an Ancient Egyptian Frontier Canal, *Scientific American* 63 (1977): 542-548; W.H. Shea, A Date for the Recently Discovered Eastern Canal of Egypt, *BASOR* 226 (1966): 31-38.

[49] M. Bietak, *Tell el-Dabᶜa* II. Vienna 1975: 135f.

[50] W.H. Shea, A Date for the Recently Discovered Eastern Canal of Egypt. *BASOR* 226 (1977): 31-37.

[51] J.A. Wilson, The Prophecy of Neferty. Pp. 444-446 in *ANET*, ed. J.B. Pritchard. Princeton: Princeton University Press 1955.

[52] J.A. Wilson, The Instructions for Merikare. Pp. 414-418 in *ANET*, ed. J.B. Pritchard, Princeton, NJ: Princeton University Press 1955.

[53] J.A. Wilson, The Story of Sinuhe. Pp. 18-22 in *ANET*, ed. J.B. Pritchard. Princeton, NJ: Princeton University Press 1955.

[54] Papyrus Anastasi VI (British Museum). See *ANET*: 259.

[55] Papyrus Anastasi V (British Museum). See *ANET*: 259.

[56] G.I. Davies, *The Way of the Wilderness. A Geographical Study of the Wilderness Itineraries in the Old Testament*. Cambridge: Cambridge University Press 1979: 81.

[57] E.D. Oren, How Not to Create a History of the Exodus - A Critique of Professor Goedicke's Theories. *BAR* 7/6 (1981): 46-53.

[58] N. Snaith, יַם-סוּף: The Sea of Reeds: The Red Sea. *VT* 15 (1965): 395-398; B.F. Batto, Red Sea or Reed Sea? *BAR* 10/4 (1984): 56-63.

[59] H. Shanks, The Exodus and the Crossing of the Red Sea, According to Hans Goedicke. *BAR* 7/5 (1981): 42-50; C.R. Krahmalkov, A Critique of Professor Goedicke's Exodus Theories. *BAR* 7/5 (1981): 51-54.

[60] S.C. Bartlett, *From Egypt to Palestine through the Wilderness and the South Country*. 131.

[61] The discovery of a cylinder seal on the floor of a 18th century B.C. Palace at Tell el-Dabᶜa (identified with Avaris, the capital of the *Hyksos*, and Qantir, the *Pi-ramesse*, the delta capital of the 19th and 20th Dynasties) depicting the Phoenician god *Baal Zaphon* merely reflects the long-term commercial connection with the Phoenician coastal cities (especially Byblos) by way of the Pelusiac branch of the Nile. See M. Bietak, Canaanites in the Eastern Nile Delta. Pp. 41-56 in *Egypt, Israel, Sinai*, ed. A.F. Rainey. Tel Aviv: Tel Aviv University, 1987.

[62] J. Gray, The Desert Sojourn of the Hebrews and the Sinai-Horeb Tradition. *VT* 4 (1954): 148-154.

[63] G.I. Davies, The Wilderness Itineraries and the Composition of the Pentateuch. *VT* 33 (1983): 1-13.

[64] T. Barron, *The Topography and Geology of the Peninsula of Sinai*. 37.

[65] See M. Harel, *The Sinai Journeys: The Route of the Exodus*. San Diego, CA: Ridgefield Publishing Co., 1983: 420-424. 'Jebel Sin Bisher' may have the meaning, 'Mountain of the Announcement of the Law' or 'Mountain of the Laws of Man,' with 'sin' derived from *suna* meaning 'tradition' or *sana* meaning 'to promulgate a law,' and 'bisher' coming from *busher* meaning 'to make an auspicious announcement,' or *bashar* meaning 'man.' Jebel Sin Bisher appears to be the only mountain in the whole of the Sinai, Midian and Edom that has retained the form 'sin,' possibly having reference to the 'tooth (shape or projection) of a mountain.'

[66] Based on the military annals of Thutmose III and the detailed description of his march across the northern Sinai along the Via Maris, the Sile to Raphia distance, approximately 150 miles, was covered in not more than 10 days, or fifteen miles a day. One may draw the assumption that a day's journey is a reference to distance and not to time. Thus, a *three days' journey* may reasonably be a distance of about 45 miles.

[67] G.I. Davies, Hagar, el-Heǧra and The Location of Mt. Sinai. *VT* 22 (1972): 152-163.

[68] *Antiquities of the Jews* II: XII, 1.

[69] Charles H. Beke, *Sinai in Arabia and of Midian*. London: Trubner & Co., 1878.

[70] A. Lucas, *The Route of the Exodus of the Israelites from Egypt*. London: E. Arnold, 1938.

[71] D. Nielsen, *The Site of the Biblical Mount Sinai*. Copenhagen, 1928.

[72] A. Perevolotsky and I. Finkelstein, The Southern Sinai Exodus Route in Ecological Perspective. *BAR* 11/4 (1985): 26-41.

[73] E. Robinson, *Biblical Researches in Palestine, Mount Sinai and Arabia Petraea*. London, 1838; *Biblical Researches in Palestine and in the Adjacent Regions*, I-III. 2nd ed. London, 1850.

[74] Y. Aharoni, Kadesh-Barnea and Mount Sinai. In Beno Rothenberg, *God's Wilderness: Discoveries in Sinai*. London: Thames and Hudson, 1961: 167.

[75] H. Sadek, *The Principal Structural Features of the Peninsula of Sinai*. Madrid: Congress Geologique International: 1928.

[76] A. Rabinovich, Is Har Karkom the real Mt. Sinai? *The Jerusalem Post International Edition*. Jerusalem, Israel. June 9, 1990: 11.

[77] E. Anati, Has Mt. Sinai Been Found? *BAR* 11/4 (1985): 42-57.

[78] The identification of Jebel Sin Bisher with Mount Sinai belongs to Menashe Harel. The complete rationale is delineated in his book, *The Sinai Journeys: The Route of the Exodus*. San Diego, CA: Ridgefield Publishing Co., 1983.

Chapter IV

FROM SINAI TO KADESH-BARNEA

In the afterglow of the Ten Commandments that sealed the covenant between Yahweh and his emancipated people and the formulation of the constitution that would guide their behavior in the Land of Promise came an awareness of the stark realities of the Sinai environment. The highlights of the Mount Sinai experience were dimmed by the jeopardy of the northern Sinai desert as they prepared for the next phase of their migration: the scarcity of food, the limited water supplies (even if and when they reached the next oasis), and the constant threat of marauding nomads or trading caravans who would challenge the Israelite presence. The greater concern came with the realization that soon they would be on the borders of Canaan where any attempt to claim their ancestral Promised Land would not go unchallenged. The time for military preparedness had come. The Canaanites would not passively acquiesce to their intrusion. Thus, in the shadow of Sinai, the *mountain of God,* Israel prepared for the anticipated conflict for control of Canaan.

The 'Numberings' at Mount Sinai and the Jordan River

The Lord spoke to Moses in the wilderness of Sinai, 'Take a census...' (Num. 1:1,2)

To overcome the traditional misconceptions of this crucial event in the life of Israel, two important socio-political factors of this period in Israel's history must be recognized.

1. The history of Israel from the patriarchal period into the times of the United Monarchy is based in a patriarchal-tribal structure. The events of the biblical period must be understood in that context and the meaning of many biblical passages, even some in the New Testament, reflect the residual effects of a long social and political history of tribal beginnings. The father as the head and sole authority of his immediate *family* with time became the 'patriarch' of the extended family, or *clan,* and in succeeding generations the continued ethnic union of a series of clans formed the *tribe.* The confederation

of the 12 tribes of Israel, joined in obedience to, and reliance on, Yahweh by the Sinaitic covenant continued as the ultimate political structure to the period of the monarchy. Within the tribal structure, the patriarch of the clan was the ultimate authority.

2. Nowhere does the Bible give any indication that the purpose of the census, either at Mount Sinai or at the Jordan River some thirty-eight years later, was to determine the size of the Israelite population emigrating from Egypt. On the other hand, the Bible is very explicit in stating clearly both the purpose and the procedure of the 'numbering.' Historically, the casual acceptance of Numbers 1 and 26 as a general census for the purpose of determining the size of the Moses-led exodus has created no end of credibility problems for the biblical text. As a careful review of the biblical text will reveal, the number of unknown variables related to an extension from the actual purpose of the *census* to the calculation of the total population make such an effort and its results highly suspect. Even the attempted calculation of any reasonable approximation of the actual number who escaped Egypt under Moses' leadership may be too much to expect.

The 'numbering' was required to determine the military strength of Israel. Both at Mount Sinai and at the Jordan, Israel anticipated a serious challenge to their takeover in Canaan. The purpose, therefore, was perfectly clear:

...Take a census of all the congregation of the people of
Israel,...every male,...all in Israel who are able to go forth to war,...
(Num. 1:2,3)

In planning and establishing a realistic strategy for the anticipated assault on Canaan Moses required a precise clarification of Israel's own military strength. Later, as we will see, the report of the twelve spies provided vital information for the implementation of those plans.

The Census Procedure

...you (Moses) and Aaron shall number them,...and these are the
names of the men who shall attend you,...chosen from the
congregation, leaders of their ancestral tribes, the heads of the
clans of Israel. (Num. 1:3,5,16)

Moses and Aaron were assisted by respected, representative patriarchs from each of the twelve tribes. The serious nature of the procedure seemed to require reputable and equal representation. The burden of responsibility could not be allowed to rest wholly on their two leaders. The census, in fact, was a form of conscription that required the authority of the most highly respected members of the congregation.

The procedure was intended to provide a two-fold record:

The Family 'Company'

...Take a census...by families, by fathers' houses,...you and Aaron shall number them, company by company. (Num. 1:2,3)

The basic fighting unit of the tribe was determined within the extended-family (clan) unit. The patriarch of the clan had the sole authority and responsibility for committing eligible males to a tribal cause. Tribal pride tended to maintain the distinct separateness of the family unit to be registered as a fighting unit; thus, the requirement that they were recorded *company by company*. The initial goal within each tribe was to determine the number of families that could provide a group of fighting men for the common cause.

'Individual' Conscription

The strategy of an extended confrontation in Canaan obviously required a more precise understanding of military strength than a *company* registry could provide. Thus, the census required an additional, more detailed record:

...Take a census...according to the number of names, every male, head by head. (Num. 1:3)

The registration of every male by name resulted in an actual head count in addition to the number of fighting units. This procedure at Mount Sinai, repeated in the biblical narrative in reference to each of the twelve tribes, appears to be basically the same at the River Jordan. The following chart provides the results of the two 'numberings' for comparative study:

	Mount Sinai Census (1)		Jordan River Census (26)	
REUBEN	46 *elaphim*	500 *'men'*	43 *elaphim*	730 *'men'*
SIMEON	59 *elaphim*	300 *'men'*	22 *elaphim*	200 *'men'*

GAD	45 *elaphim*	650 *'men'*	40 *elaphim*	500 *'men'*
JUDAH	74 *elaphim*	600 *'men'*	76 *elaphim*	500 *'men'*
ISSACHAR	54 *elaphim*	400 *'men'*	64 *elaphim*	300 *'men'*
ZEBULUN	57 *elaphim*	400 *'men'*	60 *elaphim*	500 *'men'*
EPHRAIM	40 *elaphim*	500 *'men'*	32 *elaphim*	500 *'men'*
MANASSEH	32 *elaphim*	200 *'men'*	52 *elaphim*	700 *'men'*
BENJAMIN	35 *elaphim*	400 *'men'*	45 *elaphim*	600 *'men'*
DAN	62 *elaphim*	700 *'men'*	64 *elaphim*	400 *'men'*
ASHER	41 *elaphim*	500 *'men'*	53 *elaphim*	400 *'men'*
NAPHTALI	53 *elaphim*	400 *'men'*	45 *elaphim*	400 *'men'*
TOTAL	598 *elaphim*	5,550 *'men'*	596 *elaphim*	5,930 *'men'*

Comparison of Conscription Totals

Preconceptions aside, the logical conclusion of a casual summary of the biblical statements on the purpose and procedure of the Israelite census is that the two categories, 'fighting units' and 'individual conscript' (*head by head*) clearly are represented in the two columns of figures in the chart above: a total of 598 fighting units (*elaphim*) and 5,550 fighters for the Mount Sinai Census and 596 fighting units and 5,930 fighters anticipating the crossing of the Jordan River some 38 years later.

The question then arises as to the meaning of the Hebrew term *eleph* (sing.) or *elaphim* (pl.). This word, appearing repeatedly in the biblical text, ultimately was given the numerical value of 'one thousand.' In the early biblical narratives the word is used most consistently in a military sense, in most cases suggesting the relative sizes of the opposing factions or armies. The usage is clear, for instance, following the confrontation of the Israelites and Philistines in which David killed Goliath. Part of the jubilation that greeted the

Israelite army on its return to Bethlehem suggests the military sense of the word:

...*And the women sang to one another as they made merry, "Saul has slain his 'elaphim,' and David his ten 'elaphim.'"* (I Sam. 18:7) The suggestion has been that the term referred to a fighting unit, obviously within a tribal structure of varying size, dependent on the number of eligible fighting men within the extended family. With the establishment of the Israelite monarchy and the wholesale conscription by the king for the nation's standing armies, the consistent size of a military unit was 1,000 men. As a result, a term for a military unit from tribal societies ultimately assumed a specific value, and in future generations the term quite naturally consistently was translated 'thousand,' even within such earlier contexts.

A census conducted by David at the height of the united monarchy provides interesting comparative results. Again, the primary purpose was a determination of the military strength of Israel when the kingdom extended from the Arnon in the Transjordan through the Gilead to Dan and Tyre in the north and Beersheba in the Negev in the south (2 Sam. 24:5-7). This comprehensive study of Israel's population that consumed nine months and twenty days resulted in an identification of 800 thousand fighting men in Israel and 500 thousand in Judah for an accumulative total of 1,300 thousand fighting men. At this point within the unified administrative system of the monarchy, the military unit (*eleph*) consisted of 1,000 men. An insistence on that value for the term during the Sinai and Jordan River census would imply that at the height of David's military strength and the widest extension of the monarchy, the military strength of Israel was only slightly greater than twice the number coming out of Egypt. Such a situation seems totally unrealistic and therefore, it seems clear that the results of the census for the earlier period must be understood in another way.

An evaluation of the chart suggests that the results of the census at Mount Sinai and the Jordan were basically the same. The average number of fighting men per unit was just under ten. With this realization, some of Israel's military encounters in the land begin to make sense. For example, when Joshua's spies returned with their report on conditions at ᶜAi, their recommendation to Joshua was followed:

> ...*Let not all the people do up, but let about two or three 'elaphim' of men go up and attack ᶜAi; do not make the whole people toil up there, for they are but few.*
> *So about three 'elaphim' went up there...* (Joshua 7:3,4)

The result of the attack on ᶜAi later was a devastating defeat for the Israelites with thirty-six killed. The impact of the defeat was so great that even Joshua regretted not having settled in the Transjordan:

> ...*Alas, O Lord God, why hast thou brought this people over the Jordan at all, to give us into the hands of the Amorites, to destroy us? Would that we had been content to dwell beyond the Jordan!...* (Joshua 7:7)

Obviously, the gravity of the situation is enhanced if the three fighting units sent to ᶜAi (presumably, three of the larger units) totalled 40 to 50 in number. To have their units practically wiped out would have been a dramatic blow to the Israelites following the unique victory at Jericho.

The Punishment of Simeon and Levi

The census comparison suggests little change in the relative strength of Israel from the beginning to the end of the wilderness sojourn. However, within the individual tribes, a number of very significant changes were taking place. The census clearly reflects conditions that are described in other parts of the biblical narrative. Simeon seems to have experienced a significant decline.[1] The explanation may be found in Jacob's final blessing on his sons:

> *Simeon and Levi are brothers; weapons of violence are their swords.*
> *O my soul, come not into their council;*
> *O my spirit, be not joined to their company;*
> *for in their anger they slay men,*
> *and in their wantonness they hamstring oxen.*
> *Cursed be their anger, for it is fierce;*
> *And their wrath, for it is cruel!*
> *I will divide them in Jacob and scatter them in Israel.* (Gen. 49:5-7)

Whatever the thinking about Simeon and Levi's revenge against those who had raped their sister Dinah (Genesis 34), punitive action was to be taken against them. Levi appears to have been disinherited from sharing in the tribal allotments within the Promised Land. Theirs was an appointment to 48 Levitical cities that would serve various roles in the subsequent development of the nation from civil defense to the collection of the tax and the tithe.

In the case of Simeon, the biblical description of land allotment is equally interesting:

> ...The...lot...for Simeon...its inheritance was in the midst of the inheritance of the tribe of Judah...formed part of the territory of Judah; because the portion of the tribe of Judah was too large for them, the tribe of Simeon obtained an inheritance in the midst of their inheritance. (Josh. 19:1,9)

Simeon clearly did not receive a tribal allotment in his own right. Even a casual acquaintance with the location of the towns within his territory in the arid region of the Eastern Negev suggests extended droughts and occasional famine. No wonder that very early in the history of Israel in the land, the tribe of Simeon ceased entirely as a separate entity. This prejudicial treatment of the tribe appears to be in effect already during the wilderness wanderings. The dramatic decline in the relative strength of its fighting units (= extended families) and the total number of fighting men realistically also reflects a comparable decline in the general population.

The Prominence of Joseph's Sons

The 'numbers' on Manasseh also suggest a significant change. It is interesting to note in that connection that when Joshua was ratifying the boundary descriptions, the sons of Joseph complained, on the basis of population, about receiving only one portion:

> ...And the tribe of Joseph spoke to Joshua, saying, 'Why have you given me but one lot and one portion as an inheritance, although I am a numerous people, since hitherto the Lord has blessed me?' (Josh. 17:14)

As a result of that complaint, both Ephraim and Manasseh received territories within the central hill country with Joshua's encouragement that conditions gradually would improve for them as they were able to reduce the forests for good agricultural land and gain control over the Canaanites and their superior weaponry (*chariots of iron*).[2] But in addition to the double portion, even after the respective boundaries for the tribes had been established, a special concession to claim lands assigned to adjoining tribes was made to the tribe of Manasseh:

...Also in Issachar and in Asher Manasseh had Beth-shean and its villages, and Ibleam and its villages, and the inhabitants of Dor and its villages, and the inhabitants of En-dor and its villages, and the inhabitants of Ta'anach and its villages, and the inhabitants of Megiddo and its villages; the third is Naphath. (Josh. 17:11)

Manasseh's dramatic population increase clearly is reflected in the census.

In conclusion, the 'numberings' or census was intended to determine the military strength of the Israelite migrants in terms of extended-family units that would be expected to form a 'company' of fighting men, and secondly to have a 'head' count of all males over the age of twenty and able to fight. Their name registration appears to have been a formal conscription and induction under the supervision of a respected patriarch of their own tribe. The action was a necessary prelude to the next phase of their migration across the Sinai since the border of Canaan and hostile Canaanites awaited them at the conclusion of the trip.

The Route from Mount Sinai

A year, a month and twenty days after the departure from Egypt, the stay at Sinai was terminated and the Hebrews moved from the Sinai Desert (the immediate vicinity of the mount) into the Desert of Paran (a term that clearly refers to the entire central Sinai peninsula). It is interesting to note that following the departure from Mount Sinai conditions appear to have become more harsh and the complaints concerning those conditions created a serious crisis. Seemingly the region in which they had camped for almost a year had provided adequate grazing and water for the flocks and herds, and the changes of diet and life style had not been too dramatic.

...If only we had meat to eat! We remember the fish we ate in Egypt at no cost -- also the cucumbers, melons, leeks, onions and garlic. (Num. 11:4,5) The outbreak of a fire that destroyed the outskirts of the camp and a subsequent plague were viewed as divine retribution and, as a result, the location of this crisis was identified as *Taberah* 'burning' and *Kibroth-Hattaavah*, 'the graves of the cravers or lusters' (Num. 11:3,34). Tension and dissension continued to plague the leadership and contributed to an extended stay at the next oasis identified in the itinerary as *Hazeroth* 'enclosures' or 'corrals' located in the Desert of Paran (Num. 12:16). It would seem that even a brief stay in one location required, for the sake of convenience, the construction of rock fences or enclosures for controlling or protecting the livestock.

To anyone familiar with the nature of the Sinai peninsula, the difficulty in retracing the route of the exodus and locating, with any measure of certainty, the supposed place names provided by the biblical text is obvious. The inhospitable environment of the region precluded continuous occupation and the transmission of historical events and traditions from one generation to the next. The region is largely devoid of settlement and apart from the transitory nomadic tribes and the commercial caravans that followed the clearly defined trails connecting the oases, the population of the region historically has been meager indeed. A reasonable consideration of the biblical data suggests that the identification of events was unique to the Hebrews during their sojourn in the Sinai, and where those events or stops along the route were identified in the biblical text with cultural or architectural features, their indistinctive nature or description makes certain geographical identification impossible. For the most part the supposed place names are merely descriptions of the locale or event that the Hebrews encountered.

If, however, such place names as Marah and Elim can be identified along the route from the border of Egypt to Mount Sinai, then another name may be significant in attempting to identify the specific locale of the holy mountain. The topographical list identifies the next camp site as Rithmah (Num. 33:18). An oasis with the modern name of Ein Rithmah is located about twenty kilometers east of Jebel Sin Bisher in Wadi Suder. If nothing more, these names form a most interesting

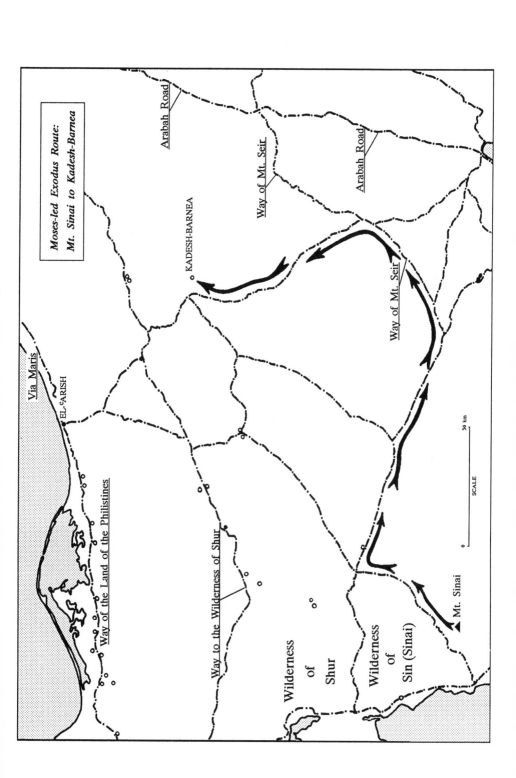

Moses-led Exodus Route:
Mt. Sinai to Kadesh-Barnea

coincidence. But, if, in fact, these identifications have historical and traditional value, the historical event of the giving of the law must have occurred in the immediate vicinity.

In the Exodus diary, it is from this locale that the representative scouting party was sent into Canaan to determine the nature of the land and the difficulties the Hebrews might encounter in their attempts at capturing the territory. Moses' instructions to the twelve spies is most informative. They were to penetrate the Negev and proceed into the hill country to:

...See what the land is like and whether the people who live there are strong or weak, few or many. What kind of land do they live in? Is it good or bad? What kind of towns do they live in? Are they unwalled or fortified? How is the soil? Is it fertile or poor? Are there trees on it or not? Do your best to bring back some of the fruit of the land. (Num. 13:18,19)

Two primary concerns are evident: the nature of the resistance they might encounter during the conquest, and the conditions for establishing an economy based on agriculture. Unfortunately, the report of the exploration in the land overwhelmed the limited resolve of the Hebrews and their decision not to challenge the Canaanites resulted in the forty-year sojourn in the Sinai.

It is interesting to note that the contingent sent into the land returned to make its report at Kadesh where the Hebrews then established their tribal religious center. The Exodus narrative recalls very few camping sites along the itinerary from the Egyptian border to Kadesh-barnea: Marah, Elim, Rephidim in the Wilderness of Sin, Horeb (the mountain of God) or Sinai in the Wilderness of Sinai, Taberah or Kibroth-Hattaavah, and Hazeroth. A comparison with Numbers 33 suggests a much more comprehensive listing, especially between Sinai and Kadesh, where the clear implication is that a major detour was taken to Ezion-Geber at the head of the eastern arm of the Red Sea before turning northward to Kadesh (Num. 33:35,36). A calculation of the distance between the two places assumes the same route:

...It takes eleven days to go from Horeb to Kadesh Barnea by the Mount Seir road. (Deut. 1:2)

The narrative 'diary-type' account of the itinerary from Egypt to Kadesh-barnea appears clear and forthright. We must question, therefore, the general purpose of the Numbers 33 listing and the specific reason for the inclusion of many place names that seem removed from the narrative itinerary, even with the detour *by the Mount Seir road.*

In the Vicinity of Kadesh-Barnea

Kadesh-barnea (also, Meribath-Kadesh, *'waters of strife at Kadesh'*) is identified in the Bible as an oasis on the southern border of Canaan on the edge of both the Wilderness of Paran and the Wilderness of Zin (Num. 34:4,5; Ezek. 47:19; 48:28) between the Brook of Egypt (Wadi el-ᶜArish) and territory controlled by the king of Edom. This general location with its four springs, ᶜAin Qadeis, ᶜAin Qudeirat, ᶜAin Muweileh and ᶜAin Quseimeh, clustered within an extended drainage system, may be identified with four biblical place names: Kadesh (Kadesh-barnea), Addar or Hazar-Addar (Num. 34:4; Josh. 15:13), Karka and Azmon. The arrival of the Hebrews at an oasis with insufficient water named 'Kadesh' is best identified with ᶜAin Qadeis, a shallow pool with a limited, uncertain capacity located about 6 miles south of the more luxuriant valley of the ᶜAin Qudeirat-Quseimeh system. Surrounded by a desert wasteland, ᶜAin Qadeis was totally unsuited for any long-term settlement.

Subsequent Israelite history in the area tends to support an identification of ᶜAin Qudeirat with the amphictyonic center maintained during the 38 years of wilderness wanderings. It is located in a deep, relatively narrow valley of the Wadi el-ᶜAin at the intersection of two primary trade routes of antiquity: *the Way of Shur*, leading from Edom and the Arabah down to Egypt, and the way from Elath and the Central Negev to Arad and Hebron. Its springs are the most abundant in the Sinai and water the largest oasis in the northern Sinai. The establishment of a major fortress at ᶜAin Qudeirat as a part of the Solomonic trade system during the tenth century B.C. took advantage of this abundant spring with its extensive grazing area. Large collections of 'Negeb' ware at ᶜAin Qudeirat, usually has been attributed to the temporary settlements of migratory or trading groups.

Although distinctive Late Bronze Age pottery appears to be lacking at
ᶜAin Qudeirat,[2] the abundant presence of 'Negeb' ware certainly is not
inconsistent with the extended encampment of the Hebrews during the
thirteenth century B.C., the period to which the earliest context of
'Negeb' ware found elsewhere belongs. The Sinai always has required
a nomadic lifestyle and there is no basis for assuming that evidences
of nomadic presence increase over time. Argumentation against
reconciliation of the biblical data and a lack of archaeological
evidence is an argument from silence.

The other springs, ᶜAin Muweileh and ᶜAin Quseimeh, may be
identified with Karka and Azmon respectively.[3] Thus, the description
of Judah's southern border south of Kadesh-barnea proceeds from
Hezron and Addar (or Hazar-Addar) through Karka, passing Azmon,
toward the Brook of Egypt (Josh. 15:3,4).

Spying in the Promised Land

The spying expedition into Canaan was a fact-finding mission. The
return of the spies was planned to coincide with Moses' arrival at
Kadesh-barnea. Their report was expected to provide strategic
information for planning an immediate assault on the Promised Land.
There clearly was no intention of making Kadesh a long-term tribal
center. Thus, the nature of the eyewitness report and evaluation of the
land Moses required was detailed specifically:

1. A general description of the land.
*Go up into the Negev yonder, and go up into the hill country, and
see what the land is,...*(Num. 13:17,18)

2. The size and military strength of the population.
*...whether the people who dwell in it are strong or weak,...whether
they are few or many...*(13:18)

3. The fertility and productivity of the land.
...whether the land that they dwell in is good or bad,...(13:19)

4. The nature of urban settlements, unfortified encampments or
fortified strongholds.
*...whether the cities that they dwell in are camps or
strongholds,...*(13:19)

5. The relative prosperity of the land.

...whether the land is rich or poor,...(13:20)
    6. The relation of wooded to agricultural lands.
...whether there is wood in it or not. (13:20)
Additionally, Moses requested the return of samples of the current crops.

Such detailed instructions suggest Moses' desire for a comprehensive understanding of the land and its people in determining the most feasible strategy in establishing a territorial foothold and in ultimately gaining total control of the region. We can only assume that the decision to request permission to pass through Edomite territory to gain access to the Kings' Highway rather than to proceed northward directly through the Negev was made on information received from the spies. Later, Moses' instructions to Joshua during the transfer of leadership, at least partially, appear to have been based on information gleaned by the spies as well.

...And when you have passed over the Jordan, you shall set up these stones,...on Mount Ebal...and you shall write upon the stones all the words of this law very plainly. (Deut. 27:4,8)
Moses' instructions give the impression of some urgency to the immediate exercise of covenant recognition on the slopes of Mount Gerizim and Mount Ebal. The implication seems clear. This was not merely intended to be a reaffirmation of covenant commitment by the Israelites who had just arrived in the land. Those who had been born since the Sinai experience were circumcised and became 'sons of the Covenant' at Gilgal. The recitation of the obligations and benefits of the covenant in antiphonal response across the valley from the mountain slopes of Ebal and Gerizim was intended for the locals of kindred blood and spirit who had preceded them to the Promised Land.

There was clearly a concern about the population distribution and the opportunities that existed for immediate settlement in the land. Such settlement opportunities were dependent upon areas of relatively sparse population or local enclaves that would be amenable to the arrival and integration of the Hebrews. The nature and scope of ethnic enclaves throughout the country must be assumed to have been of particular interest.

While the reference to the descendants of Anak is not clear, the spies identified the Amalekites with the Negev, a situation that seems to have existed from patriarchal to monarchial times. The Hittites, Jebusites and Amorites had occupied the central hill country, and the Canaanites dominated the coastal regions and the Jordan Valley (Num. 13:28,29). Reference to "fortified cities" will be an important consideration in evaluating the nature of urbanization (especially in the Negev region) during the Late Bronze period and the time of the Exodus. The nature of such fortifications must be understood within the context of the subjective report of the spies.

The Wilderness Interlude

The report of a powerful population and great fortified cities in the land prompted the Hebrews' decision against attempting an immediate invasion of Canaan. As a result, the nomadic wanderings in the Sinai were extended to forty years. The assumption that Kadesh-barnea served as a cultic center to which the clans and tribes periodically returned for religious and festive occasions is not required by the biblical text. The nature of the Sinai surely forced them into a nomadic life style with its constant foraging for water and pasturage for their flocks and herds.

It is possible that the listing of place names in Numbers 33 represents not a point-to-point itinerary of the Moses-led departure from Egypt only, but rather a much more comprehensive topographical listing of all those places, oases, and campsites of significance during the Hebrews' transition from Egypt to Canaan, whether on the various routes followed or the isolated sites casually visited during the forty year sojourn. A parallel is found in the annals of Thutmose III whose scribes provided two types of records of the military expeditions of the famous pharaoh. The daily diary entries consisted of a narrative outline of the events of each day. Thus we have insights into most of the sixteen campaigns conducted by Thutmose in his attempt to reestablish Egyptian control over the city-states of Syria/Palestine. In addition, however, we have an exhaustive topographical list of all the cities and towns affected by those military incursions. The scope of the 350 place names that appear in Thutmose III's listing is best understood as a comprehensive compilation of all those urban centers affected by the campaigns during his lifetime. It is logical to assume that the early Hebrew traditions following over four hundred years in Egypt may have been preserved in the form of the Egyptian scribal prototypes with which they were familiar.

While Kadesh-barnea served as their religious center during the thirty-eight years of 'wilderness wanderings,' the seasonal migrations, common of modern Bedouin in the peninsula, probably took the Hebrews to all parts of the Sinai in search of pasturage and water for their flocks and herds. Reflecting these movements, the inclusion of place names with faint connections to locations in the southern peninsula reasonably can be expected in the listing of Numbers 33. And, in keeping with Thutmose's annals, the place names were organized logically according to regional proximity. It is therefore not necessary to seek a sequential itinerary in Numbers 33, but rather to recognize the primacy of the itinerary followed by Moses as provided in the 'daily-diary' format of Exodus and Numbers and an appropriate integration of all the other places of note identified either with earlier migrations (through Edomite territory and along the King's Highway) or with the 38-year Sinai delay in the Numbers 33 list.

Appeal to the King of Edom

When the final move into the Promised Land came, messengers were sent to the king of Edom requesting permission to pass through Edomite territory to the King's Highway that would ultimately lead them to the Transjordanian heights overlooking the Jordan Valley. The dialogue between Moses' messengers and the King of Edom indicates that the Edomites had extended their control westward into the immediate vicinity of Kadesh-barnea. Their request appears to anticipate Edomite objections to the Hebrew migration through their territory.

...We will not go through any field or vineyard, or drink water from any well. We will travel along the king's highway and not turn to the right or to the left until we have passed through your territory. (Num. 20:17)

It is clear that the King of Edom was not convinced of the innocence of Hebrew intentions and adamantly refused to concede to their request for the right of passage. When the messengers repeated and expanded the conditions of their passage, it appears clear that they were trying to convince someone with previous experience with such movements and the havoc the intrusion of such outsiders had created at the limited water sources and the devastation the fields and vineyards had suffered. Even the offer of payment for water and the promise of passage without overnight encampment (*We only want to pass through on foot.*) were not enough to sway the Edomites from their decision: *'You may not pass through!'* The show of strength with *a large and powerful army* convinced the Hebrews there was no possibility of following their intended itinerary.

This passage leaves the definite impression that the route along the King's Highway that the Hebrews under Moses' leadership intended to follow had been used by others before them, and that such groups had taken advantage of water sources, fields and vineyards without regard for the local population and their interests. Such activities surely may be assigned to a time when the Edomite tribes, prior to their unification, were too weak to challenge and resist nomadic incursions and migrations from the Sinai or to dominate the trade routes through their territory. The implications of this dialogue may even be more specific. Is it possible that earlier movements of Hebrews through the region had created the ill will evident in the Edomites' refusal?

It is important to note that the decision to request passage through Edomite territory obviously represented the primary route of access to the Promised Land from the Sinai. The specifics of the spies' report must have suggested that penetration through the Negev was not preferable and that the seeming detour avoided significant obstacles of a more direct approach.

Confrontation with the King of Arad

With passage along the traditional route through Edomite territory refused, the primary alternative was a direct approach along the route the spies had taken earlier, along the *Way of Atharim.* There, according to the biblical account, the Canaanite king of Arad not only challenged the Hebrews' advance but took some prisoners and successfully forced their retreat.[4] The Hebrews' vowed to avenge this defeat and its consequences. Later, Judah and Simeon, following the occupation of the central hill country of Canaan during the settlement period, occupied the Negev from the north (Judges 1:17). Moses' defeat in the Negev left no other alternative. The Hebrews were forced to the lengthy, discouraging detour southward to the headwaters of the Gulf of Aqaba and around the Edomite and Moabite territories along the Wilderness Road.[5]

This segment of the wilderness sojourn from the departure at the *mount of God* to the departure from Kadesh-barnea accounts for almost thirty-nine years of the Sinai endurance. The rather limited itinerary that was highlighted in the 'diary' narrative (the wilderness of Paran, the place of God's punitive 'fire' and the cemetery, the corrals, the way of Mount Seir, and Kadesh) must be complemented by the events and places that the Hebrews experienced during their extended stay in the Sinai. The extended list of place names in Numbers 33, some tentatively identified with various locations throughout the Sinai peninsula, logically may reflect the Hebrews' normal responses to the hostile environment to which they were condemned by unbelief. Thus, while only two names are added to the first segment of the itinerary from Rameses to Mount Sinai (Num. 33:5-15), the list is extended dramatically for the period from Mount Sinai to the departure from Kadesh-barnea (Num. 33:16-37). Only the location of ʿAin Rithmah northeast of Jebel Sin Bisher in Wadi Sudr tends to reinforce the location of the sacred mountain in the immediate vicinity. While the details of events associated with these places names are lacking, the scribal compilation was an attempt to identify the significant events and locales in the Hebrews' sojourn. Most of the names defy geographical location. Like the 'cemetery' and 'corrals,' they represent the ephemeral events of the nomadic lifestyle the Hebrews were forced to adopt for a generation.

NOTES

[1] S. Talmon, The Town Lists of Simeon. *IEJ* 15 (1965): 235-241.
[2] M. Garsiel and I. Finkelstein, The Westward Expansion of the House of Joseph in the Light of the ʿIzbet Ṣarṭah Excavations. *IEJ* 5 (1978): 192-198.

[3] M. Dothan, The Fortress at Kadesh-Barnea. *IEJ* 15 (1965): 134-143; Kadesh-Barnea. Pp. 697-699 in *EAEHL*, III. Edited by M. Avi-Yonah. Englewood Cliffs, N.J.: Prentice-Hall, 1977; R. Cohen, The Excavations at Kadesh-barnea (1976-78). *B A* 44 (1981): 93-107; Did I Excavate Kadesh-Barnea? *BAR* 7/3 (1981): 20-33.
[4] S. Cohen, Azmon. P. 327 in *IDB* I. Nashville: Abingdon Press, 1962.
[5] Num. 21:1-3; cf. Num. 33:40; Deut. 1:44.
[6] Num. 21:4; Deut. 2:1-25.

Chapter V

FROM KADESH-BARNEA TO THE PLAINS OF MOAB

The Biblical Account

Though the biblical references to the Israelite passage through the Transjordan are few and sketchy, a number of passages are crucial to a tentative reconstruction of the itinerary and the nature of the exodus as a whole. Israel's detour around Edom (20:14-21), the continuation beyond the border of Moab (21:10-20), the defeat of Sihon and Og (21:21-35) and the summary statement of the itinerary from Kadesh to the Plains of Moab (33:37-49) are paralleled by statements in Deuteronomy 2:1-3:11 and Judges 11:12-22. Additional place names associated with the period of the conquest and settlement are found in the discussion of the Transjordanian settlement of Reuben, Gad and the half tribe of Manasseh (Numbers 32; Deuteronomy 3:12-17; Joshua 13). Granted, an integration of this data is problematic. However, the fact that the location of some of the place names cannot be identified and that details defy harmony for the casual reader is not adequate reason for discounting the relevance and importance of their historical validity. Underlying the interpretative problem for some scholars has been the commitment to a single unified exodus under the leadership of Moses either at an early or late date. The inevitable consequence has been the inability to harmonize the extended detour around Edom and Moab to avoid confrontation (as presented in Numbers 20 and 21) with the more direct route along the King's Highway (reflected in Numbers 33).

Apart from place location and the nature of the archaeological context during the Late Bronze Age with reference to an early or late date for the exodus, the correlation and integration of the data in Numbers 20,21 and Numbers 33 remained problematic. A solution often has been sought in a denigration of the biblical text and a questioning of the historical validity of its data instead of seeking other possible reconstructions that do not violate the text.

The recognition of two quite different biblical traditions concerning the Israelite encounter with the Transjordanian populations often has not been coupled with the logical inference that those traditions well might represent two or more equally distinct (both in time and nature) migrations of Israelites from Egypt.[1] The original writer or compiler obviously struggled in his attempt at integrating the complexities of an extended process into a single 'exodus' narrative. The efforts of his modern day interpreters at reconciling the various aspects of that account into a single event become less and less convincing with the introduction of additional geographical and archaeological data. A firm commitment to a single exodus route, on occasion, has produced a forced interpretation of terminology in the biblical text. The Moabite wilderness (*midbar*, a term usually used to refer to uncultivated land), for example, hardly can be identified with the fertile watershed region bordering the King's Highway.[2]

Late Bronze Age Remains in Transjordan

Recent archaeological surveys and excavations in the Transjordan have clarified dramatically the nature of cultural development during the Late Bronze and Early Iron ages and have forced a reevaluation of the earlier archaeological surveys that seemed to suggest a settlement 'gap' during the second millennium B.C. Earlier surface surveys in central and southern Jordan had prompted the conclusion that virtually no sedentary communities had existed along the plateau between the eighteenth and thirteenth centuries B.C. that could have interfered with the Israelite advance. The impression was that only in the thirteenth century were nomadic tribes replaced by the sedentary populations that later were confederated into the kingdoms of Edom, Moab and Ammon. The acceptance of these tentative conclusions forced a rejection of an early date for the exodus and conquest.[3]

Unfortunately, the 'Gap' theory had been based on a seeming lack of Late Bronze material culture on the sites surveyed and partially on premature conclusions resulting from preconception and cursory, unqualified evaluation of existing evidence. Based on surface surveys at a limited number of sites, the typological ceramic sherd collection was not adequate to reflect the cultural development of the region even if a thorough and accurate interpretation had been possible. The distinctive Transjordan repertoire, quite beyond the current comprehension of those early researchers was discounted in preference to a biased conception of biblical history. Early independent research in Transjordan had been very limited. At Dibon the Early Bronze site was abandoned during the Middle and Late Bronze ages and only reoccupied at the beginning of the Iron Age I period around 1200 B.C. Similarly, Aroer, though only partially excavated, provided an uncertain picture of the existence and/or nature of Late Bronze settlement. In fact, five excavations conducted in the Moabite region, between the Arnon (Wadi el-Mujib) and the Zered (Wadi el-Ḥesā), yielded no evidence of occupation during either the Middle or Late Bronze ages in seeming support of the 'Gap' theory. As a result, the forceful eloquence of its proponents and the logical clarity of those early reconstructions of the Transjordanian cultural revival of urbanized states in the thirteenth century contributed to the longevity and widespread acceptance of the 'Gap' theory.

Ultimately, however, a major archaeological survey conducted by Emory University in central and southern Moab revealed abundant evidence of Middle and Late Bronze occupation at a number of sites, though the evidence seems to suggest a more limited population than during the Early Bronze and Iron Ages. Discovery of Late Bronze pottery during surface survey on a least five sites flanking the King's Highway indicated that the 'Gap' theory about settlement on the central highlands of Moab needed to be discarded.[4] In the south as well, Late Bronze-Iron Age I pottery at a number of sites along Wadi el-Ḥesā pushed sedentary occupation back into the Late Bronze Age.[5]

The current consensus seems to be that while northern and central Transjordan were dominated by city-state confederacies similar to those across the Jordan to the west, the population and territory of Edom to the south, though unclear, appears to have been less structured politically. Few excavations have been conducted south of the Zered and none have provided stratified Middle and Late Bronze remains.

Whatever the complete picture of cultural and political development in the Transjordan, it was adequate to capture the interest and involvement of the New Kingdom pharaohs. The topographical listing of Thutmose III implies a military incursion along the plateau from Gilead to Moab. Both the Execration Texts at the beginning of the second millennium B.C. and the Amarna Tablets in the fourteenth century B.C. indicate Egyptian interest in the northern Transjordan. The emergence of new kingdoms led to internal conflicts on both sides of the Jordan. Seti I's intervention at Beth-shean was directed against incursions from the Transjordan. Midianite intervention along established trade routes also followed. Midian appears to have been a significant tribal league during the Late Bronze Period that finally succumbed to the emerging kingdoms about the mid-eleventh century B.C.[6] As a result Egypt felt the need to intervene in the Transjordan to quell further attacks against Canaan from the east. A text from the reign of Ramesses II mentioning Dibon is probably a reference to Moab,[7] since evidence of the 19th Dynasty pharaohs is reflected in a Seti I stele at Tel esh-Shihab and a Ramesses II stele at Sheikh Zayid. This Egyptian intervention in Moab and Edom during Ramesses' second decade appears subsequently to have prompted the Amorite seizure of Moabite territory north of the Arnon.

References to *Shasu* in the Land of Seir, found in early Egyptian records, appear again in the records of Ramesses II and III. Papyrus Anastasi 6, dated to the late Nineteenth Dynasty (late 13th century B.C.), refers to *Shasu* tribes in Edom. While the references to the *Shasu* are more general and do not make reference to actual Egyptian presence or involvement in the region, the Ramesses II text from Luxor mentions a military campaign and his capture of the town of Boteroth(?) in the land of Moab. These references are adequate to suggest that, in keeping with earlier policies and actions regarding the Transjordan, the pharaohs of the Eighteenth and Nineteenth Dynasties were concerned enough with nationalistic 'stirrings' in the Transjordan to mount military expeditions against key locations along the King's Highway. Whatever conditions along the plateau were during the Middle Bronze Age, the Late Bronze Age saw the formation of sedentary forces dominating the primary north-south trade route. The historical sources do not require extensive Edomite, Moabite or Ammonite kingdoms, nor does most recent archaeological research in the region exclude the possibility of the formative stages of the kingdoms adequate to frustrate free access and passage along the King's Highway on the part of the Moses-led Hebrews coming out of Egypt. The general impression of the archaeological evidence in the Transjordan seems to be that while the northern and central plateau developed a system of city states similar to contemporaneous Palestine, the southern regions were slightly later in their development.

Recent archaeological activity and a reevaluation of cultural data from the Transjordan have identified Late Bronze and Iron Age sites along the entire length of the Transjordanian plateau (in northern Jordan, the East Jordan Valley, the Hesban region and the Medeba plains). Late Bronze remains have been noted at a series of major sites throughout this region: Sahab, Jalul, Tell Safut, Tell el-Husn, Tell Irbid, Talbaqat Fahl, Tell es-Saʿidiyeh, Tell el-Mazar, Tell Deir ʿAlla, the Amman Airport 'Temple,' Amman and its citadel, Medeba, the Beqʿah Valley, Quweilbeh, and Qataret es-Samra.[8]

Analysis of the first Late Bronze pottery found at Amman proved to be slightly different than contemporary ware west of the Jordan River.[9] The Amman Temple was founded initially just before 1400 B.C. and went out of use during the thirteenth century B.C. Associated with a fire cult, its remains included enormous quantities of animal, bird and human bones and an abundant evidence of fire.

It appears that the Egyptians viewed the *Shasu* tribes as nomads or at least semi-nomadic, rather than sedentary and urbanized. Since the cultural prototypes of the Bronze ages are to be sought in the north, it is reasonable to assume that in the peripheral arable lands along the desert frontier, urbanization and sophisticated political structures should reflect a chronological lag to developments west of the Jordan and that such advancement should be much more gradual.

The 'King's Highway' Route

...And they set out from Mount Hor...and encamped in the plains of Moab by the Jordan at Jericho. (Num. 33:41-49)

A comparison of the biblical passages describing the Israelite passage from Kadesh-Barnea to the Jordan River gives the firm impression that two distinct routes are delineated. The list of place names in Num. 33:41-47 identifies sites located on a direct route from

Mt. Hor eastward through the Arabah and north along the King's Highway. It is precisely this route that was avoided by Moses following rejection by the King of Edom. His route is vividly described as a long, discouraging detour, avoiding Edomite and Moabite territories and following the wilderness road on their eastern frontiers. It is simply not possible to harmonize these two descriptions into a single route. There obviously were two distinct itineraries used by the Hebrews emigrating from Egypt to the Promised Land. To highlight the implications of this distinction and to avoid the inherent potential for confusion, the *King's Highway* itinerary used by the early 'escapees' and the route of the final, *Moses-led exodus* will be considered separately.

The place names listed in Num. 33:1-40 readily may be identified with the leadership of Moses and Aaron and are consistent with the details provided in the Exodus narratives. Though this listing of place names is far more comprehensive than the simple itinerary the Exodus narrative suggests, the individual place identifications may be integrated into a Moses-led exodus experience from Ramesses to Kadesh-barnea. The introduction of a short narrative section (33:38-40) seems to provide a break, not only in the form of the document, but also in the itinerary. The continuation of the itinerary in Num. 33:41-49 simply cannot be reconciled with Numbers 21:4 which states categorically that the Moses-led itinerary did not go through Edomite or Moabite territory and did not follow the King's Highway. On the other hand, there is no denying that this passage presents an itinerary of stages and stops followed by Israelites during their exodus journey from Kadesh-Barnea to the Plains of Moab.

The location of Mount Hor, the place of Aaron's burial, must be sought along *the way of the Atharim*, probably a fairly direct line between Kadesh-barnea and the region of the eastern Negev (Num. 20:22-29; 21:1; 33:37-39; Deut. 32:50). A brief identification of the place names integrated into the itinerary will help to clarify the route:

Zalmonah
...And they set out from Mount Hor, and encamped at Zalmonah.
(Num. 33:41)

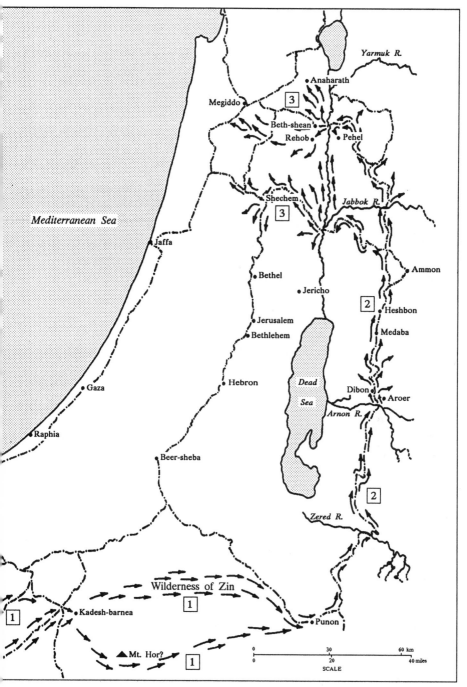

Migration and Infiltration Route of Early Hebrew Departures from Egypt

1. Direct Routes Across Sinai
2. Along King's Highway in Transjordan
3. Penetration into Northern Hill Country and Lower Galilee

The specific location of Zalmonah is uncertain, though the name
(*Calamona*) is preserved at a Roman fort in the Arabah.[10]

Punon

...And they set out from Zalmonah, and encamped at Punon. (33:42)

Punon is unknown elsewhere in the Hebrew Bible. It may be
identified with Khirbet el-Feinan in Wadi el-Feinan though there is
little archaeological evidence available from the site. It was a major
copper mining center located ca. 20 miles southeast of ᶜAin Ḥusb.[11]
This locale easily could have served as the setting for Israel's
punishment with fiery serpents and Moses' brazen serpent (Num. 21:5-
9). The connection clearly was made in the biblical text and as a
result, the itinerary that follows (Num. 21:10-20), a summary from the
Book of the Wars of the Lord, was inserted into the sequence of the
Moses-led itinerary from Kadesh-barnea to the eastern frontier of
Sihon's kingdom. Additional place names, such as Beer (Beer-Elim in
Isa. 15:8), Mattanah (possibly Khirbet el-Mudeiniyeh), Nahaliel
(unknown), and Bamoth (Bamoth-baal in Num. 22:41 and Josh. 13:17)
provide additional stations along the King's Highway, sites that easily
could have played a role in any of the migratory groups passing along
that route during the earlier periods.

Oboth

...And they set out from Punon, and encamped at Oboth. (33:43;
21:10)

ᶜAin el-Weibeh, opposite Punon on the western side of the Arabah,
has been suggested for the location of Oboth. Its sequence in the list
rather would seem to suggest a location to the east of Punon, possibly
approaching or on the King's Highway.

Iye-abarim, in Moabite Territory

*...And they set out from Oboth, and encamped at Iye-abarim, in the
territory of Moab.*

*...And they set out from Oboth, and encamped at Iye-abarim, in the
wilderness which is opposite Moab, toward the sunrise.* (33:44;
21:11)

The name of this location possibly should be translated *'the ruins on the other side'* even though its name may be retained in the modern village of ᶜAi, ca. 10 km southwest of Kerak.[12] Its location on the Edom/Moab border at the ford of the Zered should be located in the southeastern fringe of Moabite territory.

Dibon-gad

...And they set out from Iyim, and encamped at Dibon-gad. (33:45)[13]

Dhībān (biblical Dibon), located ca. 4 km north of the Arnon River (Wadi el-Mūjib), was first settled in the Early Bronze Age. Excavations indicate that Dibon was deserted at the end of the third millennium and reoccupied only in the beginning of the Iron Age about 1200 B.C.[14] (No evidence of the Middle and Late Bronze Ages was found.) The Transjordan plateau north of the Arnon shared by the tribes of Reuben and Gad was described as sheep and cattle grazing tableland (Num. 32:3, 34-37). In reference to the towns of the region, the Bible seems to hint at the nature of the confusion that plagues the identification of the biblical sites in the Transjordan. About some of the towns we are told:

...And the sons of Reuben built Heshbon, Elealeh, Kiriathaim, Nebo, and Baal-meon (their names to be changed), and Sibmah; and they gave other names to the cities which they built. (Num. 32: 37,38)

This transferring of names obviously must be taken into account in problems that have arisen in identifying the biblical place names. The biblical statement provides a very reasonable explanation for Iron Age cities that bear the names of more ancient sites.

Almon-diblathaim

...And they set out from Dibon-gad, and encamped at Almon-diblathaim. (33:46)

Almon-diblathaim clearly corresponds with Beth-diblathaim mentioned among the towns of Moab in Jer. 48:22 and the Mesha Inscription. According to the Mesha Stela, Beth-diblathaim should be located southeast of Baal-meon (Māon, Māᶜīn) and Medeba (Mādabā)[15] near the King's Highway.

Mountains of Abarim, before Nebo

...And they set out from Almon-diblathaim, and encamped in the mountains of Abarim, before Nebo. (33:47)[16]

The Mountains of Abarim may be identified with the rugged plateau overlooking the northeastern shore of the Dead Sea. From this vicinity of Mount Nebo, easy access northward along the Transjordanian plateau and westward into the Jordan Valley provided the Hebrews ample opportunity for infiltration into sparsely populated regions to establish their earliest settlements. Periodical arrivals of additional emigrants from Egypt gradually led to the Hebrew domination of some locales both on the eastern plateau and in the hilly regions of Samaria (e.g., Shechem) and the Galilee. Later the Moses-led contingent arrived at Mount Nebo as well., following their successful military encounter with the Amorite King of Heshbon.

The 'Moses-led Exodus' Route

The general biblical portrayal of the Hebrew passage through the Transjordan to the Jordan Valley north of the Dead Sea is of a series of kingdoms in their formative, or at least early, stages.[17] Whether in a semi-nomadic or sedentary state, their cohesive and military strength is presented as adequate to challenge the Israelite passage. The nature of their early settlement and domination of the Transjordan plateau has been sought in archaeological evidence.

Edomite Approach

The biblical account identifies at least four distinct ethnic groups along the course the Israelites followed through the Transjordan: Edomites, Moabites, Amorites and Ammonites. Their domination of territories along the plateau appears to have complicated the Israelite movement and ultimately resulted in the formation of kingdoms that vied with Israel and Judah for territorial and commercial rights. The general assumption has been that the direct route along the King's Highway was blocked by a sedentary, urbanized Edomite state. The Bible merely states that the relative strength of Israelite and Edomite forces precluded an Israelite attempt at penetrating territory the

Edomites claimed to be theirs. The implication of the request for passage and subsequent argumentation suggests that such passage by similar groups in earlier times, had provided the Edomites with adequate evidence for what they could expect if they granted the Israelites' current request for passage. Nowhere does the biblical text imply a socio-political structure advanced to extensive urbanization with sophisticated fortification systems. In fact, the initial concern of military confrontation (on departure from Egypt) and the subsequent failure against the King of Arad seem to imply a lack of confidence and military prowess on the part of the Israelites. In terms of the biblical account, it is sufficient to view the Edomite 'show of strength' as adequate to overcome Israelite commitment. The biblical description of the Transjordan populations requires no elaborate reconstruction of ethnic political and cultural sophistication including monarchical central control and extensive defensive and offensive systems.

The existence of Edom as a political entity first became noticeable at the time of the rise of the Israelite monarchy (I Sam. 14:47). However, the constant reference to *Shasu* by the Egyptians, from the second quarter of the fourteenth century B.C. to the reign of Ramesses III in the twelfth century B.C., may have included the emerging Edomites. They were a 'Bedouin' type identified with the Transjordan-Arabah locale.[18]

Mount Hor

...And they journeyed from Kadesh, and...came to Mount Hor...on the border of the land of Edom...From Mount Hor they set out by the way to the Red Sea, to go around the land of Edom... (Num. 20:22,23; 21:4)

Mount el-Sabha (elev. 449 m), overlooking an important road junction, north of Kadesh-barnea, or Mount Hamran (elev. 717 m), to the northeast, may provide reasonable locations for Mount Hor.

Negev Approach and the King of Arad

The Israelite confrontation with the King of Arad poses a serious problem in the correlation of archaeological and biblical data. The Early Bronze city of Arad was destroyed and deserted toward the end

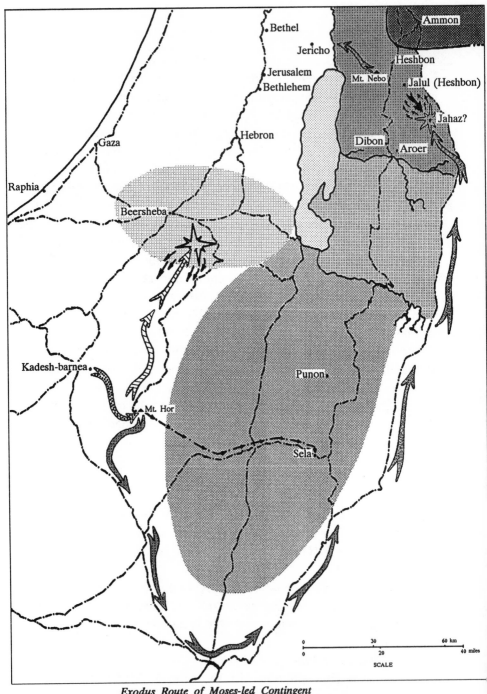

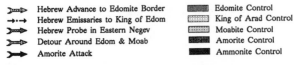

Exodus Route of Moses-led Contingent

⊱═⊰►	Hebrew Advance to Edomite Border	▦	Edomite Control
←•─•►	Hebrew Emissaries to King of Edom	▦	King of Arad Control
⊱═⊰►	Hebrew Probe in Eastern Negev	▦	Moabite Control
⊱═⊰►	Detour Around Edom & Moab	▦	Amorite Control
►═►	Amorite Attack	▦	Ammonite Control

of the third millennium B.C. and not reoccupied until the Israelites established a fortress on the summit overlooking the ruins of the EB site. Attempts to resolve this dilemma have sought other sites in the Negev that possibly could have served as the capital or administrative center for the Late Bronze region of Arad, the name of the EB metropolis having been preserved in the locale.

In the eastern Negev, two fortified Middle Bronze IIB enclosures at Tel Masos (20 dunams) and Tel Malḥata (10-15 dunams) appear to have replaced Arad following its destruction at the end of the Early Bronze Period. Their demise came with the expulsion of the *Hyksos* and the founding of the New Kingdom, ca. 1570 B.C. An occupation gap followed until the beginning of the Israelite period, a period in which no settlement existed in the whole eastern Negev. Life returned to the region after 300 years in the thirteenth century B.C. with new unfortified villages everywhere suggesting the arrival of the Israelite tribes.

...And the descendants of [Hobab (LXX)] the Kenite, Moses' father-in-law, went up with the people of Judah from the city of palms into the wilderness of Judah, which lies in the Negeb near Arad; and they went and settled with the people. (Judg. 1:16)

At the present time it appears impossible from an archaeological standpoint to speak of the conquest of Late Bronze Canaanite cities in the Negev. The suggestion that the 'Arad' and 'Hormah' of the biblical narratives are in reality Tel Masos and Tel Malḥata of the Middle Bronze Age is not particularly appealing. In that case, however, the biblical exodus account would reflect a collection of traditions of exploits of different groups over a longer period of time, with the sequence of those events established on the basis of external criteria, particularly archaeological evidence.[19]

The nature of Israelite settlement in the Negev is relatively clear. Settlement in Canaanite territory was highly unsuccessful. Thus, in the Negev, extensive settlement occurred in those unpopulated areas where the new settlements were not subject to actual danger and saw no need for fortifications. The attraction of uninhabited or sparsely populated regions gave rise to hundreds of such settlements in the Upper Galilee, the Central hill country and the Negev. In the Negev, the settlements of Simeon and the other Negev families flourished until the end of the eleventh century B.C. (I Chron. 4:31; 4:39-40). The Amalekite destruction came during the Israelite-Philistine conflict. When David restored the region to Israelite control it was as a royal enterprise. The traditional family-tribe designation ceased and a new era began in the Negev.[20]

The Way to the Red Sea

...From Mount Hor they set out by the way to the Red Sea, to go around the land of Edom; and the people became impatient (discouraged) on the way. (Num. 21:4)

Having failed in their attempt to follow the tradition migration route through Edomite and Moabite territory along the King's Highway, and having failed in their attempt to penetrate the Negev, the only option remaining was the long and tedious detour completely around the southern and eastern frontiers of Edomite territorial control. The *way to the Red Sea*, therefore, represented a retracing of part of the route they had used approximately 38 years before. The primary route from Kadesh-barnea southward ultimately would bring them to the headwaters of the Gulf of Aqaba. The elaboration of this discouraging detour is provided in Deut. 2:1: *...for many days we went around Mount Seir.*

The Arabah Road

...So we went on, away from our brethren the sons of Esau who live in Seir, away from the Arabah road from Elath and Ezion-geber. (Deut. 2:8)

When finally they were instructed to *turn northward*, it is clear they had arrived at the head of the gulf where they would leave Elath and Ezion-geber.[21] Since the stated purpose of this detour had been to avoid the Edomites, the Arabah road that led directly north along the Great Rift also was avoided. The only remaining option at this point was the ascent across the rugged Edomite mountains bordering the Arabah on the east and continuation northward along the wilderness road, *in the direction of the wilderness of Moab* (Deut. 2:8).

The Wilderness of Edom

The point of departure from the Gulf of Aqaba and the ultimate approach to both Ammonite and Amorite territory from the wilderness of Kedemoth precluded any turn to the interior and an approach along the King's Highway. The term מדבר (*midbar*) may refer to 'uncultivated land' in general. But in this case, the context seems to prefer the nomadic migration route that followed the fringe of the desert, removed from the populations controlling the more productive regions to the west. Only this wilderness approach would allow the Israelites the option of challenging the Ammonites directly rather than the Amorites. When they were instructed not to *harass* the Ammonites, the Amorites became the 'chosen people.'

The Brook Zered

...So we went over the Brook Zered. (Deut. 2:13)

Having skirted Edomite territory on the east, the Israelites crossed the traditional border between Edomite and Moabite territory, the Zered or Wādī el-Ḥesā, near the secondary watershed at the fringe of the desert.

The Wilderness of Moab at Ar

...'This day you are to pass over the boundary of Moab at Ar.' (Deut. 2:18)

After having skirted Moabite territory and crossed the Wādī el-Mūjib, the Israelites continued their northward course along the wilderness road. Directly to the north lay the territory of the Ammonites, to their west, the land of the Amorites.

Ammonite Territory[22]

...and when you approach the frontier of the sons of Ammon, do not harass them or contend with them, for I will not give you any of the land of the sons of Ammon as a possession,... (Deut. 2:19)

The injunction not to confront or challenge the Ammonites left only one option for the Israelite advance toward Canaan. That option existed through Amorite territory. This injunction concerning non-involvement with the Ammonites has special interest in reference to a territorial controversy the Ammonites later had with the Israelite

Judge Jephthah (Judg. 11:12-28). Jephthah's reply had a direct bearing on the itinerary followed by Moses:

...Then they journeyed through the wilderness, and went around the land of Edom and the land of Moab, and arrived on the east side of the land of Moab, and camped on the other side of the Arnon; but they did not enter the territory of Moab, for the Arnon was the boundary of Moab. (Judg. 11:18)

It is simply impossible to reconcile this statement with an exodus route along the King's Highway on the watershed through the center of Edomite and Moabite territory. Clearly the Israelite approach under Moses' leadership was beyond the eastern frontier of these two territories.

Change of Direction

...So I sent messengers from the wilderness of Kedemoth to Sihon the king of Heshbon, with words of peace,... (Deut. 2:26)

The request directed to Sihon involved a westward movement across Amorite territory to the Plains of Moab directly across the Jordan from Jericho. The Israelites encamped on the eastern frontier in the vicinity of Jahaz...at least, it was there the Amorite king challenged the Israelite advance.

Wilderness of Kedemoth

Kedemoth in northern Moab is located on the eastern frontier facing the desert (Josh. 13:17-20; 21:37; I Chron. 6:34). Its location supports the contention that the Israelite approach was along the nomadic wilderness route on the fringe of the desert.

The Amorite Confrontation

...Then Sihon came out against us, he and all his people, to battle at Jahaz. (Deut. 2:32)

Moving northward along the Wilderness Road beyond the sources of the Arnon River, the Hebrews, anticipating westward movement toward the Jordan Valley, sent messengers from Kedemoth (*'eastern regions'*) to the king of Heshbon, Sihon, requesting passage through Amorite territory. When Sihon refused peaceful passage and moved his troops against the Hebrews' advance and major battle ensued at

Jahaz in which the Hebrews were victorious.[23] The site of the battle at Jahaz presumably was located in the vicinity of Kedemoth near the eastern frontier of Amorite territory.

The Amorite penetration into territory north of the Arnon consistently claimed by the Moabites to be theirs may have been the aftermath of Egyptian intervention by Ramesses II and his invasion of the Dibon region. Intermittent contact by the Egyptians later possibly was intended to deter Moabite expansion beyond the Arnon in deference to the Amorites.[24]

A comparison of the biblical passages recounting the Israelite settlement in the Transjordan indicates the complexity of the Israelite arrival and challenge of the various ethnic groups established there.[25] Again there is a conflation in the biblical text of the accounts of those arriving along the King's Highway *(We will go by the King's Highway, until we have passed through your territory...)* and those arriving along the Wilderness Road *(So I sent messengers from the wilderness of Kedemoth...)* Later Jephthah, in his dispute with the Ammonites over the Israelites' rightful claim over the territory north of the Arnon, recounted the Israelites' march around Edomite and Moabite lands, but then insisted that Israel already had dwelt in Heshbon, Aroer and cities north of the Arnon for three hundred years.[26] It seems most feasible that the earliest penetration by migrating Hebrews from Egypt and their occupation of some Amorite cities north of the Arnon occurred by way of the King's Highway a number of generations prior to the arrival of the Moses-led contingent. The account of the occurrences involving Moses appears far too explicit in reference to avoiding Edomite and Moabite lands to support a single exodus event and an integration of so many contradictory statements, both in terms of time and place. A commitment to the historicity of the biblical statements demands as much.

Sihon, King of Heshbon[27]

Tell Hesban, located about 16 km southwest of ᶜAmman and 6 km northeast of Mount Nebo, and guarding the northern edge of the Moabite Plain appeared ideally situated to thwart the Israelites' advance to the Plains of Moab and the Jordan River just 24 km to the west. Excavation of the site, however, revealed that the nineteen superimposed strata of the site covered the period from ca. 1200 B.C. to A.D. 1500 without evidence of Late Bronze occupation. The earliest occupation dated to the 12th-11th centuries appeared to be a small unfortified village dependent upon an agrarian-pastoral economy.

Recent surveys, however, have identified other Late Bronze and Iron Age sites along the entire length of the Transjordanian plateau (in northern Jordan, the East Jordan Valley, the Heshbon region, and the Medeba plains). Excavation efforts have been directed at the major Bronze/Iron Age sites of Jalul and Tell el-Umeiri nearby. There are other possible explanations,[28] but it appears likely that Late Bronze Heshbon was located to Jalul and the name was adopted by the tribe of Reuben when they built a new Israelite town at Tell Hesban. Tell el-Umeiri, a 16-acre tell located between Hesban and Amman, also contains both Bronze and Iron Age remains and is a possible candidate for Sihon's Heshbon.

Battle of Jahaz

...He gathered all his men together, and went out against Israel to the wilderness, and came to Jahaz, and fought against Israel. (Num. 21:23)

The location of Jahaz on the eastern frontier of Amorite territory has been suggested at two sites near the origin of Wadi el-Wale, the northern tributary of the Arnon: Khirbet ʿAleiyān[29] and Khirbet el-Medeiyineh.[30] Either location is consistent with the desert detour described in the biblical account of the Moses-led exodus. On the other hand, an identification of Jahaz with Khirbet Libb directly on the King's Highway is consistent with the confusion that results from attempting an integration of the two distinct routes that the Israelites followed. Khirbet Libb cannot be reconciled with the Amorite confrontation on the eastern frontier.

Mount Nebo

The defeat of Sihon, the Amorite king of Heshbon, and occupation of Amorite territory north of the Arnon gave the Hebrews access to Mount Nebo, overlooking the Plains of Moab in the Jordan Valley north of the Dead Sea. It was at Mount Nebo, 18 km east of the mouth of the Jordan, that Moses died and was buried in the land of Moab without having gained access to his 'Promised Land.' After a thirty-day mourning period in the Plains of Moab, the Israelites, now under Joshua's leadership, were ready to begin their occupation of the land of Canaan.

The Plains of Moab by the Jordan at Jericho

...And they set out from the mountains of Abarim, and encamped in the plains of Moab by the Jordan at Jericho. (33:48)

Moabite territory originally extended into the Jordan Valley north of the Dead Sea. The penetration of the Amorites prior to the arrival of the Israelites reduced Moabite occupation to the area between the Arnon and Zered ravines.

Beth-jeshimoth and Abel-shittim

...they encamped by the Jordan from Beth-jeshimoth as far as Abel-shittim in the plains of Moab.(33:49)

Beth-jeshimoth (Jeshimon) appears to be located at Tell ᶜAzeimeh, while its name is probably preserved at Khirbet es-Suweimeh.[31] Shittim has been identified with Tell Kefrein and Tell el-Hammām (preferable).

Settlement in the Transjordan

Aroer

...From Aroer, which is on the edge of the valley of the Arnon, and from the city that is in the valley, as far as Gilead, there was not a city too high for us... (Deut. 2:36)

The southern extent of the Transjordan conquest is identified with Aroer and probably Khirbet Bālūᶜ, that has been identified with Ar, a major city site guarding the ford and facing Aroer on one of the southern tributaries of the Arnon.[32] Aroer is identified with Khirbet ᶜArāᶜir on the northern rim of the Arnon ravine southeast of Dibon.[33]

Although Aroer has been partially excavated, the situation there seems to be unclear. After a gap of settlement during the Middle Bronze period, it was resettled toward the end of the Late Bronze and beginning of the Iron Age. It was this settlement that appears to have been conquered and fortified by Mesha king of Moab.[34]

Reuben and Gad

Land settlement traditions about the tribes of Reuben and Gad show an early connection with the area immediately north of the Arnon (Num. 32:1-5; 32:34-38) while the families of Machir and Jair, identified with the tribe of Manasseh, were settled in the Gilead and Bashan (Num. 32:39-42). The effectiveness of Reuben to withstand the constant pressure of the Moabites in their attempts to reclaim lands north of the Arnon is not entirely clear. David's suppression of Moab effectively integrated these lands into the kingdom. Periods of internal weakness and north-south tensions between the tribes west of the Jordan provided opportunities for Moabite incursion and ultimate open rebellion under Mesha.[35]

Summary

The behavior of the Hebrews following the 'wilderness wanderings' and departure from Kadesh-barnea provides relatively clear insights into the greater complexity of the exodus event than most reconstructions tend to recognize. The biblical narratives related to the Kadesh-barnea/Plains of Moab segment reflect two independent exodus routes that have far-reaching implications for understanding the nature of the conquest and settlement. The explicit description of a long, tedious, discouraging detour around the Edomite, Moabite and Ammonite territories and a military confrontation with the Amorites is attributed to the Moses-led contingent that represents the last of the escapees from Egypt. The more desirable route through Edomite territory, along the King's Highway on the Transjordan watershed, unfortunately was denied to Moses' emissaries by the Edomite king who reinforced his words with a military show of strength. The Hebrews' rationale to convince the Edomite king to permit passage along the more convenient route clearly was intended to overcome misgivings based on earlier experiences with migrating peoples who tended to ravage the local economy. We can only assume that earlier groups of Hebrews, fleeing the deteriorating conditions in Egypt, passed along the King's Highway at a time when the Edomite king was unable to stop their intrusion into Edomite territorial lands.

These earlier migrations by smaller family or clan units surely contributed to the settlement of towns north of the Arnon River on the Transjordan plateau. It is probable that Jephthah makes reference to such early infiltration in claiming Israelite territorial rights there against Ammonite counter claims. His claim about Israelite settlement during a 300-year period seems to suggest Hebrew arrival as early as the beginning of the fourteenth century B.C.

NOTES

[1] J. Maxwell Miller, The Israelite Journey Through (Around) Moab and Moabite Toponymy. *JBL* 108 (1989): 577-595.

[2] For example, J. Maxwell Miller, The Israelite Journey Through (Around) Moab and Moabite Toponymy. *JBL* 108 (1989): 582.

[3] N. Glueck, Explorations in Eastern Palestine, I,II,III,IV. *AASOR*, Vols. 14 (1934): 15 (1935), 18-19 (1939): 25-28 (1951). New Haven, CT.: American Schools of Oriental Research; *The Other Side of the Jordan*. New Haven: ASOR, 1940 (rev. ed., 1970); Transjordan. *BA* 9 (1946): 45-61; The Civilization of the Edomites. *BA* 10 (1947): 77-84; Transjordan. Pp. 428-453 in *Archaeology and Old Testament Study*, ed. D. Winton Thomas. London: Oxford University Press, 1967.

[4] J.M. Miller, Archaeological Survey of Central Moab, 1978. *BASOR* 234 (1979): 43-52.

[5] B. MacDonald, The Wadī el-Hasā Survey 1979 and Previous Archaeological Work in Southern Jordan. *BASOR* 245 (1982): 35-52.

[6] W.J. Dumbrell, Midian - A Land or a League? *VT* 25 (1975): 323-337.

[7] K.A. Kitchen, Some New Light on the Asiatic Wars of Rameses II. *JEA* 50 (1964): 47-70, Pls. III-VI; D.B. Redford, Contact Between Egypt and Jordan in the New Kingdom: Some Comments on Sources. Pp. 115-119 in *Studies in the History and Archaeology of Jordan, I*, ed. A. Hadidi. Amman: Department of Antiquities, 1982.

[8] J.A. Sauer, Transjordan in the Bronze and Iron Ages: A Critique of Glueck's Synthesis. *BASOR* 263 (1986): 1-26.

[9] G.L. Harding, Recent Discoveries in Jordan. *PEQ* 90 (1958): 7-18; J.B. Hennessy, Excavation of a Late Bronze Age Temple at Amman. *PEQ* 98 (1966): 155-162.

[10] Y. Aharoni, *The Land of the Bible*, 202.

[11] N. Glueck, Explorations in Eastern Palestine, III. *ASOR* 18-19 (1939): 68f.

[12] J.M. Miller, The Israelite Journey Through (Around) Moab and Moabite Toponymy. *JBL* 108 (1989): 581.

[13] F.V. Winnett and W.L. Reed, The Excavations at Dibon (Dhibân) in Moab. *AASOR* 36-37 (1961); A.D. Tushingham, The Excavations at Dibon (Dhibân) in

Moab: The Third Campaign 1952-53. *AASOR* 40 (1972): 1-171; Dibon. Pp. 330-333 in *EAEHL* I, ed, M. Avi-Yonah. Jerusalem: The Israel Exploration Society and Massada Press.

[14] W.L. Reed and F.V. Winnett, *The Excavations at Dibon (Dhibân) in Moab.* (*AASOR* 36-37) New Haven: American Schools of Oriental Research, 1961; A.D. Tushingham, *The Excavations at Dibon (Dhibân) in Moab, 1952-53.* (*AASOR* 40) Cambridge, MA: American Schools of Oriental Research, 1972.

[15] M. Avi-Yonah, Medeba (Madeba). Pp. 819-823 in *EAEHL* II, ed. M. Avi-Yonah. Jerusalem: IES and Massada Press, 1977.

[16] B. Bagatti, Nebo, Mount. Pp. 923-26 in *EAEHL* III, ed. M. Avi-Yonah. Jerusalem: The Israel Exploration Society and Massada Press, 1977.

[17] J.R. Bartlett, The Land of Seir and the Brotherhood of Edom. *Journal of Theological Studies* 20 (1969): 1-20.

[18] J.R. Bartlett, The Land of Seir and the Brotherhood of Edom. *JTS* 20 (1969): 1-20; The Rise and Fall of the Kingdom of Edom. *PEQ* 104 (1972): 26-37. The Moabites and Edomites. Pp. 229-258 in *Peoples of Old Testament Times,* ed. D.J. Wiseman. Oxford: Oxford University Press, 1973.

[19] Y. Aharoni, Nothing Early and Nothing Late: Rewriting Israel's Conquest. *BA* 39 (1976): 55-76.

[20] Y. Aharoni, Problems of the Israelite Conquest in the Light of Archaeological Discoveries. *Antiquity and Survival* 2 (1957): 131-150.

[21] N. Glueck, The Topography and History of Ezion-geber and Elath. *BASOR* 72 (1938): 2-13.

[22] G.M. Landes, The Material Civilization of the Ammonites. *BA* 24 (1961): 66-86.

[23] Numbers 21:21-31; Deuteronomy 2:24-37.

[24] K.A. Kitchen, Some New Light on the Asiatic Wars of Rameses II. *JEA* 50 (1964): 47-70.

[25] J. Van Seters, The Conquest of Sihon's Kingdom: A Literary Examination. *JBL* 91 (1972): 182-97; J.R. Bartlett, A Conquest of Sihon's Kingdom: A Literary Re-examination. *JBL* 97 (1978): 347-51; J. Van Seters, Once Again - the Conquest of Sihon's Kingdom. *JBL* 99 (1980): 117-19. Scribal conventions clearly existed in the recounting of Israel's history. But for the record of the exodus and conquest, meaningful parallels more likely are to be found in Egypt's New Kingdom than in the annals and battle reports of the Neo-Assyrian and Neo-Babylonian periods. Certainly the presence of formalized battle reports, such as the battle against Sihon (Deut. 2:32-36), and parallels and similarities in form may not be taken as a determinative for dating these literary traditions to that late period. See D.M. Gunn, The 'Battle Report': Oral or Scribal Convention? *JBL* 93 (1974): 513-18.

[26] Judges 11:12-28.

[27] S.H. Horn, The 1968 Heshbon Expedition. *BA* 32 (1969): 26-41; Heshbon. Pp. 510-514 in *EAEHL*, II, 1976; Heshbon. Pp. 410-411 in *IDB Supp.* Nashville: Abingdon Press, 1976; L.T. Geraty and L.A. Willis, Archaeological Research in Transjordan. Pp. 30-32 in *The Archaeology of Jordan and Other Studies,* eds. L.T.

Geraty and L.G. Herr. Berrien Springs, Michigan: Andrews University Press, 1986.

[28] L.T. Geraty, Heshbon: The First Casualty in the Israelite Conquest for the Kingdom of God. Pp. 239-248 in *The Quest for the Kingdom of God: Studies in Honor of George E. Mendenhall*, ed. H.B. Huffmon, F.A. Spina, and A.R.W. Green. Winona Lake, Ind.: Eisenbrauns.

[29] N. Glueck, Explorations in Eastern Palestine III, *AASOR* 18-19: 116,117; J.M. Miller, The Moabite Stone as a Memorial Stele. *PEQ* 106 (1974): 9-18.

[30] Y. Aharoni, *The Land of the Bible*, 204; J.A. Dearman, The Location of Jahaz. *ZDPV* 100 (1984): 122-126.

[31] N. Glueck, Some Ancient Towns in the Plains of Moab. *BASOR* 91 (1943): 24-25.

[32] J.M. Miller, The Israelite Journey Through (Around) Moab and Moabite Toponomy. *JBL* 108 (1989): 590-595.

[33] E. Olávarri, Sondages à ᶜArôᶜer sur L'Arnon. *RB* 72 (1965): 77-94; Fouilles à ᶜArôᶜer sur L'Arnon: Les Niveaux du Bronze Intermédiaire. *RB* 76 (1969): 250-259; Aroer. Pp. 98-100 in *EAEHL* I. ed. M. Avi-Yonah. Jerusalem: The Israel Exploration Society and Massada Press.

[34] E. Olávarri, Aroer. Pp. 98-100 in *EAEHL*, I. ed. M. Avi-Yonah. Jerusalem: The Israel Exploration Society and Massada Press; *RB* 72 (1965): 77-94; 74 (1969): 250-59.

[35] J.R. Bartlett, The Historical Reference of Numbers 21:27-30. *PEQ* 101 (1969): 94-100.

Chapter VI

CANAAN: THE PROMISED LAND

The Late Bronze - Iron Age Transition

The formative stages of Israelite tribal life in Canaan chronologically are identified with the Late Bronze - Iron Age transition. The cultural continuity that ultimately is identified with the Israelite monarchy clearly extends to the beginning of the Iron Age. Attempts at identifying distinctive cultural elements that would provide some clue as to a more precise date of beginnings of ethnic presence generally have proved frustrating. Nevertheless, a summary of the relevant archaeological data may provide some helpful insights into a possible clarification of Israelite origins in their 'Promised Land'.

The Egyptian reconquest of Canaan in the mid-sixteenth century B.C. and the aftereffects were devastating, leaving many urban centers destroyed and abandoned.[1] The Syro-Palestinian city-states did not simply transfer their allegiance from the *Hyksos* to the Eighteenth Dynasty pharaohs. As a result, the embarrassment of over a century of *Hyksos* domination and the stubborn resistance of the heavily fortified cities together heightened the severity of Egyptian punitive action. The political and economic structures of the country were totally disrupted.[2] Recent archaeological evidence has illustrated the debilitating nature of Egyptian domination. We are now forced to reject an earlier view of a rapid Canaanite cultural revival following the Egyptian expulsion of the *Hyksos* from Lower Egypt and the subsequent reconquest of Canaan. It seems highly unlikely that "...*by the last years of the 18th Dynasty...almost every town for which there is evidence in the Middle Bronze was once more flourishing and, some, such as Tell Abu Hawām, had been newly founded.*"[3] On the other hand, the opposing concept that the wealth and culture of Canaan's urban centers tended to decline steadily under Egypt's punitive measures and misrule to reach a low ebb in the thirteenth century B.C. is possibly too negative. Many internal and external factors obviously contributed to the gradual destruction of Canaanite city-states and the deterioration of their economies. Canaan's geographical position as an overland link between Egypt and its northern neighbors was especially important to Egypt. The suggestion, however, that Egypt had no economic interests in Canaan because it was poor and mainly agricultural also must be discarded.[4] The fact that the Canaanite vassals paid vast sums in silver and personnel as tribute to their Egyptian overlords would seem to suggest a measure of wealth and complex organization.

Regional surveys have shown that only 37% of the Middle Bronze cities survived into the Late Bronze period.[5] Only seventeen of 77 urban settlements reflect uninterrupted occupation from Middle Bronze to Late Bronze with many sites abandoned during at least a part of the Late Bronze Age. The population of the vibrant city-states of the sixteenth century was reduced dramatically into tiny settlements (40% of the total), small sized towns (48%), and medium-sized towns (7%). Larger towns represented only 5% of the total number of urban settlements in the country.

Only Hazor continued to be an abnormally large city during the Late Bronze, more than four times the size of Lachish (second largest), and sixteen times the size of the average 12.5-acre town. The 210-acre Hazor represented 40% of the total area of urban sites in the entire country during the fourteenth-thirteenth centuries B.C. This was surely due to the continuation of the dominant role Hazor had played during the Middle Bronze Age and gives perspective to the Israelite rationale for Joshua's northern campaign directed specifically at the confederacy of Hazor.

The fourteenth and thirteenth centuries B.C. witnessed a dramatic interchange of goods, people and ideas throughout the Levant. The primary participants in this cultural cross-fertilization were the Egyptians, the Hittites and Mitannians whose relationships were characterized by belligerency and hostility that periodically erupted into military confrontation. Intensification of Egyptian activity in response to these wider interests and actual occupation in southern coastal regions contributed to a flourishing economy in Canaan during the thirteenth century B.C. However, the economic profile of the country was dramatically changed. Political instability and various natural causes ultimately (toward the end of the 13th century B.C.)

ignited a mass displacement of peoples that completely altered the settlement patterns through the eastern Mediterranean littoral.[6]

The Late Bronze period saw a shift of settlement to the coastal plain and along important trade and communication routes. A process of desertion appears to have affected primarily the interior and hilly regions of the country. New sites developed along the northern coast to serve Egypt's growing maritime trade with Cyprus[7] and Mycenae.[8] However, in the southern coastal area not a single new harbor was established. Oppressive Egyptian measures and the establishment of Egyptian strongholds in the southern coastal plain and the Shephelah not only discouraged the construction of city fortifications but disrupted normal urban life as well.

The Egyptian role in Canaan during the Late Bronze has significant implications for understanding the nature of Israelite conquest and settlement. The examination of the 77 urban sites surveyed (representing all the regions of Palestine) indicated an absence of city walls at a great majority of the Late Bronze cities and towns.[9] Both archaeological and historical evidence leave no doubt that Megiddo existed throughout the Late Bronze period without a city wall. Similar unfortified conditions existed at Timnah,[10] Accho,[11] Ekron, and Lachish.[12] The agent for this phenomenon was Egypt whose tightened control over the area to safeguard both commercial and military interests was instrumental in eliminating or at least limiting defensive features throughout Canaan.[13] The almost total lack of town fortifications is a striking phenomenon. Apart from Egyptian intervention, the inter-city rivalries, Shasu attacks, and the ʿApiru presence affecting all the city-states naturally would have called for urban defenses.

The transition from the Late Bronze Age to the Iron Age toward the end of the thirteenth century B.C. was a period of dramatic cultural change in Palestine. The political and economic collapse of the Mycenean and Hittite civilizations sent shock waves across the eastern Mediterranean coastal regions. Many factors including the Doric invasion, a shift in weather patterns and an extended period of drought and famine have been suggested for the collapse of the Mycenean empire.[14] International trade was totally disrupted by destructive population shifts of major proportions. The eastward migration of

Aegean populations, generally referred to as 'Sea Peoples' has been blamed (possibly falsely?) for the destruction of major Cypriot and Syrian centers, including Ugarit and Alalakh. Even the Hittite kingdom, desperately weakened by the same drought and famine conditions that contributed to the Mycenean downfall, succumbed to invasion from the north and pressures of these 'Sea Peoples' from the west and south.

A reevaluation of the Ras Shamra excavations has provided startling evidence that has dramatic implications for the political upheaval throughout the Levant. When the civilization of the Late Bronze came to an end ca. 1200 B.C., Ugarit's thriving metropolis was destroyed and abandoned and remained deserted for at least five centuries. Cultural remains indicate that Ras Shamra had suffered a long period of extreme drought and heat, a condition that produced the famine experienced at Ugarit and among its neighbors. The Late Bronze strata also reflect two periods of severe earthquakes, one in the mid-fourteenth century (during the reign of Amenhotep IV in Egypt), and the second, so severe it totally destroyed the palace and large portions of the city, has been dated to the beginning of the twelfth century B.C. From the crushed kiln in the collapse of the palace walls, a cuneiform letter from the Hittite king Suppiluliumas II pleads for Hammurapi, Ugarit's king, to send provisions to relieve famine among the Hittites and weapons with which to resist a formidable enemy. A second letter from the final firing in the kiln also requests food to relieve famine in another region.[15]

This evidence seems to indicate that Ugarit (Ras Shamra) succumbed to natural disasters rather than the invasion of the Sea Peoples or Northerners. A prolonged drought and its resultant famine and the sequence of earthquakes and the conflagrations they caused ultimately forced an abandonment prior to the arrival of Sea Peoples in the region. It is possible, of course, that the knowledge of their imminent arrival contributed to the Ugarit's abandonment. It is important, however, to consider how these natural phenomena affected other regions of the Levant during this period.

In Canaan the transition to the Iron Age was even more complex. The cultural confusion evident throughout the Levant was especially dramatic with the influx of displaced populations and minority enclaves uprooted from their traditional homelands. The effect on the local urbanized population was a gradual deterioration in which ultimately some of the cities and towns, even major Canaanite cultural centers throughout the country, were destroyed during the second half of the thirteenth century B.C.[16] Egypt survived this initial crisis at the end of the Nineteenth Dynasty. The onslaught of the 'Sea Peoples' that seriously challenged Egyptian supremacy was thwarted for a time by Ramesses III. As a result Egypt enjoyed a renaissance period during the first half of the twelfth century when control over Canaan remained relatively strong. Ultimately, however, the lessening of Egyptian control was painful. Many major Palestinian cities and towns suffered one or more destructions between the reigns of Ramesses III and Ramesses VI. Following the reign of Ramesses VI, Egypt gradually succumbed to an extended period of decline. With the collapse of Egyptian control, the Philistines and other 'Sea People' tribes assumed domination of the local Canaanite population along the coast and in the Shephelah, gradually expanding their settlement from the primary pentapolis.[17]

The list of the urban casualties during the second half of the thirteenth century B.C. is dramatic: Megiddo, Beth-Shean, Tel Abu Hawam, Tel Zeror, Aphek, Gezer, Timnah, Lachish, Tell Beit Mirsim, Tel Seraᶜ, and Ashdod. The fault for their demise may be attributed to the arrival of the 'Sea Peoples' and the Israelites, to the punitive action of the Egyptians against disloyalty where control over a specific region was waning or challenged, or to inter-city rivalries when, in a period of turmoil and declining Egyptian domination in some parts of the country, local kings with 'visions of grandeur' sought to carve out their own regional empire at the expense of their reluctant neighbors. The archaeological evidence clearly suggests a variety of scenarios.

The general impression, however, is of a continuing Canaanite culture and a relatively strong Egyptian presence, especially at major centers such as Beth-Shean and Megiddo in the north, Tel Mor on the coast, Lachish in the southern Shephelah, and Tel Seraᶜ and Tell el-Farᶜah in the south.[18] Recovery in most instances was immediate. The primary Egyptian administrative, military outpost, Beth-Shean, after its destruction near the end of the thirteenth century B.C., was rebuilt and continued to thrive during the reign of Ramesses III.[19] Megiddo, as well, though destroyed possibly during the same disruption that struck Beth-Shean, also immediately recovered. Archaeological evidence suggests Egyptian ties into the reign of Ramesses VI (ca. 1156-1148 B.C.).[20] Most of the others experienced a brief rebuilding by the original population that ultimately succumbed to a second wave of destruction about fifty years later.[21] Following its thirteenth century destruction, Lachish was rebuilt retaining its Canaanite character with ample evidence of an Egyptian presence at least to the reign of Ramesses III. In the far south, the Timna[c] copper mines continued to be exploited by Egyptians into the reign of Ramesses V.[22] The thirteenth century B.C. destruction of Hazor and Aphek was followed by an occupational gap before a completely new cultural pattern emerged (Israelite settlement at Hazor, and Philistine settlement at Aphek). This turbulent, destructive phase evident at major sites throughout the country in the mid-twelfth century B.C. appears to signal the end of Egyptian control in Canaan. At Timnah, the final Canaanite town without evidence of major architectural damage passed into Philistine control.[23]

The traditional date of ca. 1200 B.C. for the end of the Late Bronze period signalled the total disruption of the international trade within the Mediterranean basin, a traumatic assault on Canaanite culture and the destruction of major urban centers with adverse conditions prevalent throughout the country. Even though the final collapse of Egyptian control only came some fifty years later, the intervening period reflected the incursion of the 'Sea Peoples' (along the coast and in the Shephelah) and the Israelites (primarily in the central hill country) and thus rightly belongs to the new age. The traumatic impact of the final collapse of Egyptian domination ca. 1150 B.C. upon cultural changes within Canaan, however, must be recognized as a distinct and separate crisis in any attempted reconstruction of Israelite settlement.[24]

The Israelite Presence in Canaan: Evidence of Demographic and Cultural Change

The reality of the Israel's United Monarchy and its subsequent history calls for a definition of the formative stages of all aspects of Israelite life and culture. The biblical account of the conquest of Canaan and Israel's settlement under charismatic leaders is portrayed as a critical struggle for survival. The settlement of the twelve tribes was a process of integration into an established Canaanite culture. The beginning of their progress from survival to independence is especially vital to understanding Israel in nationhood. Whatever the nature of Israel's arrival, at some point in the evaluation of cultural remains in the land, the continuity of cultural forms that lead to the period of the United Monarchy logically should become evident.

The process by which the Israelites achieved a foothold and ultimate control of Canaan during the Late Bronze and Early Iron ages remains one of the most intriguing and important problems in Old Testament history. In attempting to reconstruct the sequence of events that led to the Israelite monarchy, scholars consistently have struggled with the apparent evidence for both peaceful infiltration and military conquest. The general tendency has been to defend and emulate one process and depreciate the other by appealing to analogy, biblical and extra-biblical data, and ultimately to archaeological and cultural evidence. Because of the intensity of the argumentation and the rigidity with which lines of distinction have been drawn, a brief summary of the three primary scenarios may provide a meaningful basis for later integration of existing data.

The Traditional 'Conquest' Model
The traditional concept of the culmination of the Hebrews' exodus from Egypt was a frontal attack on the Canaanite population, basically consistent with the biblical description in the book of Joshua. The Israelite arrival in Canaan was followed by a series of military campaigns under Joshua's leadership against the primary city-state confederacies in both south and north and other key Canaanite centers throughout the country that could hinder their anticipated settlement. The biblical description of the conquest of Canaan in Joshua 1-12

generally has been understood as a highly successful annihilation of the populations and/or a military victory over a series of thirty-one cities (Josh. 12:7-24). The support of external evidence from archaeological excavations that tended to confirm the biblical conquest traditions produced a ready following for a "conquest" model that was in keeping with traditional biblical interpretation. The dramatic destruction of Bethel at the end of the Late Bronze period and contemporary destruction strata at Lachish and Hazor were assumed to reflect the Israelite conquest and to confirm the biblical account of Israelite 'burning' (even though Bethel is only linked with the conquest as a consequence of its close proximity to ᶜAi).[26] Some have held tenaciously to the traditional interpretation of the book of Joshua and its portrayal of an all-out comprehensive military conquest without reference to the subsequent description of the Israelites' ineffectiveness and frustration in settlement presented in the book of Judges. Additionally, proponents of the 'conquest' scenario have been accused of not taking into account the critical analysis of the biblical books, a process that would recognize much of the biblical narrative other than historical.[27]

The 'conquest' model generally, however, has been denigrated in its most elemental, outdated form. Evaluation of an Israelite military conquest must include the implications of a very problematic, ineffective settlement process, a clear indication that the annihilation of the Canaanite population lacked a certain finality. The traditional concept of the founding of Israelite settlement sites following the destruction of major Canaanite cities with a variety of explanations for various problems has continued to have some support.[28]

That the biblical accounts of the exodus and conquest are filled with contradictory data as an *a priori* assumption reveals a rather simplistic approach to the biblical narratives. A prime example of such thinking occurs in reference to the Hebrew encounter with the king of Arad at Hormah (Num. 14:44-45; 21:1-4; Judg. 1:17-18).[29] Penetration by the Moses-led contingent into Canaan clearly did not occur from the south. Retreat from the encounter with the loss of prisoners to the king of Arad, the discouraging detour required by their inability to penetrate, and the ultimate taking of the area by the tribes of Judah and Simeon, all make the failure in the Negev very clear. The biblical record is not ambiguous about the rejection of a southern assault on the Canaanite population whatever its nature at the time. Ultimate settlement of the territories occupied by Judah and Simeon was achieved from the north following an eastern penetration into the hill country.

On the other hand, there is no question that the traditional conception of the Israelites' decisive military conquest and their seeming comprehensive annihilation of the Canaanite population (suggested by a cursory reading of Joshua 10-12) requires serious qualifications. The Joshua account of the southern and northern campaigns under Joshua's leadership obviously must be understood within the context of many other passages that present less than glowing accounts of the Israelites' abilities to dominate, much less annihilate, their neighbors in Canaan. In spite of the fact that subsequent difficulties in actually appropriating and settling the lands may be explained by the Israelites' failure to take immediate advantage of Joshua's military successes, reinforcement of the validity of the 'military conquest' scenario is lacking in much of the archaeological data. The problems in correlating the traditional concept of Joshua's conquest and the archaeological evidence from the specific urban centers that supposedly suffered the dire effects of Israelite wrath are not minimal, as a regional survey of those sites will indicate.

The rejection of a 'Conquest Model,' primarily for lack of a comprehensive correlation of the biblical narratives regarding the military invasion under Joshua and the destruction levels at specific urban centers mentioned in those accounts, has led many scholars to propose a gradual migration and infiltration of families and clans from a semi-nomadic or nomadic context.

The 'Infiltration' Scenario

The development of the 'infiltration' hypothesis, based primarily on Egyptian sources, focused on the sparsely populated central highlands of Canaan where, in the fourteenth century B.C. during the Amarna Age, Shechem dominated a region between Jerusalem in the south and the Jezreel Valley in the north. For some scholars, Late Bronze nomadism should be equated with the biblical patriarchal narratives.[30]

These early Israelites, generally viewed as nomadic, seasonally grazed their flocks in the "empty" spaces between existing city-state centers and, for a time, the arriving Israelite tribes maintained a period of nomadic life in the isolated mountainous regions. This nomadic period of Israelite presence in Western Palestine was marked by the arrival of additional Israelite tribes from Transjordan as both Transjordanian tribes and Israelites moved from a nomadic lifestyle (identified as *Shasu* in Egyptian records) to sedentary village life. Ultimately, this process culminated in the villages that began to dot the central highlands during the Iron Age I period.[31] When Egyptian control dramatically declined a century later at the end of the Nineteenth Dynasty, the fragmented city-state structure rapidly gave way to the formation of larger ethnically-oriented political entities such as Edom, Moab, Ammon, Israel and the Philistines in those regions more thinly populated by the native Canaanites or other splinter ethnic clans. Biblical traditions identify the Israelite settlement in the central hill country where resistance was limited and infiltration was relatively peaceful.

Following a period of consolidation and growing prosperity, aggressive expansion resulted in conflict with neighboring city-states. This attempt on the part of individual Israelite tribes to establish their own territorial identity is reflected in the book of Judges.[32] Ultimately the consolidation of the tribes resulted in the establishment of the United Monarchy. In this 'infiltration' reconstruction the immigration phase is identified with the 'Leah' tribes and the expansionist phase is linked with the 'Rachel' tribes.[33] More recent modifications of this model have suggested infiltration by farmers and herders of small livestock (rather than nomads) who came to the central hills with established cultural patterns. Their occupation of the more marginal agricultural lands was facilitated by their technological capabilities of waterproofing cisterns for retention of runoff water for use in the dry season and the utilization of terraces along the steep hillsides that extended land surface for crop cultivation. Their arrival from the coastal lowlands to the west was a flight for refuge within the seclusion of the mountaintop villages they established, removed from the violence and warfare among the more aggressive and militant inhabitants, such as the newly arrived Sea Peoples, within the richer coastal lands.[34] The 'infiltration' hypothesis generally is criticized for its failure to explain the fall of the Canaanite city-states in view of the fact that the collapse of the Late Bronze Age cultures presents no precondition for the settlement process.

An Internal Socio-Economic Revolt

A later 'internal peasant revolt' model has rejected the Israelite infiltration into the central highlands as shepherd nomads from the east and south for an internal political and sociological upheaval in which local disenfranchised peasants and village laborers threw off the oppressive bureaucratic rule of the upper classes in the neighboring Canaanite city-states. This revolt which appears from biblical traditions to have started against Sihon of Heshbon and Og of Bashan in the Transjordan spread westward beyond the Jordan into the central hills. These peasant elements ultimately were unified in the worship of Yahweh that originally may have stimulated the revolt.[35] The history of early Israel therefore, according to this model, should be understood as an indigenous revolutionary social movement.

The major weakness of this concept is its rather laborious explanation of conditions that are conducive to revolt and reorganization without giving adequate reasons for its development in the first place. The lack of biblical data appears to be a secondary concern. Archaeological evidence also fails to support such a scenario. The fact that the Late Bronze city-state system appears to have sustained a large middle class and an equitable distribution of wealth, evident in the excavations of thriving secondary towns such as Timnah appears to undermine the possibility of an environment conducive to social upheaval and revolution. The upper class residential and public areas of the primary cities of the coastal and inland plains during the period of the Late Bronze-Early Iron Age transition provide no indication of disruption or partial destruction that could be attributed to such internal social and economic conflict.

Evidence of Cultural Change

Many new settlements established about 1200 B.C. in the central hill country, an area not extensively settled during the Late Bronze Age, were characterized by two new pottery types: a 'collared rim' storage jar and a vertical rimmed cooking pot. The 'four-room' dwellings of these new settlers also seemed to represent a new architectural style.[36] The fact that this type of house was most common in Israelite settlements, and that it was thought not to exist elsewhere seemed to be conclusive evidence that it constituted 'typical' Israelite architecture.[37] The coincidence of these innovations in Canaan and biblical statements (such as, *Pithom and Raamses*) and the renewal of Transjordanian settlement that could be equated with the arrival of Amorites, Moabites and Edomites, seemed to point to the arrival of Israelites during the thirteenth century B.C.

There is no doubt that the population of the central highlands increased dramatically at the end of the Late Bronze Age. The physical evidence of ancient agricultural terraces and small village sites between Hebron and Shechem is clear. Within an area of 4200 km², 23 Late Bronze villages were replaced by at least 114 Iron Age I settlements with a swelling of the population from about 14,000 to 38,000, an increase impossible apart from the arrival of newcomers.[38] Such new villages were constructed on earlier town sites (Ai, Bethel, Tell en-Naṣbeh, el-Jib) or previously unoccupied sites (Raddana) in the area immediately north of Jerusalem.[39] In the region north of Shechem, between Tell el-Farᶜah (N) and ᶜAfula, similar settlements with pillar-type houses typical of this period have been found at Tell el-Farᶜah (N), Taanach, Megiddo, ᶜAfula and Beth-shan.[40] The destruction of Late Bronze Shechem about 1300 B.C. seems to have ended the dominant role Shechem had played in the central hill country during the Amarna period. The rebuilt city, on a poorer and smaller scale, however appears to have maintained its own traditions well into the first century of Iron Age I when, according to Judges 9, it was destroyed by Abimelech. The characteristic pillar houses of other Iron I sites do not appear in Shechem architecture.[41] This type of house construction with a row of three or four pillars that divided the main "great room" along its long axis and supported transverse roofing beams has been noted at many sites, including Beth-shemesh and Tell Beit Mirsim in the Shephelah.[42] Tell Qasile, near the mouth of the Yarkon River on the southern edge of the Sharon Plain, and Tell Abu Hawam, near the mouth of the Kishon River on the southern edge of the Accho Plain, had similar houses early in the Iron Age.[43]

The discovery of similar construction in the central Moab plateau suggests a common architectural form that extended from the Transjordan to the Mediterranean coast. The growing evidence of pillared construction in Late Bronze towns, such as Timnah, suggests, however, the continuation and probable modification of Canaanite architectural traditions rather than innovation by newly arrived settlers.

A consistent sophistication of village planning and cistern technology made possible the establishment of permanent villages on isolated hilltops far removed from perennial natural water sources. While terracing of available slopes indicates that the primary source of livelihood was agriculture, the extensive use of space within village confines for small animal enclosures and shelters suggests a significant dependence on sheep and goats. The common features of house construction, village planning, agricultural subsistence and social organization extending far beyond the central highlands appear inconsistent with an arbitrary, sporadic infiltration and settling of nomads. They reflect ingrained traditions of settlers familiar with a sedentary lifestyle based on agriculture.[44]

The question of the origin of these Iron Age I settlers in the central highlands is of vital concern in a reconstruction of the Hebrew exodus and the nature of Israelite occupation of Canaan. Clearly the Hebrews in the land of Goshen primarily were urbanized agriculturalists, living in villages and basically committed to the exploitation of the irrigated alluvial plains of the Nile Delta. Animal and plant husbandry for them would pose no problems within the new geographical context of Canaan. Attempts at inconspicuous infiltration into Canaanite dominated regions would demand accommodation to locally existing architectural designs and village planning. The earliest Hebrew emigrants from Egypt obviously hoped to blend into the Canaanite scene by adapting their lifestyles and adopting existing traditions within the locales providing, in some cases, reluctant hospitality.

NOTES

[1] B. Mazar, Canaan and the Canaanites. *BASOR* 102 (1946): 7-12; J.M. Weinstein, The Egyptian Empire in Palestine - A Reassessment. *BASOR* 241 (1981): 1-28.

[2] A. Leonard, Jr. The Late Bronze Age. *BA* 52 (1989): 4-39.

[3] K.M. Kenyon, Palestine in the Time of the Eighteenth Dynasty. *CAH³* II, 1: 556.

[4] S. Aḥituv, Economic Factors in the Egyptian Conquest of Canaan. *IEJ* 28 (1978): 39-108.

[5] M. Broshi and R. Gophna, Middle Bronze II Palestine: Its Settlement and Population. *BASOR* 253 (1984): 41-53.

[6] R.S. Merrillees, Political Conditions in the Eastern Mediterranean During the Late Bronze Age. *BA* 49 (1985): 42-50.

[7] Pottery analysis by neutron activation has shown that Eastern Cyprus is the source of 'Palestinian' Bichrome Ware. See M. Artzy, F. Asaro and I Perlman, Pottery Analysis by Neutron Activation. *Archaeometry* 11 (1969): 21; The Origin of the 'Palestinian' Bichrome Ware. *JAOS* 93 (1973): 446-461; Imported and Local Bichrome Ware in Megiddo. *Levant* 10 (1978): 99-111.

[8] B.M. Gittlen, The Cultural and Chronological Implications of the Cypro-Palestinian Trade during the Late Bronze Age. *BASOR* 241 (1981): 49-60.

[9] R. Gonen, Urban Canaan in the Late Bronze Period. *BASOR* 253 (1984): 61-73.

[10] G.L. Kelm and A. Mazar, Three Seasons of Excavations at Tel Batash - Biblical Timnah. *BASOR* 248 (1982): 1-36.

[11] M. Dothan, Ten Seasons of Excavations at Ancient Acco. *Qadmoniot* 18 (1985): 2-14.

[12] D. Ussishkin, Level VII and VI at Tel Lachish and the End of the Late Bronze Age in Canaan. Pp. 216-217 in *Palestine in the Bronze and Iron Ages*. ed. J.N. Tubb. London: Institute of Archaeology, 1985.

[13] R. Gonen, Megiddo in the Late Bronze Age - Another Assessment. *Levant* 19 (1987): 83-100.

[14] H.E. Wright, Jr., Climatic Change in Mycenaean Greece. *Antiquity* 42 (1968): 123-27; R.A. Bryson, H.H. Lamb, and D.L. Donley, Drought and The Decline of Mycenae. *Antiquity* 48 (1974): 46-50; F.H. Stubbings, The Recession of Mycenaean Civilization. Pp. 338-58 in *CAH³*, II,2 (1975); P.P Betancourt, The End of the Greek Bronze Age. *Antiquity* 50 (1976): 40-47.

[15] C.F.A, Schaeffer, The Last Days of Ugarit. *BAR* 9/5 (1983): 74-75.

[16] P. Beck and M. Kochavi, A Dated Assemblage of the Late 13th Century B.C.E. from the Egyptian Residency at Aphek. *Tel Aviv* 12 (1985): 38. A. Mazar, *Archaeology of the Land of the Bible 10,000-586 B.C.E.* New York: Doubleday, 1990: 187-88.

[17] A. Mazar, The Emergence of the Philistine Material Culture. *IEJ* 35 (1985): 95-107; I. Singer, The Beginning of Philistine Settlement in Canaan and the Northern Boundary of Philistia. *TA* 12 (1985): 109-22.

[18] A. Mazar, *Archaeology of the Land of the Bible, 10,000 - 586 B.C.E.* New York: Doubleday, 1990: 296-300.

[19] F. James, *The Iron Age at Beth Shan: A Study of Levels VI-IV*. Philadelphia: University Museum, University of Pennsylvania, 1966; Y. Yadin and Sh. Geva, *Investigations at Beth-Shean. The Early Iron Age Strata*. (*Qedem* 23). Jerusalem:The Hebrew University, 1986.

[20] T. Dothan, *The Philistines and Their Material Culture*. New Haven and London: Yale University Press, 1982: 70-76.

[21] A. Mazar, *ibid*, 290-91.

[22] B. Rothenberg, *Timna: Valley of the Biblical Copper Mines*. London: Thames and Hudson, 1972.

[23] G.L. Kelm and A. Mazar, Three Seasons of Excavations at Tel Batash - Biblical Timnah. *BASOR* 248 (1982): 14-15; *idem*, Excavating in Samson Country. *BAR* 15/1 (1989): 41.

[24] D. Ussishkin, Lachish - Key to the Israelite Conquest of Canaan? *BAR* 13/1 (1987): 18-39; *Tufnell Festschrift:* 213-30.

[25] W.F. Albright and his students provided much of the impetus for the 'conquest' model of Israel's formative stages. See, for example, W.F. Albright, The Israelite Conquest of Canaan in the Light of Archaeology. *BASOR* 74 (1939): 11-23.

[26] W.F. Albright, The Kyle Memorial Excavation at Bethel. *BASOR* 56 (1934): 2-15.

[27] V. Fritz, Conquest or Settlement? The Early Iron Age in Palestine. *BA* 50 (1987): 84.

[28] Y. Yadin, The Transition from a Semi-Nomadic to a Sedentary Society in the Twelfth Century B.C.E. Pp. 57-68 in *Symposia*, ed. F.M. Cross. Cambridge, MA: ASOR, 1979.

[29] W.H. Stiebing, Jr. *Out of the Desert? Archaeology and the Exodus/Conquest Narratives*. Buffalo, N.Y.: Prometheus Books, 1989: 66-68.

[30] M. Weippert, The Israelite "Conquest" and the Evidence from Transjordan. In *Symposia*, ed. F.M. Cross. Cambridge, MA: ASOR, 1979: 30-34.

[31] B. Mazar, The Process of Israelite Settlement in the Hill-Country. *EI* 15 (1981): 145-149.

[32] Y. Aharoni, Nothing Early and Nothing Late: Rewriting Israel's Conquest. *BA* 39 (1976): 55-76; A.G. Auld, Judges and History: A Reconstruction. *VT* 25 (1975): 261-285.

[33] A.Alt provided the primary groundwork for the 'infiltration' theory in *Kleine Schriften zur Geschichte des Volkes Israel*, I, 89-125; *Essays on Old Testament History and Religion* (English Translation). Garden City, NY: Doubleday, 1968: 133-69; Also see: M. Weippert, *The Settlement of the Israelite Tribes in Palestine; A Critical Survey of Recent Scholarly Debate*. Trans. J.D. Martin. Studies in Biblical Theology (2nd series) 21. Naperville, IL: A.R. Allenson, 1971: 1-46.

[34] J.A. Callaway, A New Perspective on the Hill country Settlement of Canaan in Iron Age I. Pp. 31-49 in *Palestine in the Bronze and Iron Ages: Papers in Honour of Olga Tufnell*, ed.J.N. Tubb. London: Institute of Archaeology, 1985.

[35] G.E. Mendenhall, The Hebrew Conquest of Palestine. *BA* 25 (1962): 66-87; *idem, The Tenth Generation*. Baltimore: Johns Hopkins, 1973; N.K. Gottwald, Were the Early Israelites Pastoral Nomads? Pp. 223-255 in *Rhetorical Criticism: Essays in Honor of James Muilenberg*, eds. J.J. Jackson and M. Kessler. Pittsburgh: Pickwick Press, 1974; Nomadism. Pp. 629-31 in *IDB Supplementary Volume*. Nashville: Abingdon Press, 1976; Were the Early Israelites Pastoral Nomads. *BAR* 4/2 (1978): 2-7; *The Tribes of Yahweh: A Sociology of the Religion of Liberated Israel, 1250-1050 BCE*. Maryknoll, NY: Orbis, 1979: 210-219; Two Models for the Origins of Ancient Israel: Social Revolution or Frontier

Development. Pp. 5-24 in *The Quest for the Kingdom of God: Studies in Honor of George E. Mendenhall*, eds. H.B. Huffmon, F.A. Spina, and A.R.W. Green. Winona Lake, Ind.: Eisenbrauns, 1983; The Israelite Settlement as a Social Revolutionary Movement. Pp. 34-46 in *Biblical Archaeology Today: Proceedings of the International Congress on Biblical Archaeology*, Jerusalem, April 1984. Jerusalem: Israel Exploration Society, 1985; M.L. Chaney, Ancient Palestinian Peasant Movements and the Formation of Premonarchic Israel. Pp. 39-90 in *Palestine in Transition: The Emergence of Ancient Israel*, eds. D.N. Freedman and D.F. Graf. Sheffield: American Schools of Oriental Research and Almond Press, 1983.

[36] Y. Aharoni, *The Archaeology of the Land of the Israel*. trans. A.F. Rainey. Philadelphia: Westminster, 1978, 1982: 160-163, 174-176.

[37] Y. Shiloh, The Four-Room House - The Israelite Type-House? *IEJ* 11 (1961): 227-285.

[38] L.E. Stager, Highland Village Life in Palestine some Three Thousand Years Ago. *The Oriental Institute Notes and News* No. 69 (1981): 1.

[39] See, for: (Ai) J.A. Callaway, *The Early Bronze Age Citadel and Lower City at Ai (et-Tell)*. (1980): 195; (el-Jib) J.B. Pritchard, *Winery, Defenses, and Soundings at Gibeon*. Philadelphia: University Museum, 1964: 35-37, 40; (Tell en-Naṣbeh) M. Broshi, Tell en-Nasbeh. *EAEHL* III (1977): 912-914; J. Muilenberg, Mizpeh. *IDB* 3, 408; (Bethel) J.L. Kelso, The Excavation of Bethel (1934-1960). *AASOR* 39 (1968); (Raddana) J.A. Callaway and R.E. Cooley, A Salvage Excavation at Raddana, in Bireh. *BASOR* 201 (1971): 9-19.

[40] R. de Vaux, Les fouilles de Tell el-Farʿah, près Naplouse. *RB* 62 (1955): 575-580; P.W. Lapp, The 1966 Excavations at Tell Taʿannek. *BASOR* 185 (1967): 2,3,21; M. Dothan, The Excavations at ʿAfula. *ʿAtiqot* I (1955): 30ff.

[41] L.E. Toombs, Shechem: Problems of the Early Israelite Era. Pp. 69-83 in *Symposia*. F.M. Cross (ed.) (1979).

[42] Y. Shiloh, The Four-Room House - The Israelite Type-House. *EI* 11 (1973): 277-85; E. Grant and G.E. Wright, *Ain Shems Excavations IV* 24 (1938); W.F. Albright, Tell Beit Mirsim III: The Iron Age. *AASOR* 21-22.

[43] B. Mazar, The excavations at Tell Qasile. *IEJ* 1 (1951): 138; R.W. Hamilton, Excavations at Tell Abu Hawâm. *QDAP* 4 (1935): 8-9.

[44] J.A. Callaway, *op.cit.*, 37-43.

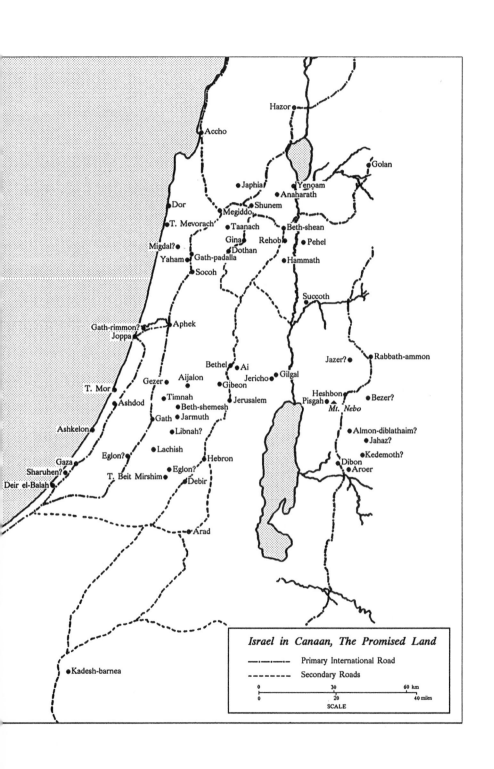

Israel in Canaan, The Promised Land

———·——— Primary International Road

- - - - - - Secondary Roads

SCALE

0   30   60 km
0   20   40 miles

Chapter VII

ISRAEL IN CANAAN, THE PROMISED LAND

Military Conquest in Canaan

The arrival of the Israelites in Canaan and their subsequent integration into the resident population and its culture, whether by infiltration or conquest, must be understood in terms of historical and archaeological data. This process legitimately may not be based on the precondition of the primacy of one form of data over the other. The objectivity of the researcher also must be tempered by humility that recognizes the resulting reconstruction as less than final. It is within the realm of a subjective process of reevaluation and review of the relevant data that we return to the question of whether the biblical presentation of an Israelite military effort in Canaan has validity.

The biblical account of the Hebrew exodus and its itinerary reflects a far more complex process than generally has been perceived in earlier reconstructions of Israel's progress toward confederation and monarchy. An extended process of emigration from Egypt culminated in a final Moses-led contingent. The scribal collation and integration of all the relevant data to form a comprehensive summary of the corporate event we now designate as the Hebrew 'Exodus' obviously was no easy matter. Even more complex was the process of Israelite integration as a covenanted people and their confrontation with the alien resident population of Canaan. The dilemma of the biblical writers in providing a meaningful summary statement of the historical ramifications of Israel's formation surely lies at the heart of our controversy over the relative merits of 'infiltration' vs. 'conflict' scenarios. Clarification hopefully will be provided through continued archaeological research. Only a constant rethinking of the growing corpus of archaeological data in reference to the biblical text will provide the insight to resolve seeming contradictions and inconsistencies within the proposed reconstructions.

The *a priori* assumption that the biblical accounts of the exodus and conquest are filled with contradictory data provides little insight into the validity of our understanding of Israel's formation. Whatever the perceived shortcomings of its historical data, the biblical narratives still form the basic source for our reconstruction of the historical background of the Israelite monarchy. Increasingly, our understanding and the implications of the biblical narratives are being clarified by relevant archaeological insights. To that end, a review of the archaeological evidence of the turbulent Late Bronze - Iron Age transition may be helpful in clarifying the validity of Israelite aggression in Canaan.

Archaeological Evidence of Military Conquest

The possibility of military action assumes a base of operations and evidence of the offending party's presence in the region, as well as the historical existence of the sites under attack. According to the biblical narratives, the prelude to overt action by the Israelites in claiming Canaan as their ancestral inheritance followed 40 years of Sinai 'wanderings.' The ephemeral evidence of those activities within the barren expanse of the Sinai is consistent with the cultural record at Kadesh-barnea, the locale on the southern fringe of the Promised Land that was assumed to have served as their cultic center during those perilous times, and in the Negev where, according to the biblical narratives, a military penetration by the Hebrews was attempted.

At Kadesh-Barnea
The area around the Kadesh-barnea oasis has yielded abundant cultural evidence of extensive settlement during the third millennium B.C. However, a thorough archaeological survey of the Kadesh-barnea oasis and surrounding terrain has not produced any ceramic or architectural evidence from the Late Bronze and Iron I Ages. The next permanent occupation at the oasis is related to the fortress and trading post that was established there during the period of the United Monarchy.

In the Negev
The biblical reference to the Israelite advance into the Negev where the Israelites were repulsed by the King of Arad has focused archaeological

research on the eastern Negev where extensive excavation and survey has discovered no evidence of Canaanite settlement during the Late Bronze Age.[1] Excavations on the acropolis at Tel ᶜArad have identified a series of fortresses dated from the Iron, Persian, Hellenistic, Roman and early Arab periods. The Iron Age construction followed a long period of abandonment during the Middle and Late Bronze periods. A large city of the Early Bronze II (ca. 2900-2700 B.C.) previously existed on the site.[2]

The mention of two Arads, the 'Great Arad' and 'Arad of the House of Yeroham,' in the campaign annals of Shishak I in the tenth century B.C. has helped to resolve the problem of the Canaanite King of Arad who confronted the Israelite advance into the Negev. A possible location shift of the king's capital during the second half of the second millennium B.C. for purposes of defense, commerce or other internal policies has prompted the search for the 'second' Arad, possibly at Tel Malḥata (Tell el-Milḥ in Arabic).[3] The possible identification of 'Arad of the House of Yeroham' (the biblical Yerahmeelites) at Tel Malḥata led to the further suggestions that Hormah was a later Israelite reference to the Canaanite capital following its destruction or that it may be located at nearby Tel Masos (Khirbet Meshâsh).[4] Archaeological excavations at both Tel Malḥata and Tel Masos, however, have produced no Late Bronze remains.[5] In fact, it seems entirely possible that no Late Bronze settlement existed in the entire eastern Negev. Both sites were fortified Middle Bronze cities dominating important water sources in the semi-arid Negev and acting as deterrents against Bedouin incursions from the desert. Their function exactly fits the nature of Arad and Hormah and the actions of the King of Arad in the biblical episode. Unfortunately, it is less than satisfying to suggest that the conquest traditions are merely recalling an earlier historical reality.[6]

The mystery concerning the location of the principal city of the king of Arad remains. It seems probable, according to the biblical text, that the king's capital and Hormah were one and the same. Tel Malḥata and Tel Masos, in the immediate vicinity of Tel Arad, appeared to be the best candidates for the 'Arad of the House of Yeroham.' It seems unreasonable to suggest that the Israelites would concoct a literary tradition about a nonexistent ruler who humiliated them in their first attempt at gaining access to the Promised Land. Consistent with the prevailing conditions in the arid regions of Canaan's southern frontier, the king and his people controlling the region identified with the great Early Bronze city were probably nomadic, or at best, semi-nomadic, of necessity and saw the Israelite advance as a major threat to their subsistent survival. The material evidence of such a population would be non-existent. On the other hand, other unexcavated sites within a wider region yet may provide a solution to this problem, though that appears very unlikely for the present.

The identification of Beersheba of the Israelite periods is clearly with Tell es-Saba[c] (Arabic) or Tel Sheba (Hebrew) where a village occupation began ca. 1200 B.C. The allotment of the Negev region to Simeon (within the tribal territory of Judah) appears to have been followed by Israelite domination and settlement.[7] By the tenth century B.C., Beersheba had become a well-planned, strongly fortified royal city.

In the Transjordan

Two different traditions reflected in the biblical text are best understood, as we have seen, in terms of two distinct routes followed by the Israelites during their migration from Egypt. The first account (Num. 20:10-11; 33:37-48), clearly outlines a route directly to the King's Highway through what would appear to have been both Edomite and Moabite territory. This account makes no reference to a confrontation with Edomite, Moabite or Amorite resistance. The second account (Num. 20:14-21; 21:4-9, 12-20; Deut. 2:1-37) relates a recognition of territorial rights for Edomites, Moabites, Amorites and Ammonites and Moses' use of emissaries to conduct negotiations for the privilege of passing through tribal lands. The failure to negotiate terms of passage resulted in a lengthy detour around Edomite and Moabite territories and finally, a successful confrontation with Sihon, the Amorite king of Heshbon, who challenged their advance from the wilderness road on his eastern frontier. Blocked in their advance to the Plains of Moab, east of the Jordan opposite Jericho, the Israelites had no alternative but to force their way through the Amorite region.

In the Jordan Valley

Gilgal

Gilgal need not have been more than a outdoor sanctuary containing twelve stones placed in a circle. Possibly, it is best identified with Suwwānet eth-Thaniya, the highest point east of Jericho, with a commanding view of the Lower Jordan Valley and Jericho.[8] Khirbet el-Mefjir, with Early and Middle Iron age remains (ca. 1200 - 600 B.C.), also has been suggested as a possible location for biblical Gilgal.[9]

Jericho

A thick streaked erosion layer of washed burnt materials above Middle Bronze buildings suggested a period of abandonment at Jericho from ca. 1560 to 1400 B.C. Above the first remains attributed to the Late Bronze Age, an unspectacular small section of floor, a small oven and a fourteenth century juglet confirmed the existence of a Late Bronze Age settlement, at least, on a part of the site. No traces of Late Bronze walls remained. The end of the latest 'Canaanite' occupation at Jericho was dated to the mid-fourteenth century B.C. Partial erosion of the building showed how the rest of the settlement disappeared.[10] For the traditional concept of the Israelite conquest of Jericho, however unorthodox its strategy, the archaeological evidence from Tell es-Sultan (biblical Jericho) is problematic. A brief review of the biblical data may provide some insights for a possible solution.

Joshua's initial confrontation with the Canaanite inhabitants of the Promised Land came at Jericho. According to the biblical account (Josh. 1-5), the advance into the Plains of Moab within the Rift Valley north of the Dead Sea was followed by a miraculous crossing of the Jordan River at flood stage and the circumcision of those males who had been born during the 38 years of 'wanderings' in the Sinai Peninsula. Of special interest for our reconstruction of the conquest is the detailed description of Joshua's strategy during this first hostile encounter. The Israelite plan was dependent upon first-hand information based on reconnaissance. Moses' sending the twelve spies into the Promised Land from the Sinai and Joshua's spies later sent to ͨAi suggest that this was a consistent strategy. We safely may assume, therefore, that Joshua's rather unorthodox plan of attack was based on the eyewitness report of the spies on conditions within Jericho that could be used to Israel's advantage. Two details reinforce this relatively safe assumption:

1. Joshua obviously had a purpose in sending the two spies into Jericho that anticipated the city's capture.

2. The details concerning Jericho included in the biblical text surely are relevant to a proper understanding of the city's capture. It is for this reason that, if any historical integrity for the biblical text is assumed in this event, serious thought must be given to the way in which some physical descriptions relate to an understanding of the event.

Joshua's instructions to the spies included observation of the terrain surrounding Jericho and specifically the nature of the city itself. Their selection of the harlot's house probably had a two-fold purpose: to minimize detection in an establishment presumably often frequented by non-residents; and, to take advantage of the location *in the wall* where defensive preparations by the local militia and the nature of the terrain around the outside of the wall could be observed. Rahab's house (Josh. 2:15), integrated into the city's defensive wall ultimately also allowed for escape through an exterior window after the city gates had been barred at sunset. It also seems clear that if Rahab's house had been constructed uniquely into the defensive system, there would have been no need for identifying her window with a scarlet cord. It, therefore, seems clear that the defensive system probably consisted of a casemate wall with its rooms (casemates), in some instances at least, converted into homes and living quarters to accommodate the overflow population of the oasis.

The ultimate strategy of marching around the city once each day during the first six days established a consistent pattern that dramatically was broken on the seventh day. The impact of the Israelites' very unusual behavior upon the residents of the city under siege, possibly a mixture of anxiety and bewilderment on the first six days, certainly became captivating curiosity on the seventh day. The shouting and blasting of trumpets must have attracted every Jerichoan to the walls to catch a glimpse of the Israelites' unusual military strategy. Since Late Bronze walls are lacking in the archaeological remains, and Egyptian restrictions seemingly limited defensive installations throughout the country, we may assume that Jericho's surviving Middle Bronze casemate walls, used primarily for living quarters, provided the defensive perimeter of Jericho. The effect of the weight of most of the population on the now fragile Middle Bronze walls, with centuries of weathering and probable deterioration of its outer foundations, easily could duplicate the biblical description of the fall of Jericho. There is absolutely no need to speculate on the possibility of an earthquake.[11] A seven-day siege, that the biblical narrative describes, obviously did not cause a food shortage. The biblical description of the city's capture suggests a strategy based on an eyewitness account of the unique conditions of Jericho's vulnerability.

The limitations of archaeological data concerning the nature of the Late Bronze city are the result of over three thousand years of erosion and a sequence of archaeological excavations that disturbed and destroyed some or most of the minimal Late Bronze remnants on the mound's surface. The prohibition against rebuilding the city precluded the sealing and protection of the Late Bronze city remains and the results of the Israelite capture and burning.

In the Judean Hill Country

ᶜAi and Bethel

Ai, which is near Beth-Aven to the east of Bethel (Josh. 7:2)

ᶜAi, identified with et-Tell, a large mound east of the village of Beitin, was a powerful Early Bronze city. The destruction of the Early Bronze city was followed by a long desertion until a small Israelite village was established there in the twelfth century B.C. Since the location of Bethel at Beitin generally is accepted in terms of geographic setting and archaeological evidence, the biblical account of Joshua's military activities in this area must be explained in reference to et-Tell. Various explanations have attempted to clarify the nature of the biblical conquest of ᶜAi in terms of the archaeological evidence. Remains at Khirbet Haiyân, a suggested location for the biblical ᶜAi, were too late for the biblical period.[12] The limited options for a biblical-archaeological correlation have led to the questionable suggestion that the Israelites captured and burned the small, unfortified Iron Age I village on the acropolis of et-Tell during the twelfth century B.C.[13]

The best explanation within the context of these limitations involves recognition of Bethel's role in the defense of the region. In view of the complementary histories that Bethel and ᶜAi appear to have, we may assume that, following the destruction of the regional capital at the end of the Early Bronze period, the principal town of the region was established to the west in closer proximity to the primary north-south road along the watershed. During the Middle and Late Bronze periods, the city of the region of ᶜAi was located at Beitin.

Having heard of the Israelite advance across the Jordan and the capture of Jericho, the king of ᶜAi (at Bethel), concerned about a front line of defense, established a garrison, or company on the mound of the 'ruin' (meaning of "ᶜAi"), using either existing remnants of structures, or hurriedly constructing emergency defenses. This situation provides a logical explanation for the report of Joshua's spies and their appraisal of the military strength of ᶜAi:

...do not make the whole people toil up there, for they are but few. (Josh. 7:3)

The disastrous consequences of their limited effort against the king of ᶜAi suggests that what the spies actually saw was misleading, a concept that is supported by what the Israelites later encountered.

There was not a man left in Ai or Bethel, who did not go out after Israel; they left the city open, and pursued Israel. (Josh. 8:17)

The biblical statement appears relatively clear in its reference to a single city. Since we know archaeologically that ᶜAi was a ruin (a situation that even the biblical record seems to recognize), the city referred to must be Bethel. And in all likelihood, it was the occasion on which Bethel was destroyed by fire. The fourteenth century B.C. town at Bethel prospered with two phases of large patrician houses. The second phase of Late Bronze Bethel was destroyed in the thirteenth century B.C. in a 'tremendous conflagration' producing a 1.5 m mass of fallen brick (burned red and black), ash-filled earth and charred and splintered debris.[14] The following Iron Age I dwellings built on the destruction level of the Late Bronze town were in stark contrast to the earlier opulence. Poorly made pottery was recovered from the floors of humble hovels.[15] Archaeological evidence for the destruction of the Late Bronze IIB town by Joshua (of the tribe of Ephraim) may quite reasonably be attributed to the House of Joseph (Judg. 1:22-25). While this reconstruction may not be totally acceptable for some, it is more satisfying than an etiological explanation for the large Early Bronze ruin at ꜥAi supposedly authored by the Iron Age Bethelites.

The problem of ꜥAi, and other sites such as Arad, in a correlation of archaeological data with the biblical narratives, has forced a redirection in thinking to a more realistic perspective in understanding Joshua 7-8. The preservation and integration of traditions in the biblical narrative, as in the case of the Book of Jasher (Josh. 10:13), without harmonizing to avoid repetitions, numerical inaccuracies and contradictions, is evidence of their authenticity and reflects a respect for those ancient written and oral traditions handed down from generation to generation.[16]

Control of the Central Hill Country

Domination of the strategic central hills was facilitated by the capitulation of the alien Hurrian (biblical Horite) population identified with a four city confederacy controlling the ridge south of Bethel and ꜥAi. Unoccupied urban sites appear to have been settled as the local population in the immediate vicinity was pacified. For example, Tell en-Nasbeh (biblical Mizpeh), after an interruption of about 2000 years, was re-occupied at the beginning of the Early Iron Age in the eleventh century B.C.[17] For the most part, however, the Israelites were forced to establish small remote settlements in undesirable areas to avoid the established Canaanite population.

The Gibeonite League: Treaty Agreement[18]

Joshua's treaty with the Gibeonites, even though achieved through trickery, illustrates the manner in which non-Israelite populations were integrated into the covenant relationship. This confederacy of four non-Semitic, Indo-European Hurrian (biblical Horite) cities, headed by Gibeon, became a part of the Israelite population. Though committed to a second-class, *corvée* role within the economic and social structure of the fledgling nation, the Gibeonites had obligated Joshua to their immediate defense.

The biblical description of Gibeon poses a serious problem for a historical reconstruction of a Late Bronze 'conquest.'

> ...Gibeon was a great city, like one of the royal cities, and because it was greater than Ai, and all its men were mighty. (Josh. 10:2)

For the present, at least, the biblical statement must be understood to refer to the city's past greatness and reputation. Its comparison with ᶜAi which we know was a ruin at the time of the Israelite conquest probably was intended to mean that at the time of ᶜAi's greatness (Early Bronze), Gibeon was even more powerful because of the bravery of its men. The fear of Adonizedek of Jerusalem came from the realization that the Gibeonite buffer on his north, whatever its strength, no longer existed.

Gibeon, identified with Tell el-Jib, just 9 km north of Jerusalem, was an extensive urban center during the Early Bronze I, Middle Bronze II and Iron Ages.[19] However, excavations failed to find evidence of a Late Bronze Age settlement or defensive walls prior to the Iron I Age. At that time a massive city wall was built around the crest of the natural hill and a tunnel with a spiral staircase provided access to the water table within the wall's protection. Late Bronze IIA pottery (fourteenth century B.C.) was recovered from tombs of secondary use. The archaeological evidence suggested a very limited occupation of the site or the use of the tombs by temporary squatters.[20]

The Jerusalem Confederacy

The displeasure of the King of Jerusalem suggests that the Gibeonite Treaty Agreement with the Israelites possibly had broken a mutual defense pact that previously had existed with Jerusalem and the other cities that immediately joined in the punitive action against Gibeon. The biblical indication that the Jebusites also were Hivites (or better, Horites) means that at least five major centers in the central hill country were populated by Hurrians (Josh. 9:7).

(Textual Break)

Joshua's southern campaign generally has been understood as a continuous military effort that saw the defeat of the Jerusalem confederacy and the destruction, in rapid succession, of a series of cities in the Shephelah and the southern hills. A textual break in the biblical narrative may indicate the need for some rethinking of this concept (Josh. 10:15). Following the extended 'mopping up' operations in the Aijalon Valley, and the editorial reference to the *Book of Jashar* as the primary source of the reference to God's miraculous intervention there, a strange assertion appears:

> Then Joshua returned, and <u>all Israel with him</u>, to the camp at Gilgal.

The continuity of the military exercises obviously was broken by an unspecified period of time with Joshua at Gilgal.

A lengthy section describing the capture and disposal of the five kings is followed by a series of very brief stylized statements concerning the siege, capture and destruction of four towns in the Shephelah and two in the southern hill country. The obvious literary imbalance between the detailed description of the aftermath of the Battle of Gibeon and the very limited stylized statements regarding Joshua's military exploits at six urban centers that are summarized as a defeat of ...*the whole land, the hill country and the Negeb and the lowland and the slopes, and all their kings; he left none remaining, but utterly destroyed all that breathed,...* leaves the reader in a quandary. Why would the detailed record of such impressive results be couched in cryptic, formalized sentences, without any elaboration apart from the reference to Gezer's interference at Lachish? The biblical author, in his formalized summary, obviously was not attempting to describe the nature of the attack and capture of the successive towns. The abrupt break from detailed description of the disposal of the five kings to the cryptic summary statements that make up the balance of the southern 'campaign' narrative prompts another serious question. Should this account of Joshua's military exploits be understood in terms of a continuous military exercise? The vagueness of the formalized text rather suggests that these towns were representative of the ongoing struggles ('war') that Joshua made *a long time with all those kings* (Josh. 11:18). If a correlation between the biblical description of the 'southern' campaign and archaeological data is possible at all, and the stylized form of the text, in fact, is not intended to be descriptive, then the actual nature of Joshua's military actions at these sites (and possibly others) may best be determined by the archaeological evidence recovered at the specific sites involved.

In the Shephelah

We may understand Joshua's initial efforts in southern Canaan best in terms of at least three major campaigns:

1. The Gibeonite war that primarily concerned the House of Joseph in what later became Benjaminite territory.

2. The conquest of the Shephelah that basically was unsuccessful in establishing Israelite control and settlement. The failure to take advantage of military successes in the region by immediate settlement later was decried by Joshua (Josh. 18:3). The distinction between the Gibeonite war and the Shephelah campaign may be reflected in the lack of correlation between the listing of the Jerusalem Confederacy members and the cities that succumbed to Joshua's punitive action.[21] For example, apart from its inclusion in the list of kings defeated by *Joshua and the people of Israel,* Jarmuth appears to have escaped Israelite attack. It seems reasonable to expect that punitive action would have been taken against Jarmuth since it was a member of the Jerusalem confederacy and the course of action, if intended in the biblical text as a continuous military operation, appears to have passed in the city's immediate vicinity.

3. The ultimate conquests of Hebron and Debir later are identified with Caleb and Kenaz and appear to be representative of actions in the southern hill country within the geographical limitations of the summary statement that follows (Josh. 10:41).

It is becoming increasingly clear that we must temper the positive successes of Joshua's conquest with the negative military and strategic failures of the Israelites hinted at by Joshua:

'How long will you be slack to go in and take possession of the land,...?' (Josh. 18:3)

and the failures openly expressed in the book of Judges:

Benjamin did not drive out the Jebusites...(Judg. 1:21)

Manasseh did not drive out the inhabitants of Beth-shean...

Taanach...Dor...Ibleam...Megiddo... but the Canaanites persisted in dwelling in that land. (Judg. 1:27)

Ephraim did not drive out the Canaanites who dwelt in Gezer; (Judg. 1:29)

Zebulun did not drive out the inhabitants of Kitron... Nahalol... (Judg. 1:30)
Asher did not drive out the inhabitants of Acco... Sidon... Ahlab... Achzib... Helbah... Aphik... Rehob... the Asherites dwelt among the Canaanites (Judg. 1:31-32)
Naphtali did not drive out the inhabitants of Beth-shemesh... Beth-anath, but dwelt among the Canaanites, the inhabitants of the land (Judg. 1:33)
The Amorites pressed the Danites back into the hill country, for they did not allow them to come down to the plain... the Amorites persisted... (Judg. 1:34)

This litany of ineffectiveness and failure must be integrated into the glowing reports of Joshua's overwhelming successes to properly appreciate the historical nature of Israelite occupation of Canaan. Many of the successes achieved by individual clans or tribes, or even notables from within a tribe (such as Caleb and Othniel) collectively may have been attributed to Joshua as the commander-in-chief, or at least have been integrated into a holistic concept of the conquest phase. Thus, the specific references to *the people of Israel* in the inventory list of defeated kings (Josh. 12) appears to have special relevance to our understanding of the nature of the 'conquest.'

Now these are the kings of the land, whom <u>the people of Israel</u> defeated... (Josh. 12:1)
And these are the kings of the land whom Joshua and <u>the people of Israel</u> defeated... (Josh. 12:7)

Makkedah
And Joshua took Makkedah on that day, and smote it... (Josh. 10:28)
The location of Makkedah, the first urban casualty among the cities that succumbed to Joshua's conquest on the western fringe of the central hills is not specifically identified in the biblical text (Josh. 10:10-29). However, the inclusion of Makkedah in the Lachish district of Judean towns in the Shephelah is clear (Josh. 15:41). While its ancient name probably is preserved in Khirbet Beit Maqdûm, a site about 11 km east-southeast of Lachish, the actual town site is relatively unimpressive.[22] Archaeological surveys of the region yielded only limited Iron Age II evidence and an abundance of Byzantine and

later pottery suggesting the possibility of a move by the Makkedah population from the confinement of an Iron Age tell in the vicinity, bringing their city's name with them. That location appears to be Khirbet el-Qôm, a sizable tell with cultural remains of the Early Bronze II-III, remains of a cyclopean city wall, a cemetery and an abundance of Iron Age II pottery.[23] Trial excavations on the site exposed five successive strata from Early Bronze to Middle Bronze I and the remains of a well-fortified Iron Age II gate constructed directly above an earlier Iron Age gate.[24]

The failure to recover any Late Bronze Age materials to this point does not conclusively negate the possible existence of the Late Bronze town. A massive destruction layer may very effectively seal in earlier strata. A prime example exists at Timnah in the northern Shephelah where five rich strata of a vibrant Late Bronze town were totally concealed from a series of surface surveys. Additional excavation may be required to determine the total sequence of settlement on the Khirbet el-Qôm site. On the other hand, as at Jarmuth where there is little question about the identification, the Late Bronze town may have yet another explanation.

Libnah

Then Joshua passed on from Makkedah, and all Israel with him, to Libnah,... (Josh. 10:29)

The possible location for Libnah is Tell Bornat, ca. 2 miles northwest of Beth Guvrin, or Tell el-Judeidah nearby. Both sites await excavation.

Lachish

And Joshua passed on from Libnah,... to Lachish,... and he took it on the second day...Then Horam king of Gezer came up to help Lachish... (Josh. 10:31,32)

The end of the Late Bronze Age in Canaan has been clarified by the excavations at Lachish (Tell ed-Duweir).[25] The sequence for the culmination of Late Bronze Lachish generally is clear. There the Late Bronze cities of both Levels VII and VI were not surrounded by city walls and possibly were not fortified at all. Unfortified Lachish VII had an important shrine (Fosse Temple III) constructed in the moat of the earlier MB defensive system. The construction of the Fosse Temple in the moat precludes its continued use as a part of a fortification system. It is possible that a continuous line of larger buildings around the upper slope of the mound formed a perimeter belt and minimal protection for the city.

The destruction of Lachish VII by fire was followed by the rebuilding of Lachish on a different plan (Lachish VI), also unfortified. The resettlement and rebuilding with a different urban plan for the final Canaanite city was immediate. The Fosse Temple remained in ruins and seemingly was replaced by a new temple on the acropolis.[26] The size of the new city appears to have been diminished. However, the final Canaanite Lachish was a large and densely populated city prior to its final destruction. Its buildings covered the entire mound and some of its slopes. Strong Egyptian influence was noted everywhere in the plan of the temple and the rich, prosperous city. Its violent, total destruction by fire (Lachish VI) came very suddenly from a strong enemy force about the mid-twelfth century B.C. The site was abandoned and left desolate for a very long time.[27]

The Fosse Temple III and Level VII clearly are contemporary and are dated to the thirteenth century B.C. Lachish VI, therefore, must be dated to the first half of the twelfth century B.C. with the final destruction by fire ca. 1150 B.C.[28] Lachish VI materials reveal strong links with Twentieth Dynasty Egypt, a relationship that may explain the city's prosperity and the absence of fortifications. Western Canaan, at least as far north as the Jezreel Plain, appears to have continued under Egyptian political, economic and military control during Ramesses III's reign.[29] The prosperity certainly demonstrates that the Egyptian empire was still in tact beyond the reign of Ramesses III, during the brief reigns of Ramesses IV (ca. 1151-1145 B.C.), Ramesses V (ca. 1145-1141 B.C.) and Ramesses VI (ca. 1141-1134/3 B.C.). Thus, Lachish in the south and Megiddo and Beth-shean in the north reflect a continuation of Egyptian hegemony until the third quarter of the twelfth century B.C. The dramatic destruction of Lachish brought Egyptian control over southern Canaan to an end. The abrupt loss of Egyptian political and military domination in the region suddenly left unfortified Lachish totally vulnerable to attack and an easy prey to any potential enemy.[30] Obviously it was not destroyed by the Egyptians.

A destruction by the Philistines has been rejected primarily on the basis of an absence of Philistine pottery at Lachish which is located in close proximity to the coastal plain controlled by the Philistines. However, a number of archaeologists have come to the conclusion, based on their independent work, that it was not until 1150 B.C. and probably slightly later, that Philistine painted pottery appeared anywhere in the country. In that case the settlement of the Philistines in southern Canaan probably would have occurred only after the total collapse of Egyptian control sometime during the reigns of Ramesses IV-VI.[31]

The absence of the distinctive Philistine painted pottery among the cultural remains of Lachish VI, however, suggests only that the two major Philistine cities, Gath (Tel Zafit?) and Ekron (Tel Miqne), in the immediate vicinity of Lachish on the north, did not coexist with Lachish since abundant evidence of wider diffusion of such pottery is found farther inland than Lachish. It would appear, therefore, that the settlement of the Philistines in southern Canaan followed the decline of Egyptian control and the death of Ramesses III. It is the appearance of Philistine painted pottery and the spread of the Philistine material culture, including the widespread use of iron, that identifies the LB/Iron Age transition.[32]

The survival and relative prosperity of Lachish together with many other Canaanite cities as political, economic and cultural centers during the first half of the twelfth century B.C. creates a chronological problem for understanding the sequence and nature of the Israelite conquest:

...Joshua passed on from Libnah, and all Israel with him, to Lachish, and laid siege to it, and assaulted it: and the Lord gave Lachish into the hand of Israel, and he took it on the second day, and smote it with the edge of the sword, and every person in it, as he had done to Libnah. (Josh. 10:31-32)

If we assume that the final destruction of Canaanite Lachish (VI) should be attributed to Joshua's southern campaign, then the Israelite conquest is firmly fixed by the archaeological evidence to the mid-twelfth century B.C. (ca. 1150). However, most authorities are agreed that the destruction of Canaanite Hazor which occurred during

Joshua's northern campaign should be dated in the thirteenth century B.C. (prior to 1230 B.C.).[33] The resolution may be found in the fact that Israelite settlement following Joshua's campaign had little impact on the political and cultural history of the country apart from the central highlands. Early settlement was delayed (a discouraging aspect for Joshua, noted in the biblical narrative) and then largely confined to more isolated and mostly unoccupied territories in the hilly regions.

Joshua's destruction of Lachish VII (rather than Lachish VI) toward the end of the thirteenth century BC solves two serious problems. The fact that the Israelites did not resettle Lachish nor any of the region in the immediate vicinity following Joshua's successful siege may be explained by continuing Egyptian domination in the region. The revival of the Canaanite town (Lachish VI) subsequently frustrated Israel's western movement beyond the slopes of the Hebron Hills, a situation that the biblical narratives seem to reflect. Lachish VI, according to this scenario, was destroyed by the Philistines who then chose two more suitable locations for their cities, Gath and Ekron, slightly farther north. It seems reasonable to suggest that the Philistine cities came into being after the Lachish destruction, and that their location was deemed preferable to the more secluded easterly position of Lachish. From this point onward, Philistine domination of the region precluded westward movement by the Israelites and the site experienced a long desertion. Not until the United Monarchy (10th century B.C.) was Israelite penetration into the southern Shephelah and the founding of the Israelite settlement at Lachish possible.

Eglon

And Joshua passed on with all Israel from Lachish to Eglon... (Josh. 10:34)

Tell el-Ḥesi on Nahal Shiqma, 7 miles southwest of Lachish, has been suggested as the location of Eglon. This large site (35-40 acres) controlled the internal road system, a branch of the *Via Maris*, that turned east at Ashkelon and passed 2.5 km north of Tell el-Ḥesi. The retention of the name at Khirbet °Ajlan north of Tell el-Ḥesi tends to support this identification over Tell Beit Mirsim and Tell °Eitun (Tel Eton). On the other hand, Tel Eton, ca. 11 miles west-southwest of Hebron, and Tell Beit Mirsim, slightly farther to the south, are in a more logical location if the sites mentioned were consecutive battles in a single military campaign. Both Tell el-Ḥesi and Tell Beit Mirsim suffered a total destruction near the end of the Late Bronze Age. The destruction of a cluster of four cities within this southern Shephelah region may rightly be called *The Lachish Campaign,* and explains the military intervention of the King of Gezer at Lachish, the largest and most central of these cities, which possibly served as the regional capital. Tell el-Ḥesi, after a period of desertion, was partially reoccupied on the acropolis, probably as a Philistine settlement. Both Lachish and Tell Beit Mirsim remained unoccupied for a longer period of time. It is this gap of occupation that is totally consistent with the biblical insistence that the individual tribes failed to take advantage of their military successes achieved under Joshua.[35]

Destruction at Other Sites

A discussion of the end of the Late Bronze period in Canaan is incomplete without a summarizing of the fate of other Canaanite towns in the Shephelah. The total list of Late Bronze cities in the Shephelah is very impressive. Gezer, a major city-state overlooking the Valley of Aijalon, dominated the northern Shephelah. Beth-shemesh and Timnah (Tel Batash, with very impressive Late Bronze ruins), controlled the Valley of Elah. Azekah (Tell Zakarîyeh), Socho (Khirbet ᶜAbbâd), Adullam (Khirbet esh-Sheikh Madhkûr), and Keilah (Khirbet Qîlā) line the Elah Valley into the central Judean Hills. On the western fringe of the Shephelah along the Elah, Tel Zafit (Tell es-Sâfi) is the probable location of Philistine Gath.[36] In the Zaphath Valley (Nahal Guvrin), Tel Burna (Tell Bornât) is the possible location of biblical Libnah. Passage along Nahal Lachish into the Hebron Hills was controlled by Lachish and Khirbet el-Qôm, possibly biblical Makkedah.[37] Along Nahal Adorayim, Tel ᶜEton (Tell ᶜAitûn) vies with Tel Ḥasi (Tell el-Ḥesī) to the west on Naḥal Shiqma as the site of biblical Eglon. Tel Nagila (Tell en-Najîleh), a very impressive tell in the southwestern Shephelah, also awaits definite identification.[38]

Gezer[39]

Gezer experienced a violent destruction in the fifteenth century B.C.

probably during Thutmose III's campaign in 1468 B.C. and remained deserted during much of the rest of the fifteenth century B.C.[40] The city recovered rapidly under strong Egyptian influence of the Amarna Age in the fourteenth century B.C. Later, Gezer appears to have experienced a partial hiatus in occupation at the very end of the thirteenth and the beginning of the twelfth century B.C. The Late Bronze IIB (ca. 13th century B.C.) city experienced a serious decline. Imported wares virtually ceased and the arrival of the Philistines in the early twelfth century B.C. came after the site already may have been partially destroyed and deserted. The cause of this disturbance possibly may be attributed to Merneptah's punitive campaign ca. 1220 B.C. It was followed by a squatters' occupation that reused the surviving elements of the former town.[41]

A series of sites not mentioned among the casualties of the Israelite conquest in the biblical narratives including Beth-Shemesh, Timnah, Tell Beit Mirsim (if we choose to identify Eglon with Tell el-Hesi) and Tel Halif (Tell el-Khuweilfeh) also suffered a tragic end. Tel Halif, located ca. 6 miles south of Tell Beit Mirsim, was the site of biblical En-rimmon, the name preserved in nearby Khirbet Umm er-Ramamin.[42] While detractors point to a litany of problems related to the integration and correlation of archaeological and biblical data, and admittedly they exist, an abundance of evidence does not contradict the biblical tradition.[43] And it is this evidence, in spite of the novel manipulations of the existing chronological structure and rejection of the historical validity of biblical narratives, that tends to support an arrival of the Moses-Joshua-led Israelites toward the end of the thirteenth century B.C.

Beth-shemesh

Beth-shemesh, though not mentioned in the biblical conquest narratives, is located on the primary north-south route in the interior of the Shephelah, at the base of the western Judean Hills, that would have been followed by a continuous military campaign from Beth-horon through the Valley of Aijalon southward to Lachish. Excavations at Beth-shemesh have provided the basic chronological sequence of the site's cultural history. The end of the Middle Bronze city (Stratum V) occurred in the mid-sixteenth century B.C., probably during the Egyptian reconquest of the region. A very prosperous Late Bronze city (Stratum IV) was destroyed at the end of the thirteenth century or the beginning of the twelfth century B.C. Later a pre-Philistine phase of Iron Age I represented by numerous silos was built on the Late Bronze ruins (as at Tell Beit Mirsim and Timnah). Furnaces for copper smelting installed in Stratum IV continued in use in Stratum III.[44] Stratum III, containing a fine collection of Philistine ware, was a flourishing town.

Timnah (Tel Batash)

Situated within the buffer zone of its more powerful neighbors and guarding a primary road between the coast and the central hills, Late Bronze Timnah survived four major destructions during the troubled fourteenth and thirteenth centuries in the northern Shephelah. The dramatic fourth destruction toward the end of the thirteenth century or early twelfth century B.C. was followed by the final rebuilding of Canaanite Timnah. It was short-lived and without evidence of destruction and with only limited modification its buildings were occupied by the Philistines.

Tel Ḥalif

Tell Ḥalif (Tell Khuweilifeh), on the eastern edge of the Shephelah, already settled during the Chalcolithic and Early Bronze Age (ca. 3200-2300 B.C.), had several occupational phases in the Late Bronze Age. An unwalled city at Tell Ḥalif (probably biblical Rimmon),[45] appears to have served the regional population alternatively with nearby Tell Beit Mirsim (8 km to the north). Its occupation followed the destruction of City D at Tell Beit Mirsim (ca. 1550 B.C.), and was destroyed early in the Amarna Age before the reoccupation of Tell Beit Mirsim after 1400 B.C.[46] Destruction again came ca. 1250 B.C. possibly related to the conquest of the incoming Israelite tribes.[47]

In the Southern Hill Country

The conquest of the towns in the southern hill country should be understood apart from the Shephelah campaign. The conquest and settlement of Hebron hills find their origin in the positive report of Joshua and Caleb following their spying expedition through the region. The concession of this region to the Calebites and their close relatives, the Kenazites, and its relationship to Joshua's campaign is unclear. The conquest of a thirteenth century Hebron also is problematic archaeologically.

Hebron
Then Joshua went up with all Israel from Eglon to Hebron... (Josh. 10:36)

Hebron, an important fortified city during the Early Bronze I and Middle Bronze II (Patriarchal) period, appears to have been uninhabited during the entire Late Bronze Age. Only in the Early Iron period was the site resettled, and later was occupied during the Hellenistic and Byzantine periods.[48]

Debir
Then Joshua, with all Israel, turned back to Debir... (Josh. 10:38)

The identification of Debir with Khirbet Rabûd, ca. 8.5 miles south-southwest of Hebron, is now generally accepted.[49] Khirbet Rabûd, together with Hebron and Anab (Khirbet ʿAnâb el-Kebîreh) ca. 4 miles southwest of Debir, form a trio of Canaanites towns in the southern Judean hill country that could be identified with the three kings, Sheshai, Ahiman, and Talmani (Judg. 1:10), who were defeated during the Judean takeover. This 15-acre Canaanite town is represented by four occupational strata and a rich cemetery. The fourteenth century B.C. represented its period of greatest prosperity.

The Sea Peoples' Occupation of the Coastal Plain

Philistine Plain
Joshua's military campaign beyond the hill country appears to have been confined to the Shephelah where ultimate Israelite settlement was delayed. The arrival of the 'Sea Peoples' during the thirteenth century B.C. seemingly precluded later attempts at western expansion by Judah in the southern coastal plain, especially against the Philistine pentapolis (their primary cities: Gath, Ekron, Ashdod, Ashkelon and Gaza).[50] The founders of Late Bronze Ashdod established a seaport at Tell Mor to serve its Mediterranean trade centers. Ashdod itself

became a great commercial and military center during the vigorous reign of the Eighteenth Dynasty pharaohs (ca. 1580-1350 B.C.). A Ras Shamra cuneiform record of linen shipments from Ashdod to Ugarit illustrates the vitality of the coastal economy during the Late Bronze Age.[51] This flourishing Canaanite city (Stratum XIV) under Egyptian supremacy was destroyed ca. 1200 B.C. shortly before the reign of Ramesses III. A smaller, unfortified city based on a different urban plan (Stratum XIII) was built by the new inhabitants whose culture showed significant Mycenaean influence. Ashdod XII was the result of a peaceful takeover of the previous population, possibly only a decade or two later, ca. 1190-1180 B.C. The new material culture is characteristic of the biblical Philistines.[52] The military prowess and superior weaponry (chariotry and iron) of these 'Sea People' tribes continued to be a scourge to the Israelites throughout the period of the Judges. Thus, Judah was incapable of advancing beyond the inner Shephelah where Joshua's military successes had been centered. Only during the United Monarchy did David make deep inroads into Philistine domination of the coastal plain.

...And the Lord was with Judah, and he took possession of the hill country, but he could not drive out the inhabitants of the plain, because they had chariots of iron. (Judg. 1:19)

To avoid the contradiction of the previous verse in the Masoretic text, we must follow the Septuagint reading:

...And Judah did not capture Gaza with its territory, and Ashkelon with its territory, and Ekron with its territory. (Judg. 1:18)

The summary statements of Joshua's military exploits and the extent of his conquests tend to avoid reference to such activity in the coastal regions. In fact, the western extent *from Kadesh-barnea to Gaza* (Josh. 10:41) seems to imply that the areas north of Gaza were not involved. A second summary statement seems to exclude the Philistine Plain from Joshua's wrath (Josh. 10:22). The nature of the defeat suffered by those kings listed in Joshua 12:7-24 is difficult to evaluate. Certainly the list provides no suggestion as to the destruction of the cities of the kings mentioned. The 'Sea Peoples' occupation of the coastal plains precluded Israelite penetration into the area.

Aphek of the Sharon

Tel Aphek, a 30-acre site at the sources of the Yarkon River, was settled at the beginning of urbanization in Israel in the final phase of the Early Bronze I Age (ca. 3000 B.C.). Middle Bronze Aphek was a walled commercial and political center with palatial buildings. During the Late Bronze Age, the governor's palace in the second half of the thirteenth century B.C. was destroyed in a dramatic conflagration. Built during Ramesses II's reign for Egyptian authorities in Canaan, it was destroyed later in Ramesses' reign and never rebuilt. A new culture established itself at Aphek early in the twelfth century B.C. At Aphek (as at Tell Abu Hawam in the mouth of the Kishon River), this culture appeared immediately upon the destruction layer of the last Canaanite city. This culture probably belonged to the 'Sea Peoples' who made Aphek their northern stronghold as early as the mid-twelfth century B.C.[53]

Dor

The first settlement was established at the beginning of the Late Bronze Age and destroyed in the thirteenth century B.C. The site was resettled in Iron Age I.[54]

Military Conquest in the North

Defeat of the Canaanite Confederacy and Destruction of Hazor

The destruction of the final Late Bronze city (Stratum XIII) at Hazor has been dated to the second third of the thirteenth century (ca. 1230 B.C.). The early Iron Age remains (Strata XII and XI) do not indicate a continuation of the Canaanite city. The Stratum XII settlement appears semi-nomadic with modest remains of walls, ovens and storage pits. Though Stratum XI includes a typical pillared house, both strata appear to represent modest groups of the Israelites who established insecure settlements that lasted only during brief intervals of the twelfth and eleventh centuries.

Datable Destruction Strata of Canaanite Cities

The list of thirty-one Canaanite kings defeated by the Israelites

(Josh. 12:7-24) provides a basis for the validity of the 'Military Conquest' scenario. The list obviously does not specify the destruction of the Canaanite cities involved in military confrontations with the Israelites. However, it is within this list that we may expect the place names that will appear among those major Canaanite urban centers with datable destruction layers during the thirteenth-twelfth centuries B.C.:

Hazor, Late Bronze Stratum XIII   (1230 B.C.)
Ashdod, Stratum XIV to XIII   (1200 B.C. or slightly later)
Megiddo, Last Canaanite city (Stratum VIIA)   (ca. 1200 B.C.)
Aphek   (ca. 1220 B.C.)
Gezer, destroyed by Merneptah   (ca. 1210 B.C.)
(However, inscriptions from the Gezer excavations mentioning Ramesses III, IV, VIII and IX of the 20th Dynasty indicate ties with Egypt during all of the 12th century B.C. Gezer became an Israelite city only in the 10th century B.C.)
Lachish, Stratum IX   (mid-13th century B.C.)

The gradual decline of Canaanite city-state structure during at least a fifty year period (ca. 1200-1150 B.C.) may be attributed to various causes: inter-city rivalries, outside military intervention, the ʿApiru element, etc. The first break came ca. 1200 B.C. followed by a period of renewal. A second break occurred following the reign of Ramesses III in the second half of the twelfth century when Egyptian control declined rapidly. The impact on settlement varied with the regions:

1. At Lachish, settlement was interrupted until the building of the Israelite town under the united monarchy of the tenth century B.C.

2. At Hazor, settlement was interrupted except for the occasional occupation by relatively small groups of Israelites.

3. At Megiddo, Aphek and Gezer settlement was continuous with the inhabitants clearly surviving Canaanites.

4. At Ashdod settlement was continuous, including the transfer to Philistine occupation in the twelfth century B.C.

An acceptance of the end of the Late Bronze Age (ca. 1230-1220 B.C.) as the time frame for the arrival of the Moses-led contingent of Israelites, does not require a rejection of the biblical account of Israel's conquest of Canaanite cities. It is just not true, that *in almost every case* the archaeological data is inconsistent with the biblical narrative. The problems that remain surely require better explanations than we now are able to provide. However, the nature of archaeological data available to us now also precludes the acceptance of other proposals that would require a radical adjustment of the chronological framework for the second millennium B.C.[56] The solutions obviously are not to be found in any simplistic correlation, but must begin with the realization that the events and environment that prompted the biblical narratives were far more complex than scholars generally have been willing to admit. As a result, the neat equations between biblical statement and archaeological evidence that have been demanded in the past realistically may be a pipedream. Certainly, the correlation has been far more taxing and problematic than most of us would have hoped. For those discouraged with the process, the solution surely is not to throw up our hands in 'Holy Horror!' nor to live in the 'Pollyanna' world of simple solutions. Our understanding of Jericho, ᶜAi, Gibeon, Hormah, and probably other sites remain major problems. Encouragement comes in comparing our level of knowledge to the 'accepted' concepts and reconstructions of 1900, or even 1940, to appreciate the contribution that archaeological research has made to our understanding of the biblical text. We are only a part of an ongoing process. It is both worthwhile and rewarding. That assurance is enough to continue...

NOTES

[1] N. Glueck, The Negev. *BA* 22 (1959): 82-97 (Discussion prior to major excavations!)

[2] Y. Aharoni and R. Amiran, Excavations at Tel Arad: Preliminary Report on the First Season, 1962. *IEJ* 14 (1964): 131-147; Arad. Pp. 74-89 in *EAEHL* I, ed. M. Avi-Yonah. Englewood Cliffs, NJ: Prentice-Hall, 1975; Y. Aharoni, Excavations at Tel Arad: Preliminary Report on the Second Season, 1963. *IEJ* 17 (1967): 133-149.

[3] B. Mazar, The Sanctuary of Arad and the Family of Hobab the Kenite. *JNES* 24 (1965): 297-303.

[4] Y. Aharoni, V. Fritz, and A. Kempinski, Excavations at Tel Masos (Khirbet El-Meshâsh). Preliminary Report on the First Season, 1972. *Tel Aviv* 1/1 (1974): 64-74; Excavations at Tel Masos (Khirbet el-Meshâsh). Preliminary Report on the

Second Season, 1974. *Tel Aviv* 2/3 (1975): 97-124; Y. Aharoni, Arad. Pp. 74-88 in *EAEHL* I, ed. M. Avi-Yonah. Englewood Cliffs, N.J.: Prentice-Hall, 1975.; Arad. Pp. 38-39 in *IDB* Supplementary Volume. Nashville: Abingdon Press, 1976; A. Kempinski and V. Fritz, Excavations at Tel Masos (Khirbet el-Meshâsh). Preliminary Report of the Third Season, 1975. *Tel Aviv* 4 (1977): 136-158.

[5] Y. Aharoni, Nothing Early and Nothing Late: Re-writing Israel's Conquest. *BA* 39 (1976): 55-76; A. Kempinski, Israelite Conquest or Settlement? New Light from Tell Masos. *BAR* 2/3 (1976): 25-30; Tel Masos. Pp. 816-819 in *EAEHL* III, ed. M. Avi-Yonah. Englewood Cliffs, N.J.: Prentice-Hall, 1977; M. Kochavi, Tel Malhata. Pp. 771-775 in *EAEHL* III, ed. M. Avi-Yonah. Englewood Cliffs, N.J.: Prentice-Hall, 1977.

[6] Y. Aharoni, Tel Masos: Historical Considerations. *Tel Aviv* 2/3 1975): 114-124.

[7] Y. Aharoni, Excavations at Tel Beer-Sheba. *Tel Aviv* 1/1 (1972): 34-42; 2/4 (1975): 146-168; Tel Beersheba. Pp. 160-68 in *EAEHL* I, ed. M. Avi-Yonah. Englewood Cliffs, N.J.: Prentice-Hall, 1975.; Z. Herzog, Beer-Sheba of the Patriarchs. *BAR* 6/6 (1980): 12-28.

[8] B.M. Bennett, Jr., The Search for Israelite Gilgal. *PEQ* 104 (1972): 111-122; N.H. Snaith, The Altar at Gilgal: Joshua 22: 23-29. *VT* 28 (1978): 330-335.

[9] J. Muilenberg, The Site of Ancient Gilgal. *BASOR* 140 (1955): 11-27.

[10] K.M. Kenyon, Excavations at Jericho, 1954. *PEQ* 86 (1954): 45-63; A.D. Tushingham, Excavation at Old Testament Jericho. *BA* 16 (1953): 46-67; *idem, BA* 17 (1954): 98-104.

[11] B.G. Wood, Did the Israelites Conquer Jericho? *BAR* 16/2 (1990): 44-59.

[12] J.A. Callaway and M.B. Nicol, A Sounding at Khirbet Haiyân. *BASOR* 183 (1966): 12-19.

[13] J.A. Callaway, The 1966 °Ai (Et-Tell) Excavations. *BASOR* 196 (1969): 2-16.

[14] W.F. Albright, The Kyle Memorial Excavation at Bethel. *BASOR* 56 (1934): 2-15; J.L. Kelso, Excavations at Bethel. *BA* 19 (1956): 36-43.

[15] J.L. Kelso, The Excavation at Bethel (1934-1960). *AASOR* 39. Cambridge, MA: ASOR, 1968; Bethel. Pp. 207-212 in *EAEHL* I, ed. M. Avi-Yonah. Englewood Cliffs, NJ: Prentice-Hall, 1975.

[16] J.A. Callaway, Was My Excavations of Ai Worthwhile? *BAR* 11/2 (1985): 68-69.

[17] G.E. Wright, Tell en-Nasbeh. *BA* 10 (1947): 69-77; M. Broshi, Tell en-Nasbeh. Pp. 912-914 in *EAEHL* III, ed. M. Avi-Yonah and E. Stern. Jerusalem: IES and Massada Press, 1977.

[18] F.C. Fensham, The Treaty Between Israel and the Gibeonites. *BA* 27 (1964): 96-100.

[19] J.B. Pritchard, *Hebrew Inscriptions and Stamps from Gibeon.* Philadelphia: The University Museum, 1959: 1-17,17; *Winery, Defenses, and Soundings at Gibeon.* Philadelphia: The University Museum, 1964: 24-27; Gibeon. *EAEHL* II. ed. M. Avi-Yonah. Jerusalem: IES and Massada Press. 446.

[20] J.B. Pritchard, Culture and History. *The Bible in Modern Scholarship.* ed. J.P. Hyatt. Nashville: Abingdon Press, 1965: 318-319.

[21] Y. Aharoni, *The Land of the Bible,* 218-219.

[22] J. Simons, *The Geographical and Topographical Texts of the Old Testament,*

Leiden: E.J. Brill, 1959: 273.

[23] D.A. Dorsey, The Location of Biblical Makkedah. *Tel Aviv* 7 (1980): 185-193; W.G. Dever, Iron Age Epigraphic Material from the Area of Khirbet el-Kom. *HUCA* 40-41 (1969-1970): 139-204.

[24] J.S. Holladay, Khirbet el-Qom. *IEJ* 21 (1971): 175-177.

[25] D. Ussishkin, Lachish. Pp. 735-753 in *EAEHL* III, ed. M. Avi-Yonah. Englewood Cliffs, NJ: Prentice-Hall, 1977.

[26] C. Clamer and D. Ussishkin, A Canaanite Temple at Tell Lachish. *BA* 40 (1977): 71-76.

[27] D. Ussishkin, Level VII and VI at Tel Lachish and the End of the Late Bronze Age in Canaan. Pp. 213-230 in *Palestine in the Bronze and Iron Ages*. ed. J.N. Tubb. London: Institute of Archaeology, 1985.

[28] G.R.H. Wright, Pre-Israelite Temples in the Land of Canaan. *PEQ* 103 (1971): 17-32.

[29] J.M. Weinstein, The Egyptian Empire in Palestine: A Reassessment. *BASOR* 241 (1981): 22-23; P. Beck and M. Kochavi, The Egyptian Governor's Palace at Aphek. *Qadmoniot* 16 (1983): 47-51 (Hebrew); idem, A Dated Assemblage of the Late 13th Century BCE from the Egyptian Residency at Aphek. *Tel Aviv* 12 (1985): 29-42.

[30] D. Ussishkin, Excavations at Tel Lachish: 1973-1977, Preliminary Report. *TA* 5 (1978): 1-97; Answers at Lachish. *BAR* 5/6 (1979): 16-39; Excavations at Tel Lachish: 1978-1983. Second Preliminary Report. *TA* 10 (1983): 97-168; Lachish - Key to the Israelite Conquest of Canaan? *BAR* 13/1 (1987): 18-41.

[31] D. Ussishkin, Lachish - Key to the Israelite Conquest of Canaan? *BAR* 13/1 (1987): 18-41.

[32] T. Dothan, *The Philistines and Their Material Culture*. New Haven and London: Yale University Press, 1982: 91-93.

[33] Y. Yadin, *Hazor: the Head of All Those Kingdoms*. (The Schweich Lectures of the British Academy, 1970.) London: Oxford University Press, 1972: 108; K.M. Kenyon, *Archaeology in the Holy Land*. 4th ed. London and New York: Ernest Benn, 1979: 209.

[34] J. Simon, *The Geographical and Topographical Texts of the Old Testament*. Leiden: E.J. Brill, 1959: 147; R. Amiran and J.E. Worrell, Hesi, Tel. Pp. 514-520 in *EAEHL* II, ed. M. Avi-Yonah. Englewood Cliffs, NJ: Prentice-Hall, 1976.

[35] Y. Aharoni, *The Land of the Bible*. Philadelphia: Westminster, 1967: 218-219.

[36] E. Stern, Es-Safi, Tell. Pp. 1024-1027 in *EAEHL* IV, ed. M. Avi-Yonah. Englewood Cliffs, NJ: Prentice-Hall, 1978.

[37] D.A. Dorsey, The Location of Biblical Makkedah. *TA* 7 (1980): 185-193.

[38] A.F. Rainey, The Biblical Shephelah of Judah. *BASOR* 251 (1983): 1-22.

[39] H.D. Lance, Gezer in the Land and in History. *BA* 30 (1967): 34-47; J.F. Ross, Gezer in the Tell el-Amarna Letters. *BA* 30 (1967): 62-70.

[40] W.G. Dever, Excavations at Gezer. *BA* 30 (1967): 47-62.

[41] W.G. Dever, et al., Further Excavations at Gezer, 1967-71. *BA* 34 (1971): 94-132; Gezer II: Report of the 1967-70 Seasons in Field I and II. *Annual of the Hebrew Union College Nelson Glueck School of Biblical Archaeology*. Jerusalem: Keter, 1974: 52,53; W.G. Dever, Gezer. Pp. 428-443 in *EAEHL* II, ed. M. Avi-

Yonah and E. Stern. Jerusalem: IES and Massada Press, 1976.

[42] Y. Aharoni, *The Land of the Bible*. 262.

[43] A. Mazar, *Archaeology of the Land of the Bible*. 332.

[44] G.E. Wright, Beth-Shemesh. Pp. 248-253 in *EAEHL* I, ed. M. Avi-Yonah. Englewood Cliffs, NJ: Prentice-Hall, 1975.

[45] O. Borowski, The Biblical Identification of Tel Halif. *BA* 51 (1988): 21-27. A tentative identification with Ziklag was suggested by J.D. Seger, The Location of Biblical Ziklag. *BA* 47 (1984): 47-53.

[46] J.D. Seger, Investigations at Tell Halif, Israel, 1976-1980. *BASOR* 252 (1983): 1-24.

[47] J.D. Seger and O. Borowski, The First Two Seasons at Tell Halif. *BA* 40 (1977): 156-166.

[48] P.C. Hammond, Hebron. *Revue Biblique* 72 (1965): 267-270; 73 (1966): 566-569; 75 (1968): 253-258.

[49] M. Kochavi, Khirbet Rabûd = Debir. *Tel Aviv* 1 (1974): 2-33; Debir (City). *IDB* Supplementary Volume, 1976. 222; Rabud, Khirbet. *EAEHL* IV, 1978: 995.

[50] I. Singer, The Beginning of Philistine Settlement in Canaan and the Northern Boundary of Philistia. *TA* 12 (1985): 109-122.

[51] D.N. Freedman, The Second Season at Ancient Ashdod. *BA* 26 (1963): 134-139.

[52] M. Dothan, Ashdod at the End of the Late Bronze Age and the Beginning of the Iron Age. Pp. 125-131 in *Symposia,* ed. F.M. Cross.Cambridge, MA: ASOR, 1979.

[53] M. Kochavi, The History and Archeology of Aphek-Antipatris. *BA* 44 (1981): 75-86.

[54] G. Foerster, Dor. Pp. 334-337 in *EAEHL*, I. ed. M. Avi-Yonah. Jerusalem: IES and Massada Press, 1975.

[55] Y.Yadin, Further Light on Biblical Hazor. *BA* 20 (1957): 34-47; The Third Season of Excavation at Hazor, 1957. *BA* 21 (1958): 30-47; Excavations at Hazor, 1957,1958. Preliminary Communiqués. *IEJ* 8 (1958): 1-14; 9 (1959): 74-88; Excavations at Hazor, 1968-1969. Preliminary Communiqué. *IEJ* 19 1969): 1-19; The Fifth Season of Excavations at Hazor, 1968-1969. *BA* 32 (1969): 50-71; *Hazor, the Head of All Those Kingdoms* (Schweich Lectures). London: Oxford University Press, 1972; *Hazor: The Rediscovery of a Great Citadel of the Bible*. New York: Random House, 1975; Hazor. Pp. 474-495 in *EAEHL*. II, ed. M. Avi-Yonah. Jerusalem: The IES and Massada Press, 1976. J. Gray, Hazor. *VT* 16 (1966): 26-52.

[56] J.J. Bimson and D. Livingston, Redating the Exodus. *BAR* 13/5 (1987): 40-53, 66-68; W.H. Stiebing, Jr. Should the Exodus and the Israelite Settlement be Redated? *BAR* 11/4 (1985): 58-69.

Chapter VIII

ISRAELITE SETTLEMENT IN CANAAN

Infiltration in Canaan

The Hebrew struggle for settlement in Canaan has long been equated with the troublesome elements that disrupted Egyptian control in the region during the New Kingdom period. The apparent similarity between the *ʿApiru (Ḥabîru)* and the Hebrews was used to support the traditional 'single' Exodus concept and the early (ca. 1400 B.C.) date for the Israelite conquest. When, however, archaeological data appeared to discredit this 'early' date in deference to a 'late' date for both exodus and conquest (ca. 1230 B.C.), the disruptive elements that plagued the Egyptian administration in Canaan required other explanations. The possibility of an extended period of infiltration was suggested by the contents of the Beth-shean Stele of Seti I. Seti's conflict with *ʿApiru* seemed to favor the arrival of the Hebrews in the area long before the end of the thirteenth century B.C. Thus the settlement of the House of Joseph (Ephraim and Manasseh) early in the fourteenth century B.C., apart from and much earlier than the exodus under Moses during the reign of Ramesses II and the military campaigns of Joshua toward the end of the thirteenth century B.C. appeared compatible with the Egyptian record.[1]

The nature of the *ʿApiru* of the Egyptian sources and especially the Amarna tablets and their relationship to the Hebrews is still in question. The direct equation "*ʿApiru* = Hebrews' has been modified by the suggestion that pre-Israelite groups of semi-nomads became amalgamated with the incoming tribes of Israel to form the early infiltrators.[2] This scenario seemed to provide the necessary ingredients for the intrigue and rivalry portrayed in the Amarna tablets. More recently it has been convincingly argued that the *ʿApiru,...outcasts and outlaws from the established society, have nothing to do either linguistically or socially with the ʿibrîm (Hebrews).*[3] The identification of the *ʿApiru* as the discredited, disenfranchised, disinherited princes of uncooperative or rebellious Canaanite vassal city-states, however,

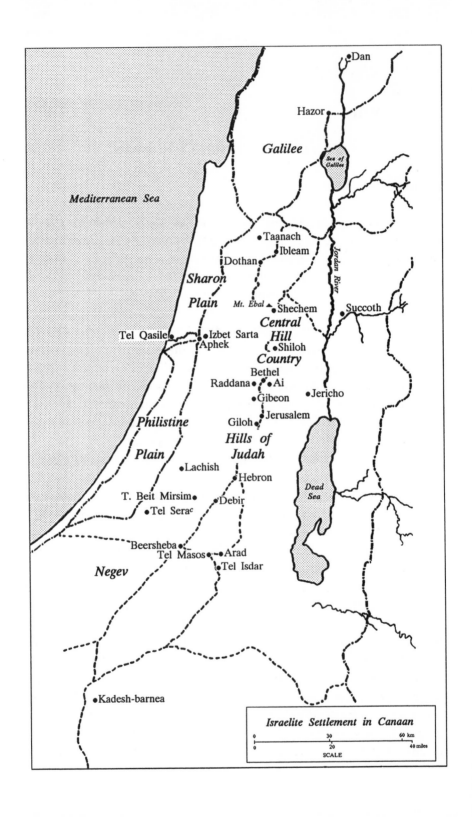

Israelite Settlement in Canaan

SCALE

0   30   60 km

0   20   40 miles

Mediterranean Sea

Galilee

Sea of Galilee

Jordan River

Dan

Hazor

Taanach

Ibleam

Dothan

Sharon Plain

Mt. Ebal

Shechem

Succoth

Central Hill Country

Tel Qasile

Izbet Sarta

Aphek

Shiloh

Bethel

Raddana

Ai

Gibeon

Jericho

Jerusalem

Giloh

Philistine Plain

Hills of Judah

Lachish

Hebron

Dead Sea

T. Beit Mirsim

Debir

Tel Serac

Beersheba

Tel Masos

Arad

Tel Isdar

Negev

Kadesh-barnea

seems too confining a qualification. Obviously, the diplomatic correspondence of the Amarna period gives every indication that such elements existed. However, the general impression of the term's usage is far more inclusive, more in keeping with a rather extensive 'unlanded' minority of whatever origin that was seeking various ways of establishing itself within the existing political, social and economic structure.

The more critical objection to the equation seems to be '...*that the society and political situation in the el-Amarna tablets leaves no room for the Israelites as we know them (an Israelite tribal league) from the Book of Judges.*' The basic problem with this objection is again the concept of a <u>single</u> exodus that must precede the arrival of the Israelites in Canaan. However, the early periodic arrival and infiltration of Hebrew family and clan units attempting to integrate themselves into the established Canaanite culture certainly would have exhibited the characteristics attributed to the ʿApiru of the Amarna period in Canaan. What is perfectly clear is the complexity of the ethnic and political interrelationships of New Kingdom Canaan that tends to preclude exclusive refinements of sociological categories.

Jephthah's argument against Ammonite territorial claims in the Transjordan seems to indicate that the period of the Judges could have begun in the early fourteenth century (ca. 1373 B.C.?) rather than the late thirteenth century (ca. 1200 B.C.)[4] Such a claim of Hebrew settlement in the Transjordan three hundred years before Jephthah's time cannot be reconciled with a single, unified exodus and conquest and/or infiltration at the end of the thirteenth century B.C.

The tendency among biblical scholars for a preference and generalization of one of the settlement models and a rejection of the others on the presumed assumption that consistent conditions in every region evoked a common response among the Israelite clans and tribes has been unfortunate. A careful reading of the biblical account of settlement conditions suggests a highly complex process that varies from region to region and tribe to tribe, a picture that has been reinforced by archaeological evidence.

The Nature of Israelite Settlement

The overwhelming archaeological evidence for the period of Israelite occupation of Canaan has been viewed by some as a gradual settling down of pastoralists during the thirteenth to eleventh centuries B.C.[5] This type of long-term infiltration of pastoralists following patient probing of defensive borders on the fringes of desirable agricultural lands appeared consistent with the Bible's presentation of the Hebrews' lot.[6]

While limiting the infiltrators to 'pastoralists' may be questionable, recent archaeological evidence has supported the historical sources, both biblical and extra-biblical, in undermining the concept of the Israelite settlement as the result of an internal social revolutionary process.[7] The Bible describes these settlers as coming from outside the land. Their infiltration is from the east, across the Jordan Valley from the Transjordanian plateau into the central hill country. This new population, unified by common origin, established a dominance in the region later identified with Ephraim and Benjamin. Special military operations in the Benjaminite territory provoked a regional challenge to the Israelite incursion and resulted in an extended campaign in the Shephelah and the Hebron hill country. While the Ephraimite territory was spared from Joshua's military exploits, the biblical impression of Ephraimite settlement is one of extended hardship (1 Chr. 7:20-29). This settlement phase, distinct from earlier infiltration, resulted from the penetration of the Moses-led exodus at the end of the thirteenth century B.C.

Regional surveys and a number of recent excavations in Israel have provided new insights into the nature of these early Israelite settlements. One of the most important insights has been that ...*it is practically impossible to make fine chronological distinctions in the pottery from settlement sites*.[8] In other words, pottery has assisted very little in recognizing Israelite presence, or any ethnicity (with the possible exception of the Philistines). As a result, the extent of early Israelite occupation in Canaan has been defined on the basis of the biblical narratives. Canaanites and Philistines in Iron I are assumed to control the coastal plain, the Shephelah and the northern valleys. Ephraim is assumed to be the very heart of early Israelite settlement.

In the Beersheba Basin of the Negev, Israelite settlement was understood as an ...*intensive wave of settlement manifest in all of the earliest sites, and in places that had never been inhabited...there was now a chain of established settlements that inaugurated a period of flourishing occupation...*[9] The beginning of this settlement was dated at the end of the thirteenth or during the twelfth century B.C.[10] However, as at most other sites, the identity of new settlers in the Beersheba Basin has been difficult to determine with certainty. At Aroer, Tel Malḥata and Tel ʿIra, no Iron I remains have been found. Tel Malḥata appears not to have been settled before the tenth century B.C. Tel Esdar Stratum III, dated to the eleventh century B.C., consisted of an oval band of unattached dwellings that formed a large, open courtyard. Originally, these pillared 'broad-room' dwellings with beaten-earth floors were attributed to nomadic or semi-nomadic tribes initiating a sedentary lifestyle, that is, Israelite settlement in the Negev. After a partial destruction (by Amalekites?), the village revived as an agricultural settlement in the tenth century B.C. (Stratum II).[11] In fact, however, Stratum III, correctly dated to the second half of the eleventh century B.C., may represent desert dwellers who established a network of sites in the Negev highlands.

The abandonment of Tel Arad from Early Bronze II to the Iron I period created a major problem for understanding the confrontation of the Israelites at Arad in the Late Bronze period, as seemingly described in the Bible. The first Iron Age level at Arad (Stratum 12) in two phases (A and B) originally was dated to the eleventh century B.C.

Recent archaeological insights into the nature of Israelite settlement in both Palestine and Transjordan suggest that the earliest period was marked by territorial shifting and regional migration,[12] an aspect of the settlement process clearly presented in the biblical narrative. The assignment of tribal units to their respective territories based on the feasibility study that Joshua commissioned (Josh. 18:1-10) required periodic adjustment based on the needs of the population (adequate water, food supply and suitable sites for urban development) and the availability of the territory (resistance from local Canaanite residents and integration as dominants or subservients). The shifting of clans and families within tribal territories (Machir within Manasseh, Simeon within Judah) or to other (tribal) areas (Reuben to Judah, Dan to Laish) is well known in the biblical narrative.

Excavation of Iron Age I sites provides a fairly consistent picture. The complexity of the sequence of settlement and its relationship to the demise of Canaanite cities in the respective regions precludes specific dates for a consistent settlement throughout the country. However, the general picture shows the real possibility of a clear chronological correlation between Late Bronze Canaanite destructions and the Iron I village settlements that may be attributed to the Israelites. Such a scenario, however, does not preclude the possibility of infiltration by other ethnic elements and their establishment as isolated enclaves within the dominant Canaanite population.

In the Upper Galilee

Settlement in the Upper Galilee, as well as other sites throughout the country, is identified with true Iron Age I (12th-11th century B.C.) sites and surely must be the aftermath of the destruction of some of the major Canaanite cities. The pottery suggests that the Upper Galilee settlement occurred after the destruction of Hazor.

Tel Dan

The transition from the Late Bronze Canaanite city to the Israelite occupation is unclear for lack of sufficient Late Bronze remains. The Late Bronze city appears to have been confined within the city fortifications. Possibly the Late Bronze occupation was concentrated on the western part of the mound near the spring where excavation was hindered by thick vegetation. There was limited evidence of Late Bronze destruction with the first Iron Age stratum at Dan (VI) consisting mainly of pits and silos (some stone-lined) and other structures built over walls of the Late Bronze Age buildings. There was no evidence of an occupational gap between the Late Bronze and Iron Age settlements. A collection of pottery from a sealed locus in a covered silo was dated to the twelfth century B.C. This early Iron Age settlement appears to have belonged to a semi-sedentary tribe that ultimately built dwellings (V).[13] Its ceramic evidence contained a relatively large number of 'collared-rim' storage jars.

The cultural remains at Dan illustrate the early shifting of clans and tribes in their attempts to accommodate themselves to their hostile environment in Canaan. The Danite failure to claim their tribal inheritance in the south and their subsequent migration and conquest of Laish is dated to the first half of the twelfth century B.C. The Danite town flourished until its destruction in the mid-eleventh century B.C., about the same time as Shiloh's demise.

In the Lower Galilee

A survey of the entire Lower Galilee found only three or four major sites settled during the Late Bronze Period (ca. 1550-1200 B.C.). This decline in population contributed to a renewal of the region's oak forests and a renewed need for deforestation as a precondition to the establishment of viable Israelite settlements in the twelfth century B.C.

In the Iron Age I (ca. 1200-1000 B.C.), small rural sites in a new settlement pattern appeared primarily in the Nazareth hills region. These settlements may be attributed to the Tribe of Zebulun. Naphtali and Asher seemingly experienced similar settlement to the north and northwest of Zebulun. Such 'Israelite' settlement sites, however, do not exist in the Eastern Lower Galilee where supposedly the tribe of Issachar was assigned. In this region cultural evidence of Israelite settlement appears late, during the United Kingdom period (10th century B.C.).[14]

The settlement of Issachar is somewhat unique in its avowed intention to settling in the most desirable lands available, that is, in the Lower Galilee.[15] Volitional subjugation to the Canaanite population in that area would have required total integration into the existing culture, a situation that hardly would recognizable in the cultural remains of the region.[16] The more valid scenario is to be found in a recognition of the infiltration of Issachar as early as the fourteenth century B.C. (the Amarna Age) with local Canaanite dominance continuing into the early part of the United Monarchy. Only with the complete integration of the Issachar tribal region into the Davidic administration was there a local adoption of cultural forms clearly identifiable as Israelite. The obscurity of Israelite distinctives may be attributed to the socio-economic subservient role Issachar assumed to assure the tribe's subsequent claim to the productive Lower Galilee.

Taanach

An impressive city during the Middle Bronze period, Taanach suffered a major catastrophe during Thutmose III's campaign in ca. 1468 B.C. A relatively modest occupation during Late Bronze I followed. The Late Bronze town ultimately grew with some substantial buildings dated to the twelfth century B.C. This evidence is consistent with the Israelites' inability to dominate the powerful Canaanite centers bordering the Jezreel Plain during the early period of settlement. In the final quarter of the twelfth century (ca. 1125 B.C.) however, Taanach suffered a violent destruction, an event that possibly may be attributed to the Deborah-Barak victory over Sisera's Canaanite forces (Judg. 4-5). Israelite settlement, however, appears to have been delayed. A period of abandonment followed to the tenth century when Taanach became an important town (under the United Monarchy of Israel), only to be destroyed again by Shishak, ca. 918 B.C.[17]

In the Jordan Valley

Historically the Jordan Valley served as a cultural and political border and a buffer against incursions from the Transjordanian plateau. However, during periods of internal disruption and political insecurity such as Canaan experienced during the Iron Age I, the Jordan Valley and its urban centers often succumbed to indigenous forces from the east.

Deir ʿAllā

At Deir ʿAlla (probably biblical Succoth), a sacred shrine had been constructed on the mound without a defensive wall. It appeared to be an open sanctuary frequented by nomads. The shrine, together with the final Late Bronze city, was destroyed in a violent conflagration following an earthquake. Without a period of desertion, a new culture was introduced by a new population that arrived with a completely different technique in pottery making. Their finer techniques were applied to the inferior clays at Deir ʿAlla. This Iron Age I (12th to 10th centuries B.C.) settlement consisted of semi-nomadic metal workers who appear to have worked bronze seasonally.[18]

Excavations at Deir ʿAllā have shown that tribes from the east had their own pottery repertoire, directly bearing on analysis of cultural changes in Transjordan of the thirteenth century B.C. and requiring a reevaluation of Transjordan as an uncivilized, unurbanized region from ca. 1750 to 1200 B.C. Early Iron Age material in Palestine developed under the influence of a large infiltration of people bringing in the type of pottery found in the latest Late Bronze sanctuary at Deir ʿAllā. Invading tribes in the thirteenth century B.C. had a pottery tradition of their own. While the Late Bronze sanctuary at Deir ʿAllā seems to have been a shrine of wanderers, the sophistication of their repertoire and imports from all parts of the known world, including Egypt,. point to the existence of 'civilized' tribes.[19] The cultural remains at Deir ʿAlla point to the probability that peoples other than Israelites (possibly Kenites) occupied the town and that much of the Jordan Valley (especially in the north) may not have been under complete Israelite control until the United Monarchy.

Jericho

Various solutions have been suggested for the Jericho problem. The failure to recover archaeological evidence for a substantial Late Bronze city at Jericho has been a perplexing problem for most biblical scholars.[20] Attempts have been made to re-date the event to fit the archaeological evidence of destruction levels.[21] Most of these solutions, unfortunately, have created more problems than have been solved.[22] An identification of the Joshua-led attack on Jericho, according to the biblical account, cannot be reconciled with either the destruction of Jericho IV at the end of the Middle Bronze Age (ca. 1550 B.C.) or the end of the Late Bronze I (ca. 1400 B.C.). The Moses-Joshua exodus contingent forms the culmination of the migration from Egypt, an event that should reflect itself in the Israelite settlement pattern in the land.

A very limited Early Iron Age settlement appears to have existed on the site late in the twelfth century and during the eleventh century for only a brief time. The site then remained uninhabited until the eighth century B.C. when again limited evidence of some brief occupation occurs.

In the Central Hill Country

Shechem

Shechem accommodated its political structure during times of political change and crisis. The Shechemites submitted to rulers from abroad whose military power was composed of aliens. During the Amarna Age, Lab῾ayu's military power probably was dependent upon the "῾Apiru' who were conscripted or mercenaries in the expansion of Shechem's borders. These ῾Apiru and other mercenaries assisted Lab῾ayu's sons in their siege of Megiddo. The strategic location of the city was a major aspect of the geopolitical and social factors that contributed to the use of mercenaries. Foreign rulers controlled the city when its territory was coveted by strangers either as a convenient pass and base of operations during the Amarna Age or as an area of settlement again in the period of the Judges.[26]

Shechem's peaceful transition into the Israelite confederacy appears evident from the archaeological evidence at Tell Balâtah. The end of the Late Bronze and the beginning of the Iron Age I (ca. 1200 B.C.) yielded no destruction level and a continued use of the 'migdal' temple with its altar and masseboth. The ultimate destruction of the temple toward the end of the twelfth century B.C. generally has been identified with the Abimelech rebellion (Judg. 9).

The covenant ritual on the slopes of Mount Gerezim and Mount Ebal, overlooking Shechem, and the affirmation of its conditions, commanded by Moses (Deut. 27) and observed by Joshua following penetration into the central hill country (Josh. 8: 30-35) were required to integrate into the covenant relationship those who previously had settled and established themselves in the Shechem area and had not been a part of the Sinai experience.[23] The sanctity of this event at Shechem obviously rivalled the earlier occasion of Covenant commitment at Mount Sinai for those who became 'Sons of the Covenant' for the first time. Apart from its ancient sacred traditions, this event established Shechem as the tribal league shrine.[24] The tribal league organizations constituted by covenant and sanctioned at and by the central shrine at Shechem became especially meaningful for the northern tribes.[25]

Mount Ebal
...Then Joshua built an altar in Mount Ebal to the Lord, the God of
Israel, as Moses the servant of the Lord had commanded the people
of Israel,... (Josh. 8:30)

The discovery on Mount Ebal of a series of cultic objects and an unique architectural installation with non-Canaanite traditions has tended to reinforce the impression of Israelite presence in the central hill country. A supposed cultic site with a ramped altar and double enclosure has been attributed to the biblical tradition of the Israelite Covenant ritual shortly after their crossing of the Jordan (Josh. 8:30-35; Deut. 27:11-13).[27] Over 50 installations containing animal bones and ashes or pottery vessels possibly for ritual purposes suggested the cultic nature of the site. Two architectural phases were noted: an earlier construction of a revetment wall to create an enclosure, and later, during a peaceful transition, the construction of larger, newly designed cultic center including a *temenos* (restricted cultic area) wall. The absence of many architectural features found at most of the other Iron Age I sites such as monolithic pillars and three- or four-room plans highlight the unique nature of this site. There are no structures apart from the 'altar' within an inner *temenos* wall. The site appears to have been deserted within fifty years of its construction for unknown reasons.[28]

Serious questions have been raised about the cultic nature of the Mt. Ebal site.[29] Whether cultic or 'a three-phase village with a watchtower' from the Israelite settlement during the Iron Age I, its origin is consistent with the dramatic settlement activity in the central hill country early in the twelfth century B.C. Other cultic activity in the central hill country has been found at an Iron Age IA (ca. 1200 B.C.) open-air cult center with a massive stone enclosure wall around an altar or *massebah*. Within the enclosure a bronze bull was found that seemingly had been used in the ritual of the site.[30]

ʿAi (et-Tell)

A violent destruction of ʿAi ca. 2400 B.C., during the Fifth Dynasty of Egypt, was followed by an invasion of nomads from the desert. The site was abandoned and left in ruins. It has been suggested that following this destruction ʿAi's residual population established the town of Bethel nearby. The site of ᶜAi continued in ruins until ca. 1220 B.C. (at the beginning of the Iron Age I) when people from the north or east established a relatively small Early Iron Age settlement (2.75 acres, with a population of not more than 150) on the Early Bronze Age acropolis terraces and seemingly assumed the name "ᶜAi' (ruin). (Though the equation ᶜAi='ruin' has been questioned on philological-etymological grounds, there appears no longer to be a basis for questioning the identification of et-Tell with ᶜAi.)[31] The Israelite settlers built their houses directly on the ruins of the Early Bronze Age floors and walls that had been abandoned since ca. 2400 B.C. Two houses were built directly inside the still standing enclosure wall of the Early Bronze Age temple. Only a few inches of soil separated the Israelite floors from the Early Bronze temple floors. The entire settlement covered only about one-tenth of the wall-enclosed EB city. Irregular three-room, pillared houses appeared to form a defensive ring. Two distinct settlement periods seemed to exist between 1220 and 1050 B.C.[32]

Though the process of urbanization during the Iron Age I requires additional clarification, the lines of three- and four-room houses and subtypes also appear at Tell en-Naṣbeh and Tell Beit Mirsim from the eleventh-tenth centuries before the construction of the later solid defensive walls.[33] The usual private dwelling of the Iron Age I, later found in every Israelite site of the Iron Age II, in terms of size and central location, appears to assume an administrative character.[34]

The Benjaminite Territory

The settlement at ᶜAi may be assigned to a similar settlement phenomenon affecting other abandoned city sites in the region, such as Tell en-Naṣbeh and Tell el-Jib (Gibeon), various new sites such as Mukhmas (biblical Michmash), Rammun (Rimmon), Taiyiba (Ophrah?), Raddana (Ataroth?) Tell el-Ful (Gibeah), and the many other smaller squatters' settlements or campsites on area hilltops. With common architectural and cultural characteristics, the remains of these sites suggest a general homogeneity for the newcomers who appear to have been unchallenged in their settlement. Most of these new settlements were relatively small (less than 5 acres) and unfortified. Their location on marginal agricultural land seemed to indicate that the better lands were controlled by others. They were committed to both cereal farming and sheep and goat herding. They sustained their water supply by cutting unplastered cisterns into the Senonian Chalk. Cisterns became an important aspect of these hilltop settlements since springs at ᶜAi, Raddana and some of the other sites were weak and located in deep valleys far from the villages.

The placid village life appears to have been disturbed during the latter half of the twelfth century (ca. 1150-1125 B.C.) when a new phase of building houses and streets began. Open areas, or courts, were filled with numerous grain silos. This transition in storage methods from large storage jars to above-ground stone granary installations indicates the possible infusion of a new population that lacked experience in village life.[35]

Such settlements existed throughout Judea and Samaria. Of the 102 villages and towns identified, about 90 were newly founded, existing in virtual isolation as single economic entities depending upon their own subsistence rather than a regional market system. Obviously, some trading existed, but the general impression based on location and cultural remains is of a tentative, fragile, subsistence economy, too insecure to risk an open market.[36]

Injection of the Benjaminites into the area of the Gibeonite confederacy, according to the biblical narratives, was slow and violent at times (2 Sam. 21:1; 2 Sam. 4:2). In fact, the general impression is that the relationship became a traditional and bloody feud with unpleasant tension continuing to the end of the monarchy.[37]

Khirbet Raddana

A new village, six km west of ᶜAi, was established ca. 1200 B.C. with three-roomed houses of monolithic stone pillars and a population of not more than 50 persons. Two phases of settlement appeared (ca. 1200-1125 and 1125-1050 B.C.). The Israelite houses in some cases stood directly on exposed rock with evidence of the earlier Early Bronze village on the site coming from depressions and crevices in the bedrock. It was abandoned in the mid-eleventh century B.C., probably for a better location.[38]

Bethel

The destruction of the Late Bronze IIB town was followed by an early Iron Age town at Bethel with pillared houses as a distinct architectural feature. Its settlement is consistent with the arrival of the Israelites and the development of the new cultural pattern in the region.

The Environs of Shiloh

To understand adequately the Israelite decision to establish their first amphictyonic center at Shiloh, a review of cultural developments during the mid-second millennium B.C. is necessary. A strong wave of Middle Bronze II settlement in the central hills resulted in more than 55 MB II cities and towns (presently known) in the Ephraimite territory. Defensive measures toward the end of the Middle Bronze period extended into the central hill country where Shiloh, apparently unfortifed during the Middle Bronze IIB (ca. 1750-1650 B.C.) received massive fortifications including a large earthen *glacis* against a solid wall in the Middle Bronze IIC (ca. 1650-1550 B.C.). This fortification wall (10-17 feet thick) established on bedrock and enclosing a settlement of over 4 acres was destroyed in the mid-sixteenth century B.C. Rooms along the interior of the fortifications and its collapsed mudbrick superstructure provided evidence of intense burning.

Such massive fortifications, including the great stone wall and the *glacis*, can hardly be explained as an indigenous building operation. A population estimated between 400 and 650 (based on the area within the walls) could not have achieved such phenomenal construction. Surface surveys in the region suggest an earlier abandonment of smaller Middle Bronze settlements in the surrounding hills. The threat of imminent danger seemingly prompted a concerted but futile effort on the part of the regional population to establish a major stronghold at Shiloh, probably to assure the protection of their regional shrine and their own preservation.

All the Middle Bronze settlements in the central hills were destroyed at the end of the period and only five Late Bronze towns of smaller proportions were reestablished on the major tells. Scattered, unfortified sites from the previous period disappeared altogether. This dramatically depicts the decline of settlement and of economic vitality that existed throughout the central hill country during the Late Bronze period prior to the arrival of the Israelites.[39] Late Bronze Shiloh had no real settlement and little activity (15th to 13th centuries B.C.). However, the cultic center on the summit of the mound appears to have been used periodically, especially during the Late Bronze I (15th century B.C.), by regional pastoral groups.

A dramatic change occurred at the beginning of Iron Age I in the twelfth century B.C. Settlement at Shiloh was renewed with buildings, stone-lined silos and other remains characteristic of Israelite villages elsewhere throughout the central hill country. A rich array of early Israelite pottery included a predominant collection of collared rim storage jars that characterize such Israelite sites. The cultic tradition that had been established at Shiloh during the Middle Bronze Age seemingly was adopted by the Israelite settlers of the twelfth-eleventh centuries B.C.

The vibrant Israelite town that was established at Shiloh succumbed to a destructive conflagration in the mid-eleventh century B.C., an event associated with the Philistine attack to Israel's interior following the battle and Israelite defeat at Ebenezer. (The Early Iron Age settlement at Shiloh was destroyed ca. 1050 B.C.) Evidence of Israelite cultic activity was recovered from the destruction debris. With its destruction by the Philistines, Shiloh never regained significant prominence. Only a small village arose on the site during Iron Age II (10th-8th centuries B.C.)[40]

The results of intensive surveys throughout the entire central hill country have shown that the earliest concentration of Israelite settlements were located in the territories of Ephraim and Manasseh (in the north) and that only later, Israelite settlements spread southward in Benjamin and Judah. The eastern desert fringe and the northern central slopes of Ephraim were overrun with new settlers during Iron Age I. In the southern central range and the southern slopes, settlement activity was very limited.[41] Clearly Shiloh, as a long-established cultic site within the seclusion of an area that was practically uninhabited by a sedentary population on the eve of extensive Israelite settlement was an ideal candidate for Israel's first cultic center.

Twenty-two of approximately 100 Israelite sites identified throughout the Ephraimite territory are located within a 3-4 mile radius of Shiloh. Two to three times the general population density throughout the region was attracted to the immediate vicinity of the tribal shrine. The 3-acre Iron Age site probably was dominated by the sacred *temenos*. Its popularity and its impact on local economy attracted about half of the surrounding settlements during its latter years prior to the Philistine attack.

The excavations at Shiloh and other sites, and the results of the extensive surveys in the central hills, suggest that the emergence of Israel as an organized sedentary population is perceptible during the second half of the twelfth century B.C. The question of isolated local groupings, however, may be another matter. The infiltration of such isolated families and clans appear totally consistent with biblical and extra-biblical data. The nature of such infiltration, in unobtrusive limited numbers, precludes the possibility of archaeological detection. To suggest, therefore, in the face of historical data, that the lack of cultural evidence from excavation and survey (*no unequivocal archaeological evidence*) negates the possibility of Israelite presence as early as the fourteenth-thirteenth centuries B.C. is highly questionable. The final chapter on this process has not been written. The settlement patterns, however are perfectly clear and consistent with an early Israelite infiltration into the northern central hill regions of Ephraim and Manasseh. Settlement in the southern hills, of Benjamin and Judah came only later (12th century B.C.) with the final wave of the Moses-led exodus.

Giloh

The 'fortified herdsmen's village' at Giloh (on a ridge midway between Jerusalem and Bethlehem) with its double outer wall (a possible forerunner of the more elaborate casemate walls of the 10th century B.C.) enclosing almost 2 acres of houses and large corrals for animals, had a population of 100-150 people. The construction of a large (ca. 11 m square) freestanding tower on the northern edge of the site overlooking the Valley of Rephaim is a unique architectural development in the Iron Age I. Such freestanding towers and forts are not a part of Late Bronze defensive architecture and appear in the Iron

Age I as a distinctive feature of Israelite settlement in the central hill country. The defensive tower (*migdal*) is identified in the biblical narratives (Migdal Eder, Migdal El, Migdal Gad, etc.) with a network of early Israelite sites along the central watershed and is a vital defensive feature consistent with the political instability of the period of the Judges. The Giloh tower appears to be one of the earliest of such towers that may be identified with Israelite settlement.[42] Its location on the slope rather than at the highest point of the hill, unlike the Iron Age II tower, suggests a reluctance to draw attention to the settlement's presence.

Pottery at the site was scarce but homogeneous, suggesting a brief occupation during the Late Bronze/Iron Age transition, ca. 1200 B.C. The presence of large collared rim pithoi which begin to appear in the country during the thirteenth century B.C. provides some basis for dating the Giloh settlement. The earliest of such distinctive storage jars at Aphek and other sites in the coastal region have been dated to the late thirteenth century B.C.

The lack of a permanent water source may explain the brief occupation of the site. However, its brief settlement is consistent with many other Iron Age I sites, especially in the territory of Benjamin and in the Upper Galilee. The unsuitability of these remote sites prompted a settlement shift consistent with any significant political change in the region. In the case of Giloh, the clustering of these early Israelite villages around Jerusalem may have followed the original, early conquest of Jerusalem (Judg. 1:8). When the Jebusites subsequently regained control, Giloh's viability and security were undermined and the site was deserted.[43] A similar picture of Israelite settlement in the Judean and Ephraimite hills between the twelfth century and the period of the monarchy has emerged from Khirbet el-Marjameh and Khirbet Abu et-Twein.[44]

In and Along the Fringe of the Coastal Plain

The arrival of the 'Sea Peoples' and the settlement of the Philistines in the coastal plain had a very negative impact on the development of those Israelite tribes committed to areas in or bordering on the coastal plain. Their ability to monopolize the developing technology and use of iron provided the Philistines with a distinctive military advantage in confrontations with the Israelites over disputed territories.[45] The distinctive nature of their material culture has provided a relatively clear understanding of the nature of their settlement and the development of their pentapolis in the southern plain. Gaza, the most southerly of the Philistine Pentapolis, had been occupied by Thutmose III ca. 1469 B.C. and served as the base of Egyptian operations in Canaan. Mentioned in the Amarna and Taanach tablets as an Egyptian administrative center, Gaza remained ethnically Canaanite into the early twelfth century B.C. when it fell under Philistine control.[46] The transition from Egyptian to Philistine control in the coastal region is clarified in the cemetery at Deir el-Balah north of Gaza. Egyptian officers and officials were buried in anthropoid coffins during the Late Bronze period and later the Philistines adopted the same custom of burying their dead. Such Philistine anthropoid coffins have been found at Beth-shean and Tell el-Farᶜa (S) as well as Deir el-Balah.[47]

Tell Qasile and Arrival of the Philistines

This Philistine settlement, on the north bank of the Yarkon River about a half mile inland from the Mediterranean, had three Early Iron Age occupational strata from the mid-twelfth century through the eleventh century B.C. Within its fortifications was a variety of three- and four-room houses and an impressive temple. This is the only site that can specifically be identified according to ethnic origin on the basis of its very distinctive Philistine pottery.[48]

The frustrated attempts of the Israelites in their efforts to move against Philistine control in the coastal plain may be evident in a number of Iron I sites on the final ridge of foothills overlooking the Sharon Plain to the east of Aphek. The remains of a series of such settlements appear to represent periodic incursions and short-lived occupation on ridges from which the rich coastal lands were accessible.

Izbet Sartah

Located 2 km east of Aphek at the headwaters of the Yarkon River, Izbet Sartah is tentatively identified with Ebenezer, the primary site involved in one of the major Philistine-Israelite confrontations of the settlement period. This village consisted of a row of moderately small houses and numerous stone-lined silos from the twelfth century B.C.

A second phase of settlement incorporated a large four-room house in the center of the village. Abandoned a second time in the mid-eleventh century B.C., it was resettled briefly until the end of the eleventh or beginning of the tenth century B.C.[49]

In the Shephelah

Tell Beit Mirsim

The profile of cultural remains at Lachish and Tell Beit Mirsim possibly provides our clearest glimpses into the historical developments in the southern Shephelah.[50] The Late Bronze/Iron Age transition has been clarified by a restudy of pottery from stone-lined silos at Tell Beit Mirsim. Following the Late Bronze Age II destruction, resettlement of the site introduced no significant architectural innovations. The nature of the previous settlement was retained with the exception of new silos that replaced a previously built-up area, an indication of declining population. Subsequent construction of fortifications and buildings around the perimeter of the town may suggest an important political change in the region and the discontinued use of the silos suggests a deterioration of the local economy as well.

The pottery evidence provided an explanation for the architectural continuity. Canaanite forms continue following the Late Bronze II destruction. New forms and techniques appear to be a continuation of Canaanite traditions in spite of some innovations. However, only in the tenth century is there a ceramic change that makes the local pottery indistinguishable from forms within the territory of Israelite Judah and suggests the arrival of an Israelite population.[51]

The cultural sequence at Tell Beit Mirsim closely parallels the latest Late Bronze phase at Lachish (VI), only 12 km away. The end of Egyptian control in southern Canaan in the second half of the twelfth century B.C. is evident both at Lachish and at Tel Sera^c.[52] The continuation of Canaanite culture did not give the impression of a small population escaping from the disintegration of the central Canaanite towns, but of a reestablished indigenous population that survived the destruction of its town and aggressively reinforced its defenses against the threat of Philistines on the west and the encroachment of the Israelites on its eastern frontier. Ultimately, however, its population appears to have succumbed to the westward push of the Israelites from the Judean highlands.

Tel Sera^c

Tel Sera^c (Tell esh-Sharia, probably biblical Ziklag) is located in the northwestern Negev, midway between Gaza and Beer-sheba. This region was the buffer zone between Egypt and Canaan. Tel Sera^c was inhabited from the Middle Bronze Age (17th century B.C.) to Byzantine times (A.D. 6th century). The impressive Late Bronze remains of the town culminated in a fiery destruction in the mid-twelfth century B.C. The profile of the last two Late Bronze periods (X-IX) had thirteenth and twelfth century destructions that coincide with the Late Bronze sequence at Lachish.[53]

The Governor's residence was a local version of the Egyptian courtyard house of the New Kingdom. Similar sun-dried brick structures at Beth-shean, Tell el-Ḥesi, Tell Jemmeh, Tell Masos, and Tell el-Far^ca (S), and possibly Aphek, suggest the nature of Egyptian administrative organization in the province of Canaan during the reign of Ramesses III. Philistine pottery did not appear before the end of Ramesses III's reign in the mid-twelfth century B.C. The destruction of the Stratum IX town at that time (either by the Philistines, or Amalekite (?) nomads) was followed by an occupational stratum with early Philistine pottery sherds. Its subsequent history appears linked with the fortunes of the Philistines.

In the Negev

Nomadic sedentarization in the Negev highlands which perhaps began as early as the twelfth century B.C. reached its zenith toward the end of the eleventh or early tenth centuries.[54]

Tel Beer-sheba (Tell es-Seba^c)

Excavation at Tel Beer-sheba yielded no evidence of habitation before ca. 1200 B.C. (the beginning of Iron Age I).[55] Three Early Iron Age strata have been dated to ca. 1200-1000 B.C. In the second phase (Stratum VIII) solid houses of the four-room type appeared. Stratum VII seems to have had a circle of four-room houses forming a defensive perimeter plan.

Tel Isdar

An Early Iron Age village was established ca. 18 km east of Beersheba in the eleventh century B.C. A series of broadroom houses were constructed in a circular, detached (no continuous closure) pattern.

Khirbet el-Meshash

A series of ovens, minor wall remnants and other disturbances provided limited evidence of a semi-nomadic squatters' settlement (Stratum IIIB) that began five phases of occupation in the twelfth century B.C. Three-room houses appeared during the second phase (IIIA). Two phases in Stratum II consisted of four-room houses, a broadroom house with pillars, a Canaanite courtyard house and a dwelling with clear Egyptian affinities. A circular arrangement of the outer houses provided a perimeter of protection for the settlement. The final phase of occupation was poorly preserved and was abandoned for some unknown reason.[56]

A complete absence of Late Bronze Age city-states in the eastern Negev region does not indicate that the 'conquest' of the Negev proceeded in a peaceful manner. The size of Tell Masos suggests a consolidation of social structures to become a village community. There was a continuity of Late Bronze pottery and metal working technology and a unique architectural style that seemingly came with the founders of the Iron Age settlement.[57]

Summary

Surface surveys and excavations from the Upper Galilee (Tel Harashim, Sasa and Har Adir) through the central region (Sharon Plain, Samaria Hills, the tribal areas of Ephraim and Benjamin) to the southern hill country and the northern Negev (Masos, Tel Esdar and Beersheba) have yielded clear evidence of the settlement of new arrivals and consequent culture modification. The subsequent cultural continuity of these new arrivals into the period of the United Monarchy leaves no question that the origin and rather dramatic proliferation of new towns and villages (sometimes in less than idea settings) and the domination of various parts of the country must be attributed to the Israelites. (The distinctive pottery and other cultural remains of the Philistines whose arrival in the land almost coincided with that of the Israelites fairly clearly defines the limits of their territorial control.) Major excavations at Dan, Hazor, Shiloh and Bethel also have contributed to an understanding of early Israelite urbanization in critical areas of their settlement. A comparable change in settlement also is noted in Transjordan where urban life related to Ammonite, Moabite and Edomite settlement in Iron Age I vied with Israelites for territorial rights.

The new settlements of the Early Iron Age in the Galilee, the central highlands and primarily in the Negev were relatively small and established far from the major Canaanite centers of the Late Bronze Age. The excavations at these Early Iron Age sites indicate a lack of uniformity in the size and nature of settlement. They varied in size from a few houses (Beit Jala, Tel Isdar) to an impressive town of 1000 to 1500 inhabitants (Kh. Meshash). Most of them (ʿAi, Kh. Raddana, Izbet Ṣarṭah, Tell es-Sebaʿ, Kh. Meshash) were founded at the beginning of the twelfth century B.C. Some were abandoned after a very short time (Hazor, Beit Jala, Tel Isdar) and none survived for the entire period. They mostly were abandoned in the middle or towards the end of the eleventh century B.C. Few survived until the end of the Iron Age IIB (Tel Qiri, between Yokneam and Megiddo, possibly because of its location, its fortunes were linked to Megiddo). The fact that very few were transformed into walled towns in the early part of the Monarchy (only Tell es-Sebaʿ) may suggest that originally they were not established in the most suitable locations. Original site selection of Israelite towns may have been based on security. In any case, settlement was not continuous from the Early Iron Age to Iron Age II.

The earliest settlement sites in the Jerusalem vicinity, including Giloh, must be dated about the same time as the destructions of Bethel, Lachish and Debir (certainly later than Lachish VII destruction). The pottery of the earliest of these sites (Izbet Ṣarṭah, Tel Masos (IIIb), earliest Beth-zur and Khirbet Raddana) is transitional Late Bronze /Iron Age I, dated ca. 1200-1150 B.C. Thus there seems to be a relationship between the establishment of these sites and the destruction of at least some of the major Canaanite cities.[58]

This transition is probably best defined between Merneptah in the late thirteenth century and the mid-twelfth century B.C., the period in which Canaanite cities were destroyed and the new Israelite pattern of settlement was established. Evidence of a possible nomadic phase in the settlement cannot be expected from archaeological data. However, the variety of archaeological finds illustrates the complexity of the Israelite conquest and settlement process.

The construction of the dwellings in the new settlements tends to show some independence. Most settlements were not fortified. However, the circular placement of houses in some suggests a concern for basic security even though a continuous perimeter was not achieved. This form of urban planning seems to stem from the Late Bronze towns where, lacking defensive city walls, the outer walls of large buildings formed a continuous protective perimeter.

Conformity in architectural method and design tends to draw on Canaanite prototypes. The monolithic pillared courtyard houses appear to continue the Canaanite courtyard houses of the Middle and Late Bronze Ages. The predominant broadroom, three-room and four-room houses, however, appear to be a new design based on practical preferences. Newly founded settlements on Canaanite city sites reflect a continuity of Canaanite building traditions and strongly suggest a return of Canaanites attempting to revive their town. Villages located in isolation from known Canaanite centers tended to reflect non-Canaanite cultural traditions.

The continuity of Canaanite traditions is evident in other cultural elements. Cultural patterns requiring greater technical skills tend to reflect a continuity rather than innovation. This is especially true in metal-crafting and ceramics. This continuity obviously is best explained by the gradual nature of the Israelites' penetration into the various parts of the country. Even this limited sampling of Early Iron Age settlements indicates an apparent irregular time frame for founding such villages. Such a settlement pattern for the Israelites tends to preclude a conquest of the country by new immigrants only if the concept of that conquest is one of total annihilation of the existing population and pervasive new beginnings by the immigrants. The variety of cultural continuity and innovation in these Early Iron Age settlements reflects a multi-faceted transition from long-established Canaanite traditions to incipient Israelite independence. The Canaanite traditions were dying and the Israelite commitments were untried and uncertain, if not unsuccessful. Clearly these villages signal the arrival of some of the Israelites. But they were not the first. Biblical and extra-biblical sources highlight the earlier infiltration of 'Hebrews' during the Late Bronze Age when their integration into the existing Canaanite population was clandestine and unpretentious. Their adoption of Canaanite cultural forms was a matter of survival and subservience. The symbiosis of nomads and their sedentary neighbors is surely not the only explanation for the fusing of Canaanite/Israelite distinctives prior to the twelfth century B.C.[59]

NOTES

[1] W.F. Albright, Archaeology and the Date of the Hebrew Conquest of Palestine. *BASOR* 58 (1935): 10-18.
[2] W.F. Albright, The Smaller Beth-shan Stele of Sethos I (1309-1290 B.C.). *BASOR* 125 (1952): 24-32.
[3] A.F. Rainey, Review of John Bimson, Redating the Exodus and Conquest. *IEJ* 30 (1980): 249-251; *Unruly Elements in Canaan during the Egyptian New Kingdom Period.* Paper delivered to the Egyptology and the History and Culture of Israel Consultation Section, AAR/SBL Annual Meeting, New Orleans, November 19, 1990.
[4] S.W. Warner, The Dating of the Period of the Judges. *VT* 28 (1978): 455-463.
[5] Y. Aharoni, The Israelite Occupation of Canaan. *BAR* 8/3 (1982): 14-23.
[6] A. Malamat, How Inferior Israelite Forces Conquered Fortified Canaanite Cities. *BAR* 8/2 (1982): 24-35; Y. Yadin, Is the Biblical Account of the Israelite Conquest of Canaan Historically Reliable? *BAR* 8/2 (1982): 16-23.
[7] Norman K. Gottwald, Were the Early Israelites Pastoral Nomads? *BAR* 42 (1978): 2-7; idem, *The Tribes of Yahweh: A Sociology of the Religion of Liberated Israel, 1250-1050 B.C.E.* Maryknoll: Orbis, 1979; idem, Early Israel and the Canaanite Socioeconomic System, in *Palestine in Transition: The Emergence of Ancient Israel*, (eds.) D.N. Freedman and D.F. Graf. The Social World of Biblical Antiquity Series 2. Sheffield: The Almond Press, 1983: 25-37; idem, Two Models for the Origins of Ancient Israel: Social Revolution or Frontier Development, in *The Quest for the Kingdom of God: Studies in Honor of George E. Mendenhall*, (eds.) H.B. Huffmon, F.A. Spina and A.R.W. Green. Winona Lake, Ind: Eisenbrauns, 1983: 5-24; idem, The Israelite Settlement as a Social Revolutionary Movement, in *Biblical Archaeology Today: proceedings of the International Congress on Biblical Archaeology*, Jerusalem, April 1984. Jerusalem: Israel Exploration Society, 1985: 34-46.
[8] I. Finkelstein, *The Archaeology of the Israelite Settlement.* Jerusalem: Israel Exploration Society, 1988: 36.
[9] Y. Aharoni, The Negev During the Israelite Period. Pp. 209-225 in *The Land of*

the Negev, I, eds. A. Shmueli and Y. Grados. Tel Aviv, 1979 (Hebrew). 211.

[10] Y. Aharoni, The Archaeology of the Land of Israel. Philadelphia: Westminster, 1978, 1982: 202; idem., The Settlement of the Tribes in the Negev -- A New Picture. Ariel 41 (1976): 3-19; idem., Nothing Early and Nothing Late. Rewriting Israel's Conquest. BA 39 (1976): 55-76; Y. Aharoni, V. Fritz and A. Kempinski, Excavations at Tel Masos (Khirbet el-Meshâsh), Preliminary Report on the Second Season, 1974. Tel Aviv 2 (1975): 97-124.

[11] M. Kochavi, Excavations at Tel Esdar. ʿAtiqot 5 (1969): 14-48 (Hebrew).

[12] A. Lemaire, Galaad et Makîr. Remarques sur la tribu de Manassē à l'est du Jourdain. VT 31 (1981): 39-61; M. Weinfeld, Historical Facts Behind the Israelite Settlement Pattern. VT 38 (1988): 324-332.

[13] A. Biran, Tel Dan. BA 37 (1974); 26-51; Dan, Tel. Pp. 313-321 in EAEHL I, ed.M. Avi-Yonah. Englewood Cliffs, NJ: Prentice-Hall, 1975; Tell Dan - Five Years Later. BA 43 (1980): 168-182; J.C.H. Laughlin, The Remarkable Discoveries at Tel Dan. BAR 7/5 (1981): 20-37.

[14] Z. Gal, Khirbet Roš Zayit - Biblical Cabul: A Historical-Geographical Case. BA 29 (1990): 88-97.

[15] Y. Aharoni, New Aspects of the Israelite Occupation in the North. Pp. 254-267 in Near Eastern Archaeology in the Twentieth Century (Glueck Festschrift), ed. J.A. Sanders. Garden City, NY: Doubleday & Co. Inc., 1970.

[16] Z. Gal, The Settlement of Issachar - Some New Observations. TA 6 (1982): 79-86.

[17] P.W. Lapp, The 1963 Excavation at Taʿannek. BASOR 173 (1964): 4-44; Taanach by the Waters of Megiddo. BA 30 (1967): 2-27; The Conquest of Palestine in the Light of Archaeology. Concordia Theological Monthly 38 (1967): 283-300; The 1966 Excavations at Tell Taʿannek. BASOR 185 (1967): 2-39; The 1968 Excavations at Tell Taʿannek. BASOR 195 (1969): 2-49; A.E. Glock, Taanach. Pp. 1138-1147 in EAEHL IV, ed. M. Avi-Yonah. Jerusalem: IES and Massada Press, 1978.

[18] H.J. Franken, The Excavations at Deir ʿAllā in Jordan. VT 10 (1960): 386-393; Excavations at Deir ʿAllā in Jordan, 2nd Season. VT 11 (1961): 361-372; Deir ʿAllā. Pp. 321-324 in EAEHL I, ed. M. Avi-Yonah. Jerusalem: IES and Massada Press 1976.

[19] H.J. Franken and W.J.A. Power, Glueck's 'Explorations in Eastern Palestine' in the Light of Recent Evidence. VT 21 (1971): 119-123.

[20] H.J. Franken, The Problem of Identification in Biblical Archaeology. PEQ 108 (1976): 3-11.

[21] P. Bienkowski, Jericho was Destroyed in the Middle Bronze Age, Not the Late Bronze Age. BAR 16/5 (1990): 45,46,69; B.G. Wood, Dating Jericho's Destruction: Bienkowski is Wrong on All Counts. BAR 16/5 (1990): 45, 47-49, 68, 69.

[22] W.H. Stiebing, Jr., Should the Exodus and the Israelite Settlement in Canaan be Redated? BAR 11/4 (1985): 58-69.

[23] M.B. Rowton, The Problem of the Exodus. PEQ 85 (1953): 46-60.

[24] E.F. Campbell, Jr., and G.E. Wright, Tribal League Shrines in Amman and Shechem. BA 32 (1969): 104-116.

[25] G.R.H. Wright, Shechem and League Shrines. 21 (1971): 572-603.
[26] H. Reviv, The Government of Shechem in the El-Amarna Period. *IEJ* 16 (1966): 252-257.
[27] A. Zertal, Has Joshua's Altar Been Found on Mt. Ebal? *BAR* 11/1 (1985): 26-43; An Early Iron Age Cultic Site on Mount Ebal: Excavation Seasons 1982-1987. *TA* 13-14 (1986-87): 105-165.
[28] A. Zertal, How Can Kempinski Be So Wrong? *BAR* 12/1 (1986): 43, 49-53.
[29] A. Kempinski, Joshua's Altar - An Iron Age I Watchtower. *BAR* 12/1 (1986): 42-49.
[30] A. Mazar, Bronze Bull Found in Israelite "High Place" from the Time of the Judges. *BAR* 9/5 (1983): 34-41.
[31] Z. Zevit, The Problem of Ai. *BAR* 11/2 (1985): 58-67.
[32] J.A. Callaway, The 1964 ʿAi (Et-Tell) Excavations. *BASOR* 178 (1965): 13-40; The 1966 ʿAi (Et-Tell) Excavations. *BASOR* 196 (1969): 2-16; The 1968 ʿAi (Et-Tell) Excavations. *PEQ* 102 (1970): 42-44; The 1968-1969 ʿAi (Et-Tell) Excavations. *BASOR* 198 (1970): 2-16.
[33] Y. Shiloh, Elements in the Development of Town Planning in the Israelite City. *IEJ* 28 (1978): 36-51.
[34] Y. Shiloh, The Four-Room House - Its Situation and Function in the Israelite City. *IEJ* 20 (1970): 180-190; The Four-Room House - The Israelite Type House? *Eretz Israel* 11 (1973): 227-285.
[35] J.A. Callaway, Ai. Pp. 36-52 in *EAEHL* I, ed, M. Avi-Yonah. Englewood Cliffs, NJ: Prentice-Hall, 1975; Excavating Ai (et-Tell): 1964-1972. *BA* 39 (1976): 18-30.
[36] J.A. Callaway, A Visit with Arrays. *BAR* 9/5 (1983): 42-53; D.C. Hopkins, Life on the Land. The Subsistence Struggles of Early Israel. *BA* 50 (1987): 178-191.
[37] S. Yeivin, The Benjaminite Settlement in the Western Part of Their Territory. *IEJ* 21 (1971): 141-154.
[38] Y. Aharoni, Khirbet Raddana and Its Inscription. *IEJ* 21 (1971): 130-135.
[39] I. Finkelstein, Excavations at Shiloh 1981-1984: Preliminary Report. *TA* 12 (1985): 123-180; *idem*. History of Shiloh from Middle Bronze Age II to Iron Age II. 159-177.
[40] I. Finkelstein, Shiloh Yields Some, But Not All, of Its Secrets. *BAR* 12/1 (1986): 22-41.
[41] I. Finkelstein, *The Archaeology of the Israelite Settlement*. Jerusalem: Israel Exploration Journal, 1988: 187.
[42] A. Mazar, Iron Age I and II Towers at Giloh and the Israelite Settlement. *IEJ* 40: 77-101.
[43] A. Mazar, Giloh: An Early Israelite Settlement Site Near Jerusalem. *IEJ* 31 (1981): 1-36.
[44] A. Mazar, Three Israelite Sites in the Hills of Judah and Ephraim. *BA* 45 (1982): 167-178.
[45] G.A. Wainwright, The Coming of Iron. *Antiquity* 10 (1936): 5-24; *idem*, Some Early Philistine History. *VT* 9 (1959): 73-84; J.D. Muhly, How Iron Technology Changed the Ancient World -And Gave the Philistines a Military Edge. *BAR* 8/6 (1982): 40-54.
[46] A. Ovadiah, Gaza. Pp. 408-417 in *EAEHL* II, ed. M. Avi-Yonah. Jerusalem: IES

and Massada Press, 1976.

[47] T. Dothan, Anthropoid Clay Coffins from a Late Bronze Age Cemetery near Deir el-Balaḥ (Preliminary Report). *IEJ* 22 (1972): 65-72; 23 (1973): 129-146; I. Perlman, F. Asaro and T. Dothan, Provenance of the Deir el-Bala.h Coffins. *IEJ* 23 (1973): 147-151.

[48] B. Mazar (Maisler), The Excavation of Tell Qasile. *BA* 14 (1951): 43-49; A. Mazar, A Philistine Temple at Tell Qasile. *BA* 36 (1973): 42-48; *idem*, Excavations at Tell Qasîle, 1973-1974. *IEJ* 25 (1975): 77-88.

[49] M. Kochavi and A. Demsky, An Israelite Village from the Days of the Judges. *BAR* 4/3 (1978): 19-22.

[50] W.F. Albright, Beit Mirsim, Tell. Pp. 171-178 in *EAEHL* I, ed. M. Avi-Yonah. Englewood, NJ: Prentice-Hall, 1975.

[51] R. Greenberg, New Light on the Early Iron Age at Tell Beit Mirsim. *BASOR* 265 (1987): 55-80.

[52] E.D. Oren, Architecture of Egyptian 'Governors' Residencies' in the Late Bronze Age Palestine. *Eretz Israel* 18 (1985): 183-199.

[53] E.D. Oren, Ziklag: A Biblical City on the Edge of the Negev. *BA* 45 (1982): 155-166; Esh-Shariᶜa, Tell. Pp. 1059-1069 in *EAEHL* IV, eds. M. Avi-Yonah and E. Stern. Jerusalem: IES and Massada Press, 1978.

[54] I. Finkelstein, The Iron Age "Fortresses" of the Negev Highlands: Sedentarization of the Nomads. *TA* 11 (1984): 189-209.

[55] Y. Aharoni, Excavations at Tel Beer-sheba. *BA* 35 (1972): 111-127; Z. Herzog, Beer-sheba of the Patriarchs. *BAR* 6/6 (1980): 12-33.

[56] A. Kempinski, Israelite Conquest or Settlement? New Light from Tel Masos. *BAR* 2/3 (1976): 25-30.

[57] V. Fritz, The Israelite 'Conquest' in the Light of Recent Excavations at Khirbet-el-Meshâsh. *BASOR* 241 (1981): 61-74.

[58] A. Mazar, Giloh: An Early Israelite Settlement Site near Jerusalem. *IEJ* 31 (1981): 1-36.

[59] V. Fritz, Conquest or Settlement? The Early Iron Age in Palestine. *BA* 50 (1987): 84-100.

CONCLUSION: HISTORICAL SUMMARY

The unfortunate, and yet propitious, sale of Joseph to the Ishmaelite caravan on its way to Egypt initiated a sequence of events that, more than any other event recorded in the Old Testament, has impacted the religious and spiritual life of Jews and Christians alike. The focal point of God's redemptive acts in the life of ancient Israel obviously came at Mount Sinai in His desire to enter into a covenant with His people. The events that preceded the Divine encounter at the sacred mount and the hardships and trials that ultimately achieved full possession of the Promised Land are, however, just as vital a part of the story. Individual man's identification with Israel's pilgrimage of faith, and unbelief, gives to the story of the 'exodus' from Egypt and the 'conquest' of Canaan a fascination and relevance that yearns for clearer understanding. The degree to which we individually attribute historical merit to the biblical narratives may vary somewhat from the fairly literalist approach taken here. The archaeological and topographical emphasis may be criticized as depreciating the miraculous nature of God's deliverance of Israel. If our concepts of the miraculous must suffer in the process of coming to a clearer understanding of Divine revelation and God's redemptive acts, so be it. Whether the objective has been achieved or not, the purpose of the study, reflected in the summary that follows, has been to provide a sequential integration of relevant biblical, extra-biblical, geographical and archaeological data that may clarify this magnificent account of God's redemptive acts.

The story begins with the call and migration of Abraham from Mesopotamian Ur where his ancestors some generations before had contributed to the downfall of that city's Third Dynasty during a major influx of 'western' Semites (*Amurru*) toward the end of the second millennium B.C. Abraham's migration with the members of his immediate family brought them back to Haran in the traditional homeland, the center from which the *Amurru* (biblical 'Amorite') expansion had engulfed, not only the Mesopotamian region, but the entire Mediterranean littoral including Syria, the Phoenician coast (Lebanon) and Canaan in what generally has been referred to as the

'Amorite invasion.' Abraham's move from Haran into his *Promised Land*' must be understood as a part of this massive Semitic expansion, based on the biblical episodes in which, in the vicinity of Gerar, he sought the king's permission to use the city's wells, an indication that urbanization and political structures were well established within the more productive coastal regions. Conflict at those wells prompted Abraham temporarily to move into the fringe Negev region before ultimately establishing himself in the southern hill country at Hebron. But even there he was forced to buy a plot of ground to bury Sarah from others who have preceded him and established a prior claim upon the land. It was this 'unlanded' status that may be inherent in the designation 'Hebrew,' the term with which the patriarchs described themselves both in Canaan and in Egypt. In any case, it is a term that was discarded, except in retrospect, following the exodus from Egypt. In other words, with the fulfillment of God's promise to Abraham and his descendants, Israel became a 'landed' people and consequently were no longer '*Hebrews.*'

The Amorite domination of Canaan was followed by an infiltration and ultimate inundation of Lower Egypt and the establishment of 'foreign' rule, known in Egypt as the 'Second Intermediate Period,' or the *Hyksos* ('foreign rulers') Period. This embarrassing 'Dark Age' in Egyptian history, a period of approximately 150 years (ca. 1720-1570 B.C.), was dominated in its early stages by this 'Amorite' influx that elevated their own to the rank of 'pharaoh' and joined Egypt to a political structure that extended along the Fertile Crescent to the northern shores of the Persian Gulf. It was within this political context that Joseph arrived in Egypt and quickly rose to the rank of 'pharaoh's deputy' (vizier). Joseph's invitation to his family during a time of famine prompted the move of 70 Hebrews from Canaan to settlement in the land of Goshen. It is conceivable that this event could have occurred early in the *Hyksos* period (ca. 1700 B.C.) when some of the 'foreign' pharaohs' names appear to be Semitic. It was this date, then, that began the 430-year Egyptian sojourn (Ex. 12:40,41) that culminated when *all the hosts of the Lord went out from the land of Egypt* under Moses' leadership.

Intensive exploration during the past two decades and the archaeological excavations at Tell ed-Dabᶜa and Tell el-Maskhuṭa have increased dramatically our knowledge of the *Hyksos*, the Second Intermediate Period and the subsequent New Kingdom. Tell ed-Dab'a and its positive identification as Avaris, the *Hyksos* capital in the Delta, has clarified the West Semitic settlement process in the eastern Delta. Their origins and homeland in Syro-Palestine are consistent with the Fifteenth Dynasty origins in the same region. Now the clear identification of Semitic names in the King List has reinforced further the basic Semitic nature of *Hyksos* domination of Lower Egypt.

During this 430-year period, there was a distinct reversal of the Hebrews' fortunes some generations following the death of Joseph. A new pharaoh ...*who did not know Joseph* (was not related ethnically to him) arose over Egypt and instituted a new policy concerning the foreign population within Egyptian borders. The biblical narrative, consistent with its primary interest in the children of Israel, attributes the concern of the Egyptian pharaoh and the effects of this new policy specifically to the Hebrews. The Egyptians obviously faced a much greater problem in the residual alien population that had invaded Egypt and grown during the 150 years of *Hyksos* rule. That non-Egyptian population had been integrated into the economic and social fiber of Lower Egypt and especially that region of the Nile Delta known as 'Goshen.'

The severity of the Egyptian pharaohs' policies intensified from simple assignment of the foreign population to public works projects to the imposition of work quotas and personal restrictions and ultimately infanticide for the purpose of limiting population growth. The biblical portrayal of the pharaoh's motivation reflects two concerns: the possibility of the foreign population, in wartime, becoming a 'fifth column' within Egypt's borders, and the possibility that they ...*escape from the land.* The primary concern reflected the political insecurity the Egyptians felt so strongly in the aftermath of almost two centuries of foreign rule. The sudden, uncontrolled departure of a major segment of the population would signal 'Egyptian instability' to enemies seeking an opportunity to attack Egypt's borders. The implication of the pharaoh's second concern was the fact that the foreign population was essential to the economic stability of the country.

It is within the historical context of 'infanticide phase' of the pharaohs' policies that Moses was born, taken into the pharaoh's courts to receive the ultimate in Egyptian education. Consistent with policies established by Thutmose III in the Eighteenth Dynasty, Moses was groomed to function in an administrative capacity among his own people. When Moses failed to meet the pharaoh's expectations, ...*he sought to kill Moses.*

Refuge among the Midianites ultimately brought Moses back, with his father-in-law's flocks, to the west side of the Sinai, where, at Horeb, the mountain of God, he received instructions for the deliverance of the Hebrews still in Egyptian bondage. The location of this mountain is repeatedly (three times) referred to as *a three days' journey* (from the border of Egypt). The pharaoh recognized the location as not being distant ('*only you shall not go very far away*').

During the sequence of punitive plagues imposed on the Egyptians to convince the pharaoh to release the Hebrews and ultimately his decision to try militarily to force their return, the ambivalence of the pharaoh surely was a balancing of the relative merits of the Hebrews' departure to the economic and political stability of his kingdom. It was specifically at this crucial juncture in the reign of Ramesses II, following his peace treaty with the Hittites that stabilized Egypt's northern frontier and stopped the steady southward encroachment by the Hittites, that such an ambivalence is easily understood. The reinforcement of such dating comes from the biblical statement of a 430-year sojourn in Egypt, which, having begun ca. 1700 B.C., ended in ca. 1270 B.C., the year of Ramesses' treaty with the Hittites.

After a conclusive decision not to take the traditional, Egyptian military road, the *Via Maris*, which was most direct, the exodus route followed a southeasterly direction from staging areas in Goshen and an approach to the frontier at Etham that suggested an intention to follow a central route across the northern Sinai to Kadesh-barnea and Canaan's southern frontier. According to the biblical narrative, Moses was instructed to *turn back* and continue in the original southeasterly direction into the impossible situation bordering the *Red Sea* where the topographical and geographical features precluded the possibility of escape. The pharaoh recognized the Hebrews' dilemma: '*They are entangled in the land; the wilderness has shut them in.*'

With their recapture by the pharaoh's military imminent, God provided the fleeing Hebrews with a miraculous escape route through the sea into the Wilderness of Shur along Egypt's eastern frontier. The biblical narrative beautifully describes the displacement of the waters, probably at the juncture of the Bitter Lakes, *by a strong east wind all night* (contrary to the Cecil B. de Mille version) that created an escape route. With the cessation of the east wind the following morning, the return of displaced waters inundated the Egyptians who had pursued the Hebrews along their escape route. This biblical description of God's deliverance of His people by means of the strong east wind at a specific location also seems to fit well the Bitter Lakes' setting in reference to the subsequent itinerary.

Following a southerly direction along the eastern shore of the 'sea' they had just crossed, the Israelites' itinerary, according to the Exodus narrative, included only three specific locations (Marah, Elim, Rephidim) and three regions (Wilderness of Shur, Wilderness of Sin, Wilderness of Sinai) between the Egyptian border and the Mount of God, Sinai. If Marah and Elim can be equated with Bir el-Murah (*well of bitterness*) and ᶜAyun Musa (*spring of Moses*) respectively, then the identification of Mount Sinai with Jebel Sin Bisher (*Mount of Proclamation?*), within *a three days' journey* from the Egyptian border on the *west side of the wilderness* appears most reasonable. This identification is reinforced by the location of Rithmah (*ᶜAyun e-Rithmah*) in Wadi Suder to the northeast of Jebel Sin Bisher on the line the Israelite reasonably could have taken following the giving of the Law. Apart from these names that may retain some reference to the biblical event, many of the place names that form the itinerary, as preserved in the biblical text, suggest the transient nature of the exodus' evidence, e.g., *Hazeroth* (corrals), *Kibroth-hattaᶜavah* (cemetery, or graves of the lusters), etc.

Again, between Mount Sinai and Kadesh-barnea, the nature of the barren northern Sinai dictated the Hebrews' progress. The complaint about lack of water was frequent. Their movement *by stages* (Ex. 17:1; Num. 10:12) possibly suggests that successive units of limited size moved from oasis to oasis. Only four specific locations are mentioned in the exodus narrative: *Taberah* (meaning 'burning') and *Kibroth-hattaᶜavah* are identified with a single event and place. The episode involved serious complaints about conditions in general that seemingly originated from among the rabble (mixed multitude, hangers-on) who came out of Egypt with the Hebrews. *Taberah* refers to the judgment of God in the form of fire that consumed *...some outlying parts of the camp,* obviously the areas in which the rabble were encamped. Possibly among the Hebrews there were casualties as well that ultimately were buried. As a result, the place was referred to as the 'cemetery of the lusters.' The next oasis appears to have been suitable for a longer stay (*...and they remained at Hazeroth*) requiring the building of corrals, or enclosures for their livestock. Hence, the name of the place was 'Corrals.' The continuation of the route is not identified by specific oases apart from the arrival at Kadesh which logically should be identified with ᶜAin Qadeis with its very limited spring: *...there was no water for the congregation... there is no water to drink* (Num.20:2,5). The ultimate location of the Hebrews' cultic center during the thirty-eight years of wilderness wanderings, Kadesh-barnea, traditionally is identified with ᶜAin Qudeirat, where the abundant springs of that expansive oasis best may be identified with the biblical *waters of Meribah* (the result of the peoples' *contention* with Moses). The absence of archaeological evidence of a permanent settlement in the oasis area would seem to suggest that such cultic activities would be limited to seasonal gatherings.

The Hebrews' route from Mount Sinai to Kadesh is identified with reference to a specific detour, *...by the way of Mount Seir* and distance, *eleven days' journey* (Deut. 1:2). Some of the oases identified in the topographical list (Num. 33) may have been located along this detour. This indirect route probably was necessitated by the size of the exodus contingent and the inadequate water sources located along the more direct routes. All other place names appearing in the topographical list for the period between the crossing of the sea and the departure from Kadesh-barnea (Num. 33:11-37) approximately forty years later that do not appear in the 'diary' description of the exodus reasonably may be attributed to the thirty-eight years of 'wilderness wanderings.' A scribal tradition based on Egyptian prototypes makes such a suggestion reasonable.

Two distinct routes used by the Hebrews between Kadesh-barnea and the Jordan Valley clearly are presented in the biblical narratives. It seems obvious that since Moses and Joshua led a final contingent along a lengthy, discouraging route around Edomite and Moabite territories, that earlier contingents must have used the more direct route through Edomite and Moabite territory along the King's Highway. Those periodic migrations preceding Moses' 'exodus' logically would have been prompted by the deterioration of living conditions for all foreigners in Lower Egypt following the expulsion of the *Hyksos* and the establishment of the New Kingdom. The existence of such periodic, small-scale emigration from Egypt provides a meaningful explanation for a series of interpretive problems, both biblical and archaeological:

1. The lack of initiative attributed to the Hebrews in Egypt (in the biblical narratives) is difficult to understand in view of the extreme hardship imposed on them by the pharaoh, including the death of their male infants. The route of escape was planned to avoid any military interference lest they voluntarily return to Egypt while en route in the Sinai. Their longing for *...cucumbers, the melons, the leeks, the onions, and the garlic* suggests an appeal greater than their freedom. Their challenge to Moses' leadership when confronted with water shortages in the desert and an expressed longing to return to the security of Egypt point to a 'slave' mentality. The nature of this behavior is more understandable if Moses was leading a residual rabble who lacked even minimal initiative to escape the progressively severe hardships of their lot in Egypt.

2. The earlier departure of relatively small, family, extended family and clan units provides a reasonable explanation for the inclusion of an 'exodus' route other than the one assigned to the Moses-led expedition.

3. Earlier encounters with such transient Hebrew groups by the King of Edom provide the background that explains the inclusion in the biblical record of the detailed conversations between the King and Moses' messengers. The specific conditions delineated by the messengers to convince the King to permit their passage clearly implies that others on previous occasions had trespassed into adjoining fields and vineyards and used water from the wells without paying for it (Num. 20:17-19).

4. Fear prompted the defensive stance of the Edomite King (*'...and they will be afraid of you... you shall purchase food... and you shall*

also buy water...' (Deut. 2:4-6). The biblical narrative presents the Edomites and Moabites as fearing the consequences of permitting the Hebrews' access within their borders. The specific instructions concerning the buying of food and water suggests the likelihood that previous groups robbed and looted the regions adjoining the route of passage.

5. Even the promises not to detour from the road (*We will go up by the highway,...*) and not to camp (*let me only pass through on foot, nothing more.*) were not adequate to convince the Edomite King to risk permission for the Hebrews' passage. Previous experiences appear to have been too unpleasant and he was willing to risk a military confrontation to thwart the Hebrews' advance.

6. We assume that the interval of 40 years of wilderness sojourn saw the consolidation of the Edomite kingdom and the development of a military sufficiently strong to defend its borders. That consolidation would have taken place during the mid-thirteenth century B.C. Since the biblical narrative neither refers to nor implies the existence of cities in the Edomite kingdom at the time of the Hebrew confrontation and rejection, the demands for archaeological evidence of urbanization in the trans-Arabah under Edomite control at the time are unfounded. Excavations and surface surveys in the Transjordan however have determined earlier development of urbanization from the Moabite plateau northward.

The arrival of smaller groups of Hebrews facilitated their infiltration and integration into Canaanite urbanized society. Their unobtrusive arrival probably precludes an identification of distinctive cultural traits even in excavations of sites where they were known or assumed to exist. The nature of their arrival required intentional accommodation to and adoption of Canaanite cultural behavior. Even in the case of the later Moses-led contingent, an attempted recognition of unique cultural forms may prove most frustrating since the 40-year nomadic lifestyle in the Sinai tended to obliterate the cultural distinctives with which they came from Egypt.

The arrival of the Hebrews in growing numbers however created some political problems that seem to surface in Egyptian annals of the Eighteenth and Nineteenth Dynasties. Infiltration into unsettled areas could accommodate the earliest arrivals. As the pressures grew in

Egypt, we may assume a growing stream of Hebrews moving across the Sinai, through the Arabah to the King's Highway and northward along the Transjordanian plateau and into the Jordan Valley. In the Transjordan, the early arrivals established themselves at least 300 years before the Judge Jephthah (dated ca. 1100 B.C.) had his famous controversy with the Ammonites about their prior claim to the area north of the Arnon first settled by Gad (note Dibon-gad) and later by Reuben. Their successful settlement in the Transjordan possibly prompted the Reubenites, Gadites and some of the Manassehites to request permission of Moses to remain on the east of the Jordan.

It seems equally logical that the early arrivals in Canaan determined to a certain extent the assignment of the tribes to their respective territorial allotments. This seems especially reasonable in reference to the tribes of Ephraim, Issachar and Asher. The ʿApiru problem so prominent in the annals of the pharaohs of the Eighteenth and Nineteenth Dynasties and the Amarna tablets was centered in the Lower Galilee, upper Jordan Valley and the vicinity of Shechem where the tribes of Issachar and Manasseh/Ephraim were settled. The Chief of Asher, dated by Papyrus Anastasi I to the reign of Ramesses II, interestingly controlled the same southern extension of the Carmel Range to which the Israelite tribe of Asher later was assigned by Joshua.

The chronological sequence of the exodus from Egypt and Israelite occupation in Canaan now seems relatively clear. Deterioration of living conditions for the Hebrews in Egypt initiated the exodus 480 years before the dedication of Solomon's temple (I Kings 6:1), the traditional date of the exodus (ca. 1440 B.C.). It was shortly after this date that the Egyptian pharaohs (in their annals) for the first time referred to ʿApiru in Canaan (Amenhotep II captured 3600 ʿApiru prisoners). (An infiltration and integration of Hebrews among other 'unlanded' elements within Canaan at the time obviously does not require a direct equating of Hebrews and ʿApiru.) The historical fact is that from this point onward, the ʿApiru became a growing problem for the Egyptians in Canaan, a possible evidence that Hebrew emigration from Egypt had increased due to worsening conditions there. This process continued to ca. 1270 B.C. when Moses demanded the release of the remaining, 'unmotivated' Hebrews from their

Egyptian overlords. After 40 years in the Sinai, the final contingent of Hebrews crossed the Jordan to begin their integration into the Canaanite culture, ca. 1230 B.C. The gradual infiltration and settlement of the Hebrews in the Transjordan and Canaan over a 190-year period may preclude the existence of a distinct cultural break that could be identified archaeologically with Hebrew arrival. The arbitrary, unstructured nature of their arrival and penetration into Canaanite economy and society also contributed to our inability to recognize their presence. Even in terms of destruction levels, the evidence is less than conclusive. The utter confusion of ethnic centers and populations during the Late Bronze/Iron Age transition and the struggles over territorial rights seriously complicates any attempts at identifying Israelite expansion or military incursions.

Obviously, the Moses-led exodus was much smaller than most literalists have imagined. The Bible gives every indication that on a number of occasions military confrontation could not be risked or was a failure --- possibly because of the Hebrews' slave mentality, the result of enduring at least 170 years of a progressively oppressive system. But the biblical narrative also indicates that the Israelite fighting force (and the number of emigrants with Moses) was fairly limited. Two midwives were adequate to care for Hebrew births (Ex. 1:15). A roving band of Amalekites, possibly traders crossing the Sinai, posed a threat of annihilation at Rephidim, reluctance to challenge Edomite strength, and defeat at the hands of the king of Arad, all point either to a lack of fighting prowess or more assuredly to a more limited size that could not overwhelm its enemies by sheer numbers. The encampment at Gilgal over an extended period of time and the nature of the siege on Jericho also point to a more manageable number than a later scribe mistakenly supplied to the military conscription lists of Numbers 1 and 26. The text clearly indicates that these census-taking events were related to determining the fighting strength of the Hebrews, first at Sinai, and then 38 years later on the banks of the Jordan in anticipation of military confrontation in Canaan. The urgency of integrating into the covenant relationship the large segments of Israelites already in the central hill country as a result of earlier infiltration also may be related to the limited strength of the Moses-led exodus. The covenant bound a fragmented, isolated group of Israelite families, clans and tribes into a confederation that ultimately achieved full control of the land of Canaan.

It is the nature of achieving that control that has been problematic in biblical studies. The conquest model seemingly so clearly elaborated in the biblical text has fallen into question. A recognition that the arrival in Canaan of a large, though fragmented force by infiltration was followed by a much smaller, final contingent led by Moses and Joshua provides clarification of the limited success in impacting the Canaanite material culture to provide the archaeologist with vivid evidence of Israelite presence. The nature of their infiltration required accommodation and obscurity. The Bible implies that type of arrival and settlement for some of the tribes, notably Gad, Ephraim and Issachar. The Moses-led contingent following a forty-year sojourn in the Sinai and Negev clearly lost distinctiveness during the nomadic lifestyle that environment forced upon them. Their arrival thus was characterized by an accommodation to prevailing customs and cultural necessities. Their presence was obscured further by a reluctance to move decisively into the territories assigned to them. The Bible narratives seem to suggest a very gradual expansion with limited confrontation or challenging of the established Canaanite populations. The fragmentation and demonstrated tribal independence so vividly evident during the settlement period of the Judges is clarified by a fragmented series of independent Hebrew 'arrivals' in the land.

Few doubt that the Hebrew exodus from Egypt was a historical event. That escape from bondage initiated an extended period of conflict that eventually resulted in the Israelite monarchy. It is the nature of that event and the historical period to which it belongs that this study has attempted to address. A disparaging of the biblical narratives and discounting of specific biblical statements can contribute little to the discussion. The ultimate reconstruction of this pivotal period in the history of Israel awaits a proper understanding of the biblical text and the results of archaeological research and a legitimate correlation and integration of that archaeological data with the relevant historical references in the biblical text and other sources. If the foregone discussion has failed adequately to resolve problems in understanding or correlation, it is at least hoped that interest may have been stimulated for ongoing study.

BIBLIOGRAPHY

Aharoni, Y.

1957   Problems of the Israelite Conquest in the Light of Archaeological Discoveries. *Antiquity and Survival* 2: 131-150.

1958   The Negev of Judah. *Israel Exploration Journal* 8: 26-38.

1960   Some Geographical Remarks Concerning the Campaigns of Amenhotep II. *Journal of Near Eastern Studies* 19: 177-183.

1961   Kadesh-Barnea and Mount Sinai. Pp. 117-170 in Beno Rothenberg, *God's Wilderness: Discoveries in Sinai*. London: Thames and Hudson.

1967a   *The Land of the Bible*, trans. A.F. Rainey. Philadelphia: Westminster Press.

1967b   Excavations at Tel Arad: Preliminary Report on the Second Season. *Israel Exploration Journal* 17: 233-249.

1969   Rubute and Ginti-Kirmil. *Vetus Testamentum* 19: 137-145.

1970   New Aspects of the Israelite Occupation in the North. Pp. 254-267 in *Near Eastern Archaeology in the Twentieth Century (Glueck Festschrift)*, ed. J.A. Sanders. Garden City, NY: Doubleday & Co. Inc.

1971   Khirbet Raddana and Its Inscriptions. *Israel Exploration Journal* 21: 130-135.

1972a   Excavations at Tel Beer-Sheba: Preliminary Report of the Fourth Season, 1972. *Tel Aviv* 1/1: 34-42.

1972b   Excavations at Tel Beer-sheba. *Biblical Archaeologist* 35: 111-127.

1975a   Arad. Pp. 74-89 in *Encyclopedia of Archaeological Excavations in the Holy Land*, Vol. I, ed. M. Avi-Yonah. Englewood Cliffs, NJ: Prentice-Hall.

1975b   Beersheba, Tel. Pp. 160-168 in *Encyclopedia of Archaeological Excavations in the Holy Land*, Vol. I, ed. M. Avi-Yonah. Englewood Cliffs, NJ: Prentice-Hall.

1975c   Excavations at Tel Beer-Sheba, Preliminary Report of the Fifth and Sixth Seasons, 1973-1974. *Tel Aviv* 2/4: 146-168.

1975d   Tel Masos: Historical Considerations. *Tel Aviv* 2/3: 114-124.

1976a   Nothing Early and Nothing Late: Re-writing Israel's Conquest. *Biblical Archaeologist* 39/2: 55-76.

1976b   Arad. Pp. 38-39 in *The Interpreter's Dictionary of the Bible*, Supplementary Volume. Nashville: Abingdon Press.

1976c   The Settlement of the Tribes in the Negev - A New Picture. *Ariel* 41: 3-19.

1978   *The Archaeology of the Land of Israel*, trans. A.F. Rainey. Philadelphia: Westminster Press.

1979a   *The Land of the Bible: A Historical Geography*, 2nd ed. trans. and ed. by A.F. Rainey. London: Burns and Oates.

1979b   The Negev During the Israelite Period. Pp. 209-225 in *The Land of the Negev*, I. Tel Aviv (Hebrew).

1982   The Israelite Occupation of Canaan. *Biblical Archaeology Review*
                8/3: 14-23.
Aharoni, Y. and R. Amiran
1964   Excavations at Arad: Preliminary Report on the First Season,
                1962. *Israel Exploration Journal* 14: 131-147.
1975   Arad. Pp. 74-89 in *Encyclopedia of Archaeological Excavations
                in the Holy Land* Vol. I, ed. M. Avi-Yonah. Englewood Cliffs, NJ:
                Prentice-Hall.
1982   *The Archaeology of the Land of Israel from the Prehistoric
                Beginnings to the End of the First Temple Period*, ed. M. Aharoni.
                Philadelphia: Westminster Press.
Aharoni, Y. and M. Avi-Yonah
1968   *The Macmillan Bible Atlas.* New York: Macmillan.
Aharoni, Y., V. Fritz and A. Kempinski.
1972   Tel Masos (Khirbet el-Meshâsh). *IEJ* 22: 243
1974   Excavations at Tel Masos (Khirbet El-Meshâsh). Preliminary
                Report on the First Season, 1972. *Tel Aviv* 1/2: 64-74.
1975   Excavations at Tel Masos (Khirbet el-Meshâsh): Preliminary
                Report on the Second Season, 1974. *Tel Aviv* 2: 97-124.
Ahituv, S.
1972   Did Ramesses II Conquer Dibon? *Israel Exploration Journal* 22:
                141-142.
1978   Economic Factors in the Egyptian Conquest of Canaan. *Israel
                Exploration Journal* 28: 39-108.
Åhlström, G.W.
1986   *Who Were the Israelites?* Winona Lake, IN: Eisenbrauns.
Åhlström, G.W. and D. Edelman
1985   Merneptah's Israel. *Journal of Near Eastern Studies* 44/1: 59-61.
Aime-Giron, N.
1940   Ba῾al Saphon et les dieux de Tahpanhes dans un nouveau Papyrus
                Phenicien. *Annales du Service des Antiquités d'Egypte* 40: 433-
                460.
Albright, W.F.
1922/23   ῾Ai and Beth-Aven. *Annual of the American Schools of Oriental
                Research* 4: 141-149.
1926   The Jordan Valley in the Bronze Age. *Annual of the American
                Schools of Oriental Research* 6. Cambridge, MA: American
                Schools of Oriental Research.
1932   The Excavations of Tell Beit Mirsim in Palestine. Vol. I: The
                Pottery of the First Three Campaigns. *Annual of the American
                Schools of Oriental Research* 12. Cambridge, MA: American
                Schools of Oriental Research.
1933   The Excavations at Tell Beit Mirsim. Vol. IA: The Bronze Age
                Pottery of the Fourth Campaign. *Annual of the American Schools
                of Oriental Research* 13. Cambridge, MA: American Schools of
                Oriental Research.

1934	The Kyle Memorial Excavation at Bethel. *Bulletin of the American Schools of Oriental Research* 56: 2-15.
1935a	Archaeology and the Date of the Hebrew Conquest of Palestine. *Bulletin of the American Schools of Oriental Research* 58: 10-18.
1935b	Presidential Address: Palestine in the Earliest Historical Period. *Journal of the Palestine Oriental Society* 15: 193-234.
1937	Further Light on the History of Israel from Lachish and Megiddo. *Bulletin of the American Schools of Oriental Research* 68: 22-26.
1938a	The Chronology of a South Palestinian City, Tell el-ᶜAjjûl. *American Journal of Semitic Languages and Literatures* 55: 337-359.
1938b	The Excavations of Tell Beit Mirsim. Vol. II: The Bronze Age. *Annual of the American Schools of Oriental Research* 17. Cambridge, MA: American Schools of Oriental Research.
1939	The Israelite Conquest of Canaan in the Light of Archaeology. *Bulletin of the American Schools of Oriental Research* 74: 11-23.
1940	New Light on the History of Western Asia in the Second Millennium B.C. *Bulletin of the American Schools of Oriental Research* 77: 20-32; 78: 23-31.
1943a	A Tablet of the Amarna Age from Gezer. *Bulletin of the American Schools of Oriental Research* 92: 28-30.
1943b	The Excavations at Tell Beit Mirsim. Vol. III: The Iron Age. *Annual of the American Schools of Oriental Research* 21-22. Cambridge, MA: American Schools of Oriental Research.
1944	A Prince of Taanach in the 15th Century B.C. *Bulletin of the American Schools of Oriental Research* 94: 24-27.
1945	The Chronology of the Divided Monarchy of Israel. *Bulletin of the American Schools of Oriental Research* 100: 16-22.
1948	The Early Alphabetic Inscriptions from Sinai and their Decipherment. *Bulletin of the American Schools of Oriental Research* 109: 6-22.
1952	The Smaller Beth-shan Stele of Sethos I (1309-1290 B.C.). *Bulletin of the American Schools of Oriental Research* 125: 24-32.
1954	Northwest-Semitic Names in a List of Egyptian Slaves from the Eighteenth Century B.C. *Journal of the American Oriental Society* 74: 222-233.
1955	Palestinian Inscriptions. Pp. 320-322 in *Ancient Near Eastern Texts Relating to the Old Testament*, 2nd ed, ed. J.B. Pritchard. Princeton, NJ: Princeton University Press.
1957	*From the Stone Age to Christianity*, 2nd ed. Baltimore: Johns Hopkins Press.
1960	*The Archaeology of Palestine*, 3rd rev. ed. Baltimore: Penguin Books.
1961	Abram the Hebrew: A New Archaeological Interpretation. *Bulletin of the American Schools of Oriental Research* 163: 36-54.

1965a   The Role of the Canaanites in the History of Civilization. Pp. 438-
             487 in *The Bible and the Ancient Near East*, ed. G.E. Wright.
             Garden City, NY: Doubleday.
1965b   Some Remarks on the Archaeological Chronology of Palestine
             before about 1500 B.C. Pp. 47-60 in *Chronologies in Old World
             Archaeology*, ed. R.W. Ehrich. Chicago: University of Chicago
             Press.
1967   Debir. Pp. 207-220 in *Archaeology and Old Testament Study*, ed.
             D. Winton Thomas. London: Oxford University Press.
1968   *Yahweh and the Gods of Canaan*. Garden City, NY: Doubleday.
1973   From the Patriarchs to Moses. *Biblical Archaeologist* 36: 5-33; 48-
             76.
1975a   The Amarna Letters From Palestine. Pp. 98-116 in *Cambridge
             Ancient History*, 3rd ed. Vol. II, Part 2, ed. I.E.S. Edwards, et al.
             Cambridge: Cambridge University Press.
1975b   Beit Mirsim, Tell. Pp. 171-178 in *Encyclopedia of Archaeological
             Excavations in the Holy Land*, Vol. I, ed. M. Avi-Yonah.
             Englewood Cliffs, NJ: Prentice-Hall.
Aldred, C.
1957   The End of the El-ʿAmārna Period. *Journal of Egyptian
             Archaeology* 43: 30-41.
1959   The Beginning of the El-ʿAmarna Period. *Journal of Egyptian
             Archaeology* 45: 19-33.
1971   Egypt: The Amarna Period and the End of the Eighteenth Dynasty.
             Pp. 49-97 in *Cambridge Ancient History*, 3rd ed. Vol. II, Part 2,
             ed. I.E.S. Edwards, et al. Cambridge: Cambridge University Press.
Alt, A.
1925   Die Landnahme der Israeliten in Palästina (Reformations program
             der Universität Leipzig 1925). In *Essays on Old Testament History
             and Religion*, trans. R.A. Wilson. Oxford: Basil Blackwell.
1954   Neue Berichte uber Feldzuge von Pharaonen des Neuen Reiches
             nach Palästina. Pp. 31-75 in *Zeitschrift des Deutschen Palästina-
             Vereins* 70.
1968   *Essays on Old Testament History and Religion* (English
             Translation). Garden City, NY: Doubleday.
Amiran, R. and A. Eitan
1963   Tel Nagila. *Israel Exploration Journal* 13: 143-144; 333-334.
1964   A Krater of Bichrome Ware from Tel Nagila. *Israel Exploration
             Journal* 14: 219-231.
1965   A Canaanite-Hyksos City at Tel Nagila. *Archaeology* 18: 113-123.
Amiran, R. and J.E. Worrell
1976   Hesi, Tel. Pp. 514-520 in *Encyclopedia of Archaeological
             Excavations in the Holy Land*, Vol. II, ed. M. Avi-Yonah.
             Englewood Cliffs, NJ: Prentice-Hall; Jerusalem: The Israel
             Exploration Society and Massada Press.

Anati, E.
1985   Has Mt. Sinai Been Found? *Biblical Archaeology Review* 11/4: 42-57.
1987   *The Mountain of God*. New York: Rizzoli Publications.
Artzy, M.
1969   Pottery Analysis by Neutron Activation. *Archaeometry* 11.
1973   The Late Bronze 'Palestinian' Bichrome Ware in its Cypriote Context. Pp. 9-16 in *Orient and Occident, Essays Presented to Cyrus H. Gordon* (= *Alter Orient und Altes Testament*, 22), ed. H.A. Hoffner, Jr.
Artzy, M., F. Asaro and I. Perlman
1973   The Origin of the 'Palestinian' Bichrome Ware. *Journal of the American Oriental Society* 93: 446-461.
1978   Imported and Local Bichrome Ware in Megiddo. *Levant* 10: 99-111.
Astour, M.
1965   New Evidence on the Last Days of Ugarit. *American Journal of Archaeology* 69: 253-258.
Avigad, N.
1978   Samaria. Pp. 1032-1050 *Encyclopedia of Archaeological Excavations in the Holy Land*, Vol. IV, ed. M. Avi-Yonah. Englewood Cliffs, NJ: Prentice-Hall; Jerusalem: The Israel Exploration Society and Massada Press.
1980   The Chief of the Corvée. *Israel Exploration Journal* 30: 170-173.
Avi-Yonah, M.
1977   Medeba (Madeba). Pp. 819-823 in *Encyclopedia of Archaeological Excavations in the Holy Land*, Vol. II, ed. M. Avi-Yonah. Englewood Cliffs, NJ: Prentice-Hall; Jerusalem: The Israel Exploration Society and Massada Press.
Auld, A.G.
1975   Judges 1 and History: A Reconstruction. *Vetus Testamentum* 25: 261-285.
Badaway, A.
1968   *A History of Egyptian Architecture, The Empire (The New Kingdom)*. Los Angeles: University of California Press.
Bagatti, B.
1977   Nebo, Mount. Pp. 923-26 in *Encyclopedia of Archaeological Excavations in the Holy Land*, Vol. III, ed. M. Avi-Yonah. Englewood Cliffs, NJ: Prentice-Hall; Jerusalem: The Israel Exploration Society and Massada Press.
Barnett, R.D.
1975a   The Sea Peoples. Pp. 359-378 in *Cambridge Ancient History*, 3rd ed. Vol. II, Part 2, ed. I.E.S. Edwards, *et al.* Cambridge: Cambridge University Press.

1975b   Phrygia and the Peoples of Anatolia in the Iron Age. Pp. 417-442
               in *Cambridge Ancient History*, 3rd ed. Vol. II, Part 2, ed. I.E.S.
               Edwards, *et al.* Cambridge: Cambridge University Press.
Bartlett, J.R.
1969a   The Land of Seir and the Brotherhood of Edom. *Journal of
               Theological Studies* 20: 1-20.
1969b   The Historical Reference of Numbers 21: 27-30. *Palestine
               Exploration Quarterly* 101: 94-100.
1970   Sihon and Og, Kings of the Amorites. *Vetus Testamentum* 20: 257-
               277.
1972   The Rise and Fall of the Kingdom of Edom. *Palestine Exploration
               Quarterly* 104: 26-37.
1973   The Moabites and Edomites. Pp. 229-258 in *Peoples of Old
               Testament Times*, ed. D.J. Wiseman. Oxford: Oxford University
               Press.
1978   The Conquest of Sihon's Kingdom: A Literary Re-examination.
               Journal of Biblical Literature 97/3: 347-351.
Bartlett, S.C.
               *From Egypt to Palestine through the Wilderness and the South
               Country.*
Batto, Bernard F.
1983   The Reed Sea: Requiescat in Pace. *Journal of Biblical Literature*
               102/1: 27-35.
1984   Red Sea or Reed Sea?: How the Mistake Was Made and What
               Yam Sûp Really Means. *Biblical Archaeology Review* 10/4: 57-63.
Beck, P., and M. Kochavi
1983   The Egyptian Governor's Palace at Aphek. *Qadmoniot* 16: 47-51
               (Hebrew).
1985   A Dated Assemblage of the Late 13th Century B.C.E. from the
               Egyptian Residency at Aphek. *Tel Aviv* 12: 29-42.
van Beek, G.W.
1962   Megiddo. Pp. 335-342 in *The Interpreter's Dictionary of the
               Bible*, III.
Beit-Arieh, I.
1983   Central-Southern Sinai in the Early Bronze II and its Relationship
               with Palestine. *Levant* 15: 39-48.
1984a   New Evidence on the Relations between Canaan and Egypt during
               the Proto-Dynastic Period. *Israel Exploration Journal* 34: 20-23.
1984b   Fifteen Years in Sinai. *Biblical Archaeology Review* 10/4: 26-54.
1987   Canaanites and Egyptians at Serabit el-Khadim. Pp. 57-68 in
               Egypt, Israel, Sinai, ed. A.F. Rainey. Tel Aviv: Tel Aviv
               University.
Beke, C.H.
1878   *Sinai in Arabia and of Midian.* London: Trubner and Co.

Bell, B.
1971   The Dark Ages in Ancient History: I. The First Dark Age in
                Egypt. *American Journal of Archaeology* 75: 1-26.
1975   Climate and the History of Egypt: The Middle Kingdom.
                American Journal of Archaeology 79: 223-269.
Bennett, B.M., Jr.
1972   The Search for Israelite Gilgal. *Palestine Exploration Quarterly*
                104: 111-122.
Bennett, C.
1972   A Brief Note on Excavations at Tawilan, Jordan, 1968-70. *Levant*
                4: v-vii and pl. II.
1973   Excavations at Buseirah, Southern Jordan, 1971: Preliminary
                Report. *Levant* 5: 1-11 and pls. I-VIII.
1974   Excavations at Buseirah, Southern Jordan, 1972: Preliminary
                Report. *Levant* 6: 1-24.
1975   Excavations at Buseirah, Southern Jordan, 1973: Third
                Preliminary Report. *Levant* 7: 1-19.
1977   Excavations at Buseirah, Southern Jordan, 1974: Fourth
                Preliminary Report. *Levant* 9: 1-10.
Ben-Tor, A.
1982   The Relations between Egypt and the Land of Canaan during the
                Third Millennium B.C. *Journal of Jewish Studies* 33: 3-18.
Betancourt, P.P.
1976   The End of the Greek Bronze Age. *Antiquity* 50: 40-47.
1987   Dating the Aegean Late Bronze Age With Radiocarbon.
                Archaeometry 29/1: 45-49.
Betancourt, P.P. and H.N. Michael
1987   Dating the Aegean Late Bronze Age With Radiocarbon:
                Addendum. *Archaeometry* 29/2: 212-213.
Betancourt, P.P. and G.A. Weinstein
1976   Carbon 14 and the Beginning of the Late Bronze Age in the
                Aegean. *American Journal of Archaeology* 80/4: 329-348.
Bienkowski, P.
1986   *Jericho in the Late Bronze Age*. Warminster, England: Aris and
                Phillips, Ltd.
1989   The Division of Middle Bronze IIB-C in Palestine. *Levant* 21:
                169-180.
1990   Jericho Was Destroyed in the Middle Bronze Age, Not the Late
                Bronze Age. *Biblical Archaeology Review* 16/5: 45,46,69.
Bierbrier, M.L.
1975   *The Late New Kingdom in Egypt (c. 1300-664 B.C.): A
                Genealogical and Chronological Investigation.* Warminster,
                England: Aris and Phillips Ltd.
Biers, W.R.
1980   *The Archaeology of Greece: An Introduction.* Ithaca, NY: Cornell
                University Press.

Bietak, M.
1975   *Tell ed-Dab^ca*. II. (Research of the Cairo Branch of the Austrian
            Archaeological Institute, I). Vienna.
1979   Archaeological Exploration in the Eastern Nile Delta. *Proceedings
            of the British Academy*, 45: 225-289.
1981   *Avaris and Piramesse: Archaeological Exploration in the Eastern
            Nile Delta*. London: Oxford University Press.
1984   Problems of Middle Bronze Age Chronology: New Evidence from
            Egypt. *American Journal of Archaeology* 88: 471-485.
1986   *Avaris and Piramesse: Archaeological Exploration in the Eastern
            Nile Delta*. London: The British Academy.
1987   Canaanites in the Eastern Nile Delta. Pp. 41-56 in *Egypt, Israel,
            Sinai*, ed. A.F. Rainey. Tel Aviv: Tel Aviv University.
1987   Comments on the 'Exodus'. Pp. 163-172 in *Egypt, Israel, Sinai*,
            ed. A.F. Rainey. Tel Aviv: Tel Aviv University.
1988   Contra Bimson, Bietak Says Late Bronze Age Cannon Begin as
            Late as 1400 B.C. *Biblical Archaeology Review* 15/4: 54-55.
Bimson, J.J.
1978   *Redating the Exodus and Conquest*. (Journal for the Study of the
            Old Testament, Supplementary Series 5). Sheffield: University of
            Sheffield.
1981   *Redating the Exodus and Conquest*, 2nd ed. Sheffield, England:
            The Almond Press.
1985   Queries and Comments - Is Et-Tell the Site of 'Ai? *Biblical
            Archaeology Review* 11/5: 78-79.
1988   A Reply to Baruch Halpern's 'Radical Exodus Dating Fatally
            Flawed,' in *BAR*, November/December 1987. *Biblical Archaeology
            Review* 15/4: 52-55.
Bimson, J.J. and D. Livingston
1987   Redating the Exodus. *Biblical Archaeology Review* 13/5: 40-53,
            66-68.
Biran, A.
1969   Tel Dan. *Israel Exploration Journal* 19: 121-123.
1974   Tel Dan. *Biblical Archaeologist* 37: 26-51.
1975   Dan, Tel. Pp. 313-321 in *Encyclopedia of Archaeological
            Excavations in the Holy Land*, Vol. I. ed. M. Avi-Yonah.
            Englewood Cliffs, NJ: Prentice-Hall.
1980   Tel Dan: Five Years Later. *Biblical Archaeologist* 43: 168-182.
1984   The Triple Arched Gate of Laish at Tel Dan. *Israel Exploration
            Journal* 34: 1-19.
1985   Tel Dan, 1984. *Israel Exploration Journal* 35: 186-189.
1987   *BAR* Interview: Avraham Biran - Twenty Years of Digging at Tel
            Dan. *Biblical Archaeology Review* 13/4: 12-25.
Bittel, K.
1970   *Hattusha, The Capital of the Hittites*. New York: Oxford
            University Press.

Blenkinsopp, J.
1985   The Documentary Hypothesis in Trouble. *Bible Review* 1/4: 22-32.
Blong, R.J.
1980   The Possible Effects of Santorini Tephra Fall on Minoan Crete. *Thera and the Aegean World*, Vol. 2, ed. C. Doumas. London: Thera and the Aegean World.
Boardman, J.
1964   *The Greeks Overseas*. Baltimore: Penguin Books.
Borowski, O.
1988   The Biblical Identification of Tel Halif. *Biblical Archaeologist* 51: 21-27.
Breasted, J.H.
1906   *Ancient Records of Egypt*, Vol. 3. Chicago: University of Chicago Press.
1909   *A History of Egypt*, 2nd ed. New York: Charles Scribner's Sons.
Bright, J.
1942   Has Archaeology Found Evidence of the Flood? *Biblical Archaeologist* 5/4: 55-62.
1956   *Early Israel in Recent History Writing*. London: SCM Press.
1981   *A History of Israel*, 3rd ed. Philadelphia: Westminster Press.
Broshi, M.
1977   Tell en-Nasbeh. Pp. 912-914 in *Encyclopedia of Archaeological Excavations in the Holy Land*, III, ed. M. Avi-Yonah and E. Stern. Jerusalem: The Israel Exploration Society and Massada Press.
Broshi, M., and R. Gophna
1984   Middle Bronze II Palestine: Its Settlements and Population. *Bulletin of the American Schools of Oriental Research* 253: 41-53.
Bryson, R.A., H.H. Lamb, and D.L. Donley
1974   Drought and the Decline of Mycenae. *Antiquity* 48: 46-50.
Buccellati, G.
1977   ʿApirū and *Munnabtūtu* - The Stateless of the First Cosmopolitan Age. *JNES* 36: 145-148.
Buhl, M.L.
1959   *The Late Egyptian Anthropoid Stone Sarcophagi*. Copenhagen: National Museum of Denmark.
Bull, R.J., and E.F. Campbell, Jr.
1968   The Sixth Campaign at Balâṭah (Shechem). *Bulletin of the American Schools of Oriental Research* 190: 2-41.
Bull, R.J., *et al.*
1965   The Fifth Campaign at Balâṭah (Shechem). *Bulletin of the American Schools of Oriental Research* 180: 7-41.
Callaway, J.A.
1965   The 1964 ʿAi (Et-Tell) Excavations. *Bulletin of the American Schools of Oriental Research* 178: 13-40.
1968   New Evidence on the Conquest of 'Ai. *Journal of Biblical Literature* 87: 312-320.

1969	The 1966 ʿAi (Et-Tell) Excavations. *Bulletin of the American Schools of Oriental Research* 196: 2-16.
1970a	The 1968-1969 ʿAi (Et-Tell) Excavations. *Bulletin of the American Schools of Oriental Research* 198: 7-31.
1970b	The 1968 ʿAi (Et-Tell) Excavations. *Palestine Exploration Quarterly* 102: 42-44.
1975	Ai. Pp. 36-52 in *Encyclopedia of Archaeological Excavations in the Holy Land*, Vol. I, ed. M. Avi-Yonah. Englewood Cliffs, NJ: Prentice-Hall.
1976a	Ai. Pp. 14-16 in *The Interpreter's Dictionary of the Bible*, Supplementary Volume. Nashville: Abingdon Press.
1976b	Excavating Ai (et-Tell): 1964-1972. *Biblical Archaeologist* 39: 18-30.
1980	*The Early Bronze Age Citadel and Lower City at Ai (et-Tell).*
1981	Review of J. Bimson, 'Redating the Exodus and Conquest.' *Biblical Archaeologist* 44: 252-253.
1983	A Visit with Ahilud. *Biblical Archaeology Review* 9/5: 42-53.
1985a	Was My Excavation of Ai Worthwhile? *Biblical Archaeology Review* 11/2: 68:69.
1985b	Queries and Comments - Joseph Callaway Replies. *Biblical Archaeology Review* 11/4: 23-24.
1985c	A New Perspective on the Hill Country Settlement of Canaan in Iron Age I. Pp. 31-49 in *Palestine in the Bronze and Iron Ages: Papers in Honour of Olga Tufnell*, ed. J.N. Tubb. London: Institute of Archaeology.
1985d	Response. Pp. 72-78 in *Biblical Archaeology Today: Proceedings of the International Congress on Biblical Archaeology, Jerusalem, April 1984*. Jerusalem: Israel Exploration Society.

Callaway, J.A., and R.E. Cooley
| 1971 | A Salvage Excavation at Raddana, in Bireh. *Bulletin of the American Schools of Oriental Research* 201: 9-19. |

Callaway, J.A., and M.B. Nicol
| 1966 | A Sounding at Khirbet Ḥaiyân. *Bulletin of the American Schools of Oriental Research* 183: 12-19. |

Calverley, A.M., and M.F. Broome
| 1933-58 | *The Temple of King Sethos I at Abydos.* 4 vols. London: The Egyptian Exploration Society and Chicago: The University of Chicago Press. |

Campbell, E.F., Jr.
1960	The Amarna Letters and the Amarna Period. *Biblical Archaeologist* 23: 2-22.
1964	*The Chronology of the Amarna Letters.* Baltimore: The Johns Hopkins University Press.
1975	Moses and the Foundations of Israel. *Interpretation* 29: 141-154.

Campbell, E.F., Jr. and J.F. Ross
1963   The Excavation of Shechem and the Biblical Tradition. *Biblical Archaeologist* 26: 2-27.
Campbell, E.F., Jr., and G.E. Wright
1969   Tribal League Shrines in Amman and Shechem. *Biblical Archaeologist* 32: 104-116.
Carpenter, R.
1968   *Discontinuity in Greek Civilization*. New York: W.W. Norton and Company.
Casperson, L.W.
1986   The Lunar Dates of Thutmose III. *Journal of Near Eastern Studies* 45/2: 139-150.
1988   The Lunar Date of Ramesses II. *Journal of Near Eastern Studies* 47/3: 181-184.
Cazelles, H.
1955   Les localisations de l'Exode et la Critique Littéraire. *Revue Biblique* 62: 321-364.
1973   The Hebrews. Pp. 1-28 in *Peoples of Old Testament Times*, ed. D.J. Wiseman. Oxford: Oxford University Press.
Černý, J.
1934   Fluctuations in Grain Prices during the Twentieth Egyptian Dynasty. *Archiv Orientalni* 6: 173ff.
1935   Semites in Egyptian Mining Expeditions to Sinai. *Archiv Orientalni* 7: 384-389.
1958   Stela of Ramses II from Beisan. *Eretz Israel* 6: 75*-82*.
1975   Egypt: From the Death of Ramesses III to the End of the Twenty-first Dynasty. Pp. 606-657 in *Cambridge Ancient History*. 3rd edition, Vol II, Part 2, ed. I.E.S. Edwards, *et al.* Cambridge: Cambridge University Press.
Chadwick, J.
1976   *The Mycenaean World*. Cambridge: Cambridge University Press.
Chadwick, J. and B. Lomond
1985   Queries and Comments - Ai and the Bible. *Biblical Archaeology Review* 11/4: 20-22.
Chaney, M.L.
1983   Ancient Palestinian Peasant Movements and the Formation of Premonarchic Israel. Pp. 39-90 in *Palestine in Transition: The Emergence of Ancient Israel*, ed. D.N. Freedman and D.F. Graf. Sheffield, England: The Almond Press.
Childs, B.S.
1970   The Red Sea Tradition. *Vetus Testamentum* 20: 406-418.
Clamer, C., and D. Ussishkin
1977   A Canaanite Temple at Tell Lachish. *Biblical Archaeologist* 40: 71-76.

Cohen, R.
1979   The Iron Age Fortresses in the Central Negev. *Bulletin of the American Schools of Oriental Research* 236: 61-79.
1981a   Did I Excavate Kadesh-Barnea? *Biblical Archaeology Review* 7/3: 20-33.
1981b   The Excavations at Kadesh-barnea (1976-78). *Biblical Archaeologist* 44: 93-107.
1983   The Mysterious MB I People - Does the Exodus Tradition in the Bible Preserve the Memory of Their Entry into Canaan? *Biblical Archaeology Review* 9/4: 16-29.
1985   The Fortress King Solomon Built to Protect His Southern Border. *Biblical Archaeology Review* 11/3: 56-70.

Cohen, S.
1962   Azmon. P. 327 in *The Interpreter's Dictionary of the Bible*. Vol. 1. Nashville: Abingdon Press.

Corney, R.W.
1962   Libnah. P. 123 in *The Interpreter's Dictionary of the Bible*. Vol. 3. Nashville: Abingdon Press.

Couroyer, B.
1946   La résidence ramesside du Delta et la Ramsès biblique. *Revue Biblique* 53: 75-98.
1954   Dieux et fils de Ramses. *Revue Biblique* 61: 108-117.

Courville, D.A.
1971   *The Exodus Problem and Its Ramifications*. 2 vols. Loma Linda, CA: Challenge Books.

Craft, C.F.
1962   *Shamgar*. Pp. 306-307 in *The Interpreter's Dictionary of the Bible*, IV.
              Nashville: Abingdon Press.

Cross, F.M.
1966   The Divine Warrior in Israel's Early Cult. Pp. 11-30 in *Biblical Motifs: Origins and Transformations*, ed. A. Altmann. Cambridge, MA: Harvard University Press.

Crowfoot, J.W. and K. Kenyon
1957   *Samaria-Sebaste III: The Objects from Samaria*. London: Palestine Exploration Fund.

Crowfoot, J.W., K. Kenyon, and E.L. Sukenik
1942   *Samaria-Sebaste II: The Buildings at Samaria*. London: Palestine Exploration Fund.

Culican, W.
1966   *The First Merchant Venturers: The Ancient Levant in History and Commerce*. London: Thames and Hudson.

Davey, C.J.
1979   Some Ancient Near Eastern Pot Bellows. *Levant* 11: 101-111.

Davies, G.I.

1972 Hagar, el-Heğra and The Location of Mt. Sinai. *Vetus Testamentum* 22: 152-163.

1979 *The Way of the Wilderness: A Geographical Study of the Wilderness Itineraries of the Old Testament.* Cambridge: Cambridge University Press.

1983 The Wilderness Itineraries and the Composition of the Pentateuch. *Vetus Testamentum* 33: 1-13.

1990 The Wilderness Itineraries and Recent Archaeological Research. *Vetus Testamentum Supplement* 41: 161-175.

Dearman, J.A.

1984 The Location of Jahaz. *Zeitschrift des Deutschen Palästina-Vereins* 100: 122-126.

Desborough, V.R. d'A.

1964 *The Last Mycenaeans and Their Successors.* Oxford: Clarendon Press.

1975 The End of the Mycenaean Civilization and the Dark Age: (a) The Archaeological Background. Pp. 658-677 in *Cambridge Ancient History.* 3rd edition. Vol. II, Part 2, ed. I.E.S. Edwards, *et al.* Cambridge: Cambridge University Press.

Dever, W.G.

1967 Excavations at Gezer. *Biblical Archaeologist* 30: 47-62.

1969-70 Iron Age Epigraphic Material from the Area of Khirbet el-Kom. *HUCA* 40-41: 139-204.

1976a The Beginning of the Middle Bronze Age in Syria-Palestine. Pp. 3-38 in *Magnalia Dei: The Mighty Acts of God*, eds. F.M. Cross, W.E. Lemke and P.D. Miller. Garden City, NY: Doubleday.

1976b Gezer. Pp. 428-443 in *Encyclopedia of Archaeological Excavations in the Holy Land.* Vol. II, ed. M. Avi-Yonah and E. Stern. Englewood Cliffs, NJ: Prentice-Hall; Jerusalem: Israel Exploration Society and Massada Press.

1980 New Vistas on the EB IV ("MB I") Horizon in Syria-Palestine. *Bulletin of the American Schools of Oriental Research* 237: 35-64.

1985a Relations Between Syria-Palestine and Egypt in the 'Hyksos' Period. Pp. 69-87 in *Palestine in the Bronze and Iron Ages: Papers in Honour of Olga Tufnell*, ed. J.N. Tubb. London: Institute of Archaeology.

1985b From the End of the Early Bronze Age to the Beginning of the Middle Bronze. Pp. 113-135 in *Biblical Archaeology Today: Proceedings of the International Congress on Biblical Archaeology, Jerusalem, April 1984.* Jerusalem: Israel Exploration Society.

1987 The Middle Bronze Age: The Zenith of the Urban Canaanite Era. *Biblical Archaeologist* 50: 149-77.

Dever, W.G., et al.
1971   Further Excavations at Gezer, 1967-71. *Biblical Archaeologist* 34:
            94-132.
1974   Gezer II: Report of the 1967-70 Seasons in Field I and II. *Annual
            of the Hebrew Union College Nelson Glueck School of Biblical
            Archaeology.* Jerusalem: Keter.
De Vries, S.J.
1962   Chronology of the OT. Pp. 580-599 in *The Interpreter's
            Dictionary of the Bible.* Vol. I. Nashville: Abingdon Press.
1976   Chronology, OT. Pp. 161-166 in *The Interpreter's Dictionary of
            the Bible.* Supplementary Volume. Nashville: Abingdon Press.
Dornemann, R.H.
1983   *The Archaeology of the Transjordan in the Bronze and Iron Ages.*
            Milwaukee: Milwaukee Public Museum.
Dorsey, D.A.
1980   The Location of Biblical Makkedah. *Tel Aviv* 7: 185-193.
Dothan, M.
1955   The Excavations at ꜥAfula. *ꜥAtiqot* 1
1965   The Fortress at Kadesh-Barnea. *Israel Exploration Journal* 15:
            134-143.
1968   Lake Sirbonis (Sabkhat el-Bardawil). *Israel Exploration Journal*
            18: 255-256.
1973   The Foundations of Tel Mor and Ashdod. *Israel Exploration
            Journal* 23: 1-17.
1977   Kadesh-Barnea. Pp. 697-699 in *Encyclopedia of Archaeological
            Excavations in the Holy Land.* Vol. III, ed. M. Avi-Yonah.
            Englewood Cliffs, NJ: Prentice-Hall.
1979   Ashdod at the End of the Late Bronze Age and the Beginning of
            the Iron Age. Pp. 125-131 in *Symposia,* ed. F.M. Cross.
            Cambridge, MA: American Schools of Oriental Research.
1985   Ten Seasons of Excavations at Ancient Acco. *Qadmoniot* 18: 2-14.
Dothan, T.
1967   *The Philistines and Their Material Culture.* Jerusalem: Bialik
            Institute and Israel Exploration Society. (Hebrew with English
            summary).
1972   Excavations at the Cemetery of Deir el-Balaḥ. *Qedem* 10.
            Jerusalem. (Monographs of the Institute of Archaeology, The
            Hebrew University of Jerusalem).
1972a   Anthropoid Clay Coffins from a Late Bronze Age Cemetery near
            Deir el-Balaḥ (Preliminary Report). *Israel Exploration Journal* 22:
            65-72.
1973   Anthropoid Clay Coffins from a Late Bronze Age Cemetery near
            Deir el-Balaḥ (Preliminary Report II). *Israel Exploration Journal*
            23: 129-146.
1979   Excavations at the Cemetery of Deir el-Balaḥ *Qedem* 10.
            Jerusalem.

1981	Notes and News: Deir el-Balah 1979-1980. *Israel Exploration Journal* 31: 126-131.
1982a	Lost Outposts of Ancient Egypt. *National Geographic Magazine* 162: 739-769.
1982b	*The Philistines and Their Material Culture.* New Haven, CT: Yale University Press.
1982c	What We Know About the Philistines. *Biblical Archaeology Review* 8/4: 20-44.
1987	The Impact of Egypt on Canaan During the 18th and 19th Dynasties in the Light of the Excavations at Deir el-Balah. Pp. 121-136 in *Egypt, Israel, Sinai.* ed. A.F. Rainey. Tel Aviv: Tel Aviv University

Dothan, T., Perlman, I and Asaro, F.
1973	Provenance of the Deir el-Balah Coffins. *Israel Exploration Journal* 23: 147-151.

Doumas, C.
1983	*Thera: Pompeii of the Ancient Aegean.* London: Thames and Hudson.

Drinkard, J.F, Jr., G.L. Mattingly, and J.M. Miller (eds.)
1988	*Benchmarks in Time and Culture: An Introduction to Palestinian Archaeology.* Atlanta, GA: Scholars Press.

Drower, M.S.
1973	Syria c. 1550-1400 B.C. Pp. 417-536 in *Cambridge Ancient History.* 3rd edition. Vol. II, Part 1, ed. I.E.S. Edwards *et al.* Cambridge: Cambridge University Press.

Dumbrell, W.J.
1971	The Tell el-Maskhuta. *Bulletin of the American Schools of Oriental Research* 203: 33-44.
1975	Midian - a land or a league? *Vetus Testamentum* 25: 323-337.

Dunayevski, I., and A. Kempinski
1973	The Megiddo Temples. *Zeitschrift des Deutschen Palästina-Vereins* 89: 161-187.

Edgerton, W.F. and John A. Wilson
1936	*Historical Records of Ramesses III.* Chicago: University of Chicago Press.

Eissfeldt, O.
1932	*Baal-Zaphon, Zeus Kasios und der Durchzug der Israeliten durchs Meer.* Halle: M. Niemeyer.
1975	Palestine in the Time of the Nineteenth Dynasty. (a) The Exodus and Wandering. Pp. 307-330 in *Cambridge Ancient History.* 3rd edition Vol. II, Part 2, ed. I.E.S. Edwards *et al.* Cambridge: Cambridge University Press.

Ellenberger, C.L.
1982	Could a Volcanic Eruption of Thera be Visible in the Nile Delta? (Queries and Comments). *Biblical Archaeology Review* 8/1: 14.

Epstein, C.
1966   *Palestinian Bichrome Ware*. Leiden: E.J. Brill.
Esse, D.L.
1988   Review of Israel Finkelstein, The Archaeology of the Israelite
                Settlement. *Biblical Archaeology Review* 14/5: 6-12.
Fairman, H.W., and B. Grdseloff
1947   Texts of Hatshepsut and Sethos I Inside Speos Artemidos. *Journal
                of Egyptian Archaeology* 33: 12-33.
Faulkner, R.O.
1942   The Battle of Megiddo. *Journal of Egyptian Archaeology* 28: 2-15.
1946   The Euphrates Campaign of Thutmosis III. *Journal of Egyptian
                Archaeology* 32: 39-42.
1947   The Wars of Setos I. *Journal of Egyptian Archaeology* 33: 34-39.
1966   Egypt: From the Inception of the 19th Dynasty to the Death of
                Ramesses III. *Cambridge Ancient History*. 3rd ed. Cambridge:
                Ch.23.
1975   Egypt: From the Inception of the 19th Dynasty to the Death of
                Ramesses III. Pp. 217-251 in *Cambridge Ancient History*. 3rd
                edition. Vol. II, Part 2, ed. I.E.S. Edwards *et al.* Cambridge:
                Cambridge University Press.
Fensham, F.C.
1964   The Treaty Between Israel and the Gibeonites. *Biblical
                Archaeologist* 27: 96-100.
Finegan, J.
1963   *Let My People Go: A Journey Through Exodus*. New York: Harper
                and Row.
1964   *Handbook of Biblical Chronology: Principles of Time Reckoning
                in the Ancient World and Problems of Chronology in the Bible.*
                Princeton, NJ: Princeton University Press.
1979   *Archaeological History of the Ancient Middle East*. Boulder, CO:
                Westview Press.
Finkelstein, I.
1984   The Iron Age 'Fortresses' of the Negev Highlands:
                Sedentarization of the Nomads. *Tel Aviv* 11: 189-209.
1985   Excavations at Shiloh 1981-1984: Preliminary Report. *Tel Aviv*
                12: 123-180.
1986a   Shiloh Yields Some, But Not All, of Its Secrets. *Biblical
                Archaeology Review* 12/1: 22-41.
1986b   The Iron Age Sites in the Negev Highlands -- Military Fortresses
                or Nomads Settling Down? *Biblical Archaeology Review* 12/4: 46-
                53.
1988a   *The Archaeology of the Israelite Settlement*. Jerusalem: Israel
                Exploration Society.
1988b   Searching for Israelite Origins. *Biblical Archaeology Review* 14/5:
                34-45.

1988c	Arabian Trade and Socio-Political Conditions in the Negev in the Twelfth-Eleventh Centuries B.C.E. *Journal of Near Eastern Studies* 47: 241-52.

Fitzgerald, G.M.

1967	Beth-shean. Pp. 185-196 in *Archaeology and Old Testament Study*, ed. D.W. Thomas. Oxford: Oxford University Press.

Foerster, G.

1975	Dor. Pp. 334-337 in *Encyclopedia of Archaeological Excavations in the Holy Land*. Vol. I, ed. M. Avi-Yonah. Englewood Cliffs, NJ: Prentice-Hall; Jerusalem: The Israel Exploration Society and Massada Press.

Franken, H.J.

1960	The Excavations at Deir ʿAllā in Jordan. *Vetus Testamentum* 10: 386-393.
1961	Excavations at Deir ʿAllā in Jordan, 2nd Season. *Vetus Testamentum* 11: 361-372.
1962	The Excavations at Deir ʿAllā in Jordan, 3rd Season. *Vetus Testamentum* 12: 378-382.
1969	*Excavations at Tell Deir ʿAlla, I. A Stratigraphical and Analytical Study of Early Iron Age Pottery*. (Documenta et monumenta orientis antiqui, Vol. 16.) Leiden: E.J. Brill.
1975	Palestine in the Time of the Nineteenth Dynasty: (b) Archaeological Evidence. Pp. 331-337 in *Cambridge Ancient History*. 3rd edition. Vol. II, Part 2, ed. I.E.S. Edwards *et al.* Cambridge: Cambridge University Press.
1976a	The Problem of Identification in Biblical Archaeology. *Palestine Exploration Quarterly* 108: 3-11.
1976b	Deir ʿAllā. Pp. 321-324 in *Encyclopedia of Archaeological Excavations in the Holy Land*. I, ed. M. Avi-Yonah. Englewood Cliffs, NJ: Prentice-Hall; Jerusalem: The Israel Exploration Society and Massada Press.

Franken, H.J., and W.J.A. Power

1971	Glueck's 'Explorations in Eastern Palestine' in the Light of Recent Evidence. *Vetus Testamentum* 21: 119-123.

Freedman, D.N.

1963	The Second Season at Ancient Ashdod. *Biblical Archaeologist* 26: 134-139.
1987	Yahweh of Samaria and His Asherah. *Biblical Archaeologist* 50/4: 241-249.

Fritz, V.

1981	The Israelite 'Conquest' in the Light of Recent Excavations at Khirbet-el-Meshâsh. *Bulletin of the American Schools of Oriental Research* 241: 61-74.
1982	The Conquest in the Light of Archaeology. *Proceedings of the Eighth World Congress of Jewish Studies*. Jerusalem: 15/21.

1987   Conquest or Settlement? The Early Iron Age in Palestine. *Biblical Archaeologist* 50/2: 84-100.

Frost, H.
1970   Some Cypriote Stone Anchors from Land Sites and From the Sea. *Report of the Department of Antiquities Cyprus*: 14-24.

Gal, Z.
1982   The Settlement of Issachar - Some New Observations. *Tel Aviv* 6: 79-86.
1990   Khirbet Roš Zayit - Biblical Cabul: A Historical-Geographical Case. *Biblical Archaeologist* 53: 88-97.

Galanopoulos, A.G. and E. Bacon
1969   *Atlantis: The Truth Behind the Legend.* Indianapolis and New York: Bobbs-Merrill Company.

Gardiner, A.H.
1916   The Defeat of the Hyksos by Kamose: The Carnarvon Tablet, No. I. *Journal of Egyptian Archaeology* 3: 95-110.
1918   The Delta Residence of the Ramessides. *Journal of Egyptian Archaeology* 5: 127-138, 179-200, 242-271.
1920   The Ancient Military Road Between Egypt and Palestine. *Journal of Egyptian Archaeology* 6: 99-116.
1922   The Geography of the Exodus. Pp. 203-215 in *Recueil d'études égyptogiques dédiées à la mémoire de J.-F. Champollion.* Paris.
1924   The Geography of the Exodus: An Answer to Professor Naville and Others. *Journal of Egyptian Archaeology.* 10: 87-96.
1933   Tanis and Pi-Ra`Messe: A Retractation. *Journal of Egyptian Archaeology* 19: 122-128.
1937   *Late Egyptian Miscellanies.* Brussels: Edition de la Fondation Egyptologique Reine Elisabeth.
1946   Davies's Copy of the Great Speos Artemidos Inscription. *Journal of Egyptian Archaeology.* 32: 43-56.
1947   *Ancient Egyptian Onomastica, I.* Oxford: Oxford University Press.
1948   *Ramesside Administrative Documents.* Oxford: Oxford University Press.
1953   The Memphite Tomb of the General Haremhab. *Journal of Egyptian Archaeology* 39: 3-12.
1960   *The Kadesh Inscriptions of Ramesses* II. Oxford: Oxford University Press.
1961   *Egypt of the Pharaohs.* Oxford: Oxford University Press.

Gardiner, A.H. and T.E. Peet
1952   *The Inscriptions of Sinai.* ed. 2, rev., J.Černý. 2 vols. London, 1952. nos. 246-50.

Garsiel, M., and I. Finkelstein
1978   The Westward Expansion of the House of Joseph in the Light of the `Izbet Ṣarṭah Excavations. *Israel Exploration Journal* 5: 192-198.

Garstang, J.
1931   *The Foundations of Bible History: Joshua, Judges.* New York: Richard R. Smith, Inc.

Garstang, J. and J.B.E. Garstang
1940   *The Story of Jericho.* London: Hodder and Stoughton.

Gelb, I.J.
1961   The Early History of the West Semitic Peoples. *Journal of Catholic Studies* 15: 27-47.

Geraty, L.T.
1983   Heshbon: The First Casualty in the Israelite Quest for the Kingdom of God. Pp. 239-248 in *The Quest for the Kingdom of God: Studies in Honor of George E. Mendenhall,* ed. H.B. Huffmon, F.A. Spina, and A.R.W. Green. Winona Lake, IN: Eisenbrauns.

Geraty, L.T., and L.A. Willis
1986   Archaeological Research in Transjordan. Pp. 30-32 in *The Archaeology of Jordan and Other Studies,* eds. L.T. Geraty and L.G. Herr. Berrien Springs, MI: Andrews University Press.

de Geus, C.H.J.
1976   *The Tribes of Israel.* Studia semitica Neerlandica 18. Assen: Van Gorcum.

Gittlen, B.M.
1981   The Cultural and Chronological Implications of the Cypro-Palestinian Trade during the Late Bronze Age. *Bulletin of the American Schools of Oriental Research* 241: 49-60.

Giveon, R.
1971   *Les Bédouins Shosou des documents égyptiens.* Leiden: E.J. Brill.
1974   Hyksos Scarabs with Names of Kings and Officials from Canaan. *Chronique d'Egypte* 49: 222-233.
1976a   New Egyptian Seals with Titles and Names from Canaan. *Tel Aviv* 3: 127-133.
1976b   The XII and XIII Dynasties in Canaan and Sinai (MB IIA). *Fourth Archaeological Congress in Israel, January 17-18 March, 1976. Lecture Summaries:* 14.
1978   *The Impact of Egypt on Canaan.* Göttingen.
1980   Some Scarabs from Canaan with Egyptian Titles. *Tel Aviv* 7: 179-184.
1987   The Impact of Egypt on Canaan in the Middle Bronze Age. Pp. 23-40 in *Egypt, Israel, Sinai.* ed. A.F. Rainey. Tel Aviv: Tel Aviv University.

Glock, A.E.
1978   Taanach. Pp. 1138-1147 in *Encyclopedia of Archaeological Excavations in the Holy Land.* Vol. IV, ed. M. Avi-Yonah. Englewood Cliffs, NJ: Prentice-Hall; Jerusalem: The Israel Exploration Society and Massada Press.

Glueck, N.
1934   Explorations in Eastern Palestine, I. *Annual of the American
             Schools of Oriental Research.* Vol. 14. New Haven: American
             Schools of Oriental Research.
1935   Explorations in Eastern Palestine, II. *Annual of the American
             Schools of Oriental Research.* Vol. 15. New Haven: American
             Schools of Oriental Research.
1938a   The Boundaries of Edom. *Hebrew Union College Annual* 11:
1938b   The Topography and History of Ezion-geber and Elath. *Bulletin
             of the American Schools of Oriental Research* 72: 2-13.
1939   Explorations in Eastern Palestine, III. *Annual of the American
             Schools of Oriental Research.* Vol. 18-19. New Haven: American
             Schools of Oriental Research.
1940   *The Other Side of the Jordan.* New Haven: American Schools of
             Oriental Research.
1943   Some Ancient Towns in the Plains of Moab. *Bulletin of the
             American Schools of Oriental Research* 91: 24-25.
1946a   *The River Jordan.* Philadelphia: Westminster Press.
1946b   Transjordan. *Biblical Archaeologist* 9: 45-61.
1947   The Civilization of the Edomites. *Biblical Archaeologist* 10: 77-
             84.
1951   Explorations in Eastern Palestine, IV. *Annual of the American
             Schools of Oriental Research.* Vol. 25-28. New Haven: American
             Schools of Oriental Research.
1955   The Age of Abraham in the Negeb. *Biblical Archaeologist* 18: 2-9.
1959   The Negev. *Biblical Archaeologist* 22: 82-97.
1967   Transjordan. Pp. 428-452 in *Archaeology and Old Testament
             Study,* ed. D. Winton Thomas. London: Oxford University Press.
1970   *The Other Side of the Jordan.* Rev. ed. Cambridge, MA: American
             Schools of Oriental Research.
Goedicke, H.
1982   Goedicke Defends His Exodus Thesis (Queries and Comments).
             Biblical Archaeology Review 8/2: 12.
1987   Exodus: The Ancient Egyptian Evidence. *A paper delivered at the
             Who Was the Pharaoh of the Exodus? Symposium, Memphis,
             Tennessee, April 23-25.*
Goetze, A.
1975   The Hittites and Syria (1300-1200 B.C.). Pp. 252-273 in
             Cambridge Ancient History. 3rd edition. Vol. II, Part 2, ed. I.E.S.
             Edwards *et al.* Cambridge: Cambridge University Press.
Gold, V.R.
1962   Beth-shemesh. Pp. 401-3 in *The Interpreter's Dictionary of the
             Bible.* I. Nashville: Abingdon Press.
1962   Makkedah. P. 228 in *The Interpreter's Dictionary of the Bible.* III.
             Nashville: Abingdon Press.

1962   Punon. P. 968 in *The Interpreter's Dictionary of the Bible*. III.
              Nashville: Abingdon Press.
Goldwasser, O.
1984   Hieratic Inscriptions from Tel Sera⁰ in Southern Canaan. *Tel Aviv*
              11(1): 77-93.
Gonen, R.
1984   Urban Canaan in the Late Bronze Period. *Bulletin of the American
              Schools of Oriental Research* 253: 61-73.
1987   Megiddo in the Late Bronze Age - Another Assessment. *Levant*
              19: 83-100.
Gophna, R.
1975   Beersheba. Pp. 152-159 in *Encyclopedia of Archaeological
              Excavations in the Holy Land*. Vol. I, ed. M. Avi-Yonah.
              Englewood Cliffs, NJ: Prentice-Hall; Jerusalem: The Israel
              Exploration Society and Massada Press.
1976   Egyptian Immigration into Southern Canaan during the First
              Dynasty. *Tel Aviv* 3: 31-37.
1987   Egyptian Trading Posts in Southern Canaan at the Dawn of the
              Archaic Period. *Egypt, Israel, Sinai*. ed. A.F. Rainey. Tel Aviv.
              13-22.
Gophna, R., and Gazit, D.
1985   The First Dynasty Egyptian Residency at ⁰En Besor. *Tel Aviv* 12:
              9-16.
Gottwald, N.K.
1974   Were the Early Israelites Pastoral Nomads? Pp. 223-255 in
              Rhetorical Criticism: Essays in Honor of James Muilenburg, ed.
              J.J. Jackson and M. Kessler. Pittsburgh: Pickwick Press.
1975   Domain Assumptions and Societal Models in the Study of Pre-
              Monarchic Israel. *Supplements to Vetus Testamentum* 28: 89-100.
1976   Nomadism. Pp. 629-631 in *The Interpreter's Dictionary of the
              Bible*. Supplementary Volume. Nashville: Abingdon Press.
1978   Were the Early Israelites Pastoral Nomads? *Biblical Archaeology
              Review* 4/2: 2-7.
1979   *The Tribes of Yahweh: A Sociology of the Religion of Liberated
              Israel, 1250-1050 B.C.E*. Maryknoll, NY: Orbis Books.
1983a   Two Models for the Origins of Ancient Israel: Social Revolution
              or Frontier Development. Pp. 5-24 in *The Quest for the Kingdom
              of God: Studies in Honor of George E. Mendenhall*, eds. H.B.
              Huffmon, F.A. Spina, and A.R.W. Green. Winona Lake, IN:
              Eisenbrauns.
1983b   Early Israel and the Canaanite Socio-Economic System. Pp. 25-37
              in *Palestine in Transition: The Emergence of Ancient Israel*, eds.
              D.N. Freedman and D.F. Graf. Sheffield, England: The Almond
              Press.

1985   The Israelite Settlement as a Social Revolutionary Movement. Pp. 34-46 in *Biblical Archaeology Today: Proceedings of the International Congress on Biblical Archaeology, Jerusalem, April 1984.* Jerusalem: Israel Exploration Society.

Gould, B.
1982   Egyptian and Egyptianizing Pottery from Late Bronze and Early Iron Age Contexts in Canaan. *Papers of the Pottery Workshop, Third International Congress of Egyptology, Toronto, September 1982,* Toronto: 21-24.

Grant, E.
1929   *Beth Shemesh (Palestine): Progress of the Haverford Archaeological Expedition.* Haverford: Privately Published.

Grant, E. and G.E. Wright
1931-39   *Ain Shems Excavations (Palestine).* 5 vols. Haverford: Privately Published.

Gray, J.
1952   Canaanite Kingship in Theory and Practice. *Vetus Testamentum* 2: 193-220.
1954   The Desert Sojourn of the Hebrews and the Sinai-Horeb Tradition. *Vetus Testamentum* 4: 148-154.
1966   Hazor. *Vetus Testamentum* 16: 26-52.
1970   *I and II Kings: A Commentary.* 2nd ed. Philadelphia: The Westminster Press, 1970.

Greenberg, M.
1955   *The Ḫab/piru.* New Haven: American Oriental Society.

Greenberg, R.
1987   New Light on the Early Iron Age at Tell Beit Mirsim. *Bulletin of the American Schools of Oriental Research* 265: 55-80.

Grintz, J.M.
1961   "Ai which is beside Beth-aven:" A Re-examination of the identity of ᶜAi. *Biblica* 42: 201-216.

Grollenberg, L.H.
1957   *Atlas of the Bible.* trans. & ed. J.M.H. Reid and H.H. Rowley. London: Nelson.

Gunn, D.M.
1974   The 'Battle Report': Oral or Scribal Convention? *Journal of Biblical Literature* 93: 513-18.

Gurney, O.R.
1981   *The Hittites.* 2nd revised edition. New York: Penguin Books.

Habachi, L.
1954   Khanta'na-Qantir: Importance. *Annales du Service des Antiquités d'Égypte* 52: 443-562.
1955   Preliminary Report on Kamose Stela and Other Inscribed Blocks found ... at Karnak. *Annales du Service des Antiquités de l'Egypte.* 53: 195-202.

1984   Certain Sites To Be Examined Before it is Too Late. *The Journal of the Society for the Study of Egyptian Antiquities* XIV:I.
Hallager, E.
1977   *The Mycenaean Palace at Knossos: Evidence for the Final Destruction in the III B Period.* Stockholm: Medelhavsmuseet.
Halpern, B.
1983   *The Emergence of Israel in Canaan.* Chico, CA: Scholars Press.
1987   Radical Exodus Redating Fatally Flawed. *Biblical Archaeology Review* 13/6: 56-61.
Hamilton, R.W.
1935   Excavations at Tell Abu Hawâm. *Quarterly of the Department of Antiquities in Palestine* 4: 1-69.
1962   Lachish. Pp. 53-57 in *The Interpreter's Dictionary of the Bible.* Vol. III. Nashville: Abingdon Press.
Hammond, P.C.
1965   Hébron. *Revue Biblique* 72: 267-270.
1966   Hébron. *Revue Biblique* 73: 566-569.
1968   Hébron. *Revue Biblique* 75: 253-258.
Hankey, V.
1974   A Late Bronze Age Temple at Amman. I: The Aegean Pottery. *Levant* 6: 131-159.
Hankey, V. and P. Warren.
1974   The Absolute Chronology of the Aegean Bronze Age. *Bulletin of the Institute of Classical Studies of the University of London* 21: 142-152.
Haran, M.
1971   The Exodus Routes in the Pentateuchal Sources. *Tarbiz* 40: 113-143.
1976   Exodus, The. Pp. 304-310 in *The Interpreter's Dictionary of the Bible.* Supplementary Volume. Nashville: Abingdon Press.
Harding, G.L.
1958   Recent Discoveries in Jordan. *Palestine Exploration Quarterly* 90: 7-18.
Harel, M.
1983   *The Sinai Journeys: The Route of the Exodus.* San Diego, CA: Ridgefield Publishing Co.
Hart, G.
1957   The Plagues of Egypt I. *Zeitschrift fur de Alttestamentliche Wissenschaft* 69: 84-102.
1958   The Plagues of Egypt II. *Zeitschrift fur de Alttestamentliche Wissenschaft* 70: 48-59.
Hart, S.
1986   Edom Survey Project, 1985. *Palestine Exploration Quarterly* 118: 77-78.
1986   Some Preliminary Thoughts on Settlement in Southern Edom. *Levant* 18: 51-58.

Hart, S. and R.K. Falkner
1985   Preliminary Report on a Survey in Edom, 1984. *Annual of the Department of Antiquities of Jordan* 29: 255-277.

Hayes, W.C.
1951   Inscriptions from the Palace of Amenhotep III. *Journal of Near Eastern Studies* 10: 35-56; 82-112; 156-183; 231-242.
1959   *The Scepter of Egypt.* Pt. II: *The Hyksos Period and the New Kingdom* (1675-1080 B.C.). New York: The Metropolitan Museum of Art.
1960   A Selection of Thutmoside Ostraca from Deir el-Bahri. *Journal of Egyptian Archaeology* 46: 29-52.
1970   Chronology: I. Egypt - to the End of the Twentieth Dynasty. Pp. 173-193 in *Cambridge Ancient History.* 3rd edition. (edited by I.E.S. Edwards *et al.* Cambridge: Cambridge University Press.
1973a   Egypt: From the Death of Ammenemes III to Seqenenre II. Pp. 42-76 in *Cambridge Ancient History.* 3rd edition. Vol. II, Part 1, ed. I.E.S. Edwards *et al.* Cambridge: Cambridge University Press.
1973b   Egypt: Internal Affairs From Tuthmosis I to the Death of Amenophis III. Pp. 42-76 in *Cambridge Ancient History.* 3rd edition. Vol. II, Part 1, ed. I.E.S. Edwards *et al.* Cambridge: Cambridge University Press.

Helck, W.
1965   <u>Tkw</u> und die Ramses-Stadt. *Vetus Testamentum* 15: 35-48.
1966   Zum Auftreten Fremder Gotter in Agypten. *Oriens Atiquus* 5: 1-14.
1968   Die Bedrohung Palästinas durch einwandernde Gruppen am Ende der 18. und am anfang der 19. Dynastie. *Vetus Testamentum* 18: 472-480.
1971   *Die Beziehungen Agyptans zur Vorderasien im 3 und 2 Jahrtausend.* Wiesbaden.

Hennessy, J.B.
1966   Excavation of a Late Bronze Age Temple at Amman. *Palestine Exploration Quarterly* 98: 155-162.

Herrmann, S.
1985   Basic Factors of Israelite Settlement in Canaan. Pp. 47-53 in *Biblical Archaeology Today: Proceedings of the International Congress on Biblical Archaeology, Jerusalem, April 1984.* Jerusalem: Israel Exploration Society.

Herzog, Z.
1980   Beer-Sheba of the Patriarchs. *Biblical Archaeology Review* 6/6: 12-28.
1984   *Beer-Sheba II: The Early Iron Age Settlements.* Tel Aviv: The Institute of Archaeology and Ramot Publishing Company.

Hestrin, R.
1970   *The Philistines and the Other Sea Peoples.* Jerusalem: The Israel Museum. (Hebrew and English).

Heusman, J.E.
1975   Archaeology and Early Israel: The Scene Today. *Catholic Biblical Quarterly* 37: 1-16.

Hoehner, H.W.
1969   The Duration of the Egyptian Bondage. *Bibliotheca Sacra* 126: 306-316.

Hoffmeier, J.K.
1989   Reconsidering Egypt's Part in the Termination of the Middle Bronze Age in Palestine. *Levant* 21: 181-193.

Holladay, J.S.
1971   Khirbet el-Qom. *IEJ* 21: 175-177.
1982   *Cities of the Delta, Part III: Tell el-Maskhuta: Preliminary Report on the Wadi Tumilat Project, 1978-79.* Malibu, CA: Undena Publications.

Holthoer, R.
1977   *New Kingdom Pharaonic Sites: The Pottery.* Uppsala (The Scandinavian Joint Expedition to Sudanese Nubia, Vol. 5:I)

Hooker, J.T.
1977   *Mycenaean Greece.* London: Routledge and Kegan Paul.

Hopkins, D.C.
1987   Life on the Land. The Subsistence Struggles of Early Israel. *Biblical Archaeologist* 50: 178-191.

Horn, S.H.
1969   The 1968 Heshbon Expedition. *Biblical Archaeologist* 32: 26-41.
1976a   Heshbon. Pp. 510-514 in *Encyclopedia of Archaeological Excavations in the Holy Land.* Vol. II, ed. M. Avi-Yonah. Englewood Cliffs, NJ: Prentice-Hall.
1976b   Heshbon. Pp. 410-411 in *The Interpreter's Dictionary of the Bible.* Supplementary Volume. Nashville: Abingdon Press.
1977   What We Don't Know About Moses and the Exodus. *Biblical Archaeology Review* 3/2: 22-31.
1986   Why the Moabite Stone Was Blown to Pieces. *Biblical Archaeology Review* 12/3: 50-61.

I.E.S. Edwards *et al.*
1978   *The Bible and Recent Archaeology.* Atlanta: John Knox Press.
1979   *Archaeology in the Holy Land.* London: Ernest Benn.
1981   *Excavations at Jericho, Vol. 3: The Architecture and Stratigraphy of the Tell,* ed. T.A. Holland.   London: British School of Archaeology in Jerusalem.

Isserlin, B.S.J.
1983   The Israelite Conquest of Canaan. *Palestine Exploration Quarterly* 115: 85-94.

Izre'el, S.
1977   Two Notes on the Gezer-Amarna Tablets. *Tel Aviv* 4: 159-167.

Jack, J.W.
1925   *The Date of the Exodus in the Light of External Evidence.*
            Edinburgh: T. & T. Clark.
James, F.W.
1966   *The Iron Age at Beth Shan: A Study of Levels VI-IV.* Philadelphia:
            University Museum, University of Pennsylvania.

1975   Beth-Shean. Pp. 207-212 in *Encyclopedia of Archaeological
            Excavations in the Holy Land.* Vol. I, ed. M. Avi-Yonah.
            Englewood Cliffs, NJ: Prentice-Hall; Jerusalem: The Israel
            Exploration Society and Massada Press.
1978   Chariot Fittings from Late Bronze Age Beth Shan. *Archaeology in
            the Levant.* (Essays for Kathleen Kenyon), ed. R. Moorey and P.
            Parr. Warminster, 102-115.
James, T.G.H.
1973   Egypt: From the Expulsion of the Hyksos to Amenophis I. Pp.
            289-312 in *The Cambridge Ancient History.* 3rd edition, Vol. II,
            1. ed. I.E.S. Edwards *et al.* Cambridge: Cambridge University
            Press.
Janssen, J.M.A.
1961   *Two Ancient Egyptian Shipdogs.* Leiden.
Kafafi, Z.
1985   Egyptian Topographical Lists on the Late Bronze Age in Jordan
            (East Bank). *Biblische Notizen* 29: 17-21.

Kallai, Z.
1983   The Wandering-Traditions from Kadesh-Barnea to Canaan: A
            Study in Biblical Historiography. Pp. 175-184 in *Essays in
            Honour of Yigael Yadin,* eds. G. Vermes and J. Neusner. Totowa,
            NJ: Allanheld, Osmun & Co.

Kantor, H.J.
1965   The Relative Chronology of Egypt and Its Foreign Correlations
            Before the Late Bronze Age. Pp. 1-46 in *Chronologies in Old
            World Archaeology,* ed. R.W. Ehrich. Chicago: University of
            Chicago Press.
Karageorghis, V.
1976   *View from the Bronze Age: Mycenaean and Phoenician
            Discoveries at Kition.* New York: E.P. Dutton.
1981   *Ancient Cyprus: 7000 Years of Art and Archaeology.* Baton
            Rouge, LA: Louisiana State University Press.
1984   Exploring Philistine Origins on the Island of Cyprus. *Biblical
            Archaeology Review* 10/2: 16-28.
Kassis, H.E.
1973   The Beginning of the Late Bronze Age at Megiddo: A Re-
            examination of Stratum X. *Berytus* 22: 5-22.

Katzenstein, H.J.
1982   Gaza in Egyptian Texts of the New Kingdom. *Journal of the American Oriental Society* 102: 111-113.
Kaufmann, Y.
1953   *The Biblical Account of the Conquest of Palestine.* Jerusalem: The Magnes Press.
1960   *The Religion of Israel From Its Beginnings to the Babylonian Exile.* (trans. & abridged by Moshe Greenberg) Chicago: University of Chicago Press.
Kelm, G.L.
1984-85   Timnah - A City of Conflict within the Traditional Buffer Zone of the Shephelah. *Bulletin of the Anglo-Israel Archaeological Society*: 54-61.
Kelm, G.L., and A. Mazar
1980   Canaanites, Philistines and Israelites at Timnah/Tel Batash. *Qadmoniot* 12/3-4: 51-52, 89-96 (Hebrew).
1982   Three Seasons of Excavations at Tel Batash - Biblical Timnah. *Bulletin of the American Schools of Oriental Research* 248: 1-36.
1985   Tel Batash (Timnah) Excavations - Second Preliminary Report (1981-1983). *Bulletin of the American Schools of Oriental Research Supplement* 23: 93-120.
1989   Excavating in Samson Country. *Biblical Archaeology Review* 15/1: 36-49.
1991   Tel Batash (Timnah) Excavations - Third Preliminary Report (1984-1988). *Bulletin of the American Schools of Oriental Research Supplement* 27 (in Press).
Kelso, J.L.
1955   The Second Campaign at Bethel. *Bulletin of the American Schools of Oriental Research* 137: 5-10.
1956   Excavations at Bethel. *Biblical Archaeologist* 19: 36-43.
1958   The Third Campaign at Bethel. *Bulletin of the American Schools of Oriental Research* 151: 3-8.
1961   The Fourth Campaign at Bethel. *Bulletin of the American Schools of Oriental Research* 164: 5-19.
1968   The Excavation of Bethel (1934-1960). *Annual of the American Schools of Oriental Research, Vol. 39.* Cambridge, MA: American Schools of Oriental Research.
1975   Bethel. Pp. 207-212 in *Encyclopedia of Archaeological Excavations in the Holy Land.* Vol. I, ed. M. Avi-Yonah. Englewood Cliffs, NJ: Prentice-Hall.
Kemp, B.J.
1981   Fortified Towns in Nubia. In Man, Settlement and Urbanism, ed. P.J. Ucko *et al.*, London.
1981   Preliminary Report on the El-ʿAmarna Expedition. *Journal of Egyptian Archaeology* 67: 5-20.

1983   Preliminary Report on the El-ᶜAmarna Expedition 1981-2. *Journal of Egyptian Archaeology* 69: 5-24.

Kempinski, A.
1974   Tell el-ᶜAjjûl - Beth Aglayim or Sharuhen? *Israel Exploration Journal* 24: 145-152.
1976   Israelite Conquest or Settlement? New Light from Tell Masos. *Biblical Archaeology Review*. 2/3: 25-30.
1977   Masos, Tel. Pp. 816-819 in *Encyclopedia of Archaeological Excavations in the Holy Land*. Vol. III, ed. M. Avi-Yonah. Englewood Cliffs, NJ: Prentice-Hall.
1978   Tel Masos. *Expedition* 20: 29-37.
1986   Joshua's Altar - An Iron Age I Watchtower. *Biblical Archaeologist Review* 12/1: 42-49.
1988   Jacob in History. *Biblical Archaeology Review* 14/1: 42-47.

Kempinski, A., and V. Fritz
1977   Excavations at Tel Masos (Khirbet el-Meshâsh). Preliminary Report of the Third Season, 1975. *Tel Aviv* 4: 136-158.

Kenyon, K.M.
1954   Excavations at Jericho, 1954. *Palestine Exploration Quarterly* 86: 45-63.
1955   Excavations at Jericho - 1955. *Palestine Exploration Quarterly* 87: 108-117.
1957   *Digging Up Jericho*. New York: Frederick A. Praeger.
1966   *Amorites and Canaanites*. Schweich Lectures. London: Oxford University Press: 76.
1967   Jericho. Pp. 264-275 in *Archaeology and Old Testament Study*, ed. D. Winton Thomas. London: Oxford University Press.
1969   The Middle and Late Bronze Age Strata at Megiddo. *Levant* 1: 25-60.
1971   Syria and Palestine c. 2160-1780 B.C.: The Archaeological Sites. Pp. 567-594 in *Cambridge Ancient History*. 3rd edition. Vol. I, Part 2, ed. I.E.S. Edwards *et al.* Cambridge: Cambridge University Press.
1973a   Palestine in the Middle Bronze Age. Pp. 77-116 in *Cambridge Ancient History*. 3rd edition. Vol. II, Part 1, ed. I.E.S. Edwards *et al.* Cambridge: Cambridge University Press.
1973b   Palestine in the Time of the Eighteenth Dynasty. Pp. 526-556 in *Cambridge Ancient History*. 3rd edition. Vol. II, Part 1, ed. Cambridge: Cambridge University Press.

Kitchen, K.A.
1964   Some New Light on the Asiatic Wars of Rameses II. *Journal of Egyptian Archaeology* 50: 47-70, Pls.III-VI.
1968   *Ramesside Inscriptions*. Oxford: Oxford University Press.
1973   The Philistines. Pp. 53-78 in *Peoples of Old Testament Times*. ed. D.J. Wiseman. Oxford: Oxford University Press.

1982	*Pharaoh Triumphant: The Life and Times of Ramesses II.* Mississauga.
1987	The Basis of Egyptian Chronology in Relation to the Bronze Age. Pp. 37-55 in *High, Middle or Low? Acts of an International Colloquium on Absolute Chronology Held in Gothenberg 20th - 22nd August 1987.* e. P.A. Åström. Gothenberg: Paul Åströms Forlag.

Kline, M.G.
1956	The Ḫa-BI-ru - Kin or Foe of Israel? Parts I, II. *Westminster Theological Journal* 19: 1-24, 170-184; Part III. 20: 46-70.

Knudtzon, J.A.
1915	*Die El-Amarna Tafeln.* 2 vols. Leipzig: Hinrichs.

Kochavi, M.
1969	Excavations at Tel Esdar. *ʿAtiqot* 5: 14-48 (Hebrew).
1972	*Judea, Samaria and the Golan, Archaeological Survey 1967-68.* Jerusalem: Carta. (Hebrew).
1974	Khirbet Rabûd = Debir. *Tel-Aviv* 1: 2-33.
1976	Debir (City). P. 222 in *The Interpreter's Dictionary of the Bible.* Supplementary Volume. Nashville: Abingdon Press.
1977	Malhata, Tel. Pp. 771-775 in *Encyclopedia of Archaeological Excavations in the Holy Land.* Vol. III, ed. M. Avi-Yonah. Englewood Cliffs, NJ: Prentice-Hall.
1978	Rabud, Khirbet. P. 995 in *Encyclopedia of Archaeological Excavations in the Holy Land.* Vol. IV, ed. M. Avi-Yonah. Englewood Cliffs, NJ: Prentice-Hall.
1981	The History and Archaeology of Aphek-Antipatris. *Biblical Archaeologist* 44: 75-86.
1985	The Israelite Settlement in Canaan in the Light of Archaeological Surveys. Pp. 54-60 in *Biblical Archaeology Today: Proceedings of the International Congress on Biblical Archaeology, Jerusalem, April 1984.* Jerusalem: Israel Exploration Society.

Kochavi, M., and A. Demsky
1978	An Israelite Village from the Days of the Judges. *Biblical Archaeology Review* 4/3: 19-22.

Kochavi, M., P. Beck, and R. Gophna
1979	Aphek-Antipatris, Tel Poleg, Tel Zeror and Tel Burga: Four Fortified Sites of the Middle Bronze IIA in the Sharon Plain. *Zeitschrift des Deutschen Palästina-Vereins* 45: 121-165.
1978	An Israelite Village from the Days of the Judges. *Biblical Archaeology Review* 4/3: 19-22.

Kraft, C.F.
1962	Judges, Book of. Pp. 1013-1023 in *The Interpreter's Dictionary of the Bible.* Vol. 2. Nashville: Abingdon Press.

Krahmalkov, C.R.
1981	A Critique of Professor Goedicke's Exodus Theories. *Biblical Archaeology Review* 6/5: 51-54.

Lance, H.D.
1967   Gezer in the Land and History. *Biblical Archaeologist* 30: 34-47.
Landes, G.M.
1961   The Material Civilization of the Ammonites. *Biblical Archaeologist* 24: 66-86.
Langdon, S., and A.H. Gardiner
1920   The Treaty of Alliance between Hattušili King of the Hittites and the Pharaoh Ramesses II of Egypt. *Journal of Egyptian Archaeology* 6: 179-205.
Lapp, P.
1964   The 1963 Excavation at Ta°annek. *Bulletin of the American Schools of Oriental Research* 173: 4-44.
1967a   Taanach by the Waters of Megiddo. *Biblical Archaeologist* 30: 2-27.
1967b   The Conquest of Palestine in the Light of Archaeology. *Concordia Theological Monthly* 38: 283-300.
1967c   The 1966 Excavations at Tell Ta°annek. *Bulletin of the American Schools of Oriental Research* 185: 2-39.
1969   The 1968 Excavations at Tell Ta°annek. *Bulletin of the American Schools of Oriental Research* 195: 2-49.
Laughlin, J.C.H.
1981   The Remarkable Discoveries at Tel Dan. *Biblical Archaeology Review* 7/5: 20-37.
Leclant, J.
1969   Tell ed-Dab°a. *Orientalia* 38: 248-251.
Lemaire, A.
1981   Galaad et Makîr. Remarques sur la tribu de Manassé à l'est du Jourdain. *Vetus Testamentum* 31: 39-61.
Lemche, N.P.
1975   The "Hebrew Slave." *Vetus Testamentum* 25: 129-144.
Leonard, A., Jr.
1987b   The Significance of the Mycenaean Pottery Found East of the Jordan River. Pp. 261-166 in *Studies in the History and Archaeology of Jordan.* Vol. 3. Amman: Department of Antiquities.
1989   The Late Bronze Age. *Biblical Archaeologist* 52: 4-39.
Livingston, D.
1970   The Location of Biblical Bethel and Ai Reconsidered. *Westminster Theological Journal* 33: 20-44.
1971   Traditional Site of Bethel Questioned. *Westminster Theological Journal* 34: 39-50.
1987   The Identity of Bethel and Ai. *A paper delivered at the "Who Was the Pharaoh of the Exodus?" symposium.* Memphis, Tennessee, April 23-25.

Lowle, D.A.
1976   A Remarkable Family of Draughtsmen-Painters from Early
            Nineteenth Dynasty Thebes. *Oriens Antiquus* S: 91-106.
Lucas, A.
1938   *The Route of the Exodus of the Israelites from Egypt.* London: E.
            Arnold.
Luce, J.V.
1969   *Lost Atlantis: New Light on an Old Legend* (British title: *The End
            of Atlantis*). New York: McGraw-Hill.
1976   Thera and the Destruction of Minoan Crete: A New Interpretation
            of the Evidence. *American Journal of Archaeology* 80: 9-16.
Luckerman, M.A.
1980   A Different View on the Chronology of Hazor. *Catastrophism and
            Ancient History* 2/2/: 95-115.
MacDonald, B.
1980   Excavations at Tell el-Maskhuta. *Biblical Archaeologist* 43: 49-
            58.
1982   The Wadī el-Ḥasā Survey 1979 and Previous Archaeological
            Work in Southern Jordan. *Bulletin of the American Schools of
            Oriental Research* 245: 35-52.
1983   The Late Bronze and Iron Age Sites of the Wadi el Hasa Survey,
            1979. Pp. 18-28 in *Midian, Moab and Edom: The History and
            Archaeology of Late Bronze and Iron Age Jordan and North-West
            Arabia*, ed. J.F.A. Sawyer and D.J.A. Clines. Sheffield, England:
            The Almond Press.
MacKie, E.
1978   Radiocarbon Dating and Egyptian Chronology. *Ages in Chaos?*
            (Proceedings of the Residential Weekend Conference, Glasgow,
            7-9 April, 1978). *S.I.S. Review* 6/1-3 (1982): 56-63.
Macqueen, J.G.
1986   *The Hittites and Their Contemporaries in Asia Minor.* Revised
            edition. New York and London: Thames and Hudson.
Malamat, A.
1954   Cushan Rishathaim and the Decline of the Near East around 1200
            B.C. *Journal of Near Eastern Studies* 13: 231-242.
1960   Hazor 'the head of all those kingdoms.' *Journal of Biblical
            Literature* 79: 12-19.
1961   Campaigns of Amenhotep II and Thutmose IV to Canaan. *Scripta
            Hierosolymitana* 8: 218-231.
1964   Military Rationing in Papyrus Anastasi I and the Bible. *The
            Military History of the Land of Israel in Biblical Times*, ed. J.
            Liver. Jerusalem: 342-349 (Hebrew).
1970   The Danite Migration and the Pan-Israelite Exodus-Conquest.
            Biblica 51: 1-16.

1979	Israelite Conduct of War in the Conquest of Canaan According to the Biblical Tradition. Pp. 35-55 in *Symposia Celebrating the Seventy-Fifth Anniversary of the Founding of the American Schools of Oriental Research (1900-1975)*, ed. Frank Moore Cross. Cambridge, MA: American Schools of Oriental Research.
1982	How Inferior Israelite Forces Conquered Fortified Canaanite Cities. *Biblical Archaeology Review* 8/2: 24-35.

Marinatos, S.
1939	The Volcanic Destruction of Minoan Crete. *Antiquity* 13: 425-439.
1972	Thera: Key to the Riddle of Minos. *National Geographic Magazine* 141/1: 40-52.

Martin, G.T.
1971	*Egyptian Administrative and Private-Name Seals*. Oxford.

Mattingly, G.L.
1983	The Exodus-Conquest and the Archaeology of Transjordan: New Light on An Old Problem. *Grace Theological Journal* 4: 245-262.
1987	Another Look At Transjordan. *A paper delivered at the "Who Was the Pharaoh of the Exodus?" symposium*. Memphis, Tennessee, April 23-25.

Mavor, J.W.
1969	*Voyage to Atlantis*. New York: G.P. Putnam's Sons.

Mayes, A.D.H.
1969	The Historical Context of the Battle Against Sisera. *Vetus Testamentum* 19: 353-360.
1983	*The Story of Israel Between Settlement and Exile: A Redactional Study of the Deuteronomistic History*. London: SCM Press.

Mazar, A.
1973	A Philistine Temple at Tell Qasile. *Biblical Archaeologist* 36: 42-48.
1975	Excavations at Tell Qasîle, 1973-1974. *Israel Exploration Journal* 25: 77-88.
1981	Giloh: An Early Israelite Settlement Site near Jerusalem. *Israel Exploration Journal* 31: 1-36.
1982a	Three Israelite Sites in the Hills of Judah and Ephraim. *Biblical Archaeologist* 45: 167-178.
1982b	The "Bull Site" - An Iron Age I Open Cult Place. *Bulletin of the American Schools of Oriental Research* 247: 27-42.
1983	Bronze Bull Found in Israelite "High Place" from the Time of the Judges. *Biblical Archaeology Review* 9/5: 34-40.
1985a	The Israelite Settlement in Canaan in the Light of Archaeological Excavations. *Biblical Archaeology Today: Proceedings of the International Congress on Biblical Archaeology, Jerusalem, April 1984*. Jerusalem: Israel Exploration Society.
1985b	The Emergence of the Philistine Material Culture. *Israel Exploration Journal* 35: 95-107.

1990	*Archaeology of the Land of the Bible, 10,000 - 586 B.C.E.* New York: Doubleday.
1991	Iron Age I and II Towers at Giloh and the Israelite Settlement. *Israel Exploration Journal* 40: 77-101.

Mazar (Maisler), B.

1946	Canaan and the Canaanites. *Bulletin of the American Schools of Oriental Research* 102: 7-12.
1951a	The Stratification of Tell Abū Huwâm on the Bay of Acre. *Bulletin of the American Schools of Oriental Research* 124: 21-25.
1951b	The Excavations at Tell Qasile. Preliminary Report. *Israel Exploration Journal* 1: 61-76; 125-140; 194-218.
1951c	The Excavation of Tell Qasile. *Biblical Archaeologist* 14: 43-49.
1965	The Sanctuary of Arad and the Family of Hobab the Kenite. *Journal of Near Eastern Studies* 24: 297-303.
1968	The Middle Bronze Age in Palestine. *Israel Exploration Journal* 18: 65-97.
1981	The Process of Settlement in the Hill-Country. *Eretz Israel* 15: 145-149.
1981	The Early Israelite Settlement in the Hill Country. *Bulletin of the American Schools of Oriental Research* 241: 75-85.

McGovern, P.E.

1986	*The Late Bronze and Early Iron Ages of Central Transjordan: The Baqᶜah Valley Project, 1977-1981.* Philadelphia: University Museum.

McKenzie, J.L.

1966	*The World of the Judges.* Englewood Cliffs, NJ: Prentice-Hall.
1983	The Sack of Israel. Pp. 25-34 in *The Quest for the Kingdom of God: Studies in Honor of George E. Mendenhall*, ed. H.B. Huffmon, F.A. Spina, and A.R.W. Green. Winona Lake, IN: Eisenbrauns.

Meek, T.J.

1960	*Hebrew Origins.* 3rd revised edition (Torchbook edition). New York: Harper and Brothers.

Mendelsohn, I.

1949	*Slavery in the Ancient Near East.* New York:
1962	On Corvée Labor in Ancient Canaanite Israel. *Bulletin of the American Schools of Oriental Research* 167: 31-53.

Mendenhall, G.E.

1962	The Hebrew Conquest of Palestine. *Biblical Archaeologist* 25: 66-87.
1973	*The Tenth Generation: The Origins of the Biblical Tradition.* Baltimore: Johns Hopkins University Press.
1976	"Change and Decay in All Around I See": Conquest, Covenant and the Tenth Generation. *Biblical Archaeologist* 39: 152-157.

1983   Ancient Israel's Hyphenated History. Pp. 91-103 in *Palestine in Transition. The Emergence of Ancient Israel,* eds. D.N. Freedman and D.F. Graf. Sheffield, England: The Almond Press.

Mercer, S.A.B.
1939   *The Tell El-Amarna Tablets.* 2 vols. Toronto: Macmillan.

Merrillees, R.S.
1970   Evidence for the Bichrome Wheel-made Ware in Egypt. *Australian Journal of Biblical Archaeology* 1: 3-27.
1971   The Early History of Late Cypriote I. *Levant* 3: 56-79.
1986   Political Conditions in the Eastern Mediterranean during the Late Bronze Age. *Biblical Archaeologist* 49: 42-50.

Meshel, Z.
1979   Did Yahweh Have a Consort? *Biblical Archaeology Review* 5/2: 24-35.

Mihelic, J.L.
1962   Red Sea. Pp. 19-21 in *The Interpreter's Dictionary of the Bible.* IV. Nashville: Abingdon Press.

Mihelic, J.L. and G.E. Wright
1962   Plagues in Exodus. Pp. 822-824 in *Interpreter's Dictionary of the Bible.* III. Nashville: Abingdon Press.

Millard, A.
1973   The Canaanites. Pp. 29-52 in *Peoples of Old Testament Times,* ed. D.J. Wiseman. Oxford: Oxford University Press.

Miller, J.M.
1974   The Moabite Stone as a Memorial Stele. *Palestine Exploration Quarterly* 106: 9-18.
1976a   Joshua, Book of. Pp. 493-496 in *Interpreter's Dictionary of the Bible.* Supplementary Volume. Nashville: Abingdon Press.
1976b   *The Old Testament and the Historian.* Philadelphia: Fortress Press.
1977a   The Israelite Occupation of Canaan. Pp. 213-284 in *Israelite and Judean History,* ed. J.H. Hayes and J.M. Miller. Philadelphia: Westminster Press.
1977b   Archaeology and the Israelite Conquest of Canaan: Some Methodological Observations. *Palestine Exploration Quarterly* 109: 87-93.
1979   Archaeological Survey of Central Moab, 1978. *Bulletin of the American Schools of Oriental Research* 234: 43-52.
1982   Recent Archaeological Developments Relevant to Ancient Moab. Pp. 169-173 in *Studies in the History and Archaeology of Jordan, I,* ed. A. Hadidi. Amman: Department of Antiquities.
1989   The Israelite Journey Through (Around) Moab and Moabite Toponymy. *Journal of Biblical Literature* 108: 577-595.

Miller, J.M. and J.H. Hayes
1986   *A History of Ancient Israel and Judah.* Philadelphia: Westminster Press.

Muhammad, M.A-K.
1959   The Administration of Syro-Palestine during the New Kingdom.
            Annales du Service des Antiquités de l'Egypte 56: 105-137.
Muhly, J.D.
1982   How Iron Technology Changed the Ancient World -- And Gave
            the Philistines a Military Edge. *Biblical Archaeology Review* 8/6:
            40-54.
Muilenberg, J.
1955   The Site of Ancient Gilgal. *Bulletin of the American Schools of
            Oriental Research* 140: 11-27.
1962   Mizpeh. P. 408 in *The Interpreter's Dictionary of the Bible*, 3.
            Nashville: Abingdon Press.
Müller, W.M.
1904   The   Egyptian   Monument   of   Tell   Esh-Shihab. *Palestine
            Exploration Fund* (1904), 78ff.
Murnane, W.J.
1975   The Earlier Reign of Ramesses II and His Coregency with Sety I.
            Journal of Near Eastern Studies 34: 153-190.
Naᶜaman, N.
1981   Economic Aspects of the Egyptian Occupation of Canaan. *Israel
            Exploration Journal* 31: 172-185.
Naveh, J.
1958   Khirbet al-Muqannaᶜ - Ekron: An Archaeological Survey. *Israel
            Exploration Journal* 8: 87-100; 165-170.
Naville, E.
1903   *The Store-City of Pithom and the Route of the Exodus*. (4th
            edition) London: Egypt Exploration Fund.
1924   The Geography of the Exodus. *Journal of Egyptian Archaeology*
            10: 18-39.
Negbi, O.
1970   *The Hoards of Goldwork from Tell el-ᶜAjjûl*. SMA 25. Göteborg:
            P. Åström.
Negbi, O., and Moskowitz, S.
1966   The 'Foundation Deposits' and 'Offering Deposits' of Byblos.
            Bulletin of the American Schools of Oriental Research 184: 21-26.
Nielsen, D.
1928   *The Site of the Biblical Mount Sinai*. Copenhagen.
Noth, M.
1930   *Das System der zwölf Stamme Israels*. Stuttgart: W. Kohlhammer.
1935   Bethel and 'Ai. *Palästinajahrbuch* 37: 7-22.

1948   *A History of Pentateuchal Traditions*. (translated and introduced
            by B.W. Anderson) Englewood Cliffs, NJ: Prentice-Hall, 1972.
1960   *The History of Israel*. (translated by P.R. Ackroyd from the 2nd
            edition of *Geschichte Israels*. New York: Harper and Brothers.

Olavarri, E.
1965   Sondages a ʿArôʿer sur L'Arnon. *Revue Biblique* 72: 77-94.
1969   Fouilles a ʿArôʿer sur L'Arnon: Les Niveaux du Bronze Intermédiaire. *Revue Biblique* 76: 250-59.
1975   Aroer. Pp. 98-100 in *Encyclopedia of Archaeological Excavations in the Holy Land.* Vol. I, ed. M. Avi-Yonah. Englewood Cliffs, NJ: Prentice-Hall.
Oren, E.D.
1973   The Overland Route Between Egypt and Canaan in the Early Bronze Age. *Israel Exploration Journal* 23: 198-205.
1973a   An Egyptian Fortress on the Military Road between Egypt and Canaan. *Qadmoniot* 6: 101-103 (Hebrew).
1973b   Bir el-ʿAbd (Northern Sinai). *Israel Exploration Journal* 23: 112-13.
1978   Esh-Shariʿa. Tell. Pp. 1059-1069 in *Encyclopedia of Archaeological Excavations in the Holy Land* IV, eds. M. Avi-Yonah and E. Stern. Jerusalem: Israel Exploration Society and Massada Press.
1980   Egyptian New Kingdom Sites in Northern Sinai. *Qadmoniot* 13: 26-33 (Hebrew).
1981   How Not to Create a History of the Exodus - A Critique of Professor Goedicke's Theories. *Biblical Archaeology Review* 7/6: 46-53.
1982a   Oren Replies to the Goedicke Letter (Queries and Comments) *Biblical Archaeology Review* 8/2: 12.
1982b   Ziklag: A Biblical City on the Edge of the Negev. *Biblical Archaeologist* 45: 155-166.
1982-83   Ancient Military Roads between Egypt and Canaan. Bulletin of the *Anglo-Israel Archaeology Society*: 20-24.
1984   Migdol: A New Fortress on the Edge of the Eastern Nile Delta. *Bulletin of the American Schools of Oriental Research* 256: 7-44.
1985a   Governors' Residencies in Canaan under the New Kingdom: A Case Study of Egyptian Administration. *The Journal for the Society for the Study of Egyptian Antiquities* 14: 37-56.
1985b   Architecture of Egyptian 'Governors' Residencies' in the Late Bronze Age Palestine. *Eretz Israel* 18: 183-199.
1985c   Response in Session IV: Israel's Neighbors in the Iron Age in the Light of Archaeological Research. Pp. 223-226 in *Biblical Archaeology Today*, ed. J. Aviram. Jerusalem: Israel Exploration Society.
1987   The 'Ways of Horus' in North Sinai. Pp. 69-120 in *Egypt, Israel, Sinai.* ed. A.F. Rainey. Tel Aviv: Tel Aviv University.
Ottosson, M.
1969   Gilead: Tradition and History. *Coniectanae Biblica: Old Testament Series, No. 3.* Lund: C.W.K. Gleerup.

Ovadiah, A.
1976   Gaza. Pp. 408-417 in *Encyclopedia of Archaeological Excavations in the Holy Land*. Vol. II, ed. M. Avi-Yonah. Englewood Cliffs, NJ: Prentice-Hall; Jerusalem: The Israel Exploration Society and Massada Press.

Owen, D.
1981   Ugarit, Canaan and Egypt. Pp. 49-53 in *Ugarit in Retrospect: Fifty Years of Ugarit and Ugaritic*. ed. G.D. Young. Winona Lake, IN: Eisenbrauns.

Parr, P.
1968   The Origin of the Rampart Fortifications of Middle Bronze Age Palestine and Syria. *Zeitschrift des Deutschen Palästina-Vereins* 84: 18-45.

Perlman, I., F. Asaro and T. Dothan
1973   Provenance of the Deir el-Balah Coffins. *Israel Exploration Journal* 23: 147-151.

Perevolotsky, A., and I. Finkelstein
1985   The Southern Sinai Exodus Route in Ecological Perspective. *Biblical Archaeology Review* 11/4: 26-41.

Posener, G.
1971   Syria and Palestine ca. 2160-1780 B.C.: Relations With Egypt. Pp. 532-558 in *Cambridge Ancient History*. 3rd edition. Vol. I, Part 2, ed. I.E.S. Edwards *et al.* Cambridge: Cambridge University Press.

Prag, K.
1974   The Intermediate Early Bronze-Middle Bronze Age: An Interpretation of the Evidence from Transjordan, Syria and Lebanon. *Levant* 6: 69-116.

1985   Ancient and Modern Pastoral Migration in the Levant. *Levant* 17: 81-88.

Pritchard, J.B.
1955   *Ancient Near Eastern Texts Relating to the Old Testament*. 2nd ed. Princeton, NJ: Princeton University Press.

1959   *Hebrew Inscriptions and Stamps from Gibeon*. Philadelphia: University Museum.

1960   Gibeon's History in the Light of Excavation. *Vetus Testamentum Supplement* 7: 1-12.

1962   *Gibeon, Where the Sun Stood Still*. Princeton, NJ: Princeton University Press.

1964   *Winery, Defenses, and Soundings at Gibeon*. Philadelphia: University Museum.

1965a   Culture and History. Pp. 313-324 in *The Bible in Modern Scholarship*, ed. J.P. Hyatt. Nashville: Abingdon Press.

1965b   A Cosmopolitan Culture of the Late Bronze Age. *Expedition* 7(4): 26-33.

1969	*The Ancient Near East In Pictures Relating to the Old Testament.* Princeton, NJ: Princeton University Press.
1975	*Sarepta, A Preliminary Report on the Iron Age.* Philadelphia: Museum Monograph.
1976	Gibeon. Pp. 446-450 in *Encyclopedia of Archaeological Excavations in the Holy Land.* Vol. II, ed. M. Avi-Yonah. Englewood Cliffs, NJ: Prentice-Hall.
1978	*Recovering Sarepta, A Phoenician City.* Princeton: Princeton University Press.
1980	*The Cemetery at Tell es-Saᶜidiyeh, Jordan.* Philadelphia: University Museum.

Raban, A., and E. Galili
1985	Recent Maritime Archaeological Research in Israel - A Preliminary Report. *The International Journal of Nautical Archaeology and Underwater Exploration* 14(4): 321-356.

Rabinovich, A.
1990	Is Har Karkom the real Mt. Sinai? *The Jerusalem Post International Edition.* Jerusalem, Israel.

Rainey, A.F.
1970	Bethel is Still Beitin. *Westminster Theological Journal* 33: 175-188.
1973	Amenhotep II's Campaign in Takhsi. *Journal of the American Research Center in Egypt* 10: 71-75.
1975	The Identification of Philistine Gath. *Eretz-Israel* 12: 63*-76*.
1976a	Eglon (City), 1. Tell ᶜAitun? P. 252 in *Interpreter's Dictionary of the Bible.* Supplementary Volume. Nashville: Abingdon Press.
1976b	Libnah (City). P. 546 in *Interpreter's Dictionary of the Bible.* Supplementary Volume. Nashville: Abingdon Press.
1978	*El Amarna Tablets 359-379: Supplement to J.A. Knudtzon, Die El-Amarna Tafeln.* Neukirchen-Vuyn: Neukirchen Verlag.
1980a	The Administrative Division of the Shephelah. *Tel Aviv* 7: 194-202.
1980b	Review of John Bimson, Redating the Exodus and Conquest. *Israel Exploration Journal* 30: 249-251.
1983	The Biblical Shephelah of Judah. *Bulletin of the American Schools of Oriental Research* 251: 1-22.
1987	Egyptian Military Inscriptions and Some Historical Implications. *Journal of the American Oriental Society* 107: 89-92.

Ramsey, G.W.
1981	*The Quest for the Historical Israel.* Atlanta: John Knox Press.

Redford, D.B.
1963	Exodus 1:11. *Vetus Testamentum* 13: 401-418.
1965	The Coregency of Thutmosis III and Amenophis II. *Journal of Egyptian Archaeology* 51: 120-122.
1967	*History and Chronology of the Eighteenth Dynasty of Egypt: Seven Studies.* Toronto: University of Toronto Press.

1970a	*A Study of the Biblical Joseph Story.* Leiden.
1970b	The Hyksos Invasion in History and Tradition. *Orientalia* 39: 1-51.
1973a	Studies in Relations Between Palestine and Egypt During the First Millennium B.C.: II. The Twenty Second Dynasty. *Journal of the American Oriental Society* 93: 3-17.
1973b	New Light on the Asiatic Campaigning of Horemheb. *Bulletin of the American Schools of Oriental Research* 211: 36-49.
1979	A Gate Inscription from Karnak and Egyptian Involvement in Western Asia during the Early 18th Dynasty. *Journal of the American Oriental Society* 99: 270-87.
1982	Contact Between Egypt and Jordan in the New Kingdom: Some Comments on Sources. Pp. 115-119 in *Studies in the History and Archaeology of Jordan, I,* ed. A. Hadidi Amman: Department of Antiquities.
1983	*King Lists, Annals and Daybooks: A Contribution to Egyptian Historiography.* Toronto.
1984	*Akhenaton: The Heretic King.* Princeton, NJ: Princeton University Press.
1986	The Ashkelon Relief at Karnak and the Israel Stele. *Israel Exploration Journal* 36: 199-200.
1987a	An Egyptological Perspective on the Exodus Narrative. Pp. 137-162 in *Egypt, Israel, Sinai: Archaeological and Historical Relationships in the Biblical Period,* ed. A.F. Rainey. Tel Aviv: Tel Aviv University.
1987b	The Monotheism of the Heretic Pharaoh. *Biblical Archaeology Review* 13/3: 16-32.

Reed, W.L.
1967	Gibeon. Pp. 231-243 in *Archaeology and Old Testament Study.* ed. D.W. Thomas. Oxford: Oxford University Press.

Reed, W.L., and F.V. Winnett
1964	*The Excavations at Dibôn (Dhibân) in Moab. Annual of the American Schools of Oriental Research* Vol. 36-37. New Haven, CT: American Schools of Oriental Research.

Reisner, G.A., C.S. Fisher, and D.G. Lyon
1924	*Harvard Excavations at Samaria.* 2 vols. Cambridge, MA: Harvard University Press.

Reviv, H.
1966	The Government of Shechem in the El-Amarna Period and in the Days of Abimelech. *Israel Exploration Journal* 16: 252-257.
1966	The Planning of an Egyptian Campaign during the Days of Amunhotep IV. *Bulletin of the Israel Exploration Society* 30: 45-51 (Hebrew).

Robinson, E.
1841	*Biblical Researches in Palestine, Mount Sinai and Arabia Patraea.* Boston: Crocker & Brewster.

1856   Biblical Researches in Palestine and in the Adjacent Regions, Vol.
                    I-III. Boston: Crocker & Brewster.
Rose, D.G.
1976   Eglon (City), 2. Tell el-Hesi? Pp. 252-253 in Interpreter's
                    Dictionary of the Bible. Supplementary Volume. Nashville:
                    Abingdon Press.
Rosen, S.A.
1988   Finding Evidence of Ancient Nomads. Biblical Archaeology
                    Review 14/5: 46-53.
Ross, J.F.
1967   Gezer in the Tell el-Amarna Letters. Biblical Archaeologist 30:
                    62-70.
Rothenberg, B.
1961   God's Wilderness. Discoveries in Sinai. London:Thames and
                    Hudson.
1972   Timna: Valley of the Biblical Copper Mines. London: Thames and
                    Hudson.
1979   Sinai. Bern.
Rowe, A.
1954   A Contribution to the Archaeology of the Western Desert, II.
                    Bulletin of the John Rylands Library 36: 484-500.
Rowley, H.H.
1942   The Exodus and the Settlement in Canaan. Bulletin of the
                    American Schools of Oriental Research 85: 27-31.
1950   From Joseph to Joshua: Biblical Traditions in the Light of
                    Archaeology. London: Oxford University Press.
Rowton, M.B.
1953   The Problem of the Exodus. Palestine Exploration Quarterly 85:
                    46-60.
1959   The Background of the Treaty between Ramesses II of Egypt and
                    Hattušiliš III. Journal of Cuneiform Studies 13: 1-11.
1974   Enclosed Nomadism. Journal of the Economy and Social History
                    of the Orient 17: 1-30.
1976   Dimorphic Structure and the Problem of the 'Apiru-'Ibrim.
                    Journal of Near Eastern Studies 35/1: 13-20.
1977   Dimorphic Structure and the Parasocial Element. Journal of Near
                    Eastern Studies 36: 181-198.
Rudman, B.S.
1981   Goedicke's Exodus Theories Anticipated by BAR Reader and
                    Others (Queries and Comments). Biblical Archaeology Review 7/6:
                    14-16.
Sadek, H.
1928   The Principal Structural Features of the Peninsula of Sinai.
                    Madrid: Congress Geologigue International.

Sandars, N.K.
1985   The Sea Peoples: Warriors of the Ancient Mediterranean.
            (Revised edition) New York and London: Thames and Hudson.
Sarna, N.M.
1986   Exploring Exodus: The Heritage of Ancient Israel. New York:
            Schocken Books.
Sauer, J.A.
1985   Ammon, Moab and Edom. Pp. 206-214 Biblical Archaeology
            Today: Proceedings of the International Conference on Biblical
            Archaeology, Jerusalem, April 1984. Jerusalem: Israel Exploration
            Society.
1986   Transjordan in the Bronze and Iron Ages: A Critique of Glueck's
            Synthesis. Bulletin of the American Schools of Oriental Research
            263: 1-26.
Säve-Söderbergh, T.
1951   The Hyksos Rule in Egypt. Journal of Egyptian Archaeology 37:
            53-71.
Schaeffer, C.F.A.
1983   The Last Days of Ugarit. An excerpt from Ugaritica 5, 1968.
            (translated by Michael D. Coogan) Biblical Archaeology Review
            9/5: 74-75.
Schulman, A.R.
1964   Some Observations on the Military Background of the Amarna
            Period. Journal of the American Research Center in Egypt 3: 51-
            69.
1978   Ankhesenamun, Nofretity, and the Amka Affair. Journal of the
            American Research Center in Egypt 15: 43-48.
1979   Diplomatic Marriage in the Egyptian New Kingdom. Journal of
            Near Eastern Studies 38: 177-193.
1980   More Egyptian Seal Impressions from ᶜEn-Besor. ᶜAtiqot 14: 17-
            33. (English Series).
1982   The Nubian War of Akhenaton. L'Egyptologie en 1979, Axes
            prioritaires de recherches, II. Paris: 299-316.
Seele, K.C.
1940   The Coregency of Ramses II with Seti I. Chicago: The University
            of Chicago Press.
Seger, J.D.
1974   The Middle Bronze IIC Date of the East Gate at Shechem. Levant
            5: 117-130.
1975   The MB II Fortifications at Shechem and Gezer - A Hyksos
            Retrospective. Eretz Israel 12: 34*-35*.
1983   Investigations at Tell Halif, Israel, 1976-1980. Bulletin of the
            American Schools of Oriental Research 252: 1-24.
1984   The Location of Biblical Ziklag. Biblical Archaeologist 47: 47-53.

Seger, J.D., and O. Borowski
1977   The First Two Seasons at Tell Halif. *Biblical Archaeologist* 40: 156-166.
Several, M.
1972   Reconsidering the Egyptian Empire in Palestine during the Amarna Period. *Palestine Exploration Quarterly* 104: 123-33.
Shanks, H.
1980   The Exodus and the Crossing of the Red Sea, According to Hans Goedicke. *Biblical Archaeology Review* 6/5: 49, 50.
Shea, W.H.
1977   A Date for the Recently Discovered Eastern Canal of Egypt. *Bulletin of the American Schools of Oriental Research* 226: 31-38.
1979   The Conquests of Sharuḥen and Megiddo Reconsidered. *Israel Exploration Journal* 29: 1-5.
1986   Some New Factors Bearing Upon the Date of the Exodus. Pp. 29-35 in *Proceeding of the Third Seminar of Catastrophism and Ancient History,* ed. M.A. Luckerman. Los Angeles: Catastrophism and Ancient History Press.
Shiloh, Y.
1970   The Four-Room House - Its Situation and Function in the Israelite City. *Israel Exploration Journal* 20: 180-190.
1973   The Four-Room House - The Israelite Type House? *Eretz Israel* 11: 277-285 (Hebrew).
1978   Elements in the Development of Town Planning in the Israelite Town. *Israel Exploration Journal* 28: 36-51.
Simons, J.
1959   *The Geographical and Topographical Texts of the Old Testament.* Leiden: E.J. Brill.
Singer, I.
1985   The Beginning of Philistine Settlement in Canaan and the Northern Boundary of Philistia. *Tel Aviv* 12: 109-122.
Smither, P.C.
1945   The Semnah Despatches. *Journal of Egyptian Archaeology* 31: 3-10.
Snaith, N.H.
1965   סוף ים: The Sea of Reeds: The Red Sea. *Vetus Testamentum* 15: 395-398.
1978   The Altar at Gilgal: Joshua 22: 23-29. *Vetus Testamentum* 28: 330-335.
Sneh, A., and T. Weissbrod
1973   Nile Delta: The Defunct Pelusiac Branch Identified. *Science* 180: 59-61.
1975   Evidence for an Ancient Egyptian Frontier Canal. *Scientific American* 63:542-548.
1979   *Brick Architecture in Ancient Egypt.* Warminster.

Spalinger, A.
1974 Some Notes on the Battle of Megiddo and Reflections on Egyptian Military Writing. *MDAIK* 30: 221-229.
1978 A New Reference to an Egyptian Campaign of Thutmose III in Asia. *Journal of Near Eastern Studies* 37: 35-41.
1979 Some Additional Remarks on the Battle of Megiddo. *MDAIK* 33: 47-54.
Spencer, A.J.
1979 Glimpses of Ancient Egypt. Pp. 132-137 in *Studies in Honour of H.W. Fairman* (ed. J. Ruffle). Warminster.
Stager, L.E.
1981 Highland Village Life in Palestine some Three Thousand Years Ago. *The Oriental Institute Notes and News* 69. Chicago.
1985a The Archaeology of the Family in Ancient Israel. *Bulletin of the American Schools of Oriental Research* 260: 1-24.
1985b Marneptah, Israel and Sea Peoples: New Light on an Old Relief. Pp. 56*-64* in *Eretz Israel* 18 (N. Avigad Volume), Jerusalem.
1985c Response. Pp. 83-86 in *Biblical Archaeology Today: Proceedings of the International Conference on Biblical Archaeology, Jerusalem, April 1984*. Jerusalem: Israel Exploration Society.
Steindorf, G., and K.C. Steele
1957 *When Egypt Ruled the East*. Chicago: University of Chicago Press.
Stern, E.
1977 A Late Bronze Temple at Tell Mevorakh. *Biblical Archaeologist* 40: 88-91.
1978 Es-Safi, Tell. Pp. 1024-1027 in *Encyclopedia of Archaeological Excavations in the Holy Land*. Vol. IV, ed. M. Avi-Yonah. Englewood Cliffs, NJ: Prentice-Hall.
1984 *Excavations at Tell Mevorakh (1973-1976), Part Two: The Bronze Age*. (Qedem 18) Jerusalem: The Hebrew University.
Stiebing, W.H., Jr.
1971 Hyksos Burials in Palestine: A Review of the Evidence. *Journal of Near Eastern Studies* 30/2: 110-117.
1980 The End of the Mycenaean Age. *Biblical Archaeologist* 43/1: 7-21.
1985 Should the Exodus and the Israelite Settlement in Canaan be Redated?. *Biblical Archaeology Review* 11/4: 58-69.
1987 The Israelite Exodus and the Volcanic Eruption of Thera. *Catastrophism and Ancient History* 9/2: 69-79.
1988a New Archaeological Dates for the Israelite Conquest, Part I: Proposals for an EB III Conquest. *Catastrophism and Ancient History* 10/1: 5-16.
1988b New Archaeological Dates for the Israelite Conquest, Part II: An MB IIc Conquest. *Catastrophism and Ancient History* 10/2 (in press).

1989   *Out of the Desert? Archaeology and the Exodus/Conquest Narratives.* Buffalo, NY: Prometheus Books.

Stubbings, F.H.
1973   The Recession of Mycenaean Civilization. Pp. 338-58 in *Cambridge Ancient History*, 3rd ed., II, 2.

Talmon, S.
1965   The Town Lists of Simeon. *Israel Exploration Journal* 15: 235-241.

Taylour, W.
1983   *The Mycenaeans.* (revised edition) New York: Thames and Hudson.

Thompson, T.L. and D. Irvin
1977   The Joseph and Moses Narratives. Pp. 149-212 in *Israelite and Judean History*, ed. John H. Hayes and J. Maxwell Miller. Philadelphia: Westminster Press.

Toombs, L.E.
1979   Shechem: Problems of the Early Israelite Era. Pp. 69-83 in *Symposia Celebrating the 75th Anniversary of the American Schools of Oriental Research (1900-1975)*, ed. F.M. Cross.

Toombs, L.E., and G.E.Wright
1961   The Third Campaign at Balâṭah (Shechem). *Bulletin of the American Schools of Oriental Research* 161: 11-54.
1963   The Fourth Campaign at Balâṭah (Shechem). *Bulletin of the American Schools of Oriental Research* 169: 1-60.

Towers, J.K.
1959   The Red Sea. *Journal of Near Eastern Studies* 18: 150-153.

Tubb, J.N.
1983   The MBIIA Period in Palestine: Its Relationship with Syria and Its Origin. *Levant* 15: 49-62.
1988   The Role of the Sea Peoples in the Bronze Industry of Palestine/Transjordan in the Late Bronze - Early Iron Age Transition. Pp. 251-270 in *Bronze Working Centres of Western Asia*, ed. J.E. Curtis. London.

Tufnell, O.
1967   Lachish. Pp. 296-308 in *Archaeology and Old Testament Study*, ed. D. Winton Thomas. London: Oxford University Press.

Tufnell, O., and W.A. Ward
1966   Relations between Byblos, Egypt and Mesopotamia at the End of the Third Millennium B.C. *Syria* 43: 165-241.

Tufnell, O., et al.
1940   *Lachish II (Tell ed-Duweir). The Fosse Temple.* London: Oxford University Press.
1953   *Lachish III (Tell ed-Duweir). The Iron Age.* London: Oxford University Press.
1958   *Lachish IV (Tell ed-Duweir). The Bronze Age.* London: Oxford University Press.

Tushingham, A.D.
1953   Excavations at Old Testament Jericho. *Biblical Archaeologist* 16: 46-67.
1954   Excavations at Old Testament Jericho. *Biblical Archaeologist* 17: 98-104.
1972   *The Excavations at Dibon (Dhiban) in Moab: The Third Campaign, 1952-53 (Annual of the American Schools of Oriental Research, Vol. 40).* Cambridge, MA: American Schools of Oriental Research.
1975   Dibon. Pp. 330-333 in *Encyclopedia of Archaeological Excavations in the Holy Land.* Vol. I, ed. M. Avi-Yonah. Englewood Cliffs, NJ: Prentice-Hall.

Uphill, E.P.
1968   Pithom and Raamses: Their Location and Significance, Part 1. *Journal of Near Easter Studies* 27: 291-316.
1969   Pithom and Raamses: Their Location and Significance, Part 2. *Journal of Near Easter Studies* 28: 15-39.

Ussishkin, D.
1977   Lachish. Pp. 735-753 in *Encyclopedia of Archaeological Excavations in the Holy Land.* Vol. III, ed. M. Avi-Yonah. Englewood Cliffs, NJ: Prentice-Hall.
1978   Excavations at Tel Lachish: 1973-1977. Preliminary Report. *Tel Aviv* 5: 1-97.
1979   Answers at Lachish. *Biblical Archaeology Review* 5/6: 16-39.
1983a   Excavations at Tel Lachish: 1978-1983. Second Preliminary Report. *Tel Aviv* 10: 91-195.
1983b   Excavations at Tel Lachish 1978-1983. Second Preliminary Report. *Tel Aviv* 10: 97-168.
1985   Level VII and VI at Tel Lachish and the End of the Late Bronze Age in Canaan. Pp. 213-230 in *Palestine in the Bronze and Iron Ages,* ed. J.N. Tubb. London: Institute of Archaeology.
1987   Lachish - Key to the Israelite Conquest of Canaan? *Biblical Archaeology Review* 13/1: 18-39.

Van Seters, J.
1966   *The Hyksos: A New Investigation.* New Haven, CT: Yale University Press.
1972a   The Terms "Amorite" and "Hittite." *Vetus Testamentum* 22: 64-81.
1972b   The Conquest of Sihon's Kingdom: A Literary Examination. *Journal of Biblical Literature* 91/2: 182-197.
1975   *Abraham in History and Tradition.* New Haven, CT: Yale University Press.
1980   Once Again - the Conquest of Sihon's Kingdom. *Journal of Biblical Literature* 99/1: 117-119.
1982   More Holes in Goedicke's Exodus Theories (Queries and Comments). *Biblical Archaeology Review* 8/1: 12.

1983   *In Search of History: Historiography in the Ancient World and the*
                Origins of Biblical History. New Haven, CT: Yale University
                Press.
de Vaux, R.
1955   Les Fouilles de Tell el-Farᶜah, prés Naplouse. *Revue Biblique* 62:
                575-580.
1970   On Right and Wrong Uses of Archaeology. Pp. 64-80 in *Near*
                Eastern Archaeology in the Twentieth Century, ed. J.A. Sanders.
                Garden City, NY: Doubleday.
1978   *The Early History of Israel*. (translated by David Smith)
                Philadelphia: The Westminster Press.
Velikovsky, I.
1952   *Ages in Chaos*. Garden City, NY: Doubleday.
Vincent, L.H.
1937   Les Fouilles d'Et-Tell. *Revue Biblique* 46: 231-266.
Wainwright, G.A.
1936   The Coming of Iron. *Antiquity* 10: 5-24.
1959   Some Early Philistine History. *Vetus Testamentum* 9: 73-84.
1960   Meneptaḥ's Aid to the Hittites. *Journal of Egyptian Archaeology*
                46: 24-28.
1961   Some Sea Peoples. *Journal of Egyptian Archaeology* 47: 71-90.
Waltke, B.K.
1972   Palestinian Artifactual Evidence Supporting the Early Date for the
                Exodus. *Bibliotheca Sacra* 129: 33-47.
Ward, W.A.
1973   A Possible New Link Between Egypt and Jordan During the Reign
                of Amenhotep III. *Annual of the Department of Antiquities of*
                Jordan and Amman 18: 45-46.
1976   Some Personal Names of the Hyksos Period Rulers and Notes on
                the Epigraphy of Their Scarabs. *Ugarit-Forschungen* 8: 353-370.
Warner, S.W.
1978   The Dating of the Period of the Judges. *Vetus Testamentum* 28:
                455-463.
Weinfeld, M
1988   Historical Facts Behind the Israelite Settlement Pattern. *Vetus*
                Testamentum 38: 324-332.
Weinstein, J.M.
1981   The Egyptian Empire in Palestine - A Reassessment. *Bulletin of*
                the American Schools of Oriental Research 241: 1-28.
1981   Egyptian Relations with Palestine in the Early Bronze I-II Period.
                Pp. 1-7 in *Annual Meeting of the Society of Biblical Literature,*
                American Academy of Religion: Papers. San Francisco.
1984   The Significance of Tel ᶜErani for Egyptian-Palestinian Relations
                at the Beginning of the Bronze Age. *Bulletin of the American*
                Schools of Oriental Research 256: 61-69.

Weippert, M.
1971   *The Settlement of the Israelite Tribes in Palestine: A Critical Survey of Recent Scholarly Debate.* trans. by J.D. Martin. Studies in Biblical Theology II, 21. London: SCM Press/ Naperville, Ill: Allenson.
1979   The Israelite 'Conquest' and the Evidence from Transjordan. Pp. 15-34 in *Symposia Celebrating the Seventy-Fifth Anniversary of the Founding of the American Schools of Oriental Research (1900-1975)*, ed. Frank Moore Cross. Cambridge, MA: American Schools of Oriental Research.

Wenham, J.W.
1967   Large Numbers in the Old Testament. *Tyndale Bulletin* 18: 19-53.

Wente, E.F.
1975   Thutmose III's Accession and the Beginning of the New Kingdom. *Journal of Near Eastern Studies* 34: 265-272.
1980   Genealogy of the Royal Family. Pp. 122-162 in *An X-Ray Atlas of the Royal Mummies*, ed. James E. Harris and Edward F. Wente. Chicago: University of Chicago Press.

Wente, E.F. and C.C. Van Siclen, III
1976   A Chronology of the New Kingdom. Pp. 217-261 in *Studies in Honor of George R. Hughes. (Chicago Studies in Ancient Oriental Civilization* 39). Chicago: The Oriental Institute.

Wilson, I.
1985   *Exodus: The True Story Behind the Biblical Account.* San Francisco: Harper and Row.

Wilson, J.A.
1927   The Texts of the Battle of Kadesh. *American Journal of Semitic Languages and Literatures* 43: 266-287.
1951   *The Burden of Egypt: An Interpretation of Ancient Egyptian Culture.* Chicago: University of Chicago Press.
1955a   Egyptian Historical Texts, Egyptian Hymns and Prayers, and Egyptian Oracles and Prophecies. Pp. 227-264, 325-381, 441-449 in *Ancient Near Eastern Texts Relating to the Old Testament.* 2nd ed, ed. James B. Pritchard. Princeton, NJ: Princeton University Press.
1955b   An Egyptian Letter. Pp. 475-479 in *Ancient Near Eastern Texts Relating to the Old Testament.* Princeton, NJ: Princeton University Press.
1956   *The Culture of Ancient Egypt.* Chicago: University of Chicago Press.

Winnett, F.V.
1937   The Founding of Hebron. *Bulletin of the Canadian Society of Biblical Studies* 3: 21-29.
1949   *The Mosaic Tradition.* Toronto: University of Toronto Press.
1965   Re-examining the Foundations. *Journal of Biblical Literature* 84: 1-19.

Winnett, F.V., and W.L. Reed
1961   The Excavations at Dibon (Dhibân) in Moab. *Annual of the American Schools of Oriental Research* 36-37.
Wiseman, D.J.
1975   Assyria and Babylonia c. 1200-1000 B.C. Pp. 443-481 in *Cambridge Ancient History*. 3rd edition. Vol. II, Part 2, ed. I.E.S. Edwards *et al.* Cambridge: Cambridge University Press.
Wood, B.G.
1982   The Stratigraphic Relationships of Local and Imported Bichrome Ware at Megiddo. *Levant* 14: 73-79.
1987   The Archaeology and History of Jericho in the Late Bronze Age. *A paper presented at the "Who Was the Pharaoh of the Exodus?" Symposium, Memphis, Tennessee, April 23-25.*
1990a   Did the Israelites Conquer Jericho? *Biblical Archaeology Review* 16/2: 44-59.
1990b   Dating Jericho's Destruction: Bienkowski is Wrong on All Counts. *Biblical Archaeology Review* 16/5: 45,47-49,68,69.
Wood, L.J.
1970   The Date of the Exodus. Pp. 67-86 in *New Perspectives on the Old Testament*, ed. J. Barton Payne. Waco, TX: Word Books.
1986   *A Survey of Israel's History.* (revised and enlarged by David O'Brien) Grand Rapids, MI: Zondervan.
Wood, L.J., and B.K. Waltke
1972   Palestinian Artifactual Evidence Supporting the Early Date for the Exodus. *Bibliotheca Sacra* 129: 33-47.
Wright, G.E.
1938   *Ain Shems Excavations IV.*
1941   Archaeological Observations on the Period of the Judges and the Early Monarchy. *Journal of Biblical Literature* 60: 27-42.
1942   Two Misunderstood Items in the Exodus-Conquest Cycle. *Bulletin of the American Schools of Oriental Research* 86: 32-35.
1947   Tell en-Naṣbeh. *Biblical Archaeologist* 10: 69-77.
1956   The First Campaign at Tell Balâṭṭah (Shechem). *Bulletin of the American Schools of Oriental Research* 144: 9-20.
1957   The Second Campaign at Tell Balâṭah (Shechem). *Bulletin of the American Schools of Oriental Research* 148: 11-28.
1961   The Archaeology of Palestine. Pp. 85-139 in *The Bible and the Ancient Near East*, ed. G.E. Wright. Garden City, NY: Doubleday, Anchor.
1962a   *Biblical Archaeology.* 2nd edition. Philadelphia: Westminster Press.
1962b   Exodus, Book of. Pp. 188-197 in *The Interpreter's Dictionary of the Bible*. Vol. 2, Nashville: Abingdon Press.
1965   *Shechem: The Biography of a Biblical City.* Newark, NJ: McGraw Hill.

1966   Fresh Evidence for the Philistine Story. *Biblical Archaeologist* 29: 70-86.
1975   Beth-Shemesh. Pp. 248-253 in *Encyclopedia of Archaeological Excavations in the Holy Land*. Vol. I, ed. M. Avi-Yonah. Englewood Cliffs, NJ: Prentice-Hall.

Wright, G.R.H.
1968   Tell el-Yehudiyah and the Glacis. *Zeitschrift des Deutschen Palastina-Vereins* 84: 1-17.
1970   The Passage of the Sea. *Gottinger Miszellen* 3:55.
1971a   Pre-Israelite Temples in the Land of Canaan. *Palestine Exploration Quarterly* 103: 17-32.
1971b   Shechem and League Shrines. *Vetus Testamentum* 21: 572-603.

Wright, H.E., Jr.
1968   Climatic Change in Mycenaean Greece. *Antiquity* 42: 123-127.

Yadin, Y.
1955   Hyksos Fortifications and the Battering Ram. *Bulletin of the American Schools of Oriental Research* 137: 23-32.
1957   Further Light on Biblical Hazor. *Biblical Archaeologist* 20: 34-47.
1958a   The Third Season of Excavation at Hazor, 1957. *Biblical Archaeologist* 21: 30-47.
1958b   Excavations at Hazor, 1957. Preliminary Communiqué. *Israel Exploration Journal* 8: 1-14.
1959   Excavations at Hazor, 1958. Preliminary Communiqué. *Israel Exploration Journal* 9: 74-88.
1968   'And Dan, why did he remain in ships?' (Judges 5:17) *Australian Journal of Biblical Archaeology* 1: 9-23.
1969a   Excavations at Hazor, 1968-1969. Preliminary Communiqué. *Israel Exploration Journal* 19: 1-19.
1969b   The Fifth Season of Excavations at Hazor, 1968-1969. *Biblical Archaeologist* 32: 50-71.
1972   *Hazor, the Head of All Those Kingdoms* (Schweich Lectures). London: Oxford University Press.
1975   *Hazor: The Rediscovery of a Great Citadel of the Bible*. New York: Random House.
1976   Hazor. Pp. 474-495 in *Encyclopedia of Archaeological Excavations in the Holy Land*. Vol. II, ed. M. Avi-Yonah. Englewood Cliffs, NJ: Prentice-Hall; Jerusalem: The Israel Exploration Society and Massada Press.
1979   The Transition from a Semi-Nomadic to a Sedentary Society in the Twelfth Century B.C.E. Pp. 57-68 in *Symposia Celebrating the Seventy-Fifth Anniversary of the Founding of the American Schools of Oriental Research (1900-1975)*, ed. Frank Moore Cross. Cambridge, MA: American Schools of Oriental Research.
1982   Is the Biblical Account of the Israelite Conquest of Canaan Historically Reliable? *Biblical Archaeology Review* 8/2: 16-23.

1985   Biblical Archaeology Today: The Archaeological Aspect. Pp. 21-
               27 in *Biblical Archaeology Today: Proceedings of the
               International Congress of Biblical Archaeology, Jerusalem, April
               1984.* Jerusalem: Israel Exploration Society.
Yadin, Y., and Sh. Geva
1986   *Investigations at Beth-Shean. The Early Iron Age Strata. (Qedem
               23)* Jerusalem: The Hebrew University.
Yadin, Y., *et al.*
1958   *Hazor I.* Jerusalem: Magness Press.
1960   *Hazor II.* Jerusalem: Magness Press.
1961   *Hazor III-IV.* Jerusalem: Magness Press.
Yeivin, S.
1950   The Third District of Tuthmosis III's List of Palestino-Syrian
               Towns. *Journal of Egyptian Archaeology* 36: 51-62.
1960   Early Contact between Canaan and Egypt. *Israel Exploration
               Journal* 10: 193-203.
1967   Amenophis II's Asiatic Campaigns. *Journal of the american
               Research Center in Egypt* 6: 119-128.
1971a   *The Israelite Conquest of Canaan.* Istanbul: Nederlands
               Historisch-Archaeologisch Instituut in Het Nabije Oosten.
1971b   The Benjaminite Settlement in the Western Part of Their
               Territory. *Israel Exploration Journal* 21: 141-154.
1976   Canaanite Ritual Vessels in Egyptian Cultic Practices. *Journal of
               Egyptian Archaeology* 62: 110-114.
Yurco, F.J.
1978   Merneptah's Palestinian Campaign. *The Journal of the Society for
               the Study of Egyptian Antiquities* 8: 70ff.
1986   Merneptah's Palestinian Campaign. *Journal of the American
               Research Center in Egypt* 23: 197ff.
1990   3,200-Year-Old Picture of Israelites Found in Egypt. *Biblical
               Archaeology Review* 16/5: 20-28.
Zertal, A.
1985   Has Joshua's Altar Been Found on Mt. Ebal? *Biblical Archaeology
               Review* 11/1: 26-43.
1986   How Can Kempinski Be So Wrong? *Biblical Archaeology Review*
               12/1: 43,49-53.
1986-87   An Early Iron Age Cultic Site on Mount Ebal: Excavation Seasons
               1982-1987. *Tel Aviv* 13-14: 105-165.
Zevit, Z.
1985a   The Problem of Ai. *Biblical Archaeology Review* 11/2: 58-69.
1985b   Queries and Comments - Ziony Zevit Replies. *Biblical
               Archaeology Review* 11/4: 22-23.
1985c   Queries and Comments - Ziony Zevit Replies. *Biblical
               Archaeology Review* 11/5: 79-80.
Zori, N.
1954,55   Survey of the Beth Shan Basin. *Bulletin of the Israel Exploration
               Society* 18: 78-90; 19: 89-98.